Dubai

The Top Five

1 Dubai Creek
While away some time at the Dhow Wharfage (p51)

2 Burj Al Arab
Marvel at the landmark building, aka the 'Arabian Tower' (p58)

3 Bastakia
Chill out under the wind-towers of the Bastakia Quarter (p53)

4 Bur Dubai Souq
Hunt and gather within the restored market arcades (p53)

5 Dubai Museum
Enter the past through the doors of the old Al-Fahidi Fort (p54)

Contents

Published by Lonely Planet Publications Pty Ltd
ABN 36 005 607 983

Australia Head Office, Locked Bag 1, Footscray,
Victoria 3011, ☎ 03 8379 8000, fax 03 8379 8111,
talk2us@lonelyplanet.com.au

USA 150 Linden St, Oakland, CA 94607,
☎ 510 893 8555, toll free 800 275 8555,
fax 510 893 8572, info@lonelyplanet.com

UK 72–82 Rosebery Ave, Clerkenwell, London,
EC1R 4RW, ☎ 020 7841 9000, fax 020 7841 9001,
go@lonelyplanet.co.uk

The Authors

Terry Carter

Terry has lived in Dubai since 2003 and the United Arab Emirates (UAE) since 1998, after many years working in Sydney's publishing industry. Having erroneously concluded that travel writing was a far more glamorous occupation than designing books or websites, he's been travel writing for several years and has travelled extensively throughout the Middle East and Europe during his time in the UAE. Terry has a Master's degree in media studies and divides his time between freelance travel writing and photography and would like to *really* settle down one day, if only he could figure out where.

Lara Dunston

Despite a lifelong passion for travel – Lara has been to 50 countries at last count – moving to the UAE certainly didn't seem a logical choice for someone with a Russian-Australian heritage and a Master's degree in Latin American cinema and Spanish! But the opportunity to develop the creative talent of young Emirati women and contribute to the growth of a film culture was too hard to refuse. More than seven years later, Lara acknowledges that her students taught her as much about Dubai and Emirati culture, society and tradition, as she taught them about creativity.

PHOTOGRAPHER
Terry Carter

As well as writing, Terry's other passion is photography. He studied photography at university, and hasn't put down a camera since. He loves shooting in the Middle East where the light, places and people are a constant joy.

TERRY & LARA'S TOP DUBAI DAY

Thursday nights can be big in Dubai – sunset drinks with friends at beautiful Bahri Bar, dinner at sublime Mezzanine, post-dinner drinks at Buddha Bar, before winding up on the Lotus One dance floor. So Fridays (for recovery) are more relaxed affairs, and are our favourite days, especially in winter. On Fridays everything's shut except the malls (which never seem to shut these days), the pace is slower (as it's meant to be!) and the roads are emptier (as we wish they'd always be). As we don't own a car in Dubai (taxis are cheap) we like to hire one and get out of the city centre – we drive just 15 minutes to the Camel Race Track at Nad Al-Sheba to watch the camels train, or just take a drive through the backstreets. On the way back we go via Jumeirah Beach Road to check out the surf – flat again. If we're up for a walk, we stroll through the backstreets of Satwa (to bring us back down to earth) and if we're peckish buy some stone-oven bread from a hole-in-the-wall Afghan bakery – it's fresh, cheap and tasty.

In the late afternoon, we like to stroll through the narrow lanes of the Bastakia and visit some galleries, then through the buzzy Bur Dubai souq, busy with 'guest workers' enjoying their day off. We buy some tasty hot Indian snacks then head for Shindagha and the Heritage Village, where there's often something on – there's nothing like watching a proud Emirati mum cheer her son on in a rifle-twirling competition! Nothing beats the commotion of the Creek – the crisscrossing *abras,* the dhows being loaded, and the crazy seagulls flying about – especially at sunset when that big ball of orange sinks rapidly into the Arabian sea.

Introducing Dubai

Arabesque, Disneyesque and clearly taking growth supplements, Dubai has reached a turning point. It's famous enough so that everyone knows something about it (even if it's just a glimpse of tennis pros hitting a ball on the Burj Al Arab helipad), but not yet popular enough so that people haven't stopped asking, what's it really like?

Dubai, currently the fastest growing city in the world, is a million things, depending on who you are and why you're here. For many of the over five million visitors who fly into its sleek airport every year, it's a flashy, fun, often surreal yet uniquely Arabian city, with year-round sunshine, stunning five-star beach hotels, endless shopping, bubbling nightlife, and world-class sports events. For Emiratis it's a city that will show the rest of the world what the Arabs are capable of when given an opportunity to shine. For the educated expat here on contract, it offers the stimuli of any other multicultural melting pot but with a lifestyle that's like going from flying business-class to having your own private jet. And to the workers that are building the billion-dollar developments mushrooming in the desert it's everything from a heaven-sent opportunity to an overheated hell on earth.

So where does it go from here? There's a feeling among Emiratis that the passing of the United Arab Emirates' (UAE's) founding father, Sheikh Zayed, in 2004, followed by the death of Dubai's ruler, Sheikh Maktoum, in early 2006, was significant. With a solid foundation of peace and prosperity in place, everyone's looking to the new leader of Dubai, Sheikh Mohammed. While it's business as usual – the hard-working, ambitious Sheikh had already assumed many of the responsibilities of running Dubai a few years ago – there are some signs that further change is underway.

When the Sheikh married Princess Haya bint Al-Hussein of Jordan in 2004, she became the first 'visible' royal wife, with their wedding photo on the front page of the local newspapers – a Dubai first. The epitome of the modern Arab woman, Sheikha Haya can be seen in *Ahlan* (Dubai's version of *Hello!* magazine) attending global economic conferences one day and wearing a glamorous gown at a glitzy charity ball the next. The Sheikh's calls to the once timid self-censoring press to

become a more open media, his insistence that Dubai be technology-driven, making previously tedious bureaucratic processes painless (how many airports these days let you breeze through immigration by placing your thumbprint on a scanner?), and the government's responsiveness to workers' strikes and demands from companies to provide better conditions or get blackbanned, are all signs of Dubai's move towards becoming a more modern, open and democratic society – all good things for travellers to Dubai.

But while the speed of modernisation is rapid (so much so that many Europeans already see Dubai as a city of the future), Emiratis are proudly clinging to their traditions. Instead of discarding their national dress (like the Egyptians or Persians did when they swapped their hijab for mini-skirts and knee-high boots), Emirati women are calling attention to it – they're embellishing their *abayas* with gems and sequins, confidently drawing attention to themselves. Like Dubai, they have a sense of optimism and confidence in their identity, and they're celebrating it! In architecture, we're seeing a renewed confidence in old Arabian forms, such as Madinat Jumeirah – Dubai realises it doesn't have to have shiny skyscrapers to show the world that it's progressive (but it reserves the right to keep building them if it wants!). It's taking traditional forms such as the arabesque pattern and (just as the women are doing with their *abayas*) creating a new hybrid design that combines the traditional and modern all at once.

When people say that Dubai has no culture or history, that the city is fake, you won't hear any apologies from Emiratis for not having the pyramids, temples or museums of other Middle Eastern destinations. Dubai's history is in its songs and dance (there's nothing like coming across a traditional performance of the *liwa* in a local neighbourhood), and its culture can be found in its Bedouin heritage and Islamic religion (the sight of Muslims praying wherever they happen to be and the echoes of the call-to-prayer in a downtown city street are wonderfully moving experiences), while its sense of purpose is rooted in its identity and spirit – a spirit that's really taking the city places no city has been before. And it's this, along with the juxtaposition of the traditional past and hi-tech present, that makes Dubai such an intriguing and exciting destination for travellers and such a compelling place to visit.

ESSENTIAL DUBAI

- Bastakia Quarter (p53) Get artsy among restored Arabian courtyard houses.
- Burj Al Arab (p58) Lap up luxury at Dubai's architectural icon and '7 star' hotel.
- Deira Souqs (p50) Inhale heady aromatic spices and haggle over gold.
- Dubai Creek (p49) Crisscross Dubai's traditional trading heart by *abra*.
- Dubai Museum (p54) Trace the changes of this fast-evolving fast-paced city in this fascinating museum.

City Life ■

City Life

DUBAI TODAY

Dubai is a 21st-century phenomenon. From a small trading centre just 40 years ago to the international travel hub, tourist destination and business powerhouse it is today, its fortunes head skywards with still no end in sight. 'Seven star' hotels, international sporting events, monumental malls – if you dream it, Dubai can fund it and deliver it in short order. Like a game of SimCity that never ends, Dubai just keeps growing at a freakishly fast rate. But why Dubai? Why not neighbouring emirate, Abu Dhabi, whose oil revenues have always left Dubai in the dust? And where is it headed?

When the Al Maktoums and other members of the Bani Yas tribe left Liwa for Bur Dubai, it's almost as if they knew this was their destiny. Each successive generation has built on the achievements of the last, with no small amount of entrepreneurial skill, daring and vision. These Arab alchemists have come up with a formula that is unique to Dubai and the 'can do' spirit, coupled with an expectation of success, has made these vast achievements possible.

The other thing that has made these achievements possible is the overwhelmingly foreign workforce that has carried out the vision of the Dubai leaders, whether it's in construction, education, business or banking. While everyone who comes to live in Dubai in some way shares in its success, expats find it hard to escape the feeling that they're the 'hired help' here, which of course they are. While buying property in Dubai now allows expats to have an open-ended residency visa, it's still not citizenship – and effectively they have no political voice.

Despite this, the better-off expats feel enormous affection towards Dubai, especially the long-term residents who have watched the city bloom and their fortunes rise. However, if inflation keeps heading skyward and rental prices continue to spiral out of control, this affection might be tested in the near future.

While the wealthy expats worry about things like traffic and roadworks lengthening their commute to their multinational headquarters, Dubai's labourers have more

Traditional songs continue to be an important and relevant aspect of Dubaian culture

urgent issues, which until recently were not being addressed. In the last edition of this book we wrote about these workers being cheated out of money, often unpaid for months, or underpaid and overworked against the terms of their employment agreement. Without political representation, building workers have begun taking the matter into their own hands, protesting and striking over unpaid wages and poor living conditions. Strikes over these issues have even spread to other emirates. The government's response has been swift (if not exactly proactive, given how long these issues have been public knowledge), addressing their concerns, fining employers, and even black-banning companies who continue the practice. They've also set up a hotline for workers to report unpaid wages and unfit conditions.

However, Emiratis are having their own struggles (admittedly on a far different scale). Firstly, they know that both skilled and unskilled labour is going to be required indefinitely in Dubai. But they're also concerned that they're being unfairly squeezed out of the job market in the private sector. In Dubai, Emiratis comprise only 1% of the private sector workforce, even though they're 10% of the total population. While many private companies have local partners, these partners are essentially silent and let the expat managers run the company, leaving them free to choose their staff. The small population of Emiratis coupled with the somewhat segregated nature of Dubai society means that many managers in private enterprise don't even *know* any Emiratis, let alone employ any. Ironically, Emiratis have demonstrated that they respond well to working in these multicultural workplaces.

The major stumbling block, however, is money. The cheap labour that keeps the wheels of Dubai turning is a double-edged *khanjar*. Why train locals to do jobs like plumbing when you can hire someone to do it for one tenth of the wages an Emirati would expect? And which Emirati would be willing to attend college to learn such a trade when they could be doing MBAs?

Despite these issues, there appears to be a sense of balance in Dubai, both within the city and with its relationship with the rest of the world. Dubai today is friends with the West: for progressive Arabs it's a shining example of a modern Arab city, but for increasingly conservative branches of Islam, it's far too liberal. How Dubai manages to balance all these factors is just as important as keeping up its spectacular growth. Given the track record of Dubai's leaders over the past few decades, it would be unwise to bet against them – particularly with Sheikh Mohammed now firmly at the helm. Whatever the future for Dubai, it's currently one of the most fascinating cities on the planet.

CITY CALENDAR

For information on Dubai's holidays, see p181.

JANUARY & FEBRUARY
DUBAI MARATHON
www.dubaimarathon.org
The event offers a full marathon as well as a 10km run and a 3km 'fun run'. The January date means that it's quite pleasant – the temperature, not the run. Just don't try running down Sheikh Zayed Rd on any other day of the year…

DUBAI SHOPPING FESTIVAL
www.mydsf.com
Running for a month from mid-January, this festival is not just about shopping; it's also about shopping for stuff from all around the world at the **Global Village** (p124). The hotels

are full, there's live music and performances, fireworks every night, and the whole month is a real traffic stopper. Literally.

DUBAI INTERNATIONAL JAZZ FESTIVAL
www.dubaijazzfest.com
Held during the Shopping Festival, this increasingly popular event is staged at Dubai Media City over three nights. The festival showcases a diverse array of musical offerings, with an eclectic programme that often has only a tenuous connection to jazz.

DUBAI TENNIS CHAMPIONSHIPS
www.dubaitennischampionships.com
Held over two weeks from late February, the championships consist of a Women's Tennis Association (WTA) event followed by an Association of Tennis Professionals (ATP) event. Both the men's and women's events now attract the big guns.

The Dubai Camel Racecourse (p117), in contrast with Sheikh Zayed Rd beyond

MARCH
DUBAI DESERT CLASSIC
www.dubaidesertclassic.com
The Dubai Desert Classic lures some of the best golfers in the world to partake in one of the world's richest golf tournaments. Events of the last couple of years have been phenomenal, with the winner decided on the 18th hole of the last day.

DUBAI WORLD CUP
www.dubaiworldcup.com
The Dubai International Racing Carnival, running from February through to the end of March, culminates in the Dubai World Cup, the world's richest horse race with prize money of a dizzying US$6 million and a total purse for the event of over US$20 million. While there's no betting, many of Dubai society's women take a punt in wearing some of the silliest hats this side of the Melbourne Cup.

JUNE
DUBAI SUMMER SURPRISES
www.mydsf.com
A similar event to the Dubai Shopping Festival, this event is a more family-oriented affair and has been successful in attracting Gulf state visitors who would normally sit out the heat somewhere more pleasant than Dubai in summer. The festival lasts until the end of August – the heat, a couple of months more.

OCTOBER
UAE DESERT CHALLENGE
www.uaedesertchallenge.com
This desert rally, a round of the FIA Cross Country Rally World Cup, starts off in Abu Dhabi and finishes in Dubai. It's held over four days and heads off through some challenging terrain and attracts car, truck and motorbike riders.

DECEMBER
DUBAI INTERNATIONAL FILM FESTIVAL
www.dubaifilmfest.com
Aimed at building cultural bridges and promoting global peace, understanding and tolerance (yes, really!), along with developing the film industry, bringing Hollywood to Dubai, and entertaining the local community, the festival showcases some excellent Arab cinema and hosts some bad Hollywood premieres. In true Dubai style, there are nightly red-carpet events with lots of stars at the Madinat Jumeirah Arabian Resort.

TOP FIVE QUIRKY EVENTS

Diwali Festival It's really only during this festival of light that you realise *just* how many Indians are living in Dubai – there are candles and lights everywhere, plus enough sweets to leave the kids running around in circles in a sugar-induced high, but we can really do without the endless firecrackers.

Global Village (p124) So successful it looks like it's decided to never end, it's one of the only places in the world where you can have some Chinese takeaway, buy some African masks, then go and watch a Yemeni knife dance.

Wooden powerboat racing A crazy marriage of old and new. You take a beautiful hand-crafted wooden boat and then bolt a couple of outboards on the back and race it like there's no tomorrow.

Rock pension tours It's like playing to a captive audience. 'We'd better go see Bryan Adams because we probably won't see him again.' Wrong, wrong, wrong.

Dubai International Jazz Festival (p9) We guess it's too late to change the name of the festival, but really, when your closing act is that well-known jazz artist, Supertramp's Roger Hodgson, clearly something's gotta give.

CULTURE

IDENTITY

The best recent estimates put Dubai's population at just over 1.4 million, a giant leap from 183,200 in 1975. These statistics apply to the whole of the Dubai emirate, though the UAE is overwhelmingly urban with more than 90% of the population living in cities. The population has been growing by as much as 7% a year, and the authorities are planning for a population of two million by 2010. Only about 10% of the total population of Dubai are Emiratis; the expatriate community makes up the rest of the population – one of the most multicultural in the world.

Dubai is an extremely tolerant and easygoing society, with its cultural and social life firmly rooted in Islam. Day-to-day activities, relationships, diet and dress are very much dictated by religion (see p12). Gender roles are changing, with more and more women wanting to establish careers before marriage. With successful Emirati women such as Sheikha Lubna Al Qasimi (the first female Minister of Economy and Planning) and Dr Amena Rostamani (Director of Dubai's Media City) serving as role models, the Emirati women's contribution to the workforce has grown by 16.7% since 1995.

There may only be limited 'bricks and mortar' representation of traditional Arabic and Bedouin life in Dubai, but the cultural and national identity of Emiratis is strong. The physical representations of the past still exist in the form of the traditional architecture (see p27) on the Shindagha waterfront in Bur Dubai and Al-Ahmadiya School (p50) and Heritage House (p52) in Deira, but to gain a good insight into traditional culture, visit Dubai Museum (p54) or venture out of the city to the East Coast villages (p160) or Al-Ain (p164) where life appears little changed from the way it was before federation.

Disregard comments you may hear about Dubai being fake and a 'shopping culture' – shopping is merely a pastime and social activity but, yes, a popular one. Emirati cultural identity is expressed passionately through poetry, traditional song and dance, a love of the desert and nature, of camels, horses and falconry, all of which remain popular activities. If you're lucky enough

TOP FIVE DUBAI READS

- *Dubai Tales* by Mohammad Al-Murr – delightful short stories by Dubai's best-known writer provide an insight into Dubai life and culture.
- *Father of Dubai: Sheikh Rashid bin Saeed Al-Maktoum* by Graeme Wilson – a wonderful tribute to the founder of modern Dubai.
- *Telling Tales: An Oral History of Dubai* by Julia Wheeler and Paul Thuysbaert – touching and astonishing accounts of old Dubai from ageing Emiratis.
- *Dubai Life and Times: Through the Lens of Noor Ali Rashid* by Noor Ali Rashid – a royal photographer's pictorial history of Dubai over the last four decades.
- *The Wells of Memory, An Autobiography* by Easa Saleh Al-Gurg – the memoirs of one of Dubai's key movers and shakers.

THE FIVE PILLARS OF ISLAM

Shahadah The profession of faith: 'There is no god but God, and Mohammed is the messenger of God'.

Salat Muslims are required to pray five times every day: at dawn, noon, mid-afternoon, sunset and twilight. During prayers a Muslim must perform a series of prostrations while facing the Kaaba, the ancient shrine at the centre of the Grand Mosque in Mecca. Before a Muslim can pray, however, he or she must perform a series of ritual ablutions, and if water isn't available for this, sand or soil can be substituted.

Zakat Muslims must give a portion of their income to help the poor. How this has operated in practice has varied over the centuries: either it was seen as an individual duty or the state collected it as a form of income tax to be redistributed through mosques or religious charities.

Sawm It was during the month of Ramadan that Mohammed received his first revelation in AD 610. Muslims mark this event by fasting from sunrise until sunset throughout Ramadan. During the fast a Muslim may not take anything into his or her body. Food, drink, smoking and sex are forbidden. Young children, travellers and those whose health will not allow it are exempt from the fast, though those who are able to do so are supposed to make up the days they missed at a later time.

Haj All able Muslims are required to make the pilgrimage to Mecca at least once, if possible during a specific few days in the first and second weeks of the Muslim month of Dhul Hijja, although visiting Mecca and performing the prescribed rituals at any other time of the year is also considered spiritually desirable. Such visits are referred to as *umrah*, or 'little pilgrimages'.

to be invited to a wedding (and you should take up the offer), it's a great way to see some of these cultural traditions in action.

Dubai has been very active in preserving and publicly displaying many of the local traditions. The Dubai Museum (p54), the Bastakia (p53), Al-Ahmadiya School (p50), Heritage House (p52) and the Heritage Village (p55) in Shindagha all give good insights into traditional and cultural life, and the aim of such work is not just to attract and entertain tourists, but to educate young Emiratis about the value of their culture and heritage. Families also make an effort to maintain their heritage by taking their kids out to the desert frequently and teaching them how to continue traditional practices such as falconry.

One matter of great concern to the authorities is the ongoing trend for Emirati men to marry foreign women. One reason for the trend is the prohibitive cost of a traditional wedding, plus the dowry the groom must provide – essentially, it's cheaper and easier to marry a foreign woman. Another factor is that as Emirati women are becoming better educated, they're less willing to settle down in the traditional role of an Emirati wife. The issue comes up frequently in the Arabic press – in a culture where women who are still unmarried at the age of 26 are referred to as spinsters, or even as slighting the family's honour, the growing numbers of single women is a hot topic indeed. The UAE Marriage Fund, set up in 1994 by the federal government to facilitate marriages between UAE nationals, provides grants to pay for the exorbitant costs of the wedding and dowry and promotes mass weddings to enable nationals to save for a down payment on a house. These initiatives have reduced the rate of intermarriages between Emirati men and foreign women to a degree, but not sufficiently to ensure that every Emirati woman has a husband.

THE MAJLIS

Majlis translates as 'meeting place' or 'reception area'. The *majlis* was a forum or council where citizens could come and speak to their leaders and make requests, complaints or raise any issues. In Dubai the *majlis* system was preserved until the 1960s. In its domestic sense, a *majlis* is a reception area found in all older buildings in Dubai (such as Al-Fahidi Fort, the Dubai Museum, and the Heritage House in Al-Ahmadiya). Its Western cousin is probably the lounge room. The *majlis* is still an important room in an Arab household and is usually the domain of the male members of the family. It's a place where they can get together and talk without disturbing the women of the house, as most traditional houses still have a separate *majlis* for women.

LIFESTYLE

There's no such thing as an average Emirati, and the first myth to dispel is that there's an oil well in every back yard – most of these are offshore anyway! While the traditional tribal leaders, or sheikhs, are often the wealthiest Emiratis, many have made their fortune through good investments, often dating back to the 1970s. As befits a nation so well off, all Emiratis have free health-care and education as well as access to a marriage fund (although the budgets don't often meet the expenses of elaborate Emirati weddings). To poorer Emiratis, these types of social benefits, and charities operated by generous sheikhs, such as Sheikh Mohammed, are essential to their survival in modern Dubai.

The upper and middle classes of Emirati society generally have an expansive villa where men and women still live apart and male family members entertain guests in the *majlis* (meeting room). In all classes of Emiratis, extended families living together is the norm, with the woman moving in with the husband's family after marriage, although some young couples are now choosing to buy their own apartments for a little more privacy than the traditional arrangement allows!

Most Emiratis work in the public sector, as the short hours, good pay, benefits and early pensions are hard for young Emiratis (whose parents and grandparents still recall hard times) to refuse.

The role of Emirati women in Dubai society is changing, as there are more women than men in higher education and increasingly women are looking for more fulfilment in employment, either by establishing their own businesses or working in the private sector. Career-focused women are also marrying later, and as a result some Emirati men are looking overseas for a wife, as an educated, strong-minded Emirati woman doesn't fit many men's expectations of a 'dutiful' wife.

Living with such a large proportion of expats, and an increasing amount of Western 'culture', has seen an increasing conservatism as well as liberalisation in Dubai. This is especially noticeable among young women; some are beginning to dress in Western fashion (usually ones with foreign mothers), others are sticking with traditional dress yet individualising it, while others are 'covering up'. One aspect that's not going away is the importance of traditional dance, song and customs. All Emiratis know their traditional songs and dances, and activities such as falcony are being passed from father to son. So is the love of the desert – Emiratis are as comfortable in the sands as they are in Switzerland, where many of them take a summer break away from the heat.

As far as the foreign community goes, there are as many different lifestyles being played out in Dubai as there are grains of sand on Jumeirah Beach. Disposable income plays a big part in how people live in Dubai. At the top end of the pay scale is the professional and wealthy management class. Good salary package, nice car (most likely a Porsche Cayenne

POPULATION BREAKDOWN

The majority of Dubai's expatriate population (comprising 90% of the emirate's population) are from India (about 60%), supplying the city with cheap labour as well as filling management and professional positions. Most of Dubai's construction workers and men in low-prestige positions (taxi drivers, hotel cleaners etc) come from Kerala, a southern Indian state, while there are a lot of workers from the Indian states of Tamil Nadu and Goa. In contrast, most of the Indians in office jobs or managerial positions are recruited by agencies based in Mumbai, while IT guys come from Bangalore. All of the leading Indian mercantile communities – Jains, Sindhis, Sikhs and Marwaris – are also represented here.

About 12% of expats are from other Arab countries (mainly Lebanon, Syria, Jordan and Egypt) while there's also a substantial Iranian community. The first wave of Iranians built the Bastakia neighbourhood in the 1930s. They were mostly religiously conservative Sunnis and Shiites from southern Iran. After the 1980 Islamic revolution, a more affluent, often Western-educated, group of Iranians settled in Dubai. There is also a growing community of Filipino expatriates, as well as some Chinese, Indonesian, Malaysian and Vietnamese residents. Western expats make up about 5% of the population, once predominantly British but now also strongly represented by people from Australia, Canada, South Africa, Ireland, Germany and France.

or BMW), a large villa with a maid and nanny, and a lifestyle that allows them to travel overseas for two months a year to escape the summer heat. Housewives left with little to do at home spend much of their time with other women in similar circumstances. It's fair to say these 'Jumeirah Janes', as we like to call them, keep the cosmetics and spa industries alive and the coffee shops ticking over during the day in Dubai. These expats are generally Western, but there are plenty of Indians, Iranians and Lebanese (mainly in business) that also fall into this category.

There is another category of professional expat – the academics, health professionals, media and IT people – who earn much the same as they would back home in gross

terms; but with no tax, free housing, great holidays and other benefits like schooling and healthcare, they come out ahead in financial terms. These expats are also generally Western, but there's a large number of Indians working in the IT field and Arabs working in the media, health and education sectors. Depending on how many children they have, some families have a full-time or part-time maid or nanny. Some are here to put away as much money as possible to pay off a place back home, while others enjoy the lifestyle and leave without saving a cent, but having had a great time!

Dubai has a huge service sector and traditionally workers come from India, Pakistan and the Philippines, but now there are workers coming from other Asian countries as well. Working as line cooks, waiters and in supermarkets, these expats stand to make much more money in Dubai than at home, usually working six days a week and staying in cheap accommodation with several others from the same company. Their one day off is generally spent with friends or using Skype to chat with family back home. Many of the Pakistani and Indian men organise cricket matches and have regular meeting places where they meet to share news from home.

There is a huge number of maids employed in Dubai – check the classifieds of *Gulf News*. Indian, Pakistani and Sri Lankan live-in maids are generally paid between Dh500 and Dh800 a month, live in a tiny room in their employer's villa or share an apartment

PERSIAN PLATES

Iranian food is very different in flavour to Lebanese food. The following dishes make an excellent introduction to this wonderful cuisine.

Berenj – spicy rice dishes, usually topped with nuts and raisins.

Baghleh polow – with dill, broad beans and chicken or mutton.

Bakhtari kebab – a kebab served with grilled capsicum.

Chelow kebab – on every Persian menu, *chelow* is rice cooked separately from the other ingredients and it's topped with a grilled *kebab* (meat grilled on a skewer).

Chelow kebab barg – a variation where the kebab is thinner than usual.

Chelow kebab makhsoos – a variation where the kebab is thicker than usual.

Istanboli polow – rice with haricot beans and chicken or mutton on top.

Koresh – meat stews with vegetables.

Lari kebab – marinated kebab cooked in yogurt.

Zereshk polow – rice mixed with barberry and chicken.

with friends. While the money earned is one tenth of a Western professional's starting salary, it's still much more than unskilled work pays at home. Depending on the family, some of these maids become an integral part of their employer's family structure, forming close bonds with the children.

For a little less money Indians, Pakistanis and workers from other Arab countries in the region go about the hazardous business of construction in Dubai. These men usually work six or six-and-a-half days a week on 12-hour shifts and live in 'labour camps' (compounds) provided by the construction companies. While conditions have improved, the heat is still oppressive and the pressure to complete buildings in Dubai is enormous. Sadly, as a result, it's been widely reported in the press that the rate of suicides among Indian and Sri Lankan expatriates from this sector is on the increase.

FOOD

Local cuisine in Dubai is mainly based on Middle Eastern dishes largely borrowed from other countries in the region, in particular Lebanon, Syria and Iran. The diet of the Bedouin, who inhabited the area that is now Dubai, consisted only of fresh fish, dried fish, dates, camel meat and camel milk – and you wonder why fast food became so popular in Dubai!

The range of cuisines offered in Dubai is wide, but mainly fall into several categories. Besides Middle Eastern, there's European (plenty of Italian), Indo-Pakistani (endless curries), and Asian or Far Eastern (too much Thai!).

The most common of Middle Eastern food you'll see in Dubai is Lebanese. Lebanese restaurants are found all over Dubai and in all price ranges, from a humble Dh4 take-away shawarma to a Dh140 platter of mixed grill at a nightclub. All Lebanese dishes are served with pickles, piles of Arabic bread and a big plate of fresh salad, so you really get value for money. If you're

LEBANESE FOOD LINGO 101

Lebanese food is delicious and abundant everywhere in Dubai. Here are some of the most popular dishes you'll see:

Street Food

Felafel Deep-fried balls of chickpea paste served on flat bread

Shawarma Found outside Lebanese and other restaurants, it's the cone shaped pressed meat on a vertical spit. There's usually lamb and chicken and it's wrapped in flat bread with a little sauce and salad. More often than not, a busy shawarma stand is a good shawarma stand!

Restaurant Starters

Mezze is the term given to the selection of dip-style starters. Try:

Hummus – chickpea and garlic puree, sometimes served with lamb pieces or pine nuts – both delicious!

Kibbeh – deep-fried balls of minced meat, pine nuts, onion and cracked wheat – addictive.

Fattoush – salad of lettuce, tomato, cucumber, fried Arabic bread, and a lemon, garlic and olive-oil dressing.

Tabouleh – finely chopped parsley, tomato, cracked wheat and mint – best when super fresh.

Baba ghanooj – chargrilled eggplant with tahini, olive oil, garlic and lemon juice.

Restaurant Main Courses

Kofta – grilled skewers of spicy minced lamb.

Shish tawooq – spiced pieces of char-grilled chicken.

Kebab – pieces of grilled meat or fish on a skewer.

To try a little of everything for mains, order a 'mixed grill', which will include all the meats mentioned above (except fish).

not just grabbing a shawarma, the best way to enjoy Lebanese food is to linger for hours over mezzes and mixed grills. Throw in a belly dancer and some *sheesha* and you have the makings of a great night out...

Though there are similarities with Lebanese cooking, Iranian food has its own style and flavours. The Iranians are big on spicy rice dishes and a favourite in Iranian cooking is the buttery crust left at the bottom of the pan after rice is cooked. Anyone who doesn't serve this part of the rice dish to guests is considered either a bad cook or a bad host.

Iranian food is usually served with a plate of lettuce, cabbage, tomato and onion, with a minty yogurt sauce on the side. Naan (Iranian bread) is baked in different ways, but the most common variety in Dubai is *lavash*, which is thin, square, somewhat elastic and, for the most part, not so fantastic.

Expat workers sample the snacks at the Bur Dubai Souq (p53) on their Friday night off

FASHION

Emirati women have been showing a growing pride and renewed confidence in their own national dress, the *abaya* (black cloak) and *shayla* (black veil), despite the ever-increasing Western influences in Dubai and recent reports in the media from doctors attacking *abayas* for causing osteoporosis and recruiters saying companies won't hire women covering their face. While most Emirati women seem addicted to Western designer wear and exclusive brands – yes, that's what they wear under their *abayas*! – more recently they seem to be proudly clinging to their traditional dress with new styles of *abayas* and *shaylas* continually emerging. The latest trend is for young women to wear *abayas* and *shaylas* playfully embellished with jewels, beads, sequins, embroidery, feathers, lace, tassels and tiny plastic toys! And while Emirati men are occasionally seen in Western dress (women very rarely are, unless travelling outside the country), they're

HENNA

Henna decoration is an oriental tradition dating back to Neolithic times. The leaves of the henna shrub *(lawsonia inermis)* have been dried, ground into powder and then turned into paste for at least 6000 years. In central Turkey in 4000 BC women painted their hands in homage to the Mother Goddess. This tradition spread through the eastern Mediterranean region where the henna shrub grows wild. The paste is applied and left to stain the skin, either in shades of red, brown or black.

Emirati women decorate their hands, nails and feet for special events, such as a wedding, and it stays on for about six weeks. A few nights before the wedding night, brides-to-be are honoured with *layyat al-henna* or henna night. This is a women-only affair, part of a week of festivities and events before the wedding ceremony. At this party, the bride-to-be has her body hair removed, is anointed from head to toe with expensive perfumes and oils, has her hair washed with henna, jasmine or perfume, and her hands, wrists, ankles and feet are decorated with henna. The henna is applied in intricate, often floral patterns, but how well the henna pattern lasts has nothing to do with the henna artist! It's said to be an indication to the mother-in-law of what kind of wife the bride will make. If she's a hard worker – and therefore more desirable as a daughter-in-law – the henna will penetrate deeper into the skin of her hand and remain longer.

With the henna craze sweeping Europe and henna artists having stalls in every European flea market now, travellers to Dubai are demanding the authentic stuff. As a result you'll now find 'henna tents' all over the city. Look for the signs with painted henna hands on them in Deira City Centre (p130), BurJuman Centre (p132), Souq Madinat Jumeirah (p138), Emirates Towers (p134) and hotel lobbies.

increasingly wearing their *dishdashas* (man's shirt-dress) in smart new colours, such as slate, teal and chocolate.

Hand-in-hand with this development of national fashion is the exciting emergence of several young Emirati and Dubai-born expat or Dubai-based designers (see the boxed text, above), whose designs experiment in a tongue-in-cheek fashion with their own cultural symbols. At the same time, expats living in Dubai seem to be increasingly incorporating exotic Arabic (and Indian) dress into their own style and are wearing giant Bedouin earrings, pendants and bangles, long flowing colourful kaftans, and floaty smocks featuring embroidery, beads, jewels and gem stones. Travellers to Dubai are advised to do the same!

The older men and women still seem set in their ways, and it's common to see men wearing the white *dishdasha* and white or red-and-white checked *gutra* (headcloth) with *agal* (a black headrope used to hold the *gutra* in place), while older women still wear a black or gold burqa on their face, whether they're on the street or in the shopping mall.

CULTURE

DUBAI FASHION DESIGNERS

Many of the young Emirati and Dubai-based expatriate designers' collections can be found in Amzaan (p132), Five Green (p132) and Sauce (p137).

Raghda Bukhash Appropriates Emirati cultural symbols for her Pink Sushi label, using the *gutra* to make handbags and skirts!

Saadia Zahia Her first menswear collection, inspired by male confidence, featured clean, tailored lines contrasted by colourful silk linings with messages.

Essa Bhagoorwalla This talented young guy makes glamorous silk women's kaftans, appliquéd with Arabic-inspired decoration, jewels, beads and sequins.

Ayesha Depala The closest thing to couture in Dubai: glamorous Azzedine Alaïa–style evening wear.

Sarah Saif Belhasa Designs jewellery and embellishes *abayas* with semi-precious stones, Swarovski crystals, charms and trinkets.

SPORT

The traditional Emirati sports of horse, camel and boat racing have been supplemented by the wide variety of sports that the expat community enjoy. Even during the fiercest heat of summer you'll see people playing golf or partaking in a social game of cricket in an empty car park. Just about any sport you can think of has a small group of dedicated enthusiasts finding a way to indulge in their favourite pastime, despite the heat and often relative lack of facilities.

Given the fierce summer heat, obviously the best time to play or watch sport in Dubai is during the winter months when all of Dubai's sports lovers make the most of the marvellous weather. Tennis and golf are extremely popular as are all varieties of football, but water sports are more suitable as a year-round activity. Scuba diving, sailing and kite surfing are all popular as are skateboarding and surfing (when there are waves, that is). Of course we have to mention Ski Dubai where those who love sandboarding can discover just how much more fun it is on snow! For more on these activities, see p110.

MEDIA

The media is booming in Dubai – if the number of Porsches, Ferraris, BMWs and Mini Coopers in the Dubai Media City car park is anything to go by. Dubai's media has certainly come a long way since the 1969 opening of Dubai Television. Since its establishment in 2001, with its mission 'freedom to create', Media City has very rapidly become the Middle East media hub Sheikh Mohammed bin Rashid Al Maktoum envisaged it would be. CNN,

TOP FIVE LOCAL MAGS

- *Ahlan* – Dubai's even gossipier version of *Hello!*
- *Bidoun* – cutting-edge art and culture in the Arab diaspora
- *Viva* – glossy cross between *Elle* and *Cosmo*
- *Sourah* – design and photography by young Emiratis
- *Millionaires* – who's buying what and where you can get yours!

THE TIMES THEY ARE A-CHANGIN'

No more than a couple of years ago, the front pages of the local papers were reassuringly familiar. A Sheikh said something wise, had a successful meeting or received a message of congratulations and hardly a day went by without a call for Arab unity in the op-ed columns. And there was plenty you wouldn't read about. Local newspapers and magazines, both in Arabic and English, followed a careful policy of self-censorship. For expatriate journalists who broke the rules, the next question they'd be asking is whether their seat was aisle or window.

In an effort to avoid that hastily arranged flight home, journalists avoided criticising the government, or anyone in authority, from the Sheikh down to motorcycle policemen. There was no reporting of a crime without the police permitting it, no coverage of a court case without a briefing from the court and certainly no reporting of a civil commotion, disturbance or protest. If there was a major local or regional disturbance, journalists had to wait for the government to give the go-ahead to report it. Sometimes this came days after the event, such as the Iraqi invasion of Kuwait in 1990, and sometimes it never came at all. The news 'angle' was usually the reaction of the senior-most official responsible (for example, 'Police chief warns polluters' rather than 'Polluters threaten wildlife'). And then something happened...

It all started with the hard-hitting reporting by Al-Jazeera and Abu Dhabi TV during the US invasion of Iraq and overthrow of Saddam Hussein. This local coverage attracted much support in Dubai and the region, and itself attracted media attention and opened up discussion. Add to that media companies such as Reuters, CNN and the BBC operating freely out of Dubai Media City, reporting what they wanted. Then throw highly popular, free, outspoken daily newspaper *7 Days* into the equation. Pretty soon Sheikh Mohammed was inviting the media to the palace and speaking at global media conferences calling for a free press and for the media to be open and critical. Next, he set up the Dubai Holding–owned Arab Media Group and encouraged the journalists to be daring. Its main paper, *Emirates Today*, features strong investigative reporting on local social issues, crime and scandals, and has critically covered everything from growing domestic violence in the Emirati home and the gruesome murder of a child to strikes by Indian construction workers, the capture of a female Russian counterfeiting gang, and a man's conviction for bestiality (he claimed he was in love with the camel!). The times have certainly changed.

Reuters, MBC, CNBC, Al Arabiya, Arabian Radio Network, Lowe, and dozens of advertising agencies, newspapers, magazines and production companies have moved their regional headquarters here, working alongside scores of freelance writers, producers, directors, graphic artists, web designers, photographers, musicians, technicians and animators. The City's annual international Ibda'a (creativity) Awards for media students is bringing talent here from as far afield as South Africa and Australia. Winners receive internships with local media companies, and Media City continues to grow.

For information on the changing face of local media, see the boxed text, above.

LANGUAGE

You'll have little trouble making yourself understood in Dubai; while Arabic is the official language, English is the language of business, though it also competes with Hindi and Urdu as the lingua franca. If you venture out into rural areas, though, you'll find that English is not as widely spoken or understood as you might have thought. While signs, ATMs and automated telephone services in Dubai are generally in both Arabic and English, in smaller settlements signage is often in Arabic only.

Knowing the basic fives (hello, goodbye, yes, no and thank you) – in Arabic, Urdu, Hindi, Farsi, Sinhala, Tagalog, Malayalam, Indonesian, Nepalese, Russian

WASTA

When visiting Dubai, you might hear expats talking about *wasta*. The term translates loosely as 'influence high up' and having *wasta* can grease the wheels in just about every transaction in Dubai. Most Westerners get a little outraged at the thought of a select few receiving favours and special treatment because of powerful contacts – until, of course, they want some help themselves. Then being friends with a local who has *wasta* becomes a very desirable thing! But the funny thing is that those who claim to have *wasta* usually don't and those that do generally don't mention it!

and Vietnamese – will win you some fast friends in Dubai. All would be very useful if you aim to chat to taxi drivers, watchmen, waiters, maids, cleaners, shop assistants, bank tellers, sales staff, security guys, etc. For some useful words in Arabic, see Language (p191). If you get stuck, mime.

ECONOMY & COSTS

Oh you who believe! Eat not up your property among yourselves in vanities, but let there be amongst you traffic and trade by mutual goodwill.

Quran 4:29

Dubai is the second richest emirate in the UAE, after the capital, Abu Dhabi. While most visitors think Dubai became rich through oil, what it's actually done is used its modest oil resources to create the infrastructure for trade, manufacturing and tourism.

About 70% of the UAE's non-oil GDP is generated in Dubai, and about 93% of Dubai's GDP is not oil based. Dubai's reserves of oil and gas were never huge and Dubai's oil industry will be starting to wind down by 2010.

While many analysts believe that Dubai has expanded too far, too fast, and that its economy is heading for trouble, others believe the city has a sufficiently sturdy economic base to survive any bumps in the road – such as the current inflation level (10%) and the troubling housing crisis which saw rents go up an average of 40% in 2005.

Dubai's main exports are oil, natural gas, dates and dried fish; top export destinations are Japan, Taiwan, the UK, the US and India. Imports are primarily minerals and chemicals, base metals (including gold), vehicles and machinery, electronics, textiles and foodstuffs; the main importers into Dubai are the US, China, Japan, the UK, South Korea and India. Dubai's re-export trade (where items such as whitegoods come into Dubai from the manufacturers and then are sent onwards) makes up about 80% of the UAE's total re-export business. Dubai's re-exports go mainly to Iran, India, Saudi Arabia, Kuwait and Afghanistan.

HAWALA: THE BUSINESS OF TRUST

Imagine a money transfer system with minimal or no fees, quick delivery, and which is available to people in the poorest countries in the world. This is *hawala*, and Dubai is one of the key centres of this controversial practice.

Hawala is an Arabic term for a written order of payment. It works like this. You hand over your dirhams and the contact details of the recipient to your neighbourhood *hawala* trader. In return you get a code – say, a letter and four numbers. Then you ring up the recipient and give them the code. The trader contacts the people in his network. The next day, maybe two days later, the *hawala* trader's partner hands over the money, sometimes delivering it to the door of the recipient. The commission taken by the *hawala* traders might be as little as 1% or 2%, even zero if they can make a little profit on exchange-rate differences.

Some newspaper reports say as much as 90% of wages remitted to developing countries from the UAE were sent via this system until recently. Sending Dh100 to India via a bank would yield Rs1200, while via a *hawala* trader it yields Rs1280; while this is only US$2 difference, this amount still goes a long way in India's poorer regions and is a huge benefit to workers who can only afford to send home small amounts.

The *hawala* system has existed among Arab and Muslim traders for centuries as a defence against theft. It's a uniquely Islamic system, completely dependent on trust and honour. If a *hawala* trader breaks this trust, he'll be out of work as his reputation is crucial to his business.

The *hawala* system in Dubai grew through gold smuggling in the 1960s. Once the gold was sold in India or Pakistan, the traders couldn't get the money back to Dubai. They found their solution in the growing numbers of expatriate workers. The workers gave their wages to the gold traders in Dubai, and the gold traders in India paid their relatives.

Since the attacks of 9/11, the system is under increasing pressure as the USA – and its media outlets – has claimed that *hawala* is being used to transfer money to terrorists. In Dubai's open economy there used to be no restrictions on currency trading and no specific laws against *hawala* trading, but the authorities in the UAE have moved to set up a registration and reporting system for brokers.

Dubai is also the home to a huge dry-dock complex, the Middle East's busiest airport and duty-free operations, the UAE and region's biggest airline, and large free-trade zones at Jebel Ali, 30 minutes from the city centre, and at Dubai airport. Dubai airport is so busy now that a new airport (mainly catering for cargo) is being built at Jebel Ali. Attracting foreign business to its free-trade zones has been one of Dubai's greatest economic achievements in the last 20 years, with companies enticed here with the promise of full foreign ownership, full repatriation of capital and profits, no corporate tax for 15 years, no currency restrictions, and no personal income tax for staff.

HOW MUCH?

Short taxi ride Dh15

Movie ticket Dh30

Fresh juice cocktail Dh5

Copy of Gulf News newspaper Dh2

Abra ride (still!) Dh0.50

Beer at a 5 star hotel Dh20

18 holes of golf Dh450

Entry to Wild Wadi Dh120

A night at the Burj Al Arab Dh6000

Wasta (see the boxed text, p18) priceless

The Dubai Internet City and neighbouring Dubai Media City have been equally successful in adding a new hi-tech information and communication stratum to the city's economy as well as gaining credibility by attracting the big media players, such as CNN, to base their Middle East operations in Dubai. Other initiatives, such as Health City, have been slower to take off.

Dubai's tourism industry has also exploded. The city's tolerance of Western habits, profusion of quality hotels, long stretches of beach, warm winter weather, shopping incentives and desert activities have helped it become the leading tourist destination in the Gulf and local tourism authorities expect to attract 15 million visitors per annum by 2010.

For Emirati citizens all this prosperity translates into benefits of which the rest of the world only dreams: free health care, free education, heavily subsidised utilities and, in some cases, free housing. Dubai's per capita income is around Dh60,000 per annum, while the monthly salary of an unskilled expat labourer is anywhere between Dh500 to Dh1000 per month.

And while the globalisation of the international labour market (read: cheap foreign labour) has made the phenomenal growth of Dubai so attainable, there is one hurdle in the economy that Dubai is seeking to overcome. Dubai is highly dependent upon this expat labour and, at the same time, its citizens are having trouble finding meaningful employment. While the government in the past had made some attempt to 'Emiratise' the economy by placing nationals in the public workforce and imposing local employee quotas on private companies, this hasn't been particularly successful. Rightly seeing this as a major concern, Dubai's new ruler Sheikh Mohammed has taken over responsibility for this – and given his track record, meaningful results are expected.

One of the problems he faces with this issue is that private companies are reluctant to hire nationals, often with the misguided notion that they are lazy. However, one of the key problems is that nationals expect to start on a salary that's far above what the equivalent expat would receive – with predictable results. There is no doubt that Dubai will be dependent on foreign labour and expertise for a long time to come.

GOVERNMENT & POLITICS

Dubai is the second most powerful of the seven emirates that make up the UAE, with Abu Dhabi being both the capital and home to most of the country's oil wealth. In each emirate, power rests with a ruling tribe, which in Dubai's case is the Maktoums. As yet, there are no political parties or general elections in Dubai and, even if there were, it would be hard to imagine the Maktoums being deposed, having resided over such extraordinary growth.

With Dubai becoming so strong over the years, it has fought hardest to preserve as much of its independence as possible and to minimise the power of the country's federal institutions. Along with Ras al-Khaimah, it maintains a legal system separate from the federal judiciary.

Politically, the relative interests of the seven emirs are fairly clear. Abu Dhabi is the largest and wealthiest emirate and has the biggest population. It is, therefore, the dominant member of the federation and is likely to remain so for some time. Dubai is the second largest emirate by population, with an interest in upholding its free-trade policies and a pronounced independent streak. The other emirates are dependent on subsidies from Abu Dhabi, though the extent of this dependence varies widely.

The forum where these issues are discussed is the Supreme Council, the highest legislative body in the country. The council, which tends to meet informally, comprises the seven emirs. New federal laws can be passed with the consent of five of the seven rulers. The Supreme Council also elects one of the emirs to a five-year term as the country's president. After the death of the founder of the country and its first president, Sheikh Zayed, in late 2004, power passed peacefully to his son Sheikh Khalifa bin Zayed Al Nahyan.

There is also a cabinet and the posts within it are distributed among the emirates. Most of the federal government's money comes from Abu Dhabi and Dubai so members of these governments hold most of the important cabinet posts.

Sheikh Zayed bin Sultan Al Nahayan (left) and Sheikh Maktoum bin Rashid Al Maktoum (right), Sheikh Zayed Rd

The cabinet and the Supreme Council are advised, but cannot be overruled, by the Federation Council of Ministers, a 40-member consultative body whose members are appointed by the emirs. Abu Dhabi and Dubai hold almost half of the council's seats, and all the council's members come from leading Emirati merchant families.

DUBAI INCORPORATED & THE PORTS SCANDAL

To manage the huge number of infrastructure and investment projects that the Dubai government was undertaking, Dubai Holding was set up in 2004. Mohammed Al Gergawi, Executive Chairman of Dubai Holding, is overseeing some 19 companies that range from Dubai Media City to Dubailand. While it is government owned, it works closely with private partners on projects in Dubai, the Middle East and beyond.

Overseeing projects such as The Palm and The World is Dubai Ports World. The Dubai Ports Authority (DPA) and its international arm, DPI Terminals, merged to create the company. In 2006, as part of their global expansion, DP World bought The Peninsular and Oriental Steam Navigation Company (P&O), who just happened to manage several ports in the United States.

Of course the thought of Arabs managing some US ports drove the press and politicians into a frenzy (fuelled by the fact that two of the 9/11 bombers were from the UAE and that DP World is owned by the Dubai government). Conflating the issue was easy, and it dominated the US media for weeks, in the process dredging up every negative Arab stereotype imaginable. Perhaps sensing the press was not going to let up, DP World decided to sell the port operations to a US-based company.

Within Dubai, the Dubai Municipality is effectively the local government for the emirate, handling everything from economic planning to the rubbish collection. Above the municipality is Sheikh Mohammed's private office, The Executive Office, along with the official administrative body called the Diwan or the Ruler's Office.

ENVIRONMENT

CLIMATE

For information on Dubai's climate, see p178.

THE LAND

Dubai sits on the Gulf, in the northwest region of the UAE. This city is the capital of the emirate of the same name, which is the second largest of the seven emirates that comprise the UAE. The emirate of Dubai is 3885 sq km and the constantly expanding city is roughly 35 sq km – now nearly doubled by The Palm and The World projects. Dubai Creek, which extends 12km inland from the coast, divides the city in two.

Prior to settlement, this area was flat sabkha (salt-crusted coastal plain). The sand mostly consists of crushed shell and coral and is fine, clean and white. The sabkha was broken only by clumps of desert grasses and a small area of hardy mangroves at the inland end of the Creek. Photographs of the area from the early 20th century show how strikingly barren the landscape was.

East of the city, the sabkha gives way to north–south running lines of dunes. The farming areas of Al-Khawaneej and Al-Awir, now on the edge of Dubai's suburbia, are fed by wells. Further east the dunes grow larger and are tinged red with iron oxide. The dunes stop abruptly at the gravel fans at the base of the rugged Hajar Mountains (see p159), where there are gorges and waterholes. A vast sea of sand dunes covers the area south of the city, becoming more and more imposing as it stretches into the desert known as the Empty Quarter, which makes up the southern region of the UAE and the western region of Saudi Arabia (you can see the Empty Quarter from Al Ain, p164). North of Dubai, along the coast, the land is tough desert scrub broken by inlets similar to Dubai Creek, until you reach the mountainous northern emirates.

GREEN DUBAI

Dubai is a very clean city compared to most in the region, though air pollution from the constant traffic is starting to become an issue, and the Creek suffers from marine pollution. In contrast to Abu Dhabi's emphasis on the 'greening of the desert', Dubai's efforts are somewhat lacklustre. There are a number of well-established parks and gardens around the city (and a huge new one at Za'abeel, p56) and some major roads are lined with palm trees, shrubs, flowers and manicured lawns, but Dubai has none of the vast forestry projects that characterise Abu Dhabi emirate.

One of the biggest problems facing Dubai is that much of the population appear to be uneducated or unconcerned about street litter. You will still see rubbish left on beaches, in parks or thrown out of car windows. As a result, an enormous number of workers are employed to make sure the rubbish on the street doesn't stay around to sully the city's image, and the municipality has slapped on a Dh500 fine for littering. Dubai generates one of the highest per capita volumes of waste in the world, and the Emirates Environmental Group (www.eeg-uae.org) has opened a number of recycling centres around the city.

Because of the proximity of Dubai's oil industry to the city, there is a high risk of oil spills off the coast. Over the years the damage caused by these spills has prompted a concerted effort by government agencies to monitor and control marine pollution, not least because they threaten the city's vital desalination plants. Oil companies are required to spend money on the protection of the coast.

Muslim expats answer the call to prayer wherever they are, including Creekside Park (p54)

Local Environmental Organisations

The Federal Environmental Agency legislates on environmental issues and encourages communication on these issues between the emirates. There are also a number of NGOs concerned with the environment.

Emirates Diving Association (☎ 393 9390; www.emiratesdiving.com) This association is an active participant in local environmental campaigns, with an emphasis on the marine environment.

Emirates Environmental Group (☎ 331 8100; www.eeg-uae.org) This group organises educational programmes in schools and businesses as well as community programmes, such as clean-up drives.

PLANTS & ANIMALS

In Dubai's parks you will see indigenous tree species such as the date palm and the neem (a botanical cousin of mahogany), and a large number of imported species, including lovely smelling eucalypts. The sandy desert surrounding the city supports wild grasses and the occasional date-palm oasis.

In the salty scrublands further down the coast you might spot the desert hyacinth emerging in all its glory after the rains. It has bright yellow and deep-red dappled flowers.

Decorating the flat plains that stretch away from the foothills of the Hajar Mountains, around Hatta (see p159), are different species of flat-topped acacia trees. The ghaf also grows in this area; this big tree looks a little like a weeping willow and is incredibly hardy as its roots stretch down for about 30m, allowing it to tap into deep water reserves. The tree is highly respected in the Arab world as it provides great shade and food for goats and camels; it's also a good indicator that there's water in the surrounding vicinity.

As in any major city, you don't see much wildlife. Urbanisation, combined with zealous hunting, has brought the virtual extinction of some species. These include the houbara bustard, the striped hyena and the caracal (a cat that resembles a lynx). The Arabian oryx (also called the white oryx), however, is one success story. As part of a programme of the **Dubai Desert Conservation Reserve** (DDCR; www.ddcr.org), it has been successfully reintroduced.

On the fringes of the city, where the urban sprawl gives way to the desert, you may see a desert fox, sand cat or falcon if you are very lucky. Otherwise, the only animals you are likely to encounter are camels and goats. The desert is also home to various reptile species, including the desert monitor lizard (up to a metre long), the sand skink, the spiny-tailed agama and several species of gecko. The only poisonous snakes are vipers, such as the sawscaled viper, which can be recognised by its distinctive triangular head. There are even two remarkably adapted species of toad, which hibernate for years burrowed deep in wadis between floods.

The city is a hot spot for bird-watchers; because of the spread of irrigation and greenery, the number and variety of birds is growing. Dubai is on the migration path between Europe, Asia and Africa, and more than 320 migratory species pass through in the spring and autumn, or spend the winter here. The city's parks, gardens and golf courses sustain quite large populations, and on any day up to 80 different species can be spotted. Species native to Arabia include the crab plover, the Socotra cormorant, the black-crowned finch lark and the purple sunbird.

Artificial nests have been built to encourage flamingos to breed at the Dubai Wildlife & Waterbird Sanctuary (p57) at the inland end of Dubai Creek. In addition to flamingos, ducks, marsh harriers, spotted eagles, broad-billed sandpipers and ospreys all call the sanctuary home – for bird-watchers, this place is a must-visit.

The waters off Dubai teem with around 300 different types of fish. Diners will be most familiar with the hammour, a species of groper, but the Gulf is also home to an extraordinary range of tropical fish and several species of small sharks. Green turtles and hawksbill turtles used to nest in numbers on Dubai's beaches, but today their nesting sites are restricted to islands. Although you won't see them around Dubai, the coastal waters around Abu Dhabi are home to the Gulf's biggest remaining population of dugongs, where they feed off sea grasses in the shallow channels between islands.

Arts & Architecture

Arts & Architecture

Dubai's architecture is eclectic and audacious. The city's anything-is-possible and nothing-is-impossible attitude has resulted in some of most attention-grabbing edifices in the world. Dubai's daring buildings are the first thing you notice, and the architectural marvels that travellers most want to see. The iconic Burj Al Arab, for example, tops everybody's list of sights to tick off, with most visitors content to take a photo of its stunning exterior rather than experience its 'seven star' services. Because Dubai has no one city centre, no plaza or central square in which people can meet, sit, gather, celebrate or even protest, buildings – especially hotels and malls – become central points of social activity. The Madinat Jumeirah complex is the best example, with its three hotels, dozens of restaurants, bars, music venues, theatres, shops, sports facilities and spa, along with picturesque places to sit and watch the world go by (there are few better postcard-writing spots in Dubai than one of the cafés overlooking its amphitheatre, from where you can ponder the extraordinariness of it all). For the traveller to Dubai, it's the city's buildings that make the place so engaging.

Sheikh Zayed Rd has become synonomous with skyscrapers that have a distinctive touch

The arts scene in Dubai is at last catching up. While its newborn cinema (not to mention nonexistent literature) has a long way to go before it grows up, the city's plucky painters, photographers and musicians, like its architects and fashion designers, are starting to show a sense of precociousness in their work that we've not seen before. Perhaps it's an extension of Dubai's increasing complexity, and the renewed confidence, spirit and optimism sweeping the city. For visitors, right now Dubai is a pretty exciting place to be.

ARCHITECTURE

Surprisingly, for a city with few buildings older than 100 years, the economic boom of the last 30 years has left it an architectural mish-mash. That said, the incongruous blend of traditional Arabian architecture with modern constructions straight out of science fiction make the city an amazing sight. A boat ride along the Creek takes you from the wind-tower houses in the Bastakia Quarter of Bur Dubai to the pointed dhow-like roof of the Dubai Creek Golf & Yacht Club, via the sail-like National Bank of Dubai. As you'll notice, these modern structures sit comfortably with the traditional architecture of the cosmopolitan city, its contrast representative of other juxtapositions in Dubai – East and West, old and new. Interestingly, much of the city's recent architecture, such as Madinat Jumeirah (but also private residences), sees a return to traditional Arabian forms, although projects such as Burj Dubai show that the cloud-busting skyscraper isn't going anywhere in Dubai but up.

TRADITIONAL ARCHITECTURE

On your wanderings around the city, you'll notice that Dubai's traditional architecture consists of essentially four types of buildings – domestic (residential homes), religious (mosques), defensive (forts and watchtowers) and commercial (souqs). Readily available materials, such as gypsum and coral from offshore reefs and from the banks of the Creek, were put to use. The Sheikh Saeed al-Maktoum House (p56) in Shindagha is a fine example of this kind of construction. Limestone building blocks were also used and mud cemented the stones together. However, mud constructions suffered badly in the heat and had a limited lifespan, sometimes only a few years. Interestingly, the dimensions of buildings were often governed by the length of timber, mainly from India or East Africa, that could be loaded onto a dhow! There were two types of traditional house – the *masayf,* a summer house incorporating a wind-tower, and the *mashait,* a winter house with a courtyard. You'll see both of these in the Bastakia Quarter (p53).

When you explore the lanes surrounding Bur Dubai Souq (p53) and behind Al-Ahmadiya School (p50) in Deira, you'll see that the alleyways are narrow and the buildings close together. The lanes are narrow to increase the velocity of wind, keeping the neighbourhood cooler, while houses, souqs and mosques were built close together to provide maximum shade so that inhabitants could move around town in comfort, protected from the harsh sun.

DUBAI'S NOTABLE BUILDINGS

Burj Al Arab (p58) Sheikh Mohammed wanted a landmark to rival the Eiffel Tower or Sydney Opera House, and the Burj Al Arab (Arabian Tower) is like no other. It was completed in 1999, and is set on an artificial island 300m from the shore. The 60-floor, sail-shaped structure is 321m high. A translucent fibreglass wall serves as a shield from the desert sun during the day and a screen for an impressive light show each night. It's *the* iconic symbol of Dubai.

Dubai Creek Golf & Yacht Club (p112) When you cross the bridges over the Creek, you'll notice the pointed white roof of the clubhouse set amid artificial, undulating hillocks. The idea behind this 1993 design was to incorporate a traditional element – the white sails of a dhow – into the form and style of the building, and while this motif is becoming overused now, it's ageing well.

Dusit Dubai (p148) Sheikh Zayed Rd has many modern skyscrapers, but none as eye-catching as this one. The 153m-high building has an inverted 'Y' shape – two pillars that join to form a tapering tower. It's supposed to evoke the Thai joined-hands gesture of greeting, appropriate for this Thai hotel chain – but it's gimmicky.

Emirates Towers (p149) Designed in an ultramodern internationalist style, the twin, triangular, gunmetal-grey towers on Sheikh Zayed Rd soar from an oval base and are among the world's tallest. The taller of the two (355m) houses offices, while the other (305m) is a hotel. Balanced by the curvilinear base structure, the curved motif is also repeated in the upper storeys of the buildings. Simply stunning.

Jumeirah Beach Hotel (p150) This long S-shaped construction represents a wave, with the Gulf Sea as its backdrop. The glimmering façades of the hotel and its close neighbour, the Burj Al Arab, are achieved by the use of reflective glass and aluminium. The two structures combined – a huge sail hovering over a breaking wave – symbolise Dubai's maritime heritage.

Madinat Jumeirah (p151) A modern interpretation of the kind of ancient Arabian skyscraper city you find in Yemen and Saudi Arabia, magical Madinat Jumeirah is an expression of the city's renewed confidence and pride in the region's history and culture, and proof that it doesn't need tall shiny buildings to tell the world it's modern.

National Bank of Dubai (Map pp216–17) This shimmering building off Baniyas Rd, Deira, overlooking the Creek, has become another quintessential symbol of Dubai. Designed by Carlos Ott and completed in 1997, it combines simple shapes to represent a dhow with a sail billowing. The bronze windows reflect the activity on the Creek and at sunset, when the light is just right, it's a beautiful sight.

World Trade Centre (Map p226) As soon as rumours started to spread that they might pull down Dubai's beloved first skyscraper, built in 1979, everyone started to reappraise the city's first icon. (We always loved it!) The kind of structure *Wallpaper** likes to do photo spreads on – its beehive-like exterior is a form of sun-shading. Timeless. But who knows how much time it has left?

Wind-towers

Wind-towers, or *barjeel* in Arabic, are the Gulf's unique form of non-mechanical air-conditioning, and scores of original wind-towers still exist in the Bastakia (p53). Traditional wind-towers, rising 5m or 6m above a house, are open on all four sides to catch the breezes, which are channelled down around a central shaft and into the room below. In the process, the air speeds up and is cooled. The cooler air already in the tower shaft pulls in, and subsequently cools the hotter air outside through simple convection. It works amazingly well. Sitting beneath a wind-tower when it's a humid 40°C, you'll notice a distinct drop in temperature and a consistent breeze even when the air outside feels heavy and still. Test out the one at Dubai Museum (p54).

The wealthy Persian merchants who settled in Dubai around the beginning of the 20th century were the first to build a large number of wind-towers in the Bastakia. In some houses the tallest wind-tower was above the master bedroom, while smaller wind-towers cooled the living rooms. The merchants brought red clay from Iran, which they mixed with manure to make *saruj*. This was baked in a kiln and used to build the foundations of the wind-tower house. Other materials included coral rock and limestone for the walls and plaster for decorative work. The walls were built as thick as 60cm, so the house could be extended upwards if the family expanded. Chandel wood from East Africa, palm-frond matting, mud and straw were used to build the roofs.

> ## KEYS TO THE CITY
>
> Architectural buffs and kitsch-souvenir collectors won't be able to resist taking home one of the more practical keepsakes around (are you really going to use a Burj Al Arab paperweight?) – a key ring dangling with miniature cut-outs of Dubai's most visible architectural landmarks: Bur Al Arab, Dubai Creek Golf & Yacht Club, Jumeirah Mosque, the National Bank of Dubai and Emirates Towers.

Courtyard Houses

Houses in Dubai were traditionally built around a central courtyard. The courtyard, known as *al-housh* in Arabic, was the heart and lungs of a house. All the rooms of the traditional house surrounded the courtyard and all doors and windows opened onto it, except those of the guest rooms, which opened to the outside of the house. A veranda provided shade, kept sun out of rooms at certain times of the day, and was usually the place where the women did weaving and sewing. For great examples of courtyard houses, visit the Heritage House (p52) in Deira or XVA (p56) in the Bastakia.

Barasti

Barasti describes both the traditional Arabian method of building a palm-leaf house and the completed house itself. *Barasti* houses are made from a skeleton of wooden poles (date-palm trunks) onto which *areesh* (palm leaves) are woven to form a strong structure through which air can still circulate. They were extremely common throughout the Gulf in the centuries before the oil boom, though few examples of this type of house survive today. They were relatively easy to build and maintain since, unlike the mud-brick houses you find in the oases around Al-Ain and Buraimi, their construction didn't require water. The circulation of air through the palms also made *barasti* houses much cooler than mud-brick ones during the summer. The courtyard in the Dubai Museum (p54) and the Heritage Village (p55) in Shindagha both contain examples of *barasti* houses.

Mosques

Fundamentally simple structures, mosques are made up of a few basic elements, which are easy to identify. The most visible of these is the minaret, the tower from which the call to prayer is broadcast five times a day. Virtually every mosque in the world has a minaret; many have several. The first minarets were not built until the early 8th century, some 70 years after the Prophet's death. The idea for minarets may have originated from the bell towers that Muslim armies found attached to some of the churches they converted into mosques during the early years of Islam. The more minarets on a mosque, the more important it is. No mosque has more than seven minarets, the number on the Grand Mosque in Mecca.

A mosque must also have a mihrab, a niche in the wall facing Mecca, indicating the qibla, the direction believers must face while praying. Mihrabs were thought to have been introduced into Islamic architecture around the beginning of the 8th century, and like minarets they can be simple or elaborate. The minbar, a pulpit chair traditionally reached by three steps, dates from the Prophet's lifetime.

Mosques need to have a water supply so that worshippers can perform the wudu or ablutions required before they begin praying. Neighbourhood mosques in Dubai are visited five times a day for prayers, with worshippers travelling further afield to larger mosques for Friday prayers.

The Jumeirah Mosque (p60) is based on the Anatolian style, identified by a massive central dome, while other mosques in Dubai are based on Iranian and Central Asian models, which have more domes covering different areas of the mosque. Shiite mosques are identifiable by their exquisite green and blue faïence tile work covering the façades and main dome. One stunning example is the Iranian Mosque (p59) on Al-Wasl Rd, while the multidomed Grand Mosque (p55) in Bur Dubai is a variation on the Anatolian style.

> ## DUBAI ARCHITECTURE & DESIGN
> Architecture and design enthusiasts will get excited about this comprehensive guide to 30 of Dubai's most impressive buildings, hotels, restaurants and boutiques. Produced by daab, who have published fabulous books on Shanghai, Tokyo and New York design, this is one for city lovers and style buffs, with info about the architects and designers, and neat layouts of the stylish spaces.

MODERN ARCHITECTURE

In contrast to the traditional architecture that was all about function over form, and was built for the environment, modern architecture in Dubai (until recently) has embraced an 'anything goes' ethos with complete disregard to the climate. About 90% of Dubai's architecture can be described as cosmopolitan or international and is built using concrete, steel and glass. However, many architects have recently started to question the thinking behind building glass towers in a country with extreme heat. The huge cooling costs alone are reason to go for designs that better respond to and integrate with the weather and surroundings. Because these materials absorb heat and transfer it to other parts of the construction, they also cause damage over time. As a result, hi-tech, state-of-the-art materials with greater heat resistance are now starting to be used. Certainly some of the newer housing developments are doing so. Other developments, such as the Jumeirah Beach Residence, consist

BURJ DUBAI

It was inevitable that Dubai would want to create the world's tallest building. However, local developers Emaar aren't saying exactly how much taller the building will be than the current title-holder, Taipei 101 in Taiwan, which tops out at a staggering 509m. Predictions are that it will be a couple of hundred metres taller, thus securing its place in the record books until the next Dubai tower goes up!

Given its height, thankfully the Burj Dubai design looks elegant, inspired by the hymenocallis flower and Islamic geometric shapes. The central core of the building will be surrounded by three elements staggered in height, creating a spiral effect. In typical Dubai fast-track style, the winning design (by Chicago-based architect Adrian Smith) was picked from a competition in 2003, construction began in 2004, and by March 2005 the foundations were complete. The all-concrete tower is expected to be finished in 2008 and is going up at a staggering one floor a week with the pace expected to pick up, as the higher floors are smaller in size! In mid-2006 there was some industrial strife when the workers (angered by low salaries and mistreatment) smashed cars and offices. Though the rampage wasn't expected to have too much of an effect on the timeline, it did affect the bottom line, as they caused US$1 million worth of damage.

For the latest on Burj Dubai, see www.burjdubai.com.

of dozens of high-rise towers. One tower, however, will dwarf them all, and is set to steal the title of the world's tallest building from Taipei 101 – Burj Dubai (p29).

Designs that are ageing well – and plenty aren't – are usually the ones from established architects, such as Carlos Ott (National Bank of Dubai building). While most of Dubai's new buildings have been designed by international firms, the most significant local architect-designers happen to be members of the Sharjah royal family. Sisters Sheikha Mai and Sheikha Wafa Al Qasimini set up their own company, Ibtikari (Arabic for 'my innovation') in 2001 in association with a British architect and their commissions include both interior design (check out Amzaan boutique, p132) and architecture.

VISUAL ARTS

Dubai's visual-arts scene is at an exciting turning point. The established galleries, such as the Majlis Gallery (p56), Total Arts at The Courtyard (p57) and the Green Art Gallery (p59) now have some stiff competition from adventurous newer spaces, such as XVA (p56), Third Line (p57), B21 (p57) and Art Space (p57), and more are opening up all the time in Bur Dubai, Al Quoz and Bastakia.

XVA has a gallery, holds regular exhibitions, and is starting an artist-in-residence programme. In recent years, Total Arts' Dariush Zandi has been curating eclectic exhibitions of groundbreaking photography, painting and video by regional artists. One of the most memorable was an attempt to address post-9/11 Muslim stereotypes by Pakistani photographer Mansoora Hassan, whose self-portraits placed herself holiday snap–like in her burqa in front of well-known US monuments, such as the White House. Curator Sunny Rahbar has also been putting together some of the most exciting and innovative shows, particularly by young Emirati artists such as Lamia Gargash, and Iranian photographers like Ramin Haerizadeh, which have been a breath of fresh air for the arts scene. Palestinian artist/gallery owner, Jeffar Khaldi, has joined them, showing his own neo-expressionistic

---

TOP FIVE PHOTOGRAPHY BOOKS

- *Portrait of Jumeirah Beach Road* by Gregg Sedgwich – This book of wonderful images of everyday life on Jumeirah Beach is ideal for those looking for a souvenir of the 'real Dubai'.
- *Dubai, A City Portrait* by Patrick Lichfield – As usual with Lichfield, the quality is super, but many of the photos feel a little staged.
- *Dubai, A Collection of Mid 20th Century Photographs* by Ronald Codrai – Codrai visited Dubai in 1946 and stayed 35 years; his beautiful images of Dubai life document the city's 'coming of age'.
- *A Vanished World* by Wilfred Thesiger – These portraits of tribal peoples taken over decades of travel earned Thesiger worldwide recognition as a photographer. During five years in Arabia from 1945 to 1950 he captured his Bedu companions in their harsh desert home with great sensitivity.
- *Dubai Life & Times: Through the Lens of Noor Ali Rashid* by Noor Ali Rashid – A pictorial history of Dubai over the last four decades by the royal photographer. The photographs are absolutely stunning and very candid.

TOP FIVE ART MUSEUMS AND GALLERIES

Sharjah Art Museum (p158) The only real art museum in the UAE, it has a growing, challenging collection of contemporary art and some Orientalist painting. It also hosts the excellent cutting-edge Sharjah International Biennale.

Third Line (p57) A brave gallery (and our favourite) showing adventurous, provocative and playful work with exhibition highlights being mixed-media art by young Emirati women and Persian women's bold photography.

Majlis Gallery (p56) This beautifully restored Arabian house can prove more distracting than the art inside which is quality (but fairly mainstream) stuff.

Total Arts & The Courtyard Gallery (p57) Two strong commercial galleries focusing on Mid East and global art in this rather kitsch courtyard space.

XVA (p56) A wonderful art gallery, laid-back café, boutique hotel, and now, a film club – makes you want to move in!

work, and work by wonderful artists such as Youssef Nabil, in his gallery B21.

Although most of the art shown in the long-established galleries was primarily produced by expats, who mostly painted drab watercolours of Arabian horses and the like, more and more locals are starting to exhibit (thanks largely to the newer galleries already mentioned) and the work itself is more exciting, such as Mohammed Kanoo's Arabian pop art. More artists are experimenting in abstract and mixed-media forms, and Emirati artists in particular are producing playful works that appropriate their own cultural forms in innovative ways.

Much of the credit for the invigoration of the visual-arts scene goes to Sheikha Hoor al-Qasimi, Director of the Sharjah International Biennale, who excited art lovers once again with a provocative 7th Biennale in 2005, featuring some daring work on themes of belonging and identity, by 70 artists from 36 countries, including work by several Emirati artists. Young

Guests arrive at an exhibition of local women's art at The Third Line gallery (p57)

media graduate Nuha Hassan grabbed most of the attention with her striking piece combining large format photography and a performance with a roll of long red cloth which she draped over herself and onlookers – the performance by an Emirati woman in itself was extraordinary to see. The Sharjah Museum of Art (p156), headed by Abdul Rahim Salem, also exhibits work by locals, and a tremendous effort has been made by the Sharjah Ministry of Culture to encourage both Emiratis and resident expat artists to come together and practise their art at the various artists' studios in Sharjah.

LITERATURE

Dubai is a city with so many stories to tell, but while there's a great deal of literature in Arabic – mainly short stories – there is little available in English. Emirati writer Mohammed Al Murr has published 12 collections of short stories in Arabic, while only two of his books have been printed in English – *The Wink of the Mona Lisa* is a must-read if you want to learn more about the everyday life of Dubai's Emiratis. In *Heirloom: Evening Tales from the East,* former Iranian expat, now UAE citizen, Marian Behnam retells folk tales she recalls from the 1920s to the 1940s, many translated from Bastaki, her mother tongue.

Unfortunately, despite a number of well-meaning initiatives by cultural organisations and grass-roots projects, such as writing workshops and short-story competitions, nothing has changed – Dubai does not yet have any working authors, yet alone its great novel. Motivate Publishing is the only company releasing anything that resembles real literature, yet their focus is the glossy coffee-table photography books popular with tourists. It's curious that there aren't more expatriates documenting their travels and experiences living in the multicultural melting pot of Dubai where, on a daily basis, their lives are touched by the familiar and the foreign, the global and the local. The only UAE expat to write about her experiences is American Patricia Holton, whose *Mother Without A Mask* provides a rare insight into Emirati culture and everyday life from a foreigner's perspective. Unavailable in the UAE, Judith Caesar's nonfiction book *Writing off the Beaten Track: Reflections on the Meaning of Travel and Culture in the Middle East* includes her experiences in Dubai and the UAE.

ARAB POETRY

Nothing touches the heart of a Gulf Arab like poetry. Poetry dominates Arabian literature, and Arab cultural, intellectual and everyday life.

The Quran is regarded as divine poetry, but even before Islam the shrine of the Kaaba was bedecked with banners embroidered with poems. These poems, the *Muallaqat* (Hung Ones), are still studied at schools today.

In Bedouin culture a facility with poetry and language is greatly prized (even now). A poet who could eloquently praise his own people while pointing out the failures of other tribes was considered a great asset. Modern poets of note from the UAE include Sultan al-Owais, some of whose poems have been translated into English, and Dr Ahmed al-Madani, who wrote in the romantic *baiti* style. Palestinian resistance poets such as Mahmood Darwish and Samih al-Qasim are popular, though traditionalists complain that they have broken with the 16 classical metres of poetry developed by the 8th-century Gulf Arab scholar Al-Khalil bin Ahmed. There are currently over 50 well-known male poets in the UAE who still use the forms of classical Arabic poetry, though they often experiment by combining it with other styles. There are also some well-known female poets, most of who write in *tafila*, or prose.

Nabati, or vernacular poetry, is especially popular. The late Sheikh Zayed, former President of the UAE, and Sheikh Mohammed bin Rashid Al Maktoum, Dubai's ruler, are noted writers in this tradition. The Jebel Ali Palm Island project features small islands shaped out of Sheikh Mohammed's poetry. (If it's hard for you to get to grips with such a bizarre concept, see www.thepalm.ae and click on The Palm, Jebel Ali to view the design.) Many Arabic-language newspapers and magazines publish pages of *nabati* poetry.

Emiratis spontaneously recite poetry with their friends, during social occasions, public events and even in shopping centres. Young people publish their own poetry, particularly romantic poems, on websites and in student magazines, and produce documentaries about the Emirati passion for poetic words.

On the other hand, there is a flourishing children's literature scene, with delightful illustrated books published periodically. Julia Johnson's *Camel-o-shy* series is the most popular, and our favourite is still her *Humpy Grumpy Camel* counting book, which makes a wonderful educational souvenir for the kids, as does the *A is for Arabia* book.

While printed literature is thin on the ground, Dubai's expat bloggers at least give you some often amusing insights into living in this often frustrating city. For a sample of what's on offer, try secretdubai.blogspot.com.

CINEMA

At last, a home-grown Emirati film industry was born in 2005 with the release of the UAE's first feature film, *Al Hilm* (The Dream – appropriately titled!), by young male Dubai director, Hani Al Shabani, much to everyone's excitement. A light-hearted drama about a young writer's struggle to write a script, it was timely (if not overdue), and reflected the challenges that many young aspiring Emirati filmmakers face.

While the industry in the UAE has seen some really exciting developments – such as the establishment of the Dubai International Film Festival, and the Emirates Film Competition under the direction of Dubai local Masoud Amralla Al Ali going from strength to strength each year – there have been few initiatives that have had a direct impact on young Emiratis and their ability to make films. The shining stars of a few years ago, the young women short film–makers from the Higher Colleges of Technology, are all working in TV, advertising and marketing, and not getting a chance to fulfil their dreams of making feature films.

DUBAI ON FILM

While Western directors have chosen Dubai as a location because they wanted a generic futuristic city, to anyone watching their films who has ever been to Dubai, the city in their films could be nowhere *but* Dubai! Asian directors on the other hand have made the city the central focus of their story's subject, while Dubai's first feature-film director uses it only as a backdrop to his universal story about filmmakers struggling to tell their story.

- *Syriana* – Stephen Soderburgh (USA, 2005)
- *Code 46* – Michael Winterbottom (UK, 2004)
- *Dubai* – Rory B Quintos (Philippines, 2005)
- *Dubai Return* – Aditya Bhattacharyya (India, 2005)
- *The Dream* (Al Hilm) – Hani Al Shabani (UAE, 2005)

The cash that the Emirates Film Competition awards the young directors is not enough to make films of their own. While the Dubai film festival had an apprenticeship programme in 2005 and screened a number of short Emirati films, it has not yet started a local competition, choosing to spend its phenomenal budget on bringing big Hollywood stars to the festival instead. What the industry needs is a film commission, script fund and grants for local talent, and until that happens, your only chance of seeing Emirati films is to visit Dubai in December for the film festival, or Abu Dhabi in March for the Emirates Film Competition.

SONG & DANCE

DANCE

Dubai's contact with East and North African cultures through trade, both seafaring and by camel caravan, has brought many musical and dance influences to the UAE shores. Thus, traditional songs and dances are inspired by the environment – the sea, desert and mountains.

One of the most popular dances is the *liwa*, performed to a rapid tempo and loud drumbeat. Most likely brought to the Gulf by East African slaves, it is traditionally sung in Swahili. Another dance, the *ayyalah*, is a typical Bedouin dance, celebrating the courage, strength and unity of the tribe. The *ayyalah* is performed throughout the Gulf, but the UAE has its own variation, performed to a simple drumbeat. Anywhere between 25 and 200 men stand with their arms linked in two rows facing each other. They wave walking-sticks or swords in front of them and sway back and forth, the two rows taking it in turn to sing. It's a war dance and the words expound the virtues of courage and bravery in battle. You can see the dance on video at Dubai Museum (p54).

The instruments used at traditional musical celebrations in Dubai are the same as those used in the rest of the Gulf. The *tamboura,* a harplike instrument, has five strings made of horse gut, which are stretched between a wooden base and a bow-shaped neck. The base is covered with camel skin and the strings are plucked with sheep horns. It has a deep and resonant sound, a little like a bass violin.

A much less sophisticated instrument is the *manior*, a percussion instrument that's played with the body. It's comprised of a belt made of cotton, decorated with dried goats' hooves, which is wrapped around the player who keeps time with the beat of the *tamboura* while dancing. The *mimzar* is a wooden instrument a little like a small oboe, but it delivers a higher pitched sound, which is haunting and undeniably Middle Eastern.

An unusual instrument and one that you'll often see at song and dance performances is the *habban*, the Arabian bagpipes. Made from a goatskin sack, it has two pipes attached. The sack retains its goat shape and the pipes resemble its front legs. One pipe is used to

DUBAI INTERNATIONAL FILM FESTIVAL

Aimed at the multicultural local community and international visitors, the festival has several goals, one of which is to build cultural bridges and promote understanding, tolerance and peace. The festival is also part of a grand plan to develop Dubai as a regional film hub, and includes incentives for major players to move their base here, promoting Dubai as a location. In terms of content, the first two festivals in 2004 and 2005 were underwhelming apart from the excellent Arab programmes curated by Dubai local, Masoud Amralla Al Ali. Local residents have loudly complained that the festival seems to be all about pleasing the sponsors and getting international stars in the country and in the newspaper. If you're thinking of making the festival part of your trip to Dubai, focus on seeing the Middle Eastern films and give the others a miss.

Morgan Freeman & Mohammed Al Gergawi (Dubai Holding CEO) at the 2005 Dubai International Film Festival (p10)

blow air into the sack and the other produces the sound. The *habban* sounds much the same as the Scottish bagpipes, but is shriller in tone.

The *tabla* is a drum, and has a number of different shapes. It can resemble a bongo drum that is placed on the floor, or it can be a *jasr*, a drum with goatskin at both ends, which is slung around the neck and hit with sticks.

Traditional music and dance is performed spontaneously at weddings, social occasions and family gatherings. You may be lucky to see a performance if you're exploring an Emirati neighbourhood and come across a wedding tent; otherwise you'll have to visit the Heritage Village (p55) or catch a performance during the Dubai Shopping

DUBAI SOUNDS

- *Lemonada, The Arabian Latin Chillout Experience* – Ahmad Ghannoum's Arab fusion meets Bossa Nova sounds
- *Blue Bedouin* – Hussain Al Bagali's 'blissful and chilled-out beats from the desert'
- *Oryx* – Dubai expats combine ambient Arabian instrumentals, electronic dance music and Arabic chants.
- *Arabian Nights Party 2005* – The Arabian CD to put on at expat gatherings this year.
- *The Desert Lounge, Vol 1* – 'A musical evocation of Madinat Jumeirah' – well, Hotel Costes has its own CD!

Festival or Summer Surprises. Women should make an effort to visit the Village during the festival on a Ladies Night, when they'll get the rare opportunity to hear local women singing.

CONTEMPORARY MUSIC

Blue Bedouin, Oryx and, more recently, Ahmed Ghannoum's Lemonada are some of the more interesting contemporary sounds that have been coming out of Dubai in recent years. Ahmed Ghannoum's fusion of sounds (in the case of Lemonada, Arabic meets Brazilian Bossa Nova) is indicative of a lot of the music being produced by locals and expats at Dubai Media City – it's a direct result of creative collaboration between a culturally diverse team of musicians: a Syrian singer, Lebanese guitarist, French bassist, Sri Lankan pianist, Indian and African percussionists and a South African harpist.

A *local* live-music scene (in contrast to the expat cover bands and dull piano players that perform at most hotel bars) has been slow to take-off. Despite rare one-off performances in small venues by the odd college band, an annual Battle of the Bands competition and a small underground university music scene (with bands playing metal, punk and even ska at secret desert locations and friends' homes!), there have been no CDs released, no great discoveries, and few opportunities for the public to hear anything live, unfortunately.

The Arabic music you're most likely to hear on the radio is *khaleeji*, the traditional Gulf style, recognisable to those familiar with Arabic pop music. Popular singers include Mohammed Nasser, who had a major hit with Ya Bint, and Dubai-born Yaseer Habeeb, the first UAE national to have a hit in Europe and the Middle East.

For information on concerts and live music events, see p105.

History

History

THE RECENT PAST

Dubai is now the fastest-growing city in the world. Since its discovery of oil in 1966 – the most significant event in Dubai's recent history – and its first oil exports left its shores in 1969, Dubai's growth has accelerated at a dizzying pace, resulting in the extraordinary economic boom the city's experiencing today. But back in the late '60s, just as the revenue started to have its effect on the economy of Dubai, political changes were afoot...

When Britain announced its departure from the region in 1968, an attempt was made to create a nation that included the Trucial States (today's United Arab Emirates), Bahrain and Qatar. While the talks collapsed with Bahrain and Qatar (who both moved on to their own independence), the leaders of Abu Dhabi, Sheikh Zayed bin Sultan al-Nahyan (see the boxed text, p40), and Dubai, Sheikh Rashid bin Saeed Al Maktoum, went and strengthened their commitment to creating a single state.

After persistent persuasion by Sheikh Zayed, the federation of the United Arab Emirates (UAE) was born on 2 December 1971, consisting of the emirates of Dubai, Abu Dhabi, Ajman, Fujairah, Sharjah and Um Al Quwain, with Ras Al Kaimah joining in 1972. Impressively, the UAE remains to this day the only federation of Arab states in the Middle East.

Under that agreement, the emirs had approved a formula whereby Abu Dhabi and Dubai (in that order) would carry the most weight in the federation, but would leave each emir largely autonomous. Sheikh Zayed became the supreme ruler (or president) of the UAE, and Sheikh Rashid of Dubai assumed the role of vice-president.

Since federation, Dubai has been one of the most politically stable city-states in the Arab world; however, the fledgling nation has still had its teething problems. Border disputes between the emirates continued throughout the 1970s and '80s, and the level of independence that each emirate assumes has always been the subject of some long discussions.

SHEIKH MAKTOUM BIN RASHID AL MAKTOUM

Much of the modern-day success of Dubai is owed to Sheikh Maktoum bin Rashid Al Maktoum, who died at the age of 62 in early 2006. The ruler of Dubai, and vice-president and prime minister of the UAE, Sheikh Maktoum was the eldest and most introspective of Sheikh Rashid Al Maktoum's sons, and was appointed heir to the throne in 1958. Sheikh Maktoum studied at Cambridge in the early 1960s and was chosen to be prime minister of the UAE in the 1970s after federation. With the balance of power between Abu Dhabi and Dubai still not fully resolved, in 1979 Sheikh Maktoum ceded power to his father and an agreement between Abu Dhabi and Dubai was reached over the direction and vision for the country.

When Sheikh Rashid passed away in 1990 after a prolonged illness, Sheikh Maktoum officially succeeded his father, although in reality he'd already been working hard to ensure that the next generation of Dubai reaped the benefits of the burgeoning economy. Spreading the wealth through education, housing and greater job opportunities, and all the while diversifying Dubai's economic portfolio, his work set a solid platform for the phenomenal growth of Dubai today.

In the later years of his reign, his younger brother, Sheikh Mohammed, began working on a more active (and economically aggressive) expansion of Dubai. This formula saw Dubai's achievements grow rapidly. Also growing rapidly was the horse stable of the two brothers, Godolphin, which has gone on to make a significant mark in the history books of horse racing.

In Dubai the sheikh will most be remembered for the way he took the reigns from his father and coolly handled the rapid expansion of the city.

C 3000 BC	AD 700
The Magan civilisation dominates the world's copper trade	The Umayyads introduce Arabic and Islam to the region

KNOW YOUR HISTORY

There's lots of terrific stuff out there on Dubai history – while some of it can be fairly dry, we've selected the most fascinating reads. While not all of these books are specifically about Dubai, there's some great reading here about the region's history.

- *Father of Dubai: Sheikh Rashid bin Saeed al-Maktoum* by Graeme Wilson – A terrific photographic and narrative tribute to the founder of modern Dubai.
- *From Trucial States to United Arab Emirates* by Frauke Heard-Bey – An insight into a society in transition, including development of Dubai, by a leading scholar and long-term UAE expat.
- *Seafarers of the Emirates* by Ronald Codrai – This remarkable record recreates the lives of pearl divers, merchants, ship builders and seafarers, with photos taken in Dubai in the middle of the 20th century.
- *Arabian Destiny* by Edward Henderson – This wry memoir by a British colonial official includes perceptive observations of the society he lived in: Dubai hasn't simply changed since the 1950s, it's become a different place altogether.
- *Sheikhdoms of Eastern Arabia* by Peter Lienhardt and Ahmed Al Shahi – An insight into how oil wealth altered Arabia, tribal structure, gender relations, and the complex relationship between the ruling sheikhs and their subjects.
- *The Merchants: the Big Business Families of Saudi Arabia and the Gulf States* by Michael Field – A brief sketch of the rise of Dubai as a trading centre, and the role played by its powerful tribal relationships.

While Dubai and Abu Dhabi had an agreement to cooperate long before the nation was born, the relationship has not been without its difficulties. Achieving an equitable balance of power between the two emirates, as well as refining a unified vision for the country was much debated until 1979 when Sheikh Zayed and Sheikh Rashid sealed a formal compromise under which each gave a little ground on his respective vision of the country. The result was a much stronger federation in which Dubai remained a bastion of free trade while Abu Dhabi imposed a tighter federal structure on the other emirates. Rashid also agreed to take the title of Prime Minister as a symbol of his commitment to the federation.

Sheikh Rashid, the driving force behind Dubai's phenomenal growth and 'father of (modern) Dubai', died in 1990 after a long illness, and was succeeded as emir by the eldest of his four sons, Sheikh Maktoum bin Rashid Al Maktoum. Maktoum had been regent for his sick father for several years already, so he continued to follow in his father's footsteps with the expansion of Dubai.

Sheikh Maktoum fully realised that oil wealth was going to be merely a blip on the chart of Dubai's health, and so diversified Dubai's wealth. To his credit,oil-related revenue today accounts for less than 6% of Dubai's income. While still a relatively shy public leader, Sheikh Maktoum pursued a policy of promoting Dubai whenever and wherever possible, initiating events such as the Dubai World Cup (p10), the horse-racing event that put Dubai firmly on the world's sporting map.

However, it's the third son of the dynasty, Sheikh Mohammed bin Rashid Al Maktoum who has been the face of modern Dubai in the past few years. In early 1995, Sheikh Maktoum signed a decree that Sheikh Mohammed would be his successor, naming him Crown Prince of Dubai. By this stage though, most people had already

The house of Sheikh Saeed Al Maktoum (p56), grandfather of the current ruler of Dubai, is beautifully restored

1580	1833
Marco Polo describes Dubai as a prosperous town	Al Maktoum family arrives in Bur Dubai

acknowledged (privately, of course) that it was Sheikh Mohammed who would be taking Dubai to the next level. And with Sheikh Maktoum's death in January 2006, it meant that Dubai was going to go forward to that new stage sooner rather than later – and at a breathtaking pace!

Sheikh Mohammed, Dubai's new ruler (and now vice-president and prime minister of the UAE), is Dubai's futurist. Even with myriad projects under his belt, from the Burj Al Arab to The Palm, he's still stated that he's only achieved around 10% of his vision for Dubai. For the Burj Al Arab project, it's said that the Sheikh wanted a design that would be as resonant as the Eiffel Tower and the Sydney Opera House. And it's perhaps from this that we can get an idea of the breadth of what he wants to achieve. With the Burj Al Arab, Sheikh Mohammed wanted an iconic building, not because he wanted to ape other great cities in the world, but because all great capitals in the world have an iconic symbol. He just wanted to get Dubai on the map as soon as possible.

Sheikh Mohammed has placed his stamp on Dubai in other ways. Having married Princess Haya bint Al Hussein, the half-sister of King Abdullah II of Jordan in 2004, he is now the first Emirati leader to have a foreign wife who is both seen in public and in the daily newspapers – and managing to do it while barely raising a ripple within local society.

FROM THE BEGINNING
EARLY SETTLEMENT

Much less is known about the early history of the area that now forms the United Arab Emirates. However, archaeological remains found in Al-Qusais, on the northeastern outskirts of present-day Dubai, show evidence of humans here as far back as 8000 BC, after the end of the last Ice Age.

Up until 3000 BC the area supported nomadic herders of sheep, goats and cattle; these early inhabitants camped on the coast and fished during winter, and moved inland with their herds during summer (not so very different to what the Bedu did here just a short time ago). The first signs of trade emerged with the discovery of pottery from Ubaid (in present-day Iraq) dating back to 5000 BC. Agriculture developed with the cultivation of the date palm around 2500 BC, which not only provided food and a range of materials for building and weaving, but also shelter for smaller plants grown for food.

Archaeological evidence also suggests that this area, together with present-day Oman, was closely associated with the Magan civilisation during the Bronze Age. The Magans

---

BOOKS: ARABS & THE ARAB WORLD

Dubai may get only the briefest of mentions in these books, but they'll give you a solid understanding of the peoples and the region in which Dubai is a now a central focus.

- *The Arabs* by Peter Mansfield – This must-read book discusses Arabs, their characteristics, aspirations and future, from the pre-Islamic Arabian nomads, through the life of Prophet Mohammed, to the modern Arab renaissance.
- *Arabia and the Arabs: From the Bronze Age to the Coming of Islam* by Robert G Hoyland – From inscriptions, poetry, histories and archaeological evidence, we learn about Arabia, from ancient Sheba to the deserts and oases of the north.
- *A History of the Arab Peoples* by Albert Hourani – A bestseller when first published in 1991 (updated 2003), this superb book covers politics, culture, society, economy and thought.
- *Travellers in Arabia* by Robin Bidwell – Arabia as experienced by its earliest tourists: Burckhardt, Burton, Palgrave, Philby, Stark, Cox and Thesiger.
- *Arabian Sands* by Wilfred Thesiger – Fascinating accounts of five years spent with the Bedu of the Arabian peninsula in the Empty Quarter in the 1940s.

1841	1894
Al Maktoum's power base extends to Deira	Tax exemption for foreign traders declared

apparently dominated the ancient world's copper trade, exploiting the rich veins of copper in the hills throughout the Hajar Mountains, and near Sohar, in Oman. It's also likely that they traded pearls in Mesopotamia (now Iraq), and with the Indus Valley civilisation, in present-day Pakistan. However, all records of the Magan civilisation cease after the 2nd millennium BC, with some historians speculating that the desertification of the area hastened its demise.

There's little archaeological evidence of occupation of Dubai during the Iron Age, with the next major habitation of the area appearing to have been by the Sassanid empire. Archaeological excavations at Jumeirah reveal a caravan station dating from the 6th century AD, which is thought to have had links with the Sassanids. A dynasty that ruled in Persia from AD 224 to 636, the Sassanids wielded amazing power over the re-

Heritage House (p52) offers a glimpse of Dubai's past life

gion during this time, until the Umayyads, an Islamic tribe, uprooted them. Archaeologists seem to think that the buildings at Jumeirah were restored and extended by the Umayyad dynasty, making it the only site in the UAE to span the pre-Islamic and Islamic periods.

With the Umayyads came the Arabic language and unification with the Islamic world. Christianity made a brief appearance, in the form of the Nestorian sect, members of which had a monastery on Sir Bani Yas Island, west of Abu Dhabi, in the 5th century. However, it was the arrival of Islam that shaped the future of the region. Unfortunately the early Islamic period from the 7th to the 14th century hasn't been well documented in the UAE. All that's known is that during this period the area was loosely under the control of the Umayyads and their successors the Abbasids. After the Baghdad-based Abbasid dynasty went into decline around AD 1000, the centre of power in the Islamic world shifted to Cairo, leaving the UAE on the periphery. In the absence of centralised control, the tribes of the Arabian Peninsula asserted themselves in the hinterlands, while the coastal regions were dominated by trading ports such as Julfar, near present-day Ras al-Khaimah, and Hormuz, an island in the Strait of Hormuz.

It wasn't until the early Islamic period that the Gulf experienced its first boom in maritime trade, due to its location on the major trading routes between the Mediterranean Sea and Indian Ocean. However, trade soon became the backbone of the local economy as ships travelled as far as China, returning laden with silk and porcelain.

The West was first to hear about the settlement in Dubai from two Italian explorers: Gasparo Balbi and Marco Polo. In 1580 Marco Polo described Dubai as a prosperous town, largely dependent on pearl fishing…it would be very interesting to see how he'd describe it today!

EUROPEAN PRESENCE

Portugal became the first European power to take an interest in this part of the Gulf, attracted by lucrative trade routes with India and the Far East. The arrival of the well-armed Portuguese was a disaster for Muslim traders. The Portuguese wanted a monopoly on trade routes between Europe and India and tolerated no rivals. Local trade dried up to the extent that many coastal settlements were just about abandoned, with tribes taking refuge in oases

1930	1951
Dubai's pearling trade collapses	Trucial States Council founded

far from the coast such as Liwa and Al-Ain. While Portugal's occupation lasted until the 1630s, eventually extending as far north as Bahrain, the only evidence of their presence are the two cannons on display at the Dubai Museum (p54).

Next to arrive were the French and Dutch, who infiltrated the area in the 17th and 18th centuries and aspired to control the trading routes to the east. The Brits were equally intent on ruling the seas to protect the sea route to India, and in 1766 the Dutch finally gave way to Britain's East India Company, which had established trading links with the Gulf as early as 1616.

Throughout this time Dubai remained a small fishing and pearling hamlet, perched on a disputed border between two local powers – the seafaring Qawasim of present-day Ras al-Khaimah and Sharjah to the north, and the Bani Yas tribal confederation of what is now Abu Dhabi to the south. The region was also affected by the rivalries between bigger regional powers – the Wahhabi tribes (of what is now Saudi Arabia), the Ottoman Empire, the Persians and the British.

THE TRUCIAL COAST

At the beginning of the 19th century, Dubai was governed by Mohammed bin Hazza, who remained ruler of Dubai until the Al Bu Fasalah, a branch of the Bani Yas tribe from Abu Dhabi, came to dominate the town in 1833, severing it from Abu Dhabi. The Bani Yas were the main power among the Bedouin tribes of the interior. Originally based in Liwa, an oasis on the edge of the desert known as the Empty Quarter (Rub al-Khali) in the south of the UAE, the Bani Yas engaged in traditional Bedouin activities of camel herding, small-scale agriculture, tribal raiding and extracting protection money from merchant caravans passing through their territory! At the end of the 18th century, the leader of the Bani Yas moved from Liwa to the island of Abu Dhabi on the coast.

FATHER OF THE NATION

Visitors to Dubai will no doubt see enormous posters of a smiling sheikh in a pair of Ray Ban–style sunglasses – this is Sheikh Zayed bin Sultan al-Nahyan, the first, and up until his death in 2004, the only President of the UAE. Revered by his people, and often called 'father' by Emiratis, he commanded huge respect across the Middle East.

Sheikh Zayed was born in Abu Dhabi around 1918, and his father was ruler of Abu Dhabi from 1922 to 1926. After his dad's death in 1927, Sheikh Zayed relocated to Al Ain and spent his time studying the Quran and learning from local Bedouin tribesmen – the knowledge he gained here was crucial to his ability to pull a nation together decades later.

His first taste of politics began in 1946, when he was appointed ruler's representative in Al Ain, where he honed his famed negotiating skills. When the oil began flowing in Abu Dhabi in 1962, it soon became apparent that Sheikh Zayed had the right skills to handle the massive changes that were to come, and the sheikh soon took over from his older brother in managing Abu Dhabi's affairs. Seizing the opportunity, Sheikh Zayed built schools, hospitals and housing for his people, and when the British decided to withdraw from the Trucial States (as the UAE was known then) in 1968, he set out to federate the states and create a nation.

The act of pulling together these often-squabbling, sometimes-fighting seven states is key to Sheikh Zayed's legacy. Few thought it could be done, fewer thought it would last, but for three years Sheikh Zayed negotiated, cajoled and convinced the other states that a United Arab Emirates was the only way forward.

After he became President in 1971 (and was continually re-elected to the post up until his death), the distribution of wealth to the poorer emirates, as well as his handling of an ambitious Dubai, were key in keeping the fledgling nation together.

Sheikh Zayed had an almost obsessive ambition to 'green' the Emirates (the results of which you'll see if you visit Abu Dhabi, p168) and with keeping tradition alive. While in the Middle East it's almost obligatory to fawn and praise leaders, both past and present, in the UAE even the most cynical students of Arab politics note that the affection the people have for this leader runs far deeper than that.

1958	1966
Sheikh Rashid officially becomes ruler of Dubai	Oil discovered in Dubai

PEARLING

The heyday of pearling is laced with romanticism. But unfortunately for those who dove in the depths to collect pearls, it was a life of hardship and the rewards were no match for the dangers involved. Most of the divers were slaves from East Africa and the profits of the industry went straight to their master, the boat owner.

The only equipment the divers used was a rope tied around their waist, a turtle-shell peg on their nose and leather finger gloves to protect their hands from the sharp coral and shells. At certain times of the year they'd wear a muslin bodysuit to protect them from jellyfish stings. The best pearls were found at depths of up to 36m and divers would be underwater for around three minutes. To reach this depth they used a rope weighted with a stone, tied to the boat, and were thrown overboard.

The pearl-diving season lasted from May until September. On the ship there would be divers, men responsible for hauling up the divers after each dive, a cook, and boys employed to serve food and water, and open the oyster shells. Each boat also had a singer, called the *naham,* whose job was to lead the crew in songs or lighten their mood by singing to them. Many of the songs were about lucky men who had become rich through diving, and the joys of returning home after the diving season.

Back on shore, pearl merchants would grade the pearls according to size by using a number of copper sieves, each with different sized holes. The greatest market for pearls was originally India, but in the early 20th century the UK and US became keen buyers of the fashionable pearl. The discovery of the means to make artificial pearls in the early 20th century triggered the demise of the industry. The Dubai Museum (p54) and the Diving Village (p55) feature wonderful displays on pearling.

About 800 people from the Bani Yas tribe settled on the Bur Dubai Creek under the leadership of Maktoum bin Butti, who established the Maktoum dynasty of Dubai, which still rules the emirate today. For Maktoum bin Butti, good relations with the British authorities in the Gulf were essential to safeguard his new and small sheikhdom against attack from the larger and more powerful sheikhdoms of Sharjah to the north and Abu Dhabi to the south.

In 1841 the Bur Dubai settlement extended to Deira on the northern side of the Creek, though throughout the 19th century it largely remained a tiny enclave of fishermen, pearl divers, Bedouin, and Indian and Persian merchants. Interestingly, the Indians and Persians (now Iranians) still give much of the Creek its character today.

Things really began to change around the end of the 19th century. In 1892 the British, keen to impose their authority on the region and protect their Indian empire, extended their power through a series of so-called exclusive agreements under which the sheikhs accepted formal British protection and, in exchange, promised to have no dealings with other foreign powers without British permission. As a result of these treaties, or truces, Europeans called the area 'the Trucial Coast', a name retained until the 1971 federation.

The Al-Ahmadiya School (p50) was the oldest school in Dubai, dating back to 1912

1969
Oil exportation begins

1971
The UAE is established

41

At the end of the 19th century, Sharjah, the area's main trading centre, began losing its trade to Dubai. In 1894, Dubai's visionary ruler at the time, Sheikh Maktoum bin Hasher Al Maktoum, decided to give foreign traders tax exemptions, and the free port of Dubai was born!

Around the same time, Lingah (now Bandar-e Langeh), across the Strait of Hormuz in Iran, lost its status as a duty-free port. The Maktoums lured Lingah's disillusioned traders to Dubai at the same time as it managed to convince some of Sharjah's merchants to relocate.

At first the Persians who came to Dubai believed that it would just be a temporary move, but by the 1920s, when it became evident that the trade restrictions in southern Iran were there to stay, they took up permanent residence – in the Bastakia (p53).

More good news for Dubai came in the early 20th century when the Maktoums, probably with the assistance of the Persian merchants, prevailed on a British steamship line to switch its main port of call in the lower Gulf from Lingah to Dubai. This gave Dubai regular links with British India and the ports of the central and northern Gulf – Bahrain, Kuwait, Bushire and Basra. Dubai's importance to Britain as a port of call would remain in place for half a century, marking the beginning of Dubai's growth as a trading power and fuelling the prosperity that would follow. (Dubai's recent purchase of British company P&O, and its strategic control of ports all around the world, shouldn't really be a surprise to anyone then, should it?)

THE EXPANDING CITY

Dubai was well established as an independent town, with a population of about 10,000, by the beginning of the 20th century. Deira was the most populous area at this time, with about 1600 houses, inhabited mainly by Arabs, but also by Persians and Baluchis, who came from parts of what are now Iran, Pakistan and Afghanistan. By 1908 there were about 350 shops in Deira and another 50 in Bur Dubai, where the Indian community was concentrated. To this day the Bur Dubai Souq (p53) shows a strong Indian influence, and Bur Dubai is home to the only Hindu temple in the city.

The development of Dubai as a major trading centre was, ironically, spurred on by the collapse of the pearling trade, which had been the mainstay of its economy for centuries. The pearling trade had fallen victim both to the worldwide depression of 1929 and to the

THE RE-EXPORT TRADE

Dubai's economy is built on trade, especially the re-export trade, which started around the time of the collapse of the pearling trade in the 1930s. Its merchants imported goods, which they then sold on to other ports. In practice, this involved smuggling, especially of gold to India. The goods entered and exited Dubai legally; it was the countries at the *other* end of the trade that looked on it as smuggling.

WWII also played a role in the growth of the re-export trade. The war brought much of the trade to a standstill and this was compounded by a shortage of basic food supplies. The British government supplied the Trucial sheikhdoms with plenty of rice and sugar. Dubai merchants bought these goods cheaply and, finding themselves oversupplied, shipped them off to the black market in Iran.

It was around this time that modern Dubai began to take shape. During the 1950s, Sheikh Rashid became one of the earliest beneficiaries of Kuwait's Fund for Arab Economic Development, which loaned him money to dredge the Creek (it had become badly silted up, reducing the volume of Creek traffic) and to build a new breakwater near its mouth. The project was completed in 1963, and gold smuggling took off like a rocket, using the trade networks built up through the pearling business. India had banned gold imports after 1947 to stabilise its currency, which sent the price of gold in India soaring. In 1967 the price of gold in Dubai was US$35 an ounce, while in India it sold for US$68 an ounce. The gold trade peaked in 1997 when 660 tonnes of gold left Dubai.

Dubai's days as a smuggler's paradise are not over. The trade now supposedly focuses on Iran; dhows take cargo such as microwaves and flat-screen TVs to Iranian ports and return laden with caviar and carpets.

1979	1985
Sheikh Rashid declared prime minister of the UAE	Emirates airline is established in Dubai

RETURNING FIRE

The origins of the brief 1940 war between Dubai and Sharjah stem from a complicated struggle within the Al-Maktoum family. Sheikh Saeed Al Maktoum, the ruler of Dubai, was challenged in the 1930s by his cousin, Mani bin Rashid, who at one point controlled Deira while Sheikh Saeed held onto Bur Dubai across the Creek. Sheikh Saeed gained the upper hand and sent his cousin into exile in 1939. Mani bin Rashid and his followers then settled in Sharjah, too close to Dubai for Sheikh Saeed's comfort. Sheikh Saeed asked Sheikh Sultan of Sharjah to exile Mani bin Rashid, but Sheikh Sultan refused on the grounds that it compromised the traditions of Arab hospitality. After much fruitless diplomacy, a desultory war broke out in January 1940 between Dubai and Sharjah, all of 23km apart. The British tried to quell the war by restricting the import of firearms and ammunition. The rival forces then resorted to using ancient muzzle-loading cannons. The soldiers were sometimes able to recover the cannonballs fired at them and to fire them back.

While the war was on, Imperial Airways, a forerunner of British Airways, would still refuel its flying boats on Dubai Creek and send the passengers over to the fort at Sharjah for lunch. For this operation a truce was called, and the passengers would pass through the battlefront without, in most cases, realising anything odd was afoot.

When the ammunition and gunpowder had nearly run out, the rival sheikhs began negotiating again. Mani bin Rashid died peacefully soon after, and the matter was put to rest with him.

Japanese discovery (in 1930) of a method by which pearls could be cultured artificially. Sheikh Rashid concluded that the pearling industry was finished, and started to look for alternative forms of revenue. This chain of events heralded a new era in Dubai's trade – re-exporting (for more details see the boxed text, opposite). Spurred on by WWII, re-exporting continued to flourish thereafter, while Sheikh Rashid's forward-thinking and entrepreneurialism were traits his sons were to inherit and make good use of in their development of Dubai.

In 1939 Sheikh Rashid bin Saeed Al Maktoum took over as regent from his father, Sheikh Saeed, but he only formally succeeded to the leadership when his dad died in 1958. He quickly moved to bolster the emirate's position as the main trading hub in the lower Gulf, at the same time as the rulers of Sharjah made the costly mistake of allowing their harbour to silt up. Sheikh Rashid quickly improved facilities along the Creek, until January 1940, when war broke out briefly between Dubai and Sharjah. See the boxed text (above) for more details on the conflict.

MODERNISATION & DEVELOPMENT

Oil was first discovered near Dubai in 1966 and oil exports began three years later. However, a building boom had already begun along the Creek well before Dubai struck oil. Even after oil revenues began coming in, trade remained the foundation of the city's wealth, though oil has contributed to trade profits and encouraged modernisation since its discovery.

The first bank, the British Bank of the Middle East, was established in 1946, and when Al-Maktoum Hospital was built in 1949 it was the only centre for modern medical care on the Trucial Coast until well into the 1950s. When Sheikh Rashid officially came to power in 1958 he set up the first Municipal Council, and established a police force and basic infrastructure, such as electricity and water supply.

Until the early 1960s the only means of transport was donkey or camel. As is still the case today, abras (water taxis) were used to transport people across the Creek. Construction of the airport began in 1958 and the British Overseas Airways Corporation (BOAC) and Middle East Airlines (MEA) launched regular flights to Dubai soon after. Roads and bridges appeared in the early 1960s.

The ambitious UK£23 million Port Rashid complex began in 1967, after it became obvious that the growing maritime traffic could no longer be managed by the existing facilities, and was completed in 1972.

The mid-1970s saw the beginnings of a massive programme of industrialisation, resulting in the construction of Jebel Ali Port, the largest artificial port in the world, and the adjacent industrial centre, which was to become a free trade zone.

All of these developments brought to life Sheikh Rashid's vision of Dubai as one of the Middle East's most important commercial hubs.

1990	1995
Sheikh Maktoum becomes ruler of Dubai after Sheikh Rashid passes away	Sheikh Mohammed becomes Crown Prince of Dubai

In 1951 the Trucial States Council was founded, bringing the leaders of what would become the UAE together. The council comprised the rulers of the sheikhdoms and was the direct predecessor of the UAE Supreme Council. Then it met only twice a year, under the aegis of the British political agent in Dubai.

The end of the war, India's independence, and the decline of the British Empire saw the end of Britain's presence in the region and prompted the creation of the UAE. But before withdrawing from the region, the British set in motion the means by which the UAE borders were drawn. The British withdrawal and the discovery of oil accelerated the modernisation of the region. For more on modernisation and development, see the boxed text, p43.

Incredibly, drawing the UAE's borders involved a British diplomat spending months riding a camel around the mountains and desert, asking village heads, tribal leaders and Bedouin which sheikh they swore allegiance to!

2004	2006
Sheikh Mohammed marries Princess Haya bint Al Hussein	Sheikh Mohammed becomes ruler of Dubai after Sheikh Maktoum's passing

Sights

Sights

Dubai's myriad neighbourhoods have names but not all of them are in everyday use – telling your taxi driver your Golden Sands hotel is at 'Tawi as Saigh' will be met with a blank stare! To make things easier for visitors to the city, we've condensed a number of Dubai neighbourhoods into four main areas: Deira, Bur Dubai, Sheikh Zayed Rd and Jumeirah & New Dubai. These areas are where most of the sights are, and where you'll spend most of your time, and those names are commonly used by Dubai residents. (Many expats still confuse Deira and Bur Dubai after living in the city for some time, so once you've got these areas firmly in mind, consider yourself well on your way to being a local.)

Deira and Bur Dubai make up the centre of Dubai with the heart of the action historically focused on the Creek.

The Deira area covers Al Sabkha, the souqs area; Rigga, the Deira centre; and Al-Garhoud, the area between Al-Garhoud bridge and the airport. There are three ways to cross the Creek south to Bur Dubai other than using the *abras* (water taxis): Al Shindagha Tunnel close to the open sea, followed by Al Maktoum Bridge (to the east), then Al Garhoud Bridge (further east). Where traders once crisscrossed the calm waters between the two sides of the Creek by boat, nowadays Dubai locals do the trip at a much more leisurely pace by all deciding to drive across the two bridges or take the tunnel at the same time. Every day, twice a day. Dubai's grand transit plans involve closing one of the bridges, building an additional bridge closer to the Dubai Wildlife & Waterbird Sanctuary (which makes sense, doesn't it?!) and installing a light-rail system.

Our Bur Dubai definition takes in the area immediately south of the Creek as far as Al-Dhiyafah Rd, from the sea in the east to Al Garhoud Bridge in the southwest, including

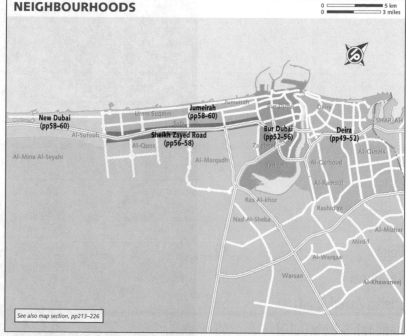

NEIGHBOURHOODS

See also map section, pp213–226

Al Shindagha waterfront area, the Bastakia heritage district, busy Al Karama, and Oud Metha, the area between Al Maktoum Bridge, Wafi City mall and the Grand Hyatt Hotel.

Sheikh Zayed Rd begins at the Trade Centre Roundabout at the edge of Karama and Bur Dubai, heading southwest towards Jebel Ali as far as Interchange No 5. There are many hotels, eateries and malls along this strip. We include Al Quoz here, an industrial area just off Sheikh Zayed Rd that's home to a growing number of art galleries and interior warehouses.

The last area we identify is Jumeirah. The spine of this sprawling suburban area is Jumeirah Beach Rd, which begins at Al-Dhiyafah Rd and runs parallel to the coast for about 16km as far as Al-Sufouh Rd, near Madinat Jumeirah. It stretches inland a couple of blocks from the sea and actually takes in a number of areas, including the three Jumeirah areas (logically named 1, 2, 3), Umm Suqeim (1 and 2), Safa, and so on. We've added a new, ritzy, rapidly growing area commonly referred to by the media and Dubai residents as New Dubai. This area begins on Sheikh Zayed around Interchange 5 and extends along the coast and inland as far as Jebel Ali, taking in new hotels, malls and high-rise developments such as the Marina and Ibn Battuta Mall.

TOP TEN FOR KIDS

- Dubai Museum (p54)
- Za'abeel Park (p56)
- Creekside Park & Children's City (p54)
- Ibn Battuta Mall (p136)
- Ski Dubai snow park (p114)
- Wild Wadi Waterpark (p60)
- Dubai Wildlife & Waterbird Sanctuary (p57)
- Dubai Desert Extreme Skate Park (p114)
- Al Mamzar Park (p50)
- Jumeirah Beach Park (p58)

ITINERARIES

One Day

Dubai life has always centred on the Creek, so with only one day, focus your exploration on the historic waterfront. Do our Wind-tower Wander (p62) through Bur Dubai first, which takes in some wonderful old architecture and history, starting with the engaging Dubai Museum (p54) for a more complex understanding of the city, the atmospheric Bastakia Quarter (p53), Bur Dubai Souq (p53) and the Shindagha area with its Sheikh Saeed al-Maktoum House

BACKSTREET DUBAI

While the glitz and glamour of Dubai is alluring, and for most visitors what the Dubai experience is all about, adventurous travellers looking for a richer and multi-layered experience should take time to explore 'backstreet Dubai', which some would argue is the 'real Dubai'. This is what we like to do on our days off:

Al-Musallah Meander (Map pp220–1, G4-5) Most people take a taxi to Bur Dubai souqs or the Bastakia but it's worth meandering there along Al-Musallah Rd and exploring its 'Little India'-like side streets with Bollywood tape shops, guys watching cricket outside cafeterias, and cheap Azerbaijani or Russian eateries.

Karama Ramble (Map pp222–3, D2) Wandering the gritty backstreets of lower-income expat community, Karama, is interesting, especially if you're sociable and chat to the affable shopkeepers. Start at Karama Souq and head towards Sheikh Khalifa bin Zayed Rd. Drop in to **Food Castle** (p83) for a Goan curry.

Satwa Dawdle (Map p226, D1-2 & E1-2) Just one block behind Sheikh Zayed Rd's swanky skyscrapers you'll find colourful houses with gates painted with palm trees, Afghani bakeries, Friday volleyball matches on sandy vacant lots, and a souq-like main shopping street. **Ravi** (p82) is the spot to refuel.

Umm Suqeim Stroll (Map pp214–15, C2 & D2) Between Jumeirah Beach Hotel, the pristine white sands of Umm Suqeim beach, and Jumeirah Beach Rd, is a laid-back Emirati neighbourhood of simple whitewashed low-rise housing, 'free range' chickens in dirt lanes, public water coolers and lush gardens of bougainvillea.

Mankhool Mosey (Map pp220–1, C5-6 & D5-6) If you're staying in Golden Sands' concrete jungle, cross Kuwait St and head toward Al-Adhid Rd to mosey around this middle-class Emirati neighbourhood of enormous villas and five-car garages, white mosques and kids playing in the street.

(p56), and **Heritage and Diving Villages** (p55). We suggest refuelling at **Kan Zaman** (p84) but you could also wander back to fabulous **Bastakiah Nights** (p86), before taking an *abra* to Deira, checking out the dhows and Creek action on the way. During the afternoon many souq shops close for prayer and lunch, so take a taxi to **Deira City Centre** (p130) for shopping and people-watching, or relax by your hotel pool, returning late afternoon or around dusk to do our Souq Saunter (p63) through old Deira. This walk starts at the **Spice Souq** (p51) and takes in **Al-Ahmadiya School** (p50), **Heritage House** (p52), the **Gold Souq** (p51) and **Deira Covered & Naif Souqs** (p50). If the shopping bug has bitten you hard, but a trip to Dubai is incomplete without a glimpse of **Burj Al Arab** (p58), kill two birds with one stone and take a taxi to **Madinat Jumeirah** (p60) for more shopping followed by a drink at beautiful **Bahri Bar** (p100) with views of the Burj. Have dinner at one of Madinat Jumeirah's many fantastic restaurants, such as **Shoo Fee Ma Fee** (p91) and round off the night with *sheesha* in the souq's central plaza or get a cab to the **Sheesha Courtyard** (p98).

Three Days

With more time, you could spread out the itinerary above over two days, doing a walk each day, and leaving more time for swimming and shopping. Keen shoppers should check out **Mall of the Emirates** (p136), **Ibn Battuta Mall** (p136) or the **BurJuman Centre** (p132), and if you're after fake brands, cheap crafts and souvenirs, visit the **Karama Shopping Centre** (p133). If you want to do something more active, head to **Wild Wadi** (p60) or **Ski Dubai** (p114). Given the misinformation in the media about Islam and Arabs, we highly recommend taking a **Jumeirah Mosque** (p60) tour. In the evenings, have a cocktail at the **Burj Al Arab** (p102) if you must, or do a sunset **Dhow Cruise** (below). Eat at one of Dubai's fine-dining restaurants, **Verre** (p82) or **Mezzanine** (p94) one night, and on the other opt for a Middle East experience at **Awtar** (p86) or **Tagine** (p93). A night out bar-hopping or clubbing is a must so follow one of our Nights on the Town itineraries (p97). On the third day, visit **Sharjah** (p156) in the morning and do our Arts Amble (p65), ideal for those looking for culture (and more shopping)! A trip to the desert is also a must, so schedule a **Desert Safari** (p155) for the late afternoon.

One Week

If the Desert Safari has whetted your appetite for more spectacular scenery, get out of town and head to a few destinations in our Excursions chapter, such as East Coast towns **Fujairah** (p162) and **Khor Fakkan** (p162), the oasis city of **Al Ain** (p164), the peaceful retreat of **Hatta** (p159) or the nation's capital **Abu Dhabi** (p168). If you're staying in the city, and looking for more than glitz and glam, take time to get off the beaten track and explore backstreet Dubai (p47). On your final day, get in some last-minute shopping: buy some gold (p124) or pick up that carpet (p124) you can't stop thinking about. In the evening, have drinks at one of Dubai's sublime al-fresco bars (p101) and dine at one of the city's many **restaurants with a view** (p81). Make your last stop the Arabian style **Rooftop Bar** (p101), where you can chill out under the stars and start planning your return visit.

ORGANISED TOURS

For desert safari tours, see p155.

Creek Cruises

BATEAUX DUBAI CRUISES Map pp220-1
☎ 399 4994; Al-Seef Rd, opp British Embassy, Bur Dubai Creek; lunch & dinner cruise 3-course set menu Dh150
This elegant boat, with a very stylish contemporary design and floor-to-ceiling glass windows, offers sophisticated lunch and dinner cruises along the Creek.

CREEKSIDE LEISURE
Map pp216-17
☎ 336 8407; www.tour-dubai.com; departs in front of Dubai Municipality Bldg, Deira; tour Dh35, dinner cruise Dh175;
⏱ tours 11.30am, 1.30pm, 3.30pm, 5.30pm, dinner cruise 8.30-10.30pm
Succinct one-hour guided dhow tours of Dubai Creek and plenty of scheduled cruise times means you get a good introduction to sights at your convenience. The licensed dinner cruise with belly dancer is popular.

DANAT DUBAI CRUISES Map pp220-1

☎ 351 1117; www.danatdubaicruises.com;
opp British Embassy, Bur Dubai Creek; sundowner
cruise adult/child Dh65/45

Boarding at 5pm, the Sundowner Cruise sails by the historical waterfront areas before entering the Gulf for sunset, returning by 6.30pm. Dinner cruises and transfers are also offered.

Bus Tours

BIG BUS COMPANY Map pp222-3

☎ 324 4187; www.bigbustours.com;
Wafi Centre, Bur Dubai; adult/child/family
Dh140/90/370, discounts online bookings

One of Dubai's surreal sights is that of the Big Bus Company's open-topped London double-decker buses plying a red city route (every half hour) and blue beach route (every hour) from 9am to 5pm every day. The 24-hour ticket allows you to get off and back on at any one of 23 well-positioned stops (maps and stops online) and includes free entry to Dubai Museum, Sheikh Saeed Al Maktoum House and a Wafi City discount card. There's a running commentary in English.

WONDER BUS TOURS Map pp220-1

☎ 359 5656; www.wonderbusdubai.com;
BurJuman Centre, cnr Khalid bin al-Waleed
(Bank St) & Trade Centre Rds, Bur Dubai;
adult/child/family Dh115/75/350

An even more surreal sight awaits you at the BurJuman Centre with the amphibious Wonder Bus. Three times a day the bus drives down to the Creek, plunges into the water, cruises the creek, and then drives back on to land and returns to the BurJuman Centre. While the trip takes two hours, the head trip (figuring out why anyone needs this attraction) could take longer.

City Tours

Both these companies are reliable, long-standing tour operators in the UAE.

ARABIAN ADVENTURES Map pp214-15

☎ 343 9966; www.arabian-adventures.com;
Emirates Holidays Bldg, Interchange No 2,
Sheikh Zayed Rd; adult/child 2-12 yrs Dh120/60

Owned by Emirates Airlines, Arabian Adventures operates half-day city tours, covering Jumeirah Rd, Jumeirah Mosque, Dubai Museum and the Deira Gold and Spice Souqs, along with half-day shopping tours to the Gold and Spice Souqs and Karama.

NET TOURS & TRAVELS Map pp218-19

☎ 266 8661; www.nettoursdubai.com;
Al-Bakhit Centre, Abu Baker al-Siddiq Rd, Hor
al-Anz; adult/child Dh110/75

Operating twice a day and starting at Jumeirah Mosque, the Dubai City Tour takes in Dubai Creek, the Bastakia, Dubai Museum, the Bur Dubai textile souq and an *abra* across the Creek to the Deira Spice and Gold Souqs.

DEIRA

Eating p79; Shopping p129; Sleeping p141

Deira has been a trading centre for centuries and nothing evokes that adventurous and difficult past more than the old wooden dhows that still ply the waters between Dubai and Iran. Take an *abra* across the Creek and you really get a feel for what it must have been like, especially after visiting Dubai Museum. Take a stroll along the Dhow Wharfage, with its extraordinary array of goods waiting to be loaded, or head into the souqs with their heady aromas of spices and perfumes, and carpet merchants armed with calculators ready for serious bargaining. Near the Gold Souq is Dubai's first school, Al-Ahmadiya, with delightful Heritage House adjoining it, while also rewarding is experiencing the Creek at sunset, on a cruise or *abra*, or just by taking a leisurely stroll along the waterfront.

www.lonelyplanet.com

Sights

DEIRA

ABRA CRUISING

Fifteen thousand people cross the Creek each day on *abras*, the traditional wooden water taxis, for just 50 fils a journey. You can hire an *abra* to do the same trip the cruise companies do – yet at water level, with the wind in your hair and the seagulls in your face. It's a more interesting experience, especially if the boat captain speaks a little English or you speak Urdu, Hindi or Arabic – you might learn a whole lot more about the Creek and those who work it. *Abras* can be hired from the *abra* stations along the creek, but try the dock near Al Seef roundabout, where they cost around Dh40 for 30 minutes or Dh60 for an hour.

AL-AHMADIYA SCHOOL Map pp216-17

☎ 226 0286; Al-Ahmadiya St, near Gold Souq;
☻ 8am-7.30pm Sat-Thu, 2.30-7.30pm Fri

Charming Al-Ahmadiya School is the oldest in Dubai, situated directly behind the Heritage House in Deira souq, which is no coincidence. Sheikh Mohammed bin Ahmed bin Dalmouk established the school in 1912, and his father, Sheikh Ahmed, owned the traditional house adjoining it. Semiformal schools such as these were set up by sheikhs and wealthy merchants to teach the Holy Quran, grammar, Arabic calligraphy, mathematics, literature and astronomy, and while students paid a couple of rupees to attend, the sheikhs paid for the poor students. Prior to this, kids only had access to education through the 'muttawa', or religious man, who taught the teachings of the Quran. While some of the displays inside are of minor interest, we love the simplicity of the architecture and the exquisite detail – check out the intricate carving within the arches of the courtyard inside and the decorative gypsum panels near the entrance outside. Touch screens take you on a tour of both the school and Heritage House (p52).

AL-MAMZAR PARK Map pp214-15

Al-Mamzar Creek; per person/car Dh5/30;
☻ 8am-10.30pm, women & children only Wed

This lush landscaped park stretching across a couple of very pleasant kilometres of a small headland on the mouth of Khor al-Mamzar is one of Dubai's gems. Situated on an attractive inlet, just across from Sharjah, there are lovely white sandy beaches, a swimming pool, barbecues, kiosks, and plenty of open

DEIRA HIGHLIGHTS

- Wander through the souqs (below), with spicy aromas, glittering gold, heady fragrances, shouting spruikers – wow!
- Step back in time at Al-Ahmadiya School (left) and Heritage House (p52) to discover the simpler life of old Dubai.
- Visit the Dhow Wharfage (opposite) and marvel at how the dhows manage to stay afloat when there's a truck, several cars and a warehouse's worth of electrical goods on deck.

spaces, play areas and a wooden castle for the kids. Lifeguards are on duty between 8am and 6pm on at least one of the small beaches. At the northern tip of the park there are 15 chalets (booking office ☎ 296 7948; per day Dh150-200; ☻ 9am-10pm), with kitchen, sitting room, bathroom and barbecue. They can be booked on a daily basis – but book well ahead.

DEIRA COVERED SOUQ & NAIF SOUQ

Map pp216-17

Covered Souq btwn Al-Sabkha Rd, 67 St & Naif Rd; Naif Souq btwn Naif South St, 9a St & Deira St

Unfortunately not much of the old covered souqs that existed around 30 years ago remain now –the Spice Souq (opposite) is all that's left of the Old Souq, once the largest in the Gulf. But after seeing photos in the Dubai Museum and Sheikh Saeed Al Maktoum house, you might just be able to close your eyes when you're exploring Deira Covered Souq and Naif Souq and imagine how it might have been. Naif Souq is covered, like traditional bazaars, while nearby

SARTORIAL SENSITIVITY

Dubai prides itself on being a very liberal Muslim state and with so many nationalities living and working here (over 100!), it's easy to lose sight of the fact that in a Muslim state you should dress with local sensitivities in mind. Over the last couple of years there's been a trend of more and more expats (who should know better) and visitors wearing beachwear and extremely revealing clothing to shopping malls and the souqs.

Beachwear is fine at a beach resort, but not at a shopping mall. The little black dress taking up one square centimetre of your luggage space? Okay for the clubs – just take a taxi there and back. Boys in shorts? Well it's funny you should mention that. One day we ran into a young Emirati friend at the mall with her mother, who was wearing the traditional burqa and doing the classic local shopping expedition where you buy cooking oil by the gallon, rice in 10kg bags and tissues by the crate. After the usual introductions, we asked our friend if she'd seen her male expat teacher, who we'd also seen at the supermarket. She said she had, but that she had to steer her mother to another aisle to avoid embarrassment. She laughed and said, 'I couldn't run the risk of him saying hello, he was wearing shorts! My mother would think he was stupid for leaving the house in his underwear!'

Deira Covered Souq is covered only in parts and is more a warren of small shops on narrow lanes spreading across a number of old Deira blocks. You'll find everything from tacky textiles and plastic kitchenware to Iranian saffron and henna, but even if you're not keen on shopping, the souqs provide an amazing insight into the lives of Emiratis and expat workers in Dubai.

DEIRA GOLD SOUQ Map pp216-17
On & around Sikkat al-Khail St, btwn Suq Deira & Old Baladiya Sts
The atmospheric wooden-latticed arcades of the Gold Souq are impressive, even to people not interested in buying gold or jewellery, for both its size – there are hundreds of shops here – and variety. Every kind of jewellery imaginable is available, from gold, diamonds and pearls, to elaborate Arabian and Indian wedding necklaces, bangles and headdresses, to more contemporary styles. It's the largest gold market in the region, and one of the largest in the world (with ambitions to rival Antwerp in diamonds); the passing people parade is almost as fascinating as the sheer amount of jewellery. Once you're done with gawking at all the jaw-dropping jewellery displays, take a seat on one of the wooden benches on the main thoroughfare and note how many different types of people are here: sun-bothered Europeans shopping for gold, blokes from the Indian Subcontinent selling copy watches and fake DVDs, sweaty Afghani guys dragging heavy carts of goods here and there, East African women in colourful caftans trading something…it's all rather extraordinary.

DEIRA SPICE SOUQ Map pp216-17
Btwn Baniyas Rd, Al Sabkha Rd & Al-Abra St Deira
The small but atmospheric covered Spice Souq, once known as the Old Souq, was the largest in the region at the beginning of the 20th century, with over 300 little shops trading their wares. Travellers shouldn't expect to see an Istanbul-like spice bazaar – they'll be disappointed – but this tiny aromatic market is still worth a half-hour of your time to take in the wonderfully restored wind-tower architecture and the pungent aromas from the jute sacks. The place is brimming with frankincense and oud, herbs and spices,

FREE AS A BIRD
While entrance fees to Dubai's official sights and museums are fairly inexpensive, for those on a tight budget, there's a great deal to do around the city that's free:

Heritage and Diving Villages (p55) Wonderful on winter evenings, when Emiratis participate in heritage activities such as rifle-throwing competitions!

Jumeirah Mosque (p60) The 'Open Doors, Open Minds' tour gets you inside the mosque and gives you a better understanding of Islam and Emirati culture.

Dhow Wharfage (below) It costs nothing to wander along the fascinating dhow wharfage and if you're good at smiling and miming you might even get invited to go onboard a boat for a look. (Unaccompanied women, of course, should refuse nicely.)

Waterfront on Friday (p52) The big day off for expats sees companies bussing workers from city-rim labour camps to the Shindagha waterfront where they hang out with friends, take snapshots for the relatives back home and play games of cricket.

dried lemons and chillies, nuts, pulses and more; it's fun to chat to the shopkeepers and guess the things you don't recognise. This is a working souq, not just a tourist attraction, so the tiny shops also sell groceries, plastics and other household goods for people living in the area and the sailors from the dhows. Good buys include incense burners, saffron, rose water, henna kits and *sheesha* pipes. When you're done here, start exploring the surrounding narrow lanes of the Old Souq, which will lead you to the Covered Souq and Gold Souq.

DHOW WHARFAGE Map pp218-19
Baniyas Rd
Strolling along the Creek on a cool evening and lingering at the Dhow Wharfage is a favourite winter pastime of many Dubai residents, locals and expats alike. Dhows are long flat, wooden sailing vessels used in the Indian Ocean and Arabian Sea, and they've docked at the Creek since the 1830s when the Maktoums established a free trade port, luring merchants away from Persia. The dhows here now trade with Iran, Iraq, Pakistan, Oman, India, Yemen, Somalia and Sudan, and you'll see all kinds of crazy cargo – air-conditioners, flat-screen TVs, mattresses, kitchen sinks, clothes, canned

food, chewing gum, car tyres, cars, even trucks (just watch them load them on!) – almost all of it re-exported after arriving by air from countries like China, South Korea and Singapore. A testament to Dubai's safety is the fact that the goods often sit on the wharves for weeks without disappearing. Try and chat to the sailors if you can – if you find one who speaks English, you'll learn that it takes a day to get to Iran by sea and seven days to Somalia, and the dhow captains often earn as little as $100 a month, the stevedores even less.

HERITAGE HOUSE Map pp216-17

☎ 226 0286; Al-Ahmadiya St; ☼ 8am-7.30pm Sat-Thu, 2.30-7.30pm Fri

Adjoining Al-Ahmadiya School, this charming renovated courtyard house, built in 1890, offers a rare opportunity to see inside a wealthy pearl merchant's residence (it once belonged to Sheikh Ahmed bin Dalmouk, whose son established Al-Ahmadiya School). Like the old Bastakia buildings, the house is built from coral and gypsum, and has a central courtyard onto which all rooms look, and verandas to prevent sunlight from heating the rooms. What's different is that it doesn't have a wind-tower. This is probably because before construction of the surrounding buildings, there was very little between the house and the water, and the airy upstairs rooms with doors and corridors facing the sea would have captured cool breezes. There are a number of delightful traditional displays inside, including – our favourites – kitsch dioramas (Dubai just loves them!) of a bride and groom and a women's majlis. Like Al-Ahmadiya School, there are touch screens here.

PERFUME SOUQ Map pp216-17

Gold Souq, on Sikkat al-Khail St

While these rows of perfume shops on a couple of aromatic blocks next to the Gold Souq hardly warrants the title 'souq', they do sell a staggering range of Arabian attars, oud and incense burners, and European perfumes, both fake and the real stuff discounted. Whether you like perfume or not, it's worth buying some as a gift for the unusual Arabian perfume bottles that come in bizarre forms (such as miniature gold coffee pot and incense

burner–shaped bottles), and the kitsch packaging. And if you truly hate the heady scents, then it's still worth a look for the insight into local culture. Emirati women adore their attars – this goes back to the days before they had air-conditioning and before they were able to wash their *abayas* every day – and it's wonderful to see the older burqa-covered ladies trying out the different perfumes and wafting the smoke from burning oud under their *abayas* as they test out the scents.

BUR DUBAI

Eating p82; Shopping p131; Sleeping p145

The Bur Dubai side of the Creek, like the Deira side, provides a slice of life from the early days, particularly the historical Bastakia Quarter with its traditional courtyard houses and wind-towers, and the Shindagha area with its fascinating Heritage Village and Diving Village, and stately former residence of Sheikh Saeed Al Maktoum. These restored areas are both wonderful places for late afternoon strolls. The Bur Dubai Souq is just as vibrant as the Deira Souqs and exploring 'Little India' in the surrounding streets can easily absorb a couple of hours of your time. Further back from the creek, past the concrete jungle (and expat neighbourhood) of Golden Sands, is Karama, home to rundown, low-cost apartment blocks housing expat workers. This area is worth a wander – it has a real community feel to it (hard to find elsewhere in Dubai), where everybody knows each other, and there's great shopping and cheap eats here too.

BUR DUBAI HIGHLIGHTS

- Visit the Dubai Museum (p54) for the fun dioramas and the way it showcases the progress of Dubai.
- Stroll through the elegantly restored Sheikh Saeed Al-Maktoum House (p56), which houses a rare collection of amazing black-and-white photographs of early Dubai.
- Wander through the re-creation of traditional Bedouin and coastal villages at the Heritage Village and Diving Village (p55) – especially in the cooler months.

Persian traders in the Bastakia Quarter once lived in these wind tower–topped homes (p28)

ALI BIN ABI TALEB MOSQUE
Map pp220-1
Ali bin Abi Taleb St
This simple yet striking mosque, in the textile area of Bur Dubai Souq, is notable for its sensuous, bulbous domes and gently tapering minaret. Its outline is best appreciated at night from Baniyas Rd in Deira, on the opposite side of the Creek, when the mosque and neighbouring wind-towers are beautifully lit up – it makes a postcard-perfect shot. Note that it's only possible to admire the mosque from outside – interiors of mosques in Dubai and the UAE are out of bounds to non-Muslims (except for the tour at Jumeirah Mosque; see p60).

BASTAKIA QUARTER Map pp220-1
With its arty feel and narrow breezy lanes, the atmospheric old Bastakia Quarter on the waterfront east of the Bur Dubai Souq is a magical place to explore. Here you'll find the highest concentration of traditional old wind-tower houses in Dubai. A characteristic feature of Central Iranian towns, wind-towers were a traditional form of air-conditioning constructed in such a way as to funnel cool air down into the house. Built at the beginning of the 20th century, these fabulous buildings were once the homes of wealthy pearl and textile merchants who came from Bastak in southern Iran, enticed to Dubai

by its free trade (what's changed?). The elegant homes the traders built were the most sophisticated in Dubai, and were only found in coastal towns where there was enough wealth to build with coral, gypsum and limestone – a big step up from palm fronds! A typical house was two-storey with a central courtyard, which most rooms opened onto, with decorative arches with intricate carvings. Generally fairly plain from the outside, they had the wonderful carved wooden doors you see today, plus crenellations, carved grilles and stucco panels on the wealthier merchants' homes – many of the Bastakia's renovated buildings, such as **XVA** (p56), **Majlis Gallery** (p56) and **Basta Art Café** (p83), have these gorgeous decorations.

BUR DUBAI SOUQ Map pp220-1
Btwn Bur Dubai waterfront & Al-Fahidi St
While not as old as the Deira souqs – in the old days Bur Dubai and Bastakia residents had to take a boat across to Deira to go shopping – this breezy renovated souq can be just as atmospheric and lively a place to visit. On a summer's evening it can also be cooler, as the breeze blows through the wooden-latticed arcades. The buzziest

---

DECONSTRUCTING THE DHOW
Just as much a feature of the city now as they were centuries ago, dhows docked in Dubai Creek give the place an unmistakably oriental feel, despite the shiny modern buildings dominating the waterfront.

Dubai was once one of the most important dhow-building centres on the Gulf coast. The dhow builders (*al-galalif* in Arabic) used very basic materials and methods to construct the enormous vessels, and the development of Dubai's maritime culture was reflected in the large number of different boats they constructed for different purposes. The larger dhows used for long-distance journeys were called *al-boom*, *al-bateel* and *al-baglah*, and were up to 60m in length. Some of them have now been turned into cruise vessels and floating restaurants. The *sambuq* was a smaller boat, never more than 30m long, mainly used for fishing. It was characterised by its single mast and square stern, which had decorative wings protruding from it. Pearling boats (*baggara*) were larger and had no mast.

When you're next by the Creek, notice how the mirrored exteriors of those modern buildings reflect the dhows sailing on the water so beautifully…

TELLING TALES

The beautiful black and white *Telling Tales: An Oral History of Dubai*, by BBC Gulf correspondent Julia Wheeler and photographer Paul Thuysbaert, offers so much more than the usual glossy coffee-table books you see on Dubai shelves. A first of its kind for Dubai publishing, it features candid oral histories and extraordinary insights from a cross-section of Emiratis – from old pearl divers, Bedu camel farmers and boat builders to some of the city's key elder statesmen and ageing movers and shakers. For instance, despite the short distance between Deira and Bur Dubai, we learn that before the tunnel and bridges some people didn't travel much at all – one elderly Bastakia woman said she'd only ever been to Deira once or twice as a child! Has anything really changed? For very different reasons, her grandkids will be telling a similar story of how they once tried to get to Deira City Centre from Bastakia in their car, but after several hours their mobile phone batteries ran flat and the talk radio became too much so they did a U-turn across several lanes of oncoming traffic and headed home…is there a book in that?

time to visit is a Friday evening when it's crowded with expat workers shopping on their day off. While you'll find some great take-home items, because this is a real working souq, what's primarily on offer are cheap clothes and shoes, and textiles, mainly purchased by expat Emirati and Indian women. The surrounding backstreets, with its tailors, textile and sari shops, may not be as aesthetically pleasing to the eye, but are still intriguing and worth taking the time to explore.

CREEKSIDE PARK Map pp222-3

Off Riyadh St, btwn Al-Garhoud & Al-Maktoum Bridges; admission Dh5; ⏰ 8am-11pm Sat-Wed, 8am-11.30pm Thu, Fri & public holidays, women & children only Wed

This lovely, lush waterfront park is one of the city's largest – running from Al-Garhoud Bridge to Al-Maktoum Bridge – and is one of our favourites. It's very peaceful and has gorgeous views across the Creek, children's play areas, *abra* rides and dhow cruises, kiosks, restaurants, an amphitheatre and beaches (though it's not advisable to swim). On weekends it's like a huge *sheesha* café, with families spread out on blankets, puffing away. There's also

a 2.5km-long cable-car ride (tickets Dh5) 30m above the shore of the Creek, with fabulous vistas. Also situated in a colourful building in the park is **Children's City** (☎ 334 0808; adult/child Dh15/10; ⏰ 9am-10pm Sat-Thu, 4pm-10pm Fri). Popular with local and expat kids, it's home to a creative, educational and entertaining kids activities centre.

DHOW-BUILDING YARD Map pp214-15

Jaddaf, Bur Dubai side of Creek

The gorgeous, traditional old dhows you see on Dubai Creek (and perhaps took a cruise on) are still built by hand in the traditional style on the Creek waterfront, in Jaddaf, about 1km south of Al-Garhoud Bridge. Here, craftsmen use basic tools (a hammer, saw, chisel, drill and plane) to curve and fit sturdy teak wooden planks, one on top of the other, before fitting the frame on the inside of the boat. Be impressed: this is in contrast to Western boat-building techniques where the frame is generally built first, and the planks fitted to it. These days, of course, the old blokes pop an engine on the back before sliding it into the Creek!

DUBAI MUSEUM Map pp220-1

☎ 353 1862; Al-Fahidi St, opp Grand Mosque & Diwan; adult/child Dh3/1; ⏰ 8.30am-8.30pm Sat-Thu, 3-9pm Fri

One of the first places most visitors head to in Dubai is this fascinating museum. Its manageable size and entertaining exhibitions mean you get a quick and easy introduction to Dubai and its history, culture and traditions. The museum occupies the early-19th-century Al-Fahidi Fort, possibly the oldest building in Dubai, and once the residence of Dubai's rulers and seat of government. Apart from a small fishing boat, traditional weapons display and a *barasti* house with wind-tower (step under it and feel the difference it makes in summer!), much of the air-conditioned museum is thankfully underground. There's an excellent (albeit somewhat dated) multimedia presentation covering the city's history and growth that gives a real understanding of how rapidly Dubai has developed. Then there are a series of wonderfully kitsch dioramas of old Dubai life supported by video, sound effects and disturbingly lifelike mannequins. A highlight for many is the complete grave from the Al-Qusais archaeological site and finds from digs at Al-Qusais (dating back to 2500 to 500 BC) and Jumeirah (6th century AD). Who said this country was young! All displays in the museum have explanations in Arabic and English. Photography is not officially permitted although many visitors find it impossible to resist posing with the mannequins in the dioramas for a sneaky snap or two…

GRAND MOSQUE Map pp220-1
Ali Bin Abi Talib St, opp Dubai Museum
This mosque, with the tallest minaret in Dubai, might appear to be as old as the Dubai Museum (across the road), but it was actually built in the 1990s. The multi-domed mosque maintains the style of the original Grand Mosque – which dated from 1900 and was knocked down to make way for another mosque in 1960 – and its sand-coloured walls and wooden shutters blend in perfectly with the surrounding old quarter of Bur Dubai. As well as being the centre of Dubai's religious and cultural life, the original Grand Mosque was also home to the town's *kuttab* school where children learnt to recite the Quran from memory.

HERITAGE & DIVING VILLAGES
Map pp220-1
☎ 393 7151; Al-Shindagha Rd; ⏰ 8am-10pm Sat-Thu, 8-11am & 4-10pm Fri
Stroll along the Creek to the old Shindagha area to wander around the charming Heritage and Diving Villages. Offering wonderful recreations of traditional Bedouin and coastal village life, complete with *barasti* homes, an old coffeehouse, a small souq where you can buy handicrafts and souvenirs, and an outdoor 'kitchen' where burqa-clad Emirati women make hot *dosa* (flat, grilled bread made of flour and water). The Diving Village also has displays on pearl diving, once the livelihood of the city, models of dhows and pearling boats, and another souq. The Villages are popular with Emirati families during the cooler winter evenings when they love to come here to participate in a variety of traditional activities, such as Rifle Throwing Competitions, many of them filmed for local TV!

'Hindi Lane' (below) is a popular destination for Dubai's Hindu community

'HINDI LANE' Map pp220-1
Behind Grand Mosque, off Ali bin Abi Talib St
If you head behind the Grand Mosque in Bur Dubai, you'll find evidence of two places of worship behind very modest exteriors – rows of shoes in shelves at the bottom of a couple of sets of stairs. One staircase leads to the Hindu **Shri Nathje Jayate Temple**, also known as the 'Krishna Mandir' (*mandir* is Hindi for temple). Shri Nathji is the main deity of Pushtimarg, a Hindu devotional sect, with its main temple in Rajastan, near Udaipur. The other house of worship is identified by a discreet sign, **Sikh Gurudaba**, and interestingly again, because a Sikh place of worship is called a *gurdwara*. A *guru* is a teacher-guide, and a *dabar* is a cheap lunch stop, but we're not sure if there's a connection. Of most interest to travellers is the small alley that expats fondly refer to as 'Hindi Lane'. Here vendors sell Hindu religious paraphernalia and offerings to take to the temples – baskets of fruit, garlands of flowers, gold-embossed holy images, sacred ash, sandalwood paste and packets of bindis, the little pendants Hindu women stick to their foreheads.

ART FLURRY

Dubai has a rapidly growing art scene that's really starting to flourish, with a flurry of galleries opening in recent times. There are too many to mention here, but standouts include the Third Line and B21 in the Bastakia area and Soho in Bur Dubai, in addition to some long-standing galleries, such as the Majlis Gallery and The Courtyard. Check the Dubai Cultural Council's website (www.dubaiculturalcouncil.ae) for a full listing and *Time Out* and *What's On* magazine for details on the latest exhibitions.

MAJLIS GALLERY Map pp220-1

☎ 353 6233; Al-Fahidi Roundabout; ⏲ 9.30am-1.30pm & 4-7.30pm Sat-Thu

In a fabulous old house in the Bastakia Quarter, Majlis Gallery is Dubai's oldest commercial gallery, established in the 1970s. It exhibits painting and calligraphy, predominantly by local and regional artists, along with old prints and maps, pottery, ceramics, glassware, sculpture and handicrafts.

SHEIKH SAEED AL-MAKTOUM HOUSE Map pp220-1

☎ 393 7139; Al-Shindagha Rd; adult/child Dh2/1; ⏲ 8.30am-9pm Sat-Thu, 3-10pm Fri

Now a wonderful museum of pre-oil times, the grand courtyard house of Sheikh Saeed, the grandfather of Sheikh Mohammed, sits splendidly on the Shindagha area waterfront, near the Heritage and Diving Villages. Built in 1896, during the reign of Sheikh Maktoum bin Hasher Al Maktoum, it served for many years as residence for the Al Maktoum family and Sheikh Saeed lived here from 1888 until his death in 1958. It houses an engaging exhibition of photographs, primarily from the 1940s, '50s and '60s, taken on the Creek, in the souqs and at traditional celebrations, illuminating the extraordinary history and rapid growth of Dubai. There are also displays of postage stamps and coins (one featuring Edward VII was known as *umm salaah*, meaning the 'bald headed one'!) and a model of Bur Dubai from the 1950s also helps tell the story. It's amazing to see how different the place looked just a very short time ago, and how quickly it's developed from a sleepy Gulf fishing village into a vibrant global hub.

XVA Map pp220-1

☎ 353 5383; xvagallery.com; behind Basta Art Café, Al Musallah Roundabout; ⏲ 9.30am-8pm, closed Fri

A peaceful retreat from the traffic chaos that's less than a block away, XVA is a contemporary art gallery, casual café and boutique hotel (see p146) in one of the Bastakia's most beautifully restored old courtyard residences. XVA holds regular exhibitions of art, sculpture and design, with splashy openings; organises Creek cruises with a difference; has a wonderful little gift shop; and has also started a film club offering regular art-house movie screenings and discussions. This is what Dubai needs more of!

ZA'ABEEL PARK Map pp222-3

☎ 800 900 (Dubai Municipality); Sheikh Khalifa bin Zayed Rd & Al-Qataiyat Rd

Opened late in 2005, this 51-hectare park, stretching over three areas, has gorgeous lakes, ponds, jogging track, sports facilities and club house, and retail and food and beverages facilities – not to mention fabulous views of the Sheikh Zayed Rd skyline. Already packed to breaking point on weekends, in the near future Za'abeel will also have an Imax Theatre, a 45m-high Panoramic Tower and a Technology Zone.

SHEIKH ZAYED ROAD

Eating p86; Shopping p134; Sleeping p147

Dubai's favourite speedway (and deadliest road) has some fabulous buildings, and the architects appear to be as competitive as the drivers who frequent this stretch. The hotels that have opened up here in the last few years (including the landmark Emirates Towers, p149) are all worth a visit. Sheikh Zayed Rd and areas nearby such as industrial Al Quoz are also home to a growing number of art galleries.

SHEIKH ZAYED ROAD HIGHLIGHTS

- Watch the pretty flamingos and water-birds just 15 minutes from Sheikh Zayed Rd at Dubai Wildlife & Waterbird Sanctuary (opposite).
- Check out some adventurous contemporary art at the Al Quoz Art Scene (opposite).

ART SPACE Map p226

☎ 332 5523; 9th fl, Fairmont Hotel,
Sheikh Zayed Rd; ◷ 10am-8.30pm Sat-Thu

There's always something interesting to see at this refreshing commercial gallery with a focus on contemporary art and a mission to promote local artists, develop an appreciation for art and to grow the local scene. Kicking off new exhibitions each month with glam opening nights, Art Space has exhibited some quality contemporary stuff, including Emirati artist Mohammed Kanoo's fun pop art and some very powerful work by Iranian women artists.

B21 GALLERY Map pp214-15

☎ 340 3965; off Sheikh Zayed Rd,
btwn Interchanges 3 & 4, Al Quoz;
◷ 10am-2pm Sat-Thu, 5-8pm Fri

In this warehouse space, new kid on the Al Quoz art block, Palestinian artist Jeffar Khaldi shows his own vibrant work, as well as rotating exhibitions of locally produced and regional work, such as Youssef Nabil's fabulous gelatin portraits. Worth a look if you're in this developing arts neighbourhood, but call first if you're not, as they could be in-between exhibitions.

COURTYARD Map pp214-15

☎ 228 2888; www.courtyard-uae.com; off Sheikh
Zayed Rd, btwn Interchanges 3 & 4, Al Quoz;
☎ 10am-1pm & 4-8pm, closed Fri

The Courtyard is home to several galleries that hold changing exhibitions of painting, calligraphy, mixed media, miniatures, rare Persian carpets and sculptures by local, Middle Eastern artists and international artists, along with interior design and handicrafts stores, and a few media/design businesses. Highlights here are Iranian expat artist, Dariush Zandi's Total Arts at The Courtyard (☎ 347 5050) and locally-owned Courtyard Gallery & Café (☎ 347 9090), run by Samia Saleh and Louis Rady.

DUBAI WILDLIFE & WATERBIRD SANCTUARY Map pp214-15

☎ 206 4240; Oud Metha Rd, Ras al-Khor;
admission free; ◷ 10am-6pm Sat-Thu

Pretty pink flamingos flock to the inland end of the Dubai Creek during the winter months. Also known as Al-Khor Nature Reserve, this sanctuary has platforms that allow visitors to get a close-up view of the birds (with fantastically sharp binoculars) without disturbing them, and the juxtaposition of these elegant birds framed against the Dubai metropolis is dramatic. Kids love it.

NAD AL-SHEBA CLUB Map pp214-15

☎ 336 3666; www.nadalshebaclub.com; Nad
al-Sheba District, 5km southeast of Dubai centre;
Morning Stable Tour; adult/child Dh130/60;
◷ 7am Sat, Mon & Wed Sep-Jun

Lovers of all things equine should not miss a chance to check out these world-class stables. The visit starts with a look at the morning training followed by a guided tour around the thoroughbred training facilities. This is followed by an excellent breakfast at 'Spikes' in the Clubhouse. You then get to check out the Millennium Grandstand and take a walk through the Godolphin Gallery – quite a trophy room. There are also displays documenting the development of Godolphin stables, but alas, no explanation as to why that Melbourne Cup win keeps eluding them!

SAFA PARK Map pp214-15

cnr Al-Wasl Rd & Al-Hadiqa St, Safa; admission Dh5;
◷ 8am-11pm, women & children only Tue

This very popular park stretches for 1km from Al-Wasl Rd to Sheikh Zayed Rd. On a crowded winter's weekend you'll hear about 20 different languages being spoken just at the swings! Lots of cricket is played on the wide grassy expanses at weekends, and after dark the rides (near Al-Wasl Rd) get busy. There is a lake where you can hire paddle boats, tennis courts, a soccer pitch, barbecues and an artificial waterfall.

THIRD LINE Map pp214-15

☎ 394 3194; www.thethirdline.com; off Sheikh
Zayed Rd, Interchange 3, Al-Quoz; ◷ 11am-8pm
Sat-Thu, 4-8pm Fri

One of Dubai's more adventurous art spaces is operated by a couple of talented young curators, Sunny Rahbar and Claudia Cellini, whose exhibitions focus on provocative contemporary art. Their shows often include work that breaks the rules of traditional arts in the region to create fresh new forms, playfully appropriating everything from Pakistani miniatures and Persian calligraphy to traditional clothing (as Emirati Raghda Burkash's work does). Recent exhibitions

PUBLIC EXPOSURE

If you're not staying at a five star with access to some sand, and want to be able to say you've swum in the Arabian Sea (or at least dipped your toes!), you've got two options: either head to one of Dubai's free public beaches or pay for a day at a beach club.

Dipping without Dirhams

Dubai's free beaches.

Russian Beach (Map pp224–5; Next to Dubai Marin Beach Resort & Spa, Jumeirah) Also known as Open Beach, it gets crowded with a mix of sun-worshippers, from Russian tourists (note the signage!) to expat residents of nearby beachfront villas, and on Fridays a large number of male guest workers on their day off. While it's safe, women won't always feel comfortable. Showers and kiosk.

Kite Beach (Map pp214–15; Behind old Wollongong University campus, Umm Suqeim 4) There's plenty of room to sunbathe comfortably on this long pristine beach, except for the kite surfers (hence the name), whose abilities range from good to good grief. No facilities.

Umm Suqeim (Map pp214–15; Btwn Jumeirah Beach Hotel & Kite Beach) This white sandy beach, with fabulous views of the Burj, is popular with Jumeirah families and a more body-conscious set. Showers and shelter.

Khor Al-Mamzar (Map pp214–15) Before you get to Al-Mamzar Park, there's a lovely long stretch of narrow beach, and while there are no waves, this calm inlet must be one of the prettiest spots to swim, with the Sharjah skyline in the distance. Showers, picnicking facilities and tour groups galore.

Beaches for Bucks

The ones that cost…

Jumeirah Beach Park (p150; per person/car Dh5/20; ☎ 8am-11pm, women & children only Sat & Mon) It's a real treat to take a walk on the grass at this verdant park, as it's a couple of degrees cooler than the beach. Fronting onto a long stretch of Jumeirah Beach, it has lifeguards on duty, a children's play area, barbecues, picnic tables, walkways and kiosks.

One&Only Royal Mirage (p149; adult/child Dh125/90) Book at least a day in advance to access this groomed beach and pool with views of The Palm development (nonguests only have access when occupancy is below 80%).

Hilton Dubai Jumeirah (p149; adult/child weekdays Dh100/40, weekends Dh130/55) Parents love the nonstop organised kids activities, water sports and comparatively low prices.

Le Meridien Mina Seyahi (p149; Sun-Wed Dh120, Thu & Sat Dh200, Fri Dh250, all including lunch) This good beach and its great pools are popular with a more body-conscious clubbing set.

---

have included a great range of works, from digital art by young Emirati women to photography by Iranian female artists.

JUMEIRAH & NEW DUBAI

Eating p89; Shopping p135; Sleeping p149

This stretch of coast with its road running parallel is home to Dubai's busy beach resorts. It's a residential area as well and if you turn in either direction off Jumeirah Rd you can snoop around some of the villas in the area. Many of the residents earn big money and there's usually a Mercedes and an expensive 4WD in the double driveways of these villas. The wives of these well-rewarded gentlemen have earned themselves a nickname – the 'Jumeirah Janes', similar to 'ladies who lunch'. To service the local residents there is an increasing number of cafés and shopping centres in the area and many residents believe this area is now the 'new Dubai centre'. This stretch is also home to some of the most remarkable construction projects on earth. The man-made islands of The Palm (p32) can be seen from space and the Burj Al Arab no longer needs an introduction.

BURJ AL ARAB Map pp214-15

☎ 301 7000; www.burj-al-arab.com; Jumeirah Rd, Umm Suqeim

Dubai has no more fitting symbol than its audacious Burj Al Arab (Arabian Tower), the self-proclaimed world's only 'seven star' hotel (actually rated five-star luxury). What it is, however, is the world's tallest dedicated hotel, and higher than the Eiffel Tower. Built on an artificial island 280m offshore from the Jumeirah Beach Hotel, the sail-shaped building tops out at 321m and was the boldest of Dubai Ruler Sheikh Mohammed's myriad 1990s projects. Construction began in 1994, with pillars of the offshore island plunging 40m into the seabed, but it wasn't until 1999 that it opened its doors. Its sleek white exterior is a dramatic sight day and night and the interior is just astonishing – not in a flattering way either. Outside it's Sydney Opera House style; inside it's the set from the genie bottle in the *I Dream of Jeannie* TV series. For information on visiting the hotel, see the **Skyview Bar** (p102).

GREEN ART GALLERY Map pp224-5
☎ 344 9888; www.gagallery.com; Behind Dubai Zoo, Jumeirah; ☯ 9.30am-1.30pm & 4.30-8.30pm, closed Fri

With regular temporary exhibitions and a growing permanent collection concentrating on the work of artists living in the UAE, this small, altruistic commercial gallery is committed to nurturing local talent and developing the art scene. It also helps educate artists about international art distribution and promotion, and their website features selections from upcoming and past exhibitions.

IRANIAN MOSQUE Map pp224-5
Al-Wasl Rd, Satwa

Shiite mosques are noteworthy for their exquisite faïence (green-and-blue coloured and glazed) tile work covering the façades

JUMEIRAH & NEW DUBAI HIGHLIGHTS

- Be astounded by Burj Al Arab (opposite), Dubai's iconic landmark that doubles as a hotel.
- Learn about Islam and Emirati culture and traditions on a tour of the Jumeirah Mosque (p60).
- Visit the Madinat Jumeirah (p60), the mesmerising Arabian-style hotel, entertainment and shopping heaven.

and main dome. A stunning Dubai example is the Iranian Mosque in Satwa – and the **Iranian hospital**, adjacent and opposite, carries this same type of tile work.

JUMEIRAH ARCHAEOLOGICAL SITE
Map pp224-5
Off 27 St (look for a large fenced-in area) near Jumeirah Beach Park, Jumeirah

Only really of interest to archaeology enthusiasts, this is one of the most significant and largest archaeological sites in the UAE, where items dating from the 6th century AD were found and can be seen at **Dubai Museum** (p54) and the **Heritage Village** (p55). Surrounded by atmosphere-inhibiting modern villas, the settlement is interesting in that it spans the pre-Islamic and Islamic eras and was once a caravan stop on a route linking Ctesiphon (now Iraq) to northern Oman. Remains from here link it

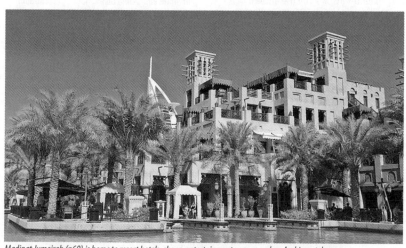

Madinat Jumeirah (p60) is home to resort hotels, shops, entertainment venues and an Arabian-style souq

with the Persian Sassanid empire, dominant in the region from the 3rd to 6th centuries AD, but wiped out by Arab tribes, and the Umayyad dynasty, with the coming of Islam in the 7th century.

JUMEIRAH MOSQUE Map pp224-5

☎ 353 6666; Jumeira Rd; tour Dh10; ⏰ 10am Thu & Sun

The splendid, intricately detailed architecture (stunningly lit at night!) and the opportunity to have a look inside (normally non-Muslims can't enter mosques here) puts Jumeirah Mosque on every visitor's sightseeing list. Aimed at fostering greater understanding between Muslims and other religions and cultures, the Sheikh Mohammed Centre for Cultural Understanding's 'Open Doors, Open Minds' tour takes visitors through the architecture of the mosque, introduces them to Islam, and Emirati culture and traditions. The Q&A session is viewed as a vital part of the visit, so read up a little first (see the boxed text, p12). It's best to pre-book as it's becoming increasingly popular, and make sure to dress modestly (no shorts, cover back and arms, and women should wear a headscarf). You'll also need to remove shoes before entering.

MADINAT JUMEIRAH Map pp214-15

Al-Sufouh Rd, Jumeirah; ⏰ 10am-11pm

You can easily lose a day at this enchanting hotel, shopping and entertainment complex, with exteriors inspired by the ancient skyscrapers found in Saudi Arabia and Yemen, and interiors influenced by old Arabian merchant houses. There are some extraordinary and exquisite details here – so if you see some stairs, take them; they'll probably lead you to a secreted terrace and wind-tower, with a mesmerising vista of the sprawling property. If you're staying at the hotel, or have a restaurant reservation, you can catch the silent *abras* cruising along the wonderful Venetian-style canals from one location to the next. Shops in the Arabian-style souq might have higher prices than the 'antique' and handicrafts stores, but the place is air-conditioned, quality is better and shopping hassle-free. There are plenty of restaurants, cafés and bars that offer breathtaking water views; Madinat Theatre (p107) plays host to

musicals, plays, opera, ballet and festivals; and during the cooler winter months, a traditional oud player enchants the *sheesha*-smoking crowd in the souq's central plaza.

MAJLIS GHORFAT UM-AL-SHEEF

Map pp214-15

17 St, near Jumeirah Beach Park; admission Dh1; ⏰ 8.30am-1.30pm & 3.30-8.30pm Sat-Thu, 3.30-8.30pm Fri

It is unusual to find a traditional building still standing so far from the Creek, but this one, south of Jumeira Beach Park, has been well restored and is worth a visit. The two-storey structure was built in 1955 and was attended in the evenings by Sheikh Rashid bin Saeed al-Maktoum. Here he would listen to his people's complaints, grievances and ideas.

The *majlis* also provided a cool retreat from the heat of the day and is made of gypsum and coral rock, traditional building materials of the Gulf, and the roof is made of palm fronds (*areesh*). The *majlis* is decorated with cushions, rugs, a coffeepot, pottery and food platters, and is pretty close to the way it would have looked in Sheikh Rashid's day. A peaceful garden of date palms and fig trees has been constructed around the *majlis*, and a traditional *barasti* café sits in one corner of the enclosure.

WILD WADI WATERPARK Map pp214-15

☎ 348 4444; www.wildwadi.com; Jumeirah Rd, Jumeirah; adult/child Dh140/120; ⏰ 11am-6pm Nov-Feb, 11am-7pm Mar-May & Sep-Oct, 11am-9pm Jun-Aug

Wild Wadi seems to satisfy everyone's needs, with dozens of ingeniously interconnected rides based on the legend of Arabian adventurer Juha and his friend, Sinbad the sailor, who are shipwrecked on a lush lagoon, beyond which lies a magical oasis. There are water-safety lessons for children, more sedate rides for young children and nervous adults, two Flowriders (artificial waves) and the truly terrifying Jumeirah Sceirah for the more adventurous among you. Many people settle in for a few hours, th body boards and tubes free, and food and beverages available via a clever debit card attached to your wrist (lifeguards are also on hand!).

Walking Tours ■

Walking Tours

Dubai is a rapidly expanding metropolis with interesting sights scattered all over the city, yet the older areas of Bur Dubai and Deira are still the most stimulating – wandering around them can be a wonderful assault upon the senses. The areas are compact and the sights worth seeing are grouped close together. Outside Deira and Bur Dubai the city's attractions are spread far and wide, and are impossible to walk unless you're prepping for a marathon, so we've included a stroll around Sharjah's splendidly rejuvenated heritage and arts areas. Traffic willing, it's just a short drive away and fascinating in its own right.

Both Dubai tours can be done in half a day, broken up with a bite for lunch and an *abra* (boat) ride across the Creek. If you're in Dubai when it's hot, we recommend starting one walking tour in the early morning and doing the other in the early evening. The Sharjah tour should take a couple of hours, or more if you can't resist the fabulous shopping in Sharjah's souqs.

WIND-TOWER WANDER

Wonderful old wind-towers are scattered throughout the historical waterfront of Bur Dubai, as you'll see on this heritage walk taking you through Dubai's oldest areas, from the beautifully restored Bastakia Quarter to the Shindagha Heritage Village and Diving Village.

Start your Bastakia exploration at Bastakiah nights 1 (p86) restaurant, near Al-Seef Rd. The courtyard house it occupies is stunningly decorated and worth a look inside (staff are happy to show you around). Spend some time wandering the quarter's atmospheric narrow lanes and peeking into the lovingly renovated wind-tower houses. Worth checking out is a section of the original city wall and several fascinating art galleries in historic courtyard houses: XVA Hotel & Art Gallery 2 (p56), Ostra 3 (p56), Majlis Gallery 4 (p56) and Basta Art Café 5 (p83).

From Basta Art Café, head along Al-Fahidi St to Dubai Museum 6 (p54), with its entrance on 62A St. Here you can easily spend an hour engaging in the history, heritage and development of Dubai, and sneaking photos of the kitsch dioramas.

Emerging from the museum, walk down 62A St to admire the reserved architectural details of the multidomed Grand Mosque 7 (p55); make a note when visiting Sheikh Saeed al-Maktoum House (No 12 on this tour) to look for the original Grand Mosque in old photos of Dubai.

Take the lane to the mosque's right-hand side, passing the humble Hindu Shri Nathje Jayate Temple 8 (p55) on your left, and continue straight ahead until you get to Hindi Lane 9 (p55), a wonderful, colourful alley lined with tiny stores selling Eastern religious paraphernalia. Along the way, you'll notice rows of shoes at the bottom of stairs that lead up to the Sikh Gurudaba 10 (p55).

At the end of the lane take a right – you are now in Bur Dubai Souq 11 (p53) – but first head towards the waterfront, past the refurbished wooden stores, until you come to a lovely open area. One of our favourite

The entrance to the Diving Village (p55), Bur Dubai

WALK FACTS

Start Al Seef Rd roundabout
End Kan Zaman restaurant
Distance 3km
Duration Three to four hours (including museum visit)

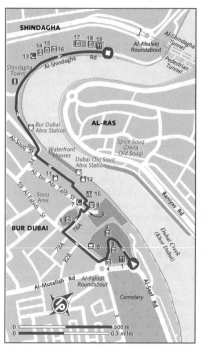

spots, it's an oasis of calm overlooking the commotion of the Creek. On the Deira side, you'll notice more restored wind-towers at the Spice Souq, while looking back to the Bur Dubai side you'll see some handsome renovated waterfront houses. Head back in the direction you came, turning right into the souq, and continue under the wooden arcades, passing scores of textile shops. Look up the lanes to the left and you'll notice even more revamped wind-towers. When you see the Dubai Old Souq Abra Station on your right, you'll also spot **Allah Din Shoes** 12 (p132) selling wonderful curly-toed slippers. Continue through the vibrant souq, generally hectic at night (chaotic on Friday evenings) but peaceful in the morning. Exit the souq at its western entrance with the Bur Dubai Abra Station ahead to your right, and walk past the *abras* and along the waterfront, passing Shindagha Tower on your left, until you arrive at a number of wonderful historic buildings. First up is tiny **Bin Suroor Mosque** 13, dating back to 1930 and frequented by local workers, followed by the **Sheikh Juma al-Maktoum House** 14, the **Sheikh Saeed al-Maktoum House** 15 (p56), once residence of Dubai's ruling Maktoum family and home to a fascinating collection of old images of Dubai, and the Islamic Centre at the **Sheikh Obaid bin Thani House** 16. You'll soon arrive at the charming **Heritage Village** 17 (p55) and **Diving Village** 18 (p55), where you can enjoy an insight into Emirati traditions, and **Kan Zaman restaurant** 19 (p84), where you can eat a tasty Arabic lunch on the waterfront.

SOUQ SAUNTER

As soon as you step off the *abra* at Deira Old Souq Abra Station, the heady scents of sumac, cinnamon, cloves and other spices will lure you across to the **Spice Souq** 1 (p51). From here we take you on a stroll through some of the absorbing backstreets of Deira's souqs.

Take some time to explore. Chat to the shopkeepers. If you can't guess what's in those sacks, ask! Buy something (see Shopping, p122): saffron is excellent value; frankincense, oud and an incense burner make a memorable souvenir; and a DIY henna kit is fun.

When you exit the souq on Al-Abra St, turn right. At the end of the street, turn

Fragrant dried spices in huge sacks at the Spice Souq (p51)

left onto Al-Ras St, continue to Al-Hadd St and turn right. The intriguing stores on these streets, selling sacks of nuts, pulses and rice, belong to wholesalers trading mainly with Iran and using the dhows to ply their goods.

At the end of the street turn right into Al-Ahmadiya St until you arrive at the beautifully restored **Heritage House 2** (p52), and behind this, the equally well-renovated **Al-Ahmadiya School 3** (p50). It's worth a brief diversion for an insight into Dubai's history and culture, and you'll enjoy the splendid architecture, exquisite detail and, everyone's favourite, more kitsch dioramas.

Continue along Al-Ahmadiya St, turning right into Old Baladiya St with more wholesalers, this time trading in *gutras* (white headcloths) and *agals* (headrobes used to hold gutras in place), sandals, cheap shoes and Chinese products. Ahead, to the left, is the wooden latticed archway that's the entrance to Dubai's famous **Gold Souq 4** (p51). Take time to drop into shops to get a closer look at the jaw-dropping jewellery. Particularly breathtaking are the elaborate gold pieces created for brides' dowries – find them by the camera flashes going off! Wander along the atmospheric narrow lanes that lead off the main arcade – you'll discover tiny teashops, simple cafeterias, busy tailors and barber shops. Exiting the souq (usually poorer than when you entered), continue along Sikkat al-Khail St to the **Perfume Souq 5** (p52). This is really just a string of shops selling heady Arabian *attars* and oud, fake European colognes and pretty tinted perfume bottles. If you need to refuel, enjoy a shawarma at **Ashwaq Cafeteria 6** (p78).

Hang a right into 107 St where it can be bedlam some nights with spruikers competing to sell off their cut-price clothes, Chinese-made shoes and kitsch souvenirs. Tucked behind these streets is **Deira Covered Souq 7** (p50), which doesn't look like a traditional souq,

WALK FACTS

Start Spice Souq
End Naif Souq
Distance 2km
Duration Three hours (including souq shopping)

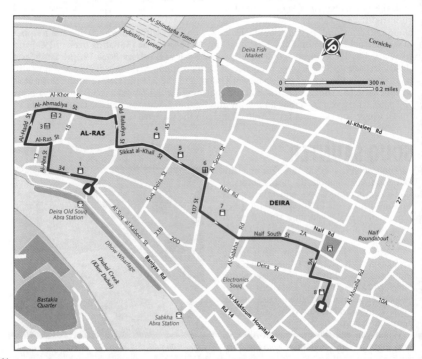

A local man at Sharjah's Souq Al-Arsa (p157)

nor is it covered – instead you'll find hundreds of little shops on alleys selling everything from textiles to luggage, groceries and *sheesha* pipes. Arriving near Al-Sabkha Rd bus station, cross the road and head into Naif South St.

Follow Naif South St, turn right into 9A St and wander down until you arrive at **Naif Souq 8** (p50), a small covered market popular with Emirati women buying copy designer Dior *shaylas* and *abayas*, children's clothes and toys – it can get crazy here at night!

ARTS AMBLE

Dubai's nearest neighbour, Sharjah, has a thriving arts scene in its revitalised Heritage and Arts precinct. It's wonderful to explore in the late afternoon or early evening, except Mondays when most sights are shut. Catch a taxi to Sharjah and then start at imposing **Al-Hisn Fort 1** (p157) for a decent introduction to local history.

Cross Al Borj Ave and head across Al Borj Rd to arrive at the atmospheric, pedestrianised Heritage Area. Ahead of you is a spacious open 'square' with a number of small museums and several narrow lanes connecting this square to another couple of open areas. Behind the restored areas are

WALK FACTS

Start Al-Hisn Fort
End Arts Café
Distance 2km
Duration Two hours

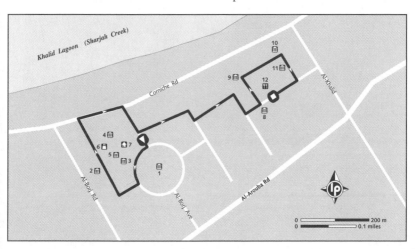

some crumbling old buildings still awaiting renovation, palm trees and the odd chicken or goat, surprising to see in the centre of the city. It's fun to wander around here.

The renovated white buildings in the Heritage Area fall under the umbrella of the Sharjah Heritage Museum, including the **Sharjah Islamic Museum** 2 (p157), the **Museum for Arabic Calligraphy & Ornamentation** 3 and **Al-Midfa House** 4 (p157), with the only round wind-tower in the Gulf. Worth a closer look is **Bait Al Naboodah** 5 for its gorgeous courtyard and small display of artefacts, jewellery and costumes.

Across from Bait Al Naboodah is the atmospheric old **Souq Al-Arsa** 6 (p157) with wonderful crafts, 'antique' and carpet shops, a traditional coffeehouse and a beautifully restored hotel, **Dar al Dhyafa** 7 (p159).

Next, head towards the water and turn right on Corniche Rd, passing by another traditional coffee shop. Notice the dhows across the road on the dock – they're worth a closer look if you have time. Head back towards Al-Hisn fort and left into the Arts Area to excellent **Sharjah Art Museum** 8 (p158), home to an interesting collection of Orientalist art and the more adventurous Sharjah Art Biennale. Across the square and off its surrounding lanes you can visit **Sharjah Art Centre** 9 in Bait Al Serkal, **Sharjah Art Galleries** 10 in Obaid Al-Shamsi house, the **Very Special Arts Centre** 11 (p158) for disabled artists, and the **Emirates Fine Arts Society** (p158), which shows local artists' work and is in the same complex as the Very Special Arts Centre. Take a well-earned rest at **Arts Café** 12.

1 *A longboarder heads into the surf, Jumeirah Beach Park (p58)* 2 *A lifeguard on patrol by the looming Burj Al Arab (p58)* 3 *The beach resort at Madinat Jumeirah (p60)* 4 *Conversation in the heat at one of Jumeirah's public beaches (p58)*

1 *Shopping in 'Hindi Lane' (p55), Bur Dubai* **2** *Expat workers (p14) sit waiting for friends on their day off* **3** *Kitchen staff at restaurant Mezzanine (p94)*

1 *Jumeirah Mosque (p60), the only mosque open to non-Muslims in Dubai* 2 *The traditional wind-towers (p28) of the Bastakia Quarter* 3 *Boat access to Madinat Jumeirah's resort hotels (p150)* 4 *Night-time view of the stunning Burj Al Arab (p58)*

1 A worker takes a break from tending his camel; camels (p116) are still of great importance to the Dubaian culture and economy
2 Enjoying the opulence of Madinat Jumeirah (p60) **3** The traditional red-and-white-checked gutra (headcloth) has become a modern fashion accessory (p129)
4 Taking a stroll along Dubai Creek (p49)

1 Camels are employed both in industry and at The Dubai Camel Racecourse (p117) **2** The traditional practice of falconry (p12) lives on **3** On the road to Hatta (p159) **4** The rugged Hajar Mountains (p159)

1 *Aladdin slippers for sale at Bur Dubai Souq (p53)* **2** *Ibn Battuta Mall (p136), styled to follow the worldly travels of Arab scholar Ibn Battuta* **3** *Bargains at Karama Shopping Centre (p133)*
4 *Hundreds of stores at the Gold Souq (p51) display their wares in a dazzling array*

local game of volleyball, a walk from glitzy Sheikh ed Road (p56) **2** A back-et bakery in colourful Satwa 7) **3** A barbershop in the ra neighbourhood (p49)

1 Reflections in a building along Dubai Creek (p49) **2** Dubai Creek dhows (p53) at sunset **3** Drivers of the local abras (water taxis; p49) wait their turn to ferry passengers across the Creek **4** A couple watches a dhow pass by the gleaming buildings of Deira (p49)

Eating

Eating

Given the mix of nationalities living in Dubai, it's no surprise that you can indulge in just about any cuisine that takes your fancy – and in just about every price range. From a simple, tasty street shawarma to the *haute cuisine* delights of Gordon Ramsay's Verre, Dubai offers a huge range of dining experiences – and we recommend that you try a bit of everything.

Start the day off with a quick pastry at one of Dubai's independent (not attached to a hotel) cafés, such as More or the Lime Tree Café. Head to the Gold Souq for some shopping and try some shawarma. Then head off for dinner at Dubai's latest gastronomic temple, such as Mezzanine, or eat somewhere more casual such as Noodle House.

Surprisingly, the hardest thing to get in Dubai is local Emirati and Gulf specialities! Unless you score an invitation to a local wedding, you're unlikely to see the local dish, *khouzi*, which consists of a whole roasted lamb or baby camel stuffed with rice and spices – it is delicious. More common is chicken, lamb or shrimp *mashbous*, where the meat is spiced and served with equally spicy rice. As Dubai is on the coast, seafood is very popular and the favourite local fish is hammour, a tasty member of the groper family – it's so abundant that there's no excuse for it not to be fresh.

Opening Hours & Meal Times

Restaurant hours are generally from noon to 3pm and from 7.30pm to midnight, while the cheap eats are generally open from 9am to midnight – shawarma places generally open in the late afternoon and stay open well past midnight. Most places are open seven days a week, with the exception of Friday lunch when some of the smaller local eateries are closed. In the top-end restaurants, if you want to eat like a local resident, your booking is for 8.30pm or 9pm, although you'll turn up fashionably late. For the Arab/Lebanese restaurants with live music, an 11pm reservation is the norm as the entertainment usually continues until 3am.

How Much?

Street food such as a shawarma costs around Dh5 and in the local restaurants dishes such as an Indian curry are about Dh8 to Dh10. At midrange eateries expect to pay around Dh25 to Dh35 for a main course, while at the top end prices are around Dh65 to

---

WINING FOR DUBAI DINING

Dubai only has two alcohol importers so you're likely to see the same wines pop up on wine lists all over town. The good news is that the wines available are a decent mix of Old and New World, so here's an eclectic range of wines to try while in Dubai.

Chateau d'Armajan des Ormes Sauternes This rich yellow-gold Bordeaux has a medium sweetness and a long finish. While it's a perfect partner for foie gras, try it with crème brûlée.

Leeuwin Estate Prelude Vineyards Chardonnay This excellent white from the Margaret River region in Australia is well-rounded, with peach and mango on the nose, tropical fruit on the palate with a buttery finish. Great with seafood, pasta and white meat.

Montes Alpha Cabernet Sauvignon This Chilean red is full of forest fruits and spices and is a great choice to accompany barbecued meats (especially Lebanese) and even Indian dishes.

Stonehedge Merlot A reliable favourite from California, it's a spicy but smooth merlot that can take on some reasonably hearty red-meat dishes.

Villa Maria Private Bin Marlborough Sauvignon Blanc This New Zealand white has a fruity nose and a lovely hint of lemongrass on the palate – try it with a cold entrée or just enjoy it by itself.

Dh100 plus. What really bumps the price of a meal into the stratosphere is alcohol. Alcohol can only be sold in restaurants/bars attached to hotels (generally three-star hotels or better) and some clubs, and the prices are pretty outrageous – expect to pay around Dh18 for a pint of beer or a glass of wine, and more at a nightclub. Even the most mundane bottle of plonk will set you back at least Dh100 a bottle. So if you're on a tight budget, don't forget to grab some duty-free on the way into Dubai! See the boxed text, opposite, for recommendations that ease the pain of paying Dh100 for a Dh15 bottle of wine. Also see Price Ranges (above).

PRICE GUIDE

Reviews in this chapter are listed under each area in order of price for a main course, from the least expensive to the wallet-busters. Here's how we break it down:

$	Under Dh15
$$	Dh16-35
$$$	Dh36-60
$$$$	Over Dh60

Booking Tables

Generally speaking, you should always book tables at restaurants in the hotels, while this is not necessary for the cheaper eateries. Restaurants usually want a mobile phone number and the better restaurants will call you if you're late for a booking. Weekend bookings for Wednesday and Thursday nights as well as Friday brunch are best made a week in advance for the more popular restaurants. Foodies should note that there are an increasing number of 'gourmet' nights in Dubai, so check *Time Out* or *What's On* magazines to see if there's something special on during your visit.

Tipping

Tipping is not compulsory and not necessarily expected, which may explain some of the comical 'service' that is rampant in Dubai. The hotel restaurants often put a service charge on the bill, which by and large goes to the hotel, not your waiter. A tip of 5% to 10% is generally the rule of thumb if you're happy with the service.

Restaurant Al Mallah (p83) is kept busy serving up Lebanese fare, with especially delicious shawarmas

SHAWARMA SHOOTOUT

Simply the best fast food ever invented, the shawarma is the stable snack food of the Middle East. While you'll hear it called many other things in many other countries – Gyros in Greece and döner kebab in Turkey – it's really only known as shawarma in Dubai (or *shwarma, shawerma, chawerma*, but let's not be too pedantic). While the Greeks might disagree, this hand-held meal originated in Turkey, where döner literally means 'one that turns'. This refers to the vertical rotisserie that the meat for the shawarma is cooked on. Strips of marinated meat (usually chicken or lamb) and fat are placed on a skewer which then rotates in front of a flame or gas grill. When you place an order the grill is usually turned up and your 'sandwich' is made fresh. One highly subjective facet of shawarma making (besides what kind of bread it should be made with – but it should *never* be a bread roll) is the number and variety of toppings. Pickles, tomato, onion and parsley are the most common additions, but really, anything goes. Dubai is blessed with an enormous number of shawarma joints, so to help you enjoy this ingenious snack we undertook a massive research project – involving count-less late-night tastings – to present to you our favourite kebabs, sorry, shawarmas:

Al Mallah (p83) This is our favourite in Dubai. Both the chicken and lamb shawarmas are sublime here – the juicy chicken meat shawarma is loaded with tasty garlic sauce and jammed with pickles, while the lamb is tender and tasty with tonnes of fresh tomato, parsley, pickles and hummus.

Ashwaq Cafeteria (Map pp216–17; cnr Al-Soor St & Sikkat al-Khail St, Bur Dubai; ☺ noon-11pm) Everyone's favourite stop on a Gold Souq shopping excursion. The simple shawarmas here are delicious – the chicken is best, juicy chicken meat, with a light spread of garlic sauce, and crunchy lettuce.

Beirut (p83) Beirut is one of the big guns in shawarmas on Al-Dhiyafah St and battles with Al Mallah for the title of best lamb shawarma, but we like the fact that they have two sizes here.

Lebanese Village (p83) The little lamb shawarmas here are zesty with loads of onion, parsley, pickles and tomato, all combining to give them a tangy flavour (and their crunchy hot felafels are also delicious). Not sure about the 'Mexican' shawarmas, though…

Saj Express (p86) Despite being the only one in this selection that looks like a real fast-food chain, its excellent fresh bread makes these shawarmas special. Try the chicken – it's delicious.

Self-Catering

Those interested in self-catering will find plenty of small grocery stores around Deira, Bur Dubai, Karama, Satwa and Rigga. They sell a good range of basic groceries as well as a small selection of fruit and vegetables, although sometimes we could swear that some of the produce has been in Dubai longer than we have…these are not always of the best quality.

For fresher produce, head to what is collectively known as the **Shindagha Market** (Map pp220–1; ☺ 7am-11pm), where there are daily fish and meat markets. There are no fixed prices, so bargaining is the order of the day. Further up Al-Khaleej Rd, near Hamriya Port, the **Wholesale Market** (Map pp216–17; ☺ 7am-11pm) is even cheaper, but most sales are in bulk quantities. Again, haggling is the norm. The huge parking area is usually filled with trucks bringing in produce from Oman.

One of the biggest supermarket chains operating in Dubai is the French-based Carrefour with branches at Bur Dubai (Map pp220–1), Deira City Centre (p130) and Mall of the Emirates (p136). It's best to visit in the mornings for the wonderful seafood and to avoid the late-afternoon and evening crowds. Another French brand, Geant, operates out of Ibn Battuta Mall (p136) and stocks roughly the same items as Carrefour. The North American **Spinney's** (☺ 8am-midnight) is the most popular supermarket with Western expats and, while it's more expensive than the rest, stocks some brands the expats can't live without – including (whisper it) pork products. There are branches on Abu Baker al-Siddiq Rd, Deira (Map pp216–17); on Al-Mankhool Rd (Map pp220–1), opposite Al-Rolla Rd; on Sheikh Khalifa bin Zayed Rd (Map pp220–1), near the corner with Kuwait St; on Jumeira Rd (Map pp224–5); on Al-Wasl Rd (Map pp214–15), in Safa; and at Mercato (p137) on Jumeira Rd. For organic produce, we have to salute Organic Foods & Café (p135) for finally bringing Dubai its first real organic supermarket.

Choitrams, geared to catering for the Indian and Pakistani communities more than West-ern expats, has much the same stuff as Spinney's at lower prices. You'll find a **Choitrams** (Map pp220–1; cnr Al-Rolla & Al-Mankhool Rds) next to Al-Khaleej Shopping Centre. There's another on Al-Wasl Rd, Jumeirah (Map pp214–15) near Safa Park.

Union Co-op Society has a good selection of cheap groceries, but no pork products. There is one shop on Al-Wasl Rd (Map pp214–15) near Safa Park and a second on Sheikh Khalifa bin Zayed Rd (Map pp222–3) in Mankhool.

DEIRA

With all the dining attention now focused down the beach, it's hard not to feel a little sorry for Deira's dining scene. But Deira offers a myriad of dining opportunities, from the shawarma at the Gold Souq to one of Dubai's best restaurants in Verre.

TOP FIVE DEIRA EATS

- Verre (p82)
- Blue Elephant (p81)
- Casa Mia (p80)
- Glasshouse Mediterranean Brasserie (p80)
- Minato (p81)

CAFÉ HAVANA Map pp218-19   Café $$

☎ 295 5238; Deira City Centre, Level II; coffee Dh12; ☼ 8am-midnight

We're not so in love with the food offerings at this mall, but the decent coffee and excellent people-watching opportunities make this café the best choice for a shopping break. For many visitors to Dubai it provides one of the only opportunities to hang with the local Emirati men who kick back here for hours.

MORE Map pp218-19   Café $$

☎ 283 0224; near Welcare Hospital, Al Garhoud; mains Dh30; ☼ 8am-11pm

One of the Dubai expat communities' favourite brunch spots, this café is a stylish escape from the bland branded cafés that dominate Dubai. While the secret is that it resembles the kind of café that the clientele would visit on a weekend back home, the food is a little hit and miss. However, the coffee, tea, attentive service and free wi-fi make up for its shortcomings.

YUM! Map pp216-17   Noodle Bar $$

☎ 222 7171; InterContinental Hotel, Baniyas St; mains Dh35; ☼ noon-1am

While it follows closely in the footsteps of the successful Noodle House (p87) chain, Yum! lacks the buzz of that Emirates Towers eatery, but makes a good alternative on this side of the Creek. Try the combination plate of spring rolls, seafood parcels and minced shrimp, and the tom kha gai (chicken and coconut soup). The wok specials such as char kway teow (fried flat noodles) are also excellent. There are only a few vegetarian dishes scattered through the menu, but they're good.

Asian cuisine at Noodle House (p87) – a popular choice at Emirates Towers

CELLAR Map pp218-19 — Fusion $$$

☎ 282 9333; Aviation Club; mains Dh40;
🕑 noon-2am
Known best for its Friday brunch, this expat favourite has lifted its gastronomic game in the past couple of years. It serves hearty and comforting stuff, with dishes such as braised lamb shank with butternut risotto a feature. Honest food, honest prices and a relaxed atmosphere make this one of Dubai's less pretentious eateries.

THAI KITCHEN Map pp218-19 — Thai $$$

☎ 602 1234; Park Hyatt Dubai; mains Dh45;
🕑 7pm-midnight, brunch 12.30-4pm Fri
While this innovative restaurant had a very bumpy take-off, it's now a fine option, serving up traditional Thai with a twist in tapas-sized portions. With its open kitchens and almost market-style ambience, you expect the food to be fresh – and it most certainly is. We love it that you can just order a couple of dishes, watch what else is coming out of the kitchen and order that as well. And it's great to see a woman chef running the show too, a rarity in Dubai.

Preparing some chicken shawarmas (p78) in a small backstreet restaurant

CASA MIA Map pp218-19 — Italian $$$

☎ 702 2506; Le Meridien Dubai, Airport Rd, Al Garhoud; mains Dh50; 🕑 12.30-2.45pm & 8-11.30pm
One of the most dependable Italian experiences in town, Casa Mia manages to transcend the somewhat odd setting of Le Meridien Village. First off, the service is friendly and efficient, as you'll note while scoffing the brilliant fresh breads. The beef carpaccio is a highlight of the starters, the fresh pastas and pizzas are delicious, and if you manage to get to *secondi piatti* (mains), we salute you. Good vegetarian options and a well-selected wine list make this a local favourite, so book ahead.

CHINA CLUB

Map pp216-17 — Contemporary Chinese $$$
☎ 222 7171; InterContinental Hotel, Baniyas St; mains Dh50; 🕑 1-3pm & 8-11pm
It's hard to decide when to visit this restaurant. The Friday Yum Cha is excellent fun (remember that in Dubai Friday is the 'Sunday' of the week!), but it's at night when this beautifully designed room is looking its best. While some of the more inventive dishes occasionally fall flat, the classics are excellent – the Peking duck is super. The service can be random but just order a good bottle from the decent wine list and enjoy.

CREEKSIDE Map pp216-17 — Japanese $$$

☎ 207 1750; Sheraton Dubai Creek, Baniyas St, Deira; mains Dh50; 🕑 12.30-3pm & 6.30pm-midnight
This is one of our favourites, and not because of the overly bright lighting and bland décor, but for the freshness of the produce, such an important component of a great Japanese meal. The sushi and sashimi are exemplary, but the hot dishes, such as teppanyaki and tempura, are enough to make us skip the brilliant green tea brûlée. Almost…

GLASSHOUSE MEDITERRANEAN BRASSERIE

Map pp216-17 — Modern Mediterranean $$$
☎ 227 1111; Hilton Dubai Creek, Baniyas Rd; mains Dh50; 🕑 12.30-3.30pm & 7-11.30pm
It must be hard for the folk at Glasshouse not to want to throw stones at its neighbouring

restaurant, Gordon Ramsay's Verre (p82). While Verre gets all the media attention, Glasshouse has gone and reinvented itself as one of Dubai's most accomplished brasserie-style restaurants. While the menu is comforting, filled with dishes such as risotto with mushrooms, and rib-eye steak with chips, it's executed with style, unlike the service, which has probably caught you sneaking glances over to Verre. Great wines by the glass.

ASHIANA Map pp216-17 — Indian $$$$
☎ 228 1707; Sheraton Dubai Creek; mains Dh75; ⏱ 12.30-3pm & 7.30pm-midnight

There's always something unsettling about recommending an upmarket Indian restaurant in a town that has an overabundance of cheap Indian eateries. After all, at a cheapie you can probably shout the whole restaurant to a free biryani for the price of a main course here. But Ashiana has great ambience, fantastic flavours, and you can have a beer with your curry while watching some live sitar-playing. Enjoy the excellent North Indian cuisine, with delectable tandoori and curry meat dishes, as well as excellent vegetarian options.

BLUE ELEPHANT Map pp218-19 — Thai $$$$
☎ 705 4660; Al-Bustan Rotana Hotel, Casablanca Rd, Al Garhoud; mains Dh75; ⏱ 12-3pm & 7-11.30pm

While the Thai village interior (complete with fish-filled lake) is disconcertingly kitsch, the warm Thai welcome and great menu removes any lingering doubts that this is the real thing. While Blue Elephant is now quite a large chain of restaurants, refined Thai cuisine is welcome in any city. Settle down to a Royal Thai Banquet, or just choose your favourites, but pay attention to the heat level! Decent vegetarian options, and a particularly good-value buffet night. Book ahead.

MINATO Map pp216-17 — Japanese $$$$
☎ 222 7171; InterContinental Hotel, Baniyas St; mains Dh75; ⏱ 1-3pm & 8-11pm

While the minimalist interior doesn't inspire here, the food certainly does. Book some seats at the tiny sushi bar or a teppanyaki table for the best ambience and order up a storm. At the sushi bar you'll find the fresh sushi and sashimi are of first-rate quality and the chef is very knowledgeable (and amusing). There are

MEALS WITH A VIEW

Dubai has restaurants with breathtaking views. Here's our top five:

Pierchic (p92) Take in the Burj Al Arab and the incredible Al Qasr.

Vu's (p89) From Sheikh Zayed Rd to the Arabian Gulf, a fantastic view.

Marina Seafood Market (p93) Brilliant views of the Burj Al Arab.

Toscana (p90) The Madinat Jumeirah waterway at its best.

Zheng He's (p92) Watch the silent *abras* float by.

also buffet deals on some nights, making it extremely good value.

MIYAKO Map pp216-17 — Japanese $$$$
☎ 209 1222; Hyatt Regency, off Al-Khaleej Rd; mains Dh75; ⏱ 12.30-3pm & 7-11pm

After an extreme makeover, this consistently outstanding Japanese restaurant now has style to match the food on offer. Tuna and salmon are usually the pick of the raw stuff on the extensive menu, but there's far more fascinating food on offer besides sushi and sashimi, and the crumbed fried oysters and braised pork belly (*kakuni*) alone are worth coming for.

M'S BEEF BISTRO
Map pp218-19 — Steakhouse $$$$
☎ 282 4040; Le Meridien Dubai, Airport Rd, Al Garhoud; mains Dh75; ⏱ 12.30-2.45pm & 7.30-11.45pm

The best choice for a hearty steak on this side of the Creek, this intimate but busy American-style steakhouse serves up US and NZ beef cooked to order. With starters such as carpaccio and tartare followed by dishes such as tenderloin with Béarnaise sauce, it's certainly no place for a vegetarian, despite the other non-meat menu items. There's a great wine selection perfectly matched to the food on offer and the service is friendly.

SHABESTAN Map pp216-17 — Persian $$$$
☎ 205 7333; InterContinental Hotel, Baniyas St; mains Dh75; ⏱ 1-3pm & 8-11pm

Get a more nuanced idea of what Middle East cuisine consists of (it's more than just

Eating

DEIRA

shawarma and mezze plates), at Shabestan: it offers a wonderful introduction to Iranian cooking. Select a table with creek views or one of the intimate niches – perfect for groups – and sample the oven-fresh bread and the great Persian band while checking out the menu. While the selection of starters is recommended – especially for vegetarians – a consistent highlight is the lamb.

SHAHRZAD Map pp216-17 · · · · · · · · · · Persian $$$$

☎ 209 1200; Hyatt Regency, off Al-Khaleej Rd; mains Dh75; 🕑 12.30-3.30pm & 7.30-11pm, closed Sat

Steeped in faux *The Thousand and One Nights* ambience, Shahrzad is a droll setting in which to sample fine Persian cooking as well as the delights of a live Persian band. Accompanied by the mouth-watering smell of bread cooked fresh in the *tanour* oven, order up some hot starters and a traditional stew as well as the obligatory kebabs.

VERRE Map pp216-17 · · · · · · · · · · Fine Dining $$$$

☎ 212 7551; Hilton Dubai Creek, Baniyas Rd; mains Dh80; 🕑 7pm-midnight

Since the heady days of Verre's opening, plenty has changed. The original chef, Angela Hartnett, has gone on to get her own Michelin Star, and the maître d' has been roped into appearing on Gordon Ramsay's awful reality TV show, *Hell's Kitchen*. However, back in the kitchen at Verre, things are humming along nicely. The team on the floor are still the best-drilled lot in Dubai, the wine list is wide and deep, and the food always sublime. Ramsay's combination of French technique and light touch (especially in his seafood dishes) works well in Dubai and we don't even mind the fact that Ramsay only visits a few times a year. For some reason the staff get very nervous when he's around…

TRAITEUR Map pp218-19 · · · · · · · · · · Fine Dining $$$$

☎ 602 1234; Park Hyatt Dubai; mains Dh100; 🕑 12.30-3.30pm & 7pm-midnight

Lured by the promise of fresh produce and groovy French lounge music, we hoped Traiteur would be another eatery that gets it right in Dubai. While the hotel and restaurant were only a couple of months old when we visited, this should have

been ample time to get the bugs ironed out of the service and food. However, as we tried to decipher the menu (ordered by ingredient) and attempted to figure out exactly what was a main or a starter, *Footsteps on the Dancefloor* played twice and the cycling coloured lights drove us to distraction. Still, the food, when we did manage to get some, was fine. Great aged beef and fresh seafood as promised. Let's hope they've found the lounge music before you book there.

BUR DUBAI

Probably the most eclectic eating area of Dubai, Bur Dubai juxtaposes great restaurants at Wafi City and the Grand Hyatt Dubai with the cheap workers' eateries at Karama and Satwa.

CHHAPPAN BHOG

Map pp222-3 · · · · · · · · · · Indian/Vegetarian $

☎ 396 8176; Sheikh Khalifa bin Zayed Rd (Trade Centre Rd), Karama; mains Dh10; 🕑 12.30-3pm & 7pm-midnight

This long-standing favourite is very popular with the local Indian population, serving up mainly North Indian dishes and fantastic naans and tandoori rotis. It has a fast-food counter and an excellent Indian sweets shop downstairs.

KARACHI DARBAR

Map pp222-3 · · · · · · · · · · Pakistani $

☎ 334 7272; Karama Shopping Centre & various locations; mains Dh11; 🕑 4am-2am

A firm favourite with 'guest workers' and Western expats with an eye for a biryani bargain, the Karachi Darbar keeps them well fed with a huge menu of Pakistani, Indian and Chinese specialities. You could try the chicken or mutton Kashmiri, but the vegetarian dishes such as fried dhal or vegetable korma are delicious with the obligatory biryani rice side dish. It's not a culinary highlight of Dubai, but it's fun and filling. No credit cards.

RAVI Map pp224-5 · · · · · · · · · · Pakistani $

☎ 331 5353; Al-Satwa Rd, Satwa; mains Dh12; 🕑 24hr

To be frank, this place is probably better known for its cheap prices and opening hours than the cuisine on offer (though several well-known chefs inexplicably love the place). Really a 'workers' café', there is a pretty direct correlation between the prices and the quality of the meat. But stick to the vegetarian dishes, order a biryani and some bread (delicious while it's hot), and you can't go wrong at these prices. Try the Punjabi sweet lassi drink – very tasty!

FOOD CASTLE Map pp222-3   Indian $
☎ 335 5717; Sheikh Mohammed Bldg, Karama; mains Dh13; ☽ 24hr

An excellent choice after a Karama shopping excursion. Settle down in the outdoor garden (complete with a cooling little fountain) and sample the *beef olathiyathu*, a spicy dry curry, the *kozhi varatharachathu* (chicken with coriander), or one of the excellent seafood curries. While there's Chinese on the menu as well, the Keralan curries are too good to go past.

AL MALLAH Map pp224-5   Lebanese $$
☎ 398 4723; Al-Dhiyafah St, Satwa; mains Dh20; ☽ 6am-4am

A local favourite, the brightly lit Al Mallah sees waves of customers converge on its outdoor seating area, even when the thermometer is about to burst in summer. They're all here for the shawarmas, served either wrapped or as a plate, and a fresh juice. The other typical Lebanese fare on the menu is excellent too and it's a great place for people-watching.

BASTA ART CAFÉ Map pp220-1   Café $$
☎ 353 5071; Al-Fahidi St, Bastakia; mains Dh20; ☽ 10am-8pm

A wonderful spot set in a traditional courtyard of a Bastakia house. The food is respectable café fare (the salads are great on a hot and humid day), but it's just so nice to sit in the courtyard of one of the original houses in the area. Check out the local art before you leave.

BEIRUT Map pp224-5   Lebanese $$
☎ 398 9822; Al-Dhiyafah St, Satwa; mains Dh20; ☽ noon-2am

Along with Al Mallah (above), this is the pick of the Lebanese places along busy Al-Dhiyafah St. The outdoor seating is the place to be – unless it's so hot that the locals are complaining about the heat – and the Lebanese menu is tasty. Besides the

shawarmas, try the hummus with pine nuts and the meat *kibbeh*. Note that the service ranges from surly to dismissive depending on the time of day and the heat.

TOP FIVE BUR DUBAI EATS

- Asha's (p84)
- Antique Bazaar (p84)
- Indochine (p86)
- Peppercrab (p86)
- Thai Chi (p85)

KWALITY Map pp220-1   Indian $$
☎ 393 6563; opposite Ascot Hotel, Khalid Bin al-Waleed Rd (Bank St); mains Dh20; ☽ 1-3pm & 8-11.45pm

A well-known chain in Dubai, where the food is dependable and the service is swift. There are no surprises on the menu, so it's hard to go wrong with hearty portions of favourite dishes such as chicken makhani (butter chicken) or rogan josh (lamb curry). As with most Indian restaurants there's a large and tasty number of vegetarian options.

GAZEBO Map pp222-3   Indian $$
☎ 397 9930; Sheikh Khalifa bin Zayed Rd (Trade Centre Rd), opposite Spinney's; mains Dh22; ☽ 10am-3.30pm & 7pm-midnight

In a neighbourhood full of Indian eateries, Gazebo stands out with incredibly tasty naan breads, juicy chicken tikka masala and great curries. Try the Banjara Gosht (mutton in special gravy made of masala, rose petals, cashew nuts and tomato) or the Gosht Achari (mutton in coriander, tomato and pomegranate). Great stuff and well-priced for the quality.

LEBANESE VILLAGE
Map pp220-1   Lebanese $$
☎ 352 2522; Al-Mankhool Rd; mains Dh22; ☽ noon-3am

One of Bur Dubai's most popular Lebanese eateries, this place comes alive late at night during the cooler months, when the outdoor seating is packed and the stereo struggles to overcome the noise of busy Al-Mankhool Rd. Besides the excellent shawarmas, the authentic grills and mezze are worth lingering over, as is the *sheesha*. There's a large dining room upstairs when the weather is too much and while the main kitchen closes at 1am, you can still get shawarma and juices until 3am.

DÔME Map pp220-1 — Café $$
☎ 355 6004; BurJuman Centre, Sheikh Khalifa bin Zayed Rd (Trade Centre Rd); mains Dh25; ⏰ 7.30am-11.30pm
A great spot to take a breather during a shopping expedition, this Australian franchise serves up decent coffee and great gourmet sandwiches and cakes. In the cooler months the outdoor seating is popular all day and night. There's a branch at Souq Madinat Jumeirah (p138) as well.

KAN ZAMAN Map pp220-1 — Arabic $$
☎ 393 9913; Heritage Village, Al Shindagha; mains Dh27; ⏰ 11am-3am
A trip to Heritage Village is almost incomplete without a visit to this Creekside favourite. During the cooler months, the large outdoor area is the place to leisurely sample some mezze and grills and watch the passing parade of boats. While there's no alcohol, puffing on *sheesha* (apple, please) long into the night is a fantastic way to end the meal.

COCONUT GROVE Map pp224-5 — Goan $$
☎ 398 3800; Rydges Plaza Hotel, Al-Diyafah St, Satwa Roundabout, Satwa; mains Dh30; ⏰ noon-3pm & 7pm-12.30am
Firstly, the food here is fantastic. The great curries and biryani bring in regular customers who love these authentic dishes from Kerala and Goa. The seafood curries are a

---

BEST LUNCH DEALS
Several of Dubai's better restaurants have better-value lunch deals. Here are our favourites:

Asha's (right) Thali lunch special for Dh65.

Awtar (p86) Mezze, main course and dessert for Dh65.

Benjarong (p88) Set menu Dh89.

Glasshouse Mediterranean Brasserie (p80) Two courses for Dh60 and three courses for Dh85.

Miyako (p81) Set-price lunch Dh55.

---

highlight. Less than a highlight though, is the overbearing, overselling service that blatantly keeps plugging away at you to order more drinks and the most expensive dishes on the menu. However, the food, the views of Dubai and the reasonable prices keep us coming back.

LEMONGRASS Map pp222-3 — Thai $$
☎ 334 2325; near Lamcy Plaza; mains Dh30; ⏰ noon-midnight
One of the most reliable Thai restaurants in Dubai, this is a great little independent (no alcohol) eatery that has been packing punters in for years now – and making our home-delivery order slower and slower! The reason this place is so busy is simple: the food is wonderfully fresh and flavourful and it's as hot as you want it (tell them your preference). Start with the Lemongrass set, a selection of starters for two, and then go for the curries – they're all good, but we really love the red duck curry. Great vegetarian options too.

AUTOMATIC Map pp220-1 — Lebanese $$
☎ 359 4300; Off Khalid bin al-Waleed Rd (Bank St); mains Dh33; ⏰ 11am-1am
A great branch of this reliable chain of Lebanese restaurants, it offers great mezze and mains in huge portions. Try the *shish taook*, the mixed grill or the grilled prawns – all delicious. There is another popular branch at the Beach Centre (Map pp224–5; Jumeira Rd).

ANTIQUE BAZAAR Map pp220-1 — Indian $$$
☎ 397 7444; Four Points Sheraton, Bank St; mains Dh50; ⏰ 12.30-3.30pm & 7.30pm-3am
Somewhat predictably, this very popular restaurant resembles a wonderful antique bazaar and the Indian food on offer is decidedly old-fashioned as well. But in this case it's a good thing as the food is rich and tasty and the service is excellent. While you might be wondering why the musicians sitting cross-legged at the front of the room look so bored, it's because the dancer has yet to strut her stuff. Odd? Yes. Fun? For sure.

ASHA'S Map pp222-3 — Contemporary Indian $$$
☎ 324 4100; Pyramids, Wafi City, Al-Qataiyat Rd; mains Dh50; ⏰ 12.30-3.30pm & 7.30pm-2am
While there are plenty of singing stars who have opened restaurants that have fallen

flatter than Madonna singing live, Asha Bhosle (of Bollywood singing fame) has a hit on her hands with this contemporary – and funky – Indian eatery. The chef's choices are excellent, but if you want traditional Indian, it's there as well. Fans of Bollywood can check out the old photos of Asha in action and the rest of you can now spend the rest of the day trying to stop singing Cornershop's hit single *Brimful of Asha*, dedicated to the singer.

IL RUSTICO Map pp224-5   Italian $$$
☎ 398 2222; Rydges Plaza Hotel, Al-Diyafah St, Satwa Roundabout; mains Dh50; ⏲ noon-3pm & 6pm-midnight
This friendly place is like a great little local Italian eatery you stroll to when you're hungry and want good, comforting food without fuss. The homemade bread, fresh pastas, wood-fired pizzas and inexpensive wines (for Dubai) are its main attractions. Because it's one of the only places that does this well, it's always packed – so book ahead.

SEVILLE'S Map pp222-3   Spanish Tapas $$$
☎ 324 7300; Pyramids, Wafi City, Al-Qataiyat Rd; mains Dh50; ⏲ noon-2am Sat-Wed, noon-3am Thu & Fri
Decent Spanish food is thin on the ground in Dubai – maybe it's because the best Spanish food usually involves pork (see the boxed text, p14). However, this *muy popular* place does a good job sating those with a craving for tapas. All of the usual suspects are on offer – the Gambas al Ajillo (prawns cooked in garlic and oil) and Chorizo a la Sidra (Spanish sausage cooked in cider) are particularly good. For something more filling, try the traditional paella with mixed seafood or chicken. With the live music and agreeable vibe it's a great place to meet up to start a big night out.

THAI CHI
Map pp222-3   Contemporary Thai & Chinese $$$
☎ 324 4100; Pyramids, Wafi City, Al-Qataiyat Rd; mains Dh50; ⏲ noon-3pm & 7.30pm-midnight
Generally, these kinds of places make us roll our eyes and move on to something that sounds more authentic – whether it be Thai or Chinese. However, at this restaurant, consisting of a stylishly traditional Thai area and a less formal Chinese one, the duality is

---

RAMADAN & IFTAR

During the holy month of Ramadan (p181), there's no eating, drinking or smoking allowed in public. While this might appear to be an inconvenient time to visit Dubai, some visitors find the more relaxed pace and quieter streets a revelation. If you're visiting during this month, your meals will be taken inside until the sun goes down, but then you get the chance to head out for Iftar, the traditional meal that breaks the fast. The Iftar meal is usually a good-value, all-you-can-eat buffet, as people tend to graze the tables for a couple of hours after fasting all day! Iftar is fun because you'll find plenty more Emiratis out eating at this time of year. Here are our favourite hotels to head to for the action:

- Dusit Dubai (p148)
- Emirates Towers Hotel (p149)
- Grand Hyatt Dubai (p146)
- The Royal Mirage (p149)
- Le Meridien Mina Seyahi (p149)

---

confirmed by having separate kitchens. The Thai menu is very extensive with good set menus and the Chinese one features some great old favourites such as the irresistible Peking Duck.

TROYKA Map pp220-1   Russian $$$
☎ 359 5908; Ascot Hotel, Khalid Bin al-Waleed Rd (Bank St); mains Dh50; ⏲ noon-3pm & 7pm-3am
An amusing slice of home for the Russian expat community and the ever-increasing number of Russian tourists in Dubai, Troyka has exactly what you need for a decent Russian night out: copious amounts of vodka, caviar, hearty main courses, and musicians and dancers blissfully unaware of how camp the whole thing is. Arrive around 10pm and get into the spirits, er, spirit.

YAKITORI Map pp220-1   Japanese $$$
☎ 352 0900; Ascot Hotel, Khalid Bin al-Waleed Rd (Bank St); mains Dh50; ⏲ 12.30-3pm & 6.30-11.30pm
This is a classic old-school Japanese restaurant, with sushi-bar seating, teppanyaki tables, a TV in the corner showing sumo matches and – reassuringly – plenty of Japanese businessmen and tourists hankering for a slice of fish and home. All of which shouldn't divert your attention from the excellent sushi and sashimi, which is pretty reasonably priced.

Eating

BUR DUBAI

85

BASTAKIAH NIGHTS

Map pp220-1   Arabian $$$

☎ 353 7772; Near the Rulers Court, off Al-Fahidi St, Bastakia; mains Dh55 ⏰ 12.30pm-midnight Sat-Thu, 2pm-midnight Fri

The old Arabian-style setting of this, the only real restaurant in a restored Bastakia house, is fabulous. It's not *The Thousand and One Nights* over-the-top style, which is a nice change in a city where too much of it is not nearly enough. The restaurant is true to its location by offering a taste of traditional Arabic food through either its set or *à la carte* menu. There are numerous private and romantic dining rooms (book ahead for these) and in the cooler months, open seating on the roof. No alcohol.

INDOCHINE Map pp214-15   Vietnamese $$$

☎ 317 1234; Grand Hyatt Dubai, Al-Qataiyat Rd; mains Dh55; ⏰ 7-11.30pm

This slice of Vietnam, hidden away in a corner of the mammoth Grand Hyatt, is a favourite for its fresh ingredients, open kitchen and fabulous flavours. While not all the dishes on the menu are traditional Vietnamese, those familiar with the cuisine can ask for dishes off the menu. If you're not familiar with Vietnamese food, just order one of the well-designed set menus. Great service and a good wine list too.

AWTAR Map pp214-15   Lebanese $$$$

☎ 317 1234; Grand Hyatt Dubai, Al-Qataiyat Rd; mains Dh75; ⏰ 12.30-3pm & 7.30pm-3am, closed Sat

An opulent Bedouin tent–like atmosphere and a warm welcome await diners here. The mezze is mouth-watering, the live music entertaining, and the belly dancer over the top. So book a table for around 10pm, fill it with mezze, order some succulent meat dishes, and graze the food for

---

TOP FIVE SHEIKH ZAYED ROAD EATS

- Benjarong (p88)
- Hoi An (p88)
- Noodle House (opposite)
- Spectrum on One (opposite)
- Trader Vic's (p88)

---

a few hours while taking in the entertainment. Excellent food, great fun.

MANHATTAN GRILL

Map pp214-15   Steakhouse $$$$

☎ 317 1234; Grand Hyatt Dubai, Al-Qataiyat Rd; mains Dh75; ⏰ 7.30-11.30pm, closed Fri

That this stylish eatery manages to feel so New York in a hotel that has dhow hulls stuck to the ceiling is no mean feat. The food manages to live up to the surroundings too, with sensational steaks: juicy, and cooked to order and perfection. Sides of mash (a creamy delight) and vegetables complement them well. Unusual for a steak restaurant, the desserts are delicious.

PEPPERCRAB Map pp214-15   Singaporean $$$$

☎ 317 1234; Grand Hyatt Dubai, Al-Qataiyat Rd; mains Dh100; ⏰ 7pm-midnight

Once you see the chefs working through a huge glass fish tank, you know this restaurant is all about the fruits of the sea. While there are plenty of interesting dishes on the menu (such as the oyster omelette), it's pretty hard to go past the succulent signature dish – it's enough to leave seafood lovers swooning. Just remember to take off the dignity-inhibiting oversized napkin when you're finished.

SHEIKH ZAYED ROAD

The hotels along the strip have really breathed life into the dining scene here. The phenomenal pace of growth in Dubai is amply demonstrated by the fact we can actually have a Top Five list – not much more than a couple of years ago we'd have been hard pressed to do anything except keep driving on to Abu Dhabi for a decent meal.

SAJ EXPRESS Map p226   Lebanese $

☎ 321 1191; Sheikh Zayed Rd; mains Dh15; ⏰ 9am-2am

The Saj Express is one of Sheikh Zayed Rd's best fast-food joints, and the fresh bread (cooked on the *saj*, a curved, iron dome-topped oven) is what makes the shawarmas here so special. They're not the cheapest shawarmas in Dubai by any means, but they're one of the best. The rest of the menu doesn't excite, but pair a shawarma with one of the fresh juices and you can't go wrong.

ZAATAR W ZEIT Map p226 — Lebanese $

☎ 800 922 827; Near the Shangri-La Hotel, Sheikh Zayed Rd; mains Dh15; ⏲ 24hr

This Lebanon-based chain is a welcome addition to Dubai's fast-food scene. In Beirut, these quick snacks are the staple diet of university students. Open 24 hours, it serves up *manaeesh* (flat bread) with toppings such as cheese and, of course, zaatar (a mix of thyme, sumac and sesame seeds). It's simple, but a very delicious snack.

AL NAFOORAH Map p226 — Lebanese $$

☎ 319 8088; Emirates Towers, Sheikh Zayed Rd; mains Dh25; ⏲ 12.30-3pm & 8pm-12.30am

It took us several months and several recommendations from foodies before we tried this Lebanese restaurant – we always find it hard to visit Emirates Towers without hitting **Noodle House** (below) for a quick meal. The nondescript interior and the same-old Lebanese menu doesn't impress…however, the food here is excellent Lebanese fare.

NOODLE HOUSE Map p226 — Asian $$

☎ 319 8757; Emirates Towers, Sheikh Zayed Rd; mains Dh25; ⏲ noon-11.30pm

Rightly packed from the first day it opened its doors, this is one of the most affordable and fun hotel eateries in Dubai. The concept is simple – everyone sits on long wooden communal benches and orders by ticking dishes on a tear-off menu pad. There's enough variety on the pan-Asian menu to please everyone – everything from curry laksa to duck pancakes – and there are good wines by the glass as well as Asian beers (Tiger beer on tap, no less). There are no bookings, so put your name down and head to the **Agency** (p99) for a tipple while you wait.

WAGAMAMA Map p226 — Noodles $$

☎ 305 6060; Crowne Plaza Hotel, Sheikh Zayed Rd; mains Dh28; ⏲ noon-midnight

The Dubai branch of this noodle chain is actually better than other ones we've experienced in the UK – probably a first for a Dubai franchise. The duck gyoza, yaki udon and chilli beef ramen noodles are our favourite dishes, but everything else besides

DID YOU KNOW?

Many hotel restaurants in Dubai have symbols on their menu indicating that a dish contains pork or has been prepared using alcohol. This information is for Muslims who, as a rule, don't partake in either. Pork is mentioned several times in the Quran as being forbidden – purely for health reasons – as pigs were seen as disease-carrying animals. Intoxicants, such as alcohol, are also forbidden under Islam as it makes followers forgetful of God and prayer.

the food (and the no-smoking policy), drives us nuts. The staff appear to think that this is everyone's first time trying anything Asian besides buying a product made by Sony – even when you've visited the restaurant several times. We also find it hard to take seriously a restaurant that actually advertises the fact that its chefs can't promise to deliver all the dishes that you've ordered for your table at the same time – and then happily watch you 'share' a bowl of ramen noodles between six people…

OLIVE HOUSE

Map p226 — Lebanese/Mediterranean $$

☎ 343 3110; Tower One; mains Dh30; ⏲ 9am-midnight

While this stylish little place has a bit of an identity crisis (is it a bakery, Lebanese restaurant, delicatessen or pizza place?), there's no crisis in the kitchen. The pizzas are fresh, wonderful wood-fired numbers, the grills and mezze are excellent quality, and with the *manaeesh* done in the wood-fired oven as well, they're about the tastiest around. A great spot for a good inexpensive lunch or snack.

SPECTRUM ON ONE

Map p226 — Modern Global $$$

☎ 332 5555; Fairmont Hotel, Sheikh Zayed Rd; mains Dh50; ⏲ 7pm-1am

A great way to solve the age-old 'can't decide where to eat' problem is to just head to the Fairmont Hotel's signature restaurant, with eight individual open kitchens representing cuisine from around the world. The food is uniformly good and while it's odd to see someone downing freshly shucked oysters next to someone tucking into an Indian curry, if it solves the diverse desires in dining dilemma, who cares!

Eating

SHEIKH ZAYED ROAD

LOTUS ONE Map p226 Fusion $$$

☎ 329 3200; Dubai International Convention Centre, off Sheik Zayed Rd; mains Dh55; 🕑 noon-2am

The cool clubbing vibe of Lotus One often overshadows the ambitious menu of the eatery. After a couple of their signature Asian-flavoured cocktails though, the food here might just be the thing you need! The menu covers everything from finger food through to grills (excellent beef) with great Thai dishes from the Thai chef and some interesting Australian dishes from the Aussie head chef. However, the menu covers far too much territory to be really focused, and while the cocktails are inventive, the short wine list doesn't have enough wines by the glass.

AL TANNOUR Map p226 Lebanese $$$

☎ 331 1111; Crowne Plaza Hotel, Sheikh Zayed Rd; mains Dh60; 🕑 8pm-3am

While its traditional village-style décor doesn't excite, the smell of the fresh bread being made all night does, as does the rest of the food – it has some of the best authentic Lebanese food in Dubai. Go with a group (it's not the spot for a romantic dinner) for a huge array of mezze and a couple of grill dishes (try the chicken). Book a table for late (10.30-ish) and watch the band and amusing (rather than accomplished) belly dancer.

MARRAKECH Map p226 Moroccan $$$$

☎ 343 8888; Shangri-La Hotel; mains Dh65; 🕑 1-3pm & 8pm-midnight

While **Tagine** (p93) and **Shoo Fee Ma Fee** (p91) have an edge on this Moroccan eatery for ambience, the food here is on par. All the Moroccan favourites are excellent – the Couscous Royale and tagines are noteworthy. The Moroccan live music isn't a patch on Shoo Fee Ma Fee's (for the moment – bands change).

BENJARONG Map p226 Thai $$$$

☎ 343 3333; Dusit Dubai; mains Dh70; 🕑 7.30pm-midnight

This elegant, welcoming restaurant serves up the best Royal Thai food in Dubai. The décor is gorgeous, the service refined, and the Thai music and dance pleasant to take in. For starters try the *gung hom sabai* (deep fried prawns wrapped in egg noodles) or the *tom yam goong* (hot prawn soup with lime, lemongrass and chilli), while the green curry is the pick of the mains. Let them know if you like it hot and they'll gladly oblige!

ORIENTALIST'S DELIGHT

If you're looking for *The Book of One Thousand and One Nights* ambience, Dubai can certainly provide that for you! Here are some great restaurants that fully satisfy those Orientalist fantasies:

Awtar (p86) The best Dubai version of the Lebanese 'big night out'.

Tagine (p93) Fez-wearing waiters and overflowing Moroccan ambience.

Shahrzad (p82) Old Persia bottled and brought to Dubai.

Bastakiah Nights (p86) Dine in old-Arabia style at this restored Bastakia house.

TRADER VIC'S Map p226 Polynesian $$$$

☎ 331 1111; Crowne Plaza Hotel, Sheikh Zayed Rd; mains Dh70; 🕑 12.30-3pm & 7.30-11.30pm

A reliable old favourite of the Dubai dining scene, this branch of the Trader Vic's empire is starting to show its age. However, when you're suitably fortified by one of the lethal signature cocktails, the Polynesian-themed interior starts to grow on you. To stop a downward slide towards inebriation, try the 'island titbits' sampling of starters – just the thing to help soak up that alcohol – and the main courses emanating from the wood-fired clay oven are all recommended. Great for groups, but you'll need to book a couple of days in advance. There's another branch at **Souq Madinat Jumeirah** (p138), but we prefer this one for atmosphere.

HOI AN Map p226 Contemporary Vietnamese $$$$

☎ 343 8888; Shangri-La Hotel; mains Dh75; 🕑 7.30pm-1am

While this stylish restaurant is named and decorated after the ancient city of Hoi An, there's nothing backward-looking about the food here. Here, the innovative French–Vietnamese cuisine is a delight, with the starters representing the best of the dishes on offer – try the crispy crab rolls. Look out for specials as well, as the chef does his best work when he lets his imagination fly.

EXCHANGE Map p226   Steakhouse $$$$
☎ 311 8000; Fairmont Hotel, Sheikh Zayed Rd; mains Dh75; ⏲ 7pm-1am
An understated but stylish steakhouse, the Exchange is modelled on New York's legendary Oak Room at the Plaza Hotel. Great service, excellent steaks and a wine list that matches well with big slabs of meat.

TOKYO@THETOWERS
Map p226   Japanese $$$$
☎ 330 0000; Emirates Towers, Sheikh Zayed Rd; mains Dh75; ⏲ 12.30-3pm & 7.30-midnight, Sun lunch 1-3pm
This small, upmarket slice of Tokyo offers first-rate sushi and teppanyaki. The tuna and salmon are always a standout and we love the tempura – the batter is the finest in Dubai. The teppanyaki chefs show off their knife skills, while not neglecting the food – which is beautifully cooked. It's the best-quality Japanese in Dubai, but watch what you order – you can run up an impressive bill here!

VU'S Map p226   Fine Dining $$$$
☎ 319 8771; Emirates Towers, Sheikh Zayed Rd; mains Dh100; ⏲ 12.30-3pm & 7.30-midnight
This chic restaurant atop Emirates Towers impresses with its spectacular views and romantic setting. The well-thought-out menu, featuring a combination of French and Italian cuisine, is excellent. However, the cooking sometimes lets it down – unforgivable when the prices are as lofty as the views, and the service is very 'kitchen knows best'. Still, it's a gorgeous room, with views that command your attention.

JUMEIRAH & NEW DUBAI

The Jumeirah Beach stretch and 'New Dubai' contain some fine dining options, exemplified by Mezzanine, as well as a few welcome oddities such as Johnny Rockets and Maria Bonita's Taco Shop. Nearly every hotel along the strip has at least one

TOP FIVE JUMEIRAH & NEW DUBAI EATS

- BiCE (p92)
- Eauzone (p92)
- Tagine (p93)
- Mezzanine (p94)
- Zheng He's (p92)

exceptional restaurant in breathtaking surroundings, and for most of the restaurants here (especially the Top Five), you need to make a reservation at least a week in advance. There are also some popular cafés, such as Lime Tree Café, where you can catch expats enjoying their downtime. For those not staying at one of the resorts, a trip down the beach is a must – combine it with some pre- and post-dinner drinks (see the boxed text, p97) and you'll have a brilliant night out.

JOHNNY ROCKETS
Map pp224-5   Hamburger Joint $$
☎ 344 7898; Juma al Majid Center, Jumeirah Rd; mains Dh20; ⏲ noon-midnight
Nestled among the beachwear shops down at Jumeirah Beach, this seems an unlikely place for an unapologetically all-American hamburger joint. And the menu makes no concessions either – artery-clogging goodness abounds. Onion rings and chilli fries (breath mints, anyone?), followed by their 12-pound hamburger, really hits the spot. There's a kids' menu too, and another branch at Dubai Marina.

LIME TREE CAFÉ Map pp224-5   Café $$
☎ 349 8498; near Jumeirah Mosque, Jumeira Rd; mains Dh20; ⏲ 7.30am-8pm
We wouldn't be surprised if the term 'Jumeirah Jane' (referring to wives of expat executives with too much time on their hands) was coined here, as during the week this bright green villa appears to be in a state of perpetual 'coffee morning'. The reason is that the excellent daily menu features delicious frittatas, quiches and salads, and there's a range of delectable cakes that those with a sweet tooth can never resist. While the weekend breakfasts are underwhelming, the people-watching opportunities make up for it.

CURRY IN A HURRY

With so many Indian and Pakistani expats living here, Dubai is blessed with a plethora of places to get some inexpensive curries. Here's a list of some of the more reliable ones:

- Chhappan Bhog (p82)
- Food Castle (p83)
- Gazebo (p83)
- Karachi Darbar (p82)
- Kwality (p83)

MARIA BONITA'S TACO SHOP

Map pp214-15   Mexican $$

☎ 395 5576; Umm al-Sheif St, Umm Suqeim; mains Dh20; ☷ 7.30am-8pm

Maria Bonita's is Dubai's only real Mexican restaurant (forget those silly 'Tex-Mex' chains around town) – the smells from the kitchen will bring a smile to the face of anyone who has spent time south of the border. This laid-back restaurant offers up tasty, authentic dishes right down to the tortilla soup, cheese quesadillas and *queso fundido*. And for those who have indulged too much the night before, the amusingly named 'Morning After Platter' is guaranteed to get you going again. Only problem is, as it's unlicensed, there's no *cerveza* on offer as a hair-of-the-dog.

TOSCANA Map pp214-15   Italian $$

☎ 366 8888; Souq Madinat Jumeirah, Al-Mina Al-Seyahi; mains Dh30; ☷ noon-1am

While all the punters are hankering for an outside table, to watch the Dubai version of Venetian gondoliers (ok, guys in motorised *abras*) sail by, the interior of this refreshingly unpretentious Souq eatery is delightfully 'rustic Italian kitchen' with jars of olives, oils and vinegars on display. The breads and virgin olive oil immediately brought to the table are delicious and the food gets pretty close to traditional, simple Tuscan cuisine – excellent carpaccio and perfect thin pizzas with just one or two toppings of the freshest ingredients. There are fantastically fresh hand-made pastas – we love the tagliatelle with pesto with green beans and potatoes. We recommend you visit this place for lunch or a late dinner.

BELLA DONNA Map pp224-5   Italian $$

☎ 344 7710; Mercato Mall, Jumeira Rd; mains Dh35; ☷ 11am-11pm

While Mercato probably wins the prize for cheesiest mall in Dubai, Bella Donna is one of the best mall eateries in the city. Thankfully, the menu and décor take no part in the mall's kitsch Italian design schizophrenia. The pasta and pizzas are honest, fresh and tasty, and the coffee's smooth and strong – just the ticket to get you out shopping again. If it's not too hot (or windy), dine *al fresco* on the tiny balcony tables.

JAPENGO CAFÉ Map pp224-5   Eclectic $$

☎ 345 4979; Palm Strip Shopping Mall, opposite Jumeirah Mosque; mains Dh35; ☷ noon-midnight

Since opening in 2000, this local café has become a landmark in Jumeirah Beach circles. The food is eclectic, featuring dishes from Lebanon, Italy and Asia, but it doesn't seem to bother the regular clientele. At the

Shoo Fee Ma Fee (p91) serves up delicious Moroccan specialities

time of research the wonderful outdoor seating was gone to make way for the silly widening of Jumeirah Rd, so check out a couple of the other branches at **Souq Madinat Jumeirah** (p138) and **Wafi City** (Map pp222–3).

ROYAL ORCHID Map pp214-15   Chinese/Thai $$
☎ 367 4040; Marina Walk, Dubai Marina; mains Dh35; ☺ 10am-midnight
An institution in neighbouring emirate Abu Dhabi, this new location is more Thai than Chinese (or Mongolian, which also features on the menu). The location is great, with outdoor seating that's very Thai as well. While we love their Peking Duck, we generally suggest sticking to the Thai dishes. Just like at the Abu Dhabi branch, the soups are tasty and the curries sublime.

CHANDELIER Map pp214-15   Lebanese $$$
☎ 366 3606; Marina Walk, Dubai Marina; mains Dh45; ☺ 8.30am-3.30pm & 6.30pm-2.30am
While there are plenty of restaurants down at the Marina Walk, you'd be forgiven for thinking that Chandelier was the only restaurant around – to most Lebanese expats, it is! This stylish slice of Downtown Beirut is known for its excellent mezze, the grilled haloumi cheese and the different styles of small tasty sausages, such as *makanek* (homemade spicy Arabian sausage with tomato, garlic and onion sauce). On a cool evening, you'll find it hard to get a table. And don't expect too many people to

leave – eating usually ends with a marathon *sheesha* session. Great fun.

SHOO FEE MA FEE
Map pp214-15   Moroccan $$$
☎ 366 8888; Souq Madinat Jumeirah, Al-Mina Al-Seyahi; mains Dh45; ☺ 7-11.30pm, drinks until 12.30am
Modern Moroccan ambience abounds at this three-floor restaurant-bar overlooking the waterways of the souq. In the main restaurant area (downstairs), the live band serves up some fine accompaniment to the competently cooked Moroccan staples, including an excellent pigeon *pastilla*. Though the modern interpretations of other dishes are unimpressive, great bread and fine tagines save the day. The more casual drinking areas upstairs are fabulous.

NINA Map pp214-15   Contemporary Indian $$$
☎ 399 9999; Arabian Court, One&Only Royal Mirage; mains Dh60; ☺ 7-11.30pm
As soon as you arrive at Nina and have your eyeballs soak up the rich orange and purple interior, you realise that this is not going to be your average Indian meal. The dishes are a mix of Indian classics with an Asian twist put together somewhere in Europe. While Indian expat families will be scratching their heads looking at the menu, just order the tasting selection of starters and mains and be seduced. Uncharted territory, sure, but a worthwhile adventure.

CHARLIE'S ANGEL
After seven years as head chef to HRH Prince Charles, chef Gary Robinson resigned to open his first restaurant, Mezzanine, at the swish Grosvenor House hotel. And it's certainly not what you'd expect. Sure, there are faux antique sideboards, but they're painted silver and reside in glass receptacles that would bring a smile to the face of British artist Damien Hirst. It's a space that's as eccentric as Robinson's former boss, but way more cool. Robinson himself is also quite a surprise package. Looking far too young for someone who has had so much responsibility, Robinson is welcoming and friendly and not at all nervous about having set up one of the riskiest restaurant ventures in Dubai. Robinson says he wanted to make a significant impact on Dubai's dining scene – and he has. Apart from Verre (p82), which we're sure he's sick of hearing about, Dubai's top-end restaurants are an uneven bunch, something that Robinson agrees with. So what does he find to be the hardest thing about setting up a restaurant of this calibre in Dubai? 'Getting good local produce and securing good local suppliers' – a refrain heard often in Dubai. There's excellent produce sourced from all over the world on the menu (and this is reflected in the price of the dishes); however, Robinson still – somewhat endearingly – follows British seasonal changes.

Standing in the kitchen about an hour before service time, we notice that Robinson's team looks like a mini UN, with 11 different nationalities from Burma to Mauritius represented, and they all clearly know they're working somewhere special. Speaking of things special, we can't help but ask Robinson what his former boss's favourite dish was. 'You know, I don't think I can remember!!' Sure, Gary, sure…

EAUZONE Map pp214-15 · Fine Dining $$$$
☎ 399 9999; One&Only Royal Mirage, Al Mina Al Siyahi; mains Dh65; 🕑 noon-3.30pm & 7.30pm-midnight
Once you've settled into your chair with a magical view across the tranquil poolside setting, you might want to have a quick look at the menu. You'll be puzzling over how the flavours are going to combine and the dishes work, but just relax again; you're in very capable hands. Our firm favourites here are the tian of scampi, and the lamb with green tea, salt and an awesome side of truffled mash potato. It's only really the unsure service that mars what is a fantastic restaurant.

LA BAIE Map pp214-15 · Fine Dining $$$$
☎ 399 4000; Ritz-Carlton Hotel, Al Mina Al Siyahi; mains Dh70; 🕑 7-11pm, closed Sun
The clubby feel of this restaurant will make fans of the Ritz-Carlton feel right at home, while others will ponder the incongruity of a formal 'gentleman's club'–style restaurant at a beach resort. As you'd expect, however, the food is refined – foie gras and plenty of meat dishes and accompanying sauces. The service is discreet and efficient, and the wine list is extensive but well chosen.

PIERCHIC Map pp214-15 · Seafood $$$$
☎ 366 6730; Al-Qasr, Madinat Jumeirah; mains Dh70; 🕑 noon-3pm & 7-11.30pm
The stroll down to this restaurant, located on a pier in front of Al-Qasr, is a very romantic one (book for dinner). If you're not lucky enough (er, or rich enough) to be staying at the Burj Al Arab or Al-Qasr, be prepared to be a little jealous as this restaurant affords you excellent views of both. Pierchic's menu tries a little too hard with great seafood, so lobster and sea bass are accompanied by far too many flavours to work for us. The seafood platter, on the other hand, is super – the perfect indulgence to go with the views.

ZHENG HE'S
Map pp214-15 · Contemporary Chinese $$$$
☎ 366 8888; Mina A'Salam, Madinat Jumeirah; mains Dh70; 🕑 noon-3pm & 7-11.30pm
In short, Zheng He's is a decadent delight. From the brilliant views across the waterway to the Burj Al Arab to the super seafood, it's not surprising that it's still hard to get a booking here after a couple of years of business. Try the dim sum for starters and move on to one of the meat or tank-fresh fish dishes (with tank-fresh prices) for a memorable meal in superlative surroundings.

BICE Map pp214-15 · Italian $$$$
☎ 399 1111; Hilton Dubai Jumeirah, Al Mina Al Siyahi; mains Dh75; 🕑 noon-3pm & 7pm-midnight
The most consistent Italian restaurant in town has been BiCE for as long as we can remember. There's no secret to it, though; it's just fresh produce (imported several times a week), well cooked and simply

---

LET'S DO BRUNCH...

First of all, get your head around the fact that Friday in Dubai is Sunday just about everywhere else. And given that for Dubai's workers, weekends can be Thursday and Friday, Friday and Saturday or just Friday, Friday is the only day that (almost) everyone has off. And Sunday (sorry, Friday), equals brunch. Easy, isn't it?

For Thursday-night partygoers looking for stomach-filling starch and a hair-of-the-dog, to families sharing what is often their only day together, there are plenty of venues across the city offering a relaxing and good-value feed. Here's a (very) short selection of the better ones on offer (bookings essential):

Carters (Map pp222–3; ☎ 324 0000; Pyramids, Wafi City; adult/child Dh75/30, incl one free drink; 🕑 11.30am-3pm) Very popular with Western expats, it's a good one for a long, long, lunch.

Glasshouse Mediterranean Brasserie (Map pp216–17; ☎ 227 1111; Hilton Dubai Creek; adult/child Dh169/150, incl free-flowing bubbly and drinks; 🕑 12.30pm onwards) After the Fairmont, this is the best brunch in the city.

Pax Romana (Map p226; ☎ 343 3333; Dusit Dubai; adult Dh95, child under 12 free, alcohol included; 🕑 noon-3pm) Quality food and a more refined ambience than many others.

Spectrum on One (Map p226; ☎ 332 5555; Fairmont Hotel; adult/child Dh288/108; 🕑 noon-3pm) The most popular brunch in town includes free-flowing bubbly. Book ahead.

Thai Kitchen (Map pp218–19; ☎ 602 1234; Park Hyatt Dubai; per person with soft drinks/alcohol Dh99/149; 🕑 12.30-4pm) For a different kind of brunch (and lovely outdoor seating) this one is quite special.

presented – just as Italian fare should be. The restaurant is understated and stylish, the service is attentive and knowledge-able, and there's always someone on hand to assist with the well-selected wine list. Remember to book a table and arrive hungry – you'll want to try the excellent cheese selection or a classic tiramisu.

TAGINE Map pp214-15
Moroccan $$$$

☎ 399 9999; One&Only Royal Mirage, Al Mina Al Siyahi; mains Dh75; ⏱ 7-11pm

Tagine offers the best Moroccan experience in Dubai. After walking through the **Sheesha Courtyard** (p98) and past a classic Moroccan tiled fountain, you're ready for a trip to Fez or Marrakesh. And this restaurant doesn't disappoint. From the fez- wearing wait-ers and the classic harira soup to the rich tagines and the live musicians, it's the real deal. Book ahead and ask for a table near the musicians.

OSSIGENO Map pp214-15
Italian $$$$

☎ 399 5555; Le Royal Meridien, Al Mina Al Siyahi; mains Dh85; ⏱ 7pm-midnight

Ossigeno is a smart and stylish Italian res-taurant that puts the emphasis on quality ingredients and decent portions. While the food's not about to change the direction of Italian cuisine, it's very competently cooked. The service is attentive and the desserts are good enough to make you want to skip *secondi*. It's a good beachside alternative if you can't get a booking at **BiCE** (opposite).

PRIME RIB Map pp214-15
Steakhouse $$$$

☎ 399 5555; Le Royal Meridien, Al Mina Al Siyahi; mains Dh85; ⏱ 7pm-midnight

The focus of this neo-deco dining room is unapologetically about serving up slabs of US Angus Beef. While there are some sea-food dishes on the menu, cow is king and it's best to stick to the meat-based dishes. The music of early jazz greats pleasantly fills the room, the staff know their stuff, and there's an excellent wine list. A sound choice for carnivorous diners.

MARINA SEAFOOD MARKET
Map pp214-15
Seafood $$$$

☎ 406 8181; Jumeirah Beach Hotel; mains Dh100; ⏱ 12.30-4pm & 7pm-2am

For a seafood lunch with sublime views of the Burj Al Arab, this is unbeatable. Situated at the end of a long curving breakwater, this restaurant serves up an impressive array of seafood, both local and flown in from around the world. The wine list is exten-sive and impressive, and if it's not too hot, there's a bar upstairs. Don't forget to book a table with a view!

BUDDHA BAR Map pp214-15
Asian $$$$

☎ 399 8888; Dubai Marina, Grosvenor House, Jumeirah; mains Dh110; ⏱ 8pm-2am

The last time we visited the original Buddha Bar in Paris, we waited in vain for some 40 minutes to order a drink and then left without anyone knowing we'd even been there. No chance of that happening at the Dubai branch of the restaurant and bar that helped put 'lounge music' on the map, be-cause here you're treated like a VIP from the moment you're guided to your table until you stagger off into the night several hours later. The food here is pan-Asian – every-thing from sushi to duck curry – great for sharing and very tasty. But it's the venue itself that is the real star. The buzzy main room is full of large groups (this is not the place for a romantic tête-à-tête) letting their hair down, probably celebrating getting a booking – this was the hottest ticket in town at the time of writing.

Mezzanine (p94) is the brainchild of the former head chef to Britain's Prince Charles, Gary Robinson

Eating

JUMEIRAH & NEW DUBAI

MEZZANINE Map pp214-15   Modern British $$$$

☎ 399 8888; Dubai Marina, Grosvenor House, Jumeirah; mains Dh138; ⏲ 7pm-midnight

The first restaurant of Gary Robinson, former head chef to Prince Charles (see the boxed text, p91), has certainly made a splash in Dubai. From the whimsical white-on-white décor to the 'serious restaurant' prices (although it's actually less expensive than equivalent restaurants in Europe), it's had foodies' tongues wagging all over town – and with good reason. Charlie's loss is most assuredly Dubai's gain, as Robinson's version of 'Modern British' is both skilful and playful, and while there'll be foie gras and caviar on the menu somewhere, there'll also be chunky chips or a shepherds pie lurking there as well. The restaurant has had the same impact on Dubai's dining scene that Gordon Ramsay's Verre (p82) did when it opened in 2001. Here's hoping the future king doesn't try to lure him back…

Entertainment ◼

Entertainment

Dubai has arrived.

The city's nightlife has been simmering away for a few years now, but with the opening of uber-cool bars like Sho Cho and Ginseng as well as decadent club Boudoir, it's really reached boiling point. The grungy club Terminal was an interesting diversion (and we wish some adventurous young entrepreneurs would take us down that road again), while the opening of MIX (Dubai's first 'super club') and Trilogy (which so successfully combined 'serious dance venue' with Oriental style) marked a sophisticated shift in Dubai's club scene. And while Planetarium's urban bass rumble is still sorely missed, its demise opened up new vistas, with swanky Vice and Chameleon taking the city down a different path. But it was the opening of one venue in particular that made Dubai's nocturnal nomads collectively think 'at last, we've arrived' – Lotus One. No other restaurant-bar-club had been as cool or as contemporary or had got its mix of style/music/atmosphere so right. And then there was funky iBO and the Asian-chic of Buddha Bar showing us what wonderfully different directions Dubai's nightlife could take us in, each as enjoyable as the other, yet propelling us on completely different journeys. We're eagerly waiting to see where the city's going to move us next…

There's a DJ spinning somewhere every night of the week in Dubai (except during Ramadan), with regular one-off dance events, and all kinds of sounds from around the globe out there – funk, soul, house, trip-hop, hip-hop, R & B, jazz, African, Arabic and Latino (and fusions of all of these). There are also more opportunities to listen to live music, with everything from jazz to Bengali and traditional Arabian oud to Moroccan music.

With so many options, nights can be long, although they'll never end at dawn – while clubs officially close at 3am, it's the practice of expats to start the night early with a sunset drink at a seaside bar, dinner, a post-dinner tipple and perhaps a bar hop before hitting a club or two. Licensing laws require venues serving alcohol to be attached to hotels or private clubs and as a result they all charge service fees. You also won't find any backstreet indie bars as you might in other cities.

As befits a port town, Dubai's nightlife can be seedy. Many of Deira and Bur Dubai's midrange hotels are home to bars and clubs where very friendly women offer fee-based hospitality, but ironically, real couples are forbidden from touching. Whereas,

GETTING OUT WITH THE IN CROWD

For entertainment listings, buy monthly magazine *What's On* and weekly *Time Out* or pick up free guides and leaflets promoting clubs, dance parties and gigs from bars, cafés, Virgin Megastore and Ohm Records. Check out club guides Mumtazz (www.mumtazz.com) and Infusion (www.infusion.ae) and promoters' sites www.9714.com and www.fluidproduction.com. For tickets to concerts and major events at Dubai Media City, the Tennis Stadium and Madinat Jumeirah, phone the Time Out ticketline on ☎ 800 4669 or buy online at www.itptickets.com or www.boxofficeme.com.

Bahri Bar (p100), one of Dubai's most popular

in the past, working girls would only show up one night a week, or late at night, now they're everywhere all the time. Single women: be prepared to get propositioned.

For travellers to Dubai, weekends are long: Thursday and Friday are holidays for the government sector, so Wednesday is their big night out. Those working in the private sector take Friday and Saturday off, while the hospitality industry heads out on Saturday night. If you still have one foot in your Western time zone, you'll still have a hangover on Monday morning.

Those looking for more low-key entertainment will be seduced by the city's many waterside bars with sea or Creek vistas – Arabian-colonial style Bahri Bar is popular with all ages, travellers and expats, who come for the wonderful breezy veranda and views of Burj Al Arab – while a quiet *sheesha* is always relaxing, especially at the Arabian Courtyard. For something different, head to the city during the Dubai International Film Festival and catch some movies from the Middle East or join local residents for a night of cinema under the stars, an increasingly popular activity.

The live music, theatre, opera, comedy and dance scenes are slowly catching up (although still have a long way to go), with Madinat Jumeirah Arena providing a breathtaking location for performances by the likes of Pavarotti, and Madinat Theatre hosting everything from the Russian Ballet to a theatrical production of Aladdin. Recent live acts to come to Dubai included Destiny's Child and the Black Eyed Peas.

NIGHTS ON THE TOWN

It's wise (and cost-effective) to stick to one area of town for a night out, particularly as there's no more effective buzz kill than Dubai's traffic chaos on weekends. Here are our favourite nights out in...

Bur Dubai

Wafi City and the Grand Hyatt Hotel are excellent options for a night out, and are within walking distance of each other if you want to combine them. If opting for Wafi, start with wine and cheese at **Vintage** (p103), tapas and sangria at **Seville's** (p85), dinner at **Asha's** (p84) or **Thai Chi** (p85), cocktails at **Ginseng** (p101), vodka at **Vice** (p104) and dancing at **Chameleon** (p104). The Grand Hyatt offers an equally lively night, starting with vino at **Vinoteca**, dinner at **Indochine** (p86) or **Peppercrab** (p86) and *sheesha* at **Awtar** (p86) while you catch a bellydancer or Lebanese singer, before joining the bongo player and podium dancers at **MIX** (p104).

Deira

Begin with a quiet pre-dinner drink at **Issimo** (p101), before having the ultimate fine-dining experience at Gordon Ramsay's **Verre** (p82). Depending on the night, check out **M-Level** (p104) for some dance action. If you feel like a quiet night, take a stroll along the waterfront and watch the dhows being loaded in the cool of the evening. If you're up for more, head to the InterContinental's **KuBu** (p101) for cocktails or the **Velvet Lounge** (p102) for Persian pop. Around midnight, take a taxi to funky **iBO** (p104), where the fun will really begin.

Sheikh Zayed Road

Start the evening with a glass of wine at the **Agency** (p99), and perhaps a starry drink at **Vu's** (p103), before lining your stomach with a delicious bowl of something from the **Noodle House** (p87). If you're in the mood for live music, pop across to the Novotel for some jazz and great beers at **Blue Bar** (p106). Stylish **Lotus One** (p101) is nearby and is a must-do for drinks, and depending on the crowd, dancing. If you don't get a boogie here, head across Sheikh Zayed Rd to **Tangerine** (p105) at the Fairmont.

Jumeirah

Mellow out with a sunset drink on the veranda at **Bahri Bar** (p100). If the Burj Al Arab is not close enough for you, take a taxi there and head to the **Skyview Bar** (p102), but remember to book ahead. Plan for a meal at one of the One&Only Royal Mirage's wonderful restaurants – **Tagine** (p93), **Eauzone** (p92) or **Nina** (p91) – then chill out at the exotic **Rooftop Bar** (p101). If you're in the mood for more relaxation, recline on the cushions at the atmospheric **Sheesha Courtyard** (p98). Up for some dancing? Wait in line to get into **Kasbar** (p104) – it's worth it! If drinking and dancing is a priority then skip dinner altogether and head to Madinat Jumeirah's **Agency** (p99) and snack on some great tapas when you get hungry, followed by drinks at **Left Bank** (p101), a *sheesha* in the **Souq plaza** (p99), a band at **Jam Base** (p106) and dancing at **Trilogy** (p105). If you need a change of scenery take a cab to **Sho Cho** (p102) and **Boudoir** (p103) to boogie the rest of the night away.

SHEESHA CAFÉS

Make some time in your busy schedule for one of Dubai's most relaxing and traditional pastimes – *sheesha*! (See the boxed text, below.) *Sheesha* cafés are open until well after midnight, much later during the cooler winter months when the city's population spends their evenings outdoors, and the going rate is Dh10 to Dh25 – all you can inhale.

COSMO CAFÉ Map p226

☎ 332 6569; The Tower, Sheikh Zayed Rd; ⏰ 8.30–1am

It wouldn't matter if this was your only visit to a *sheesha* café in Dubai – while you might be missing out on the Oriental atmosphere, you'll be getting an insight into Arab expat life in Dubai when you join the beautiful (mainly Lebanese) people for *sheesha* at this stylish spot. The food's not bad either.

KAN ZAMAN Map pp220-1

☎ 393 9914; Heritage & Diving Village, Al Shindagha, Bur Dubai; ⏰ 11am–3am

The buzzy atmosphere (especially late at night), wonderful waterfront location, and excellent mezze and sheesha, make Kan Zaman popular with Emiratis and

Arab expats – it's particularly popular with families, where the adults happily spend the night puffing away.

SHAKESPEARE & COMPANY Map p226

☎ 331 1757; Kendah House, Sheikh Zayed Rd; ⏰ 7am–1.30am

This casual and rather whimsically decorated café is not your typical *sheesha* place, but it's enjoyable all the same, and is popular with women and families.

SHEESHA COURTYARD Map pp214-15

☎ 399 9999; One&Only Royal Mirage, Jumeirah; ⏰ 7pm–1am

It might take a connoisseur to appreciate the 20 different flavours of *sheesha* on offer, but who wouldn't enjoy the aroma of apple *sheesha*, reclining on cushions in this atmospheric palm-filled Arabian courtyard. Highly recommended.

SHEESHA 101

A *sheesha* pipe, also known as a hubbly bubbly, hookah or nargileh, is a long-stemmed, glass-bottomed smoking implement about 50cm high. *Sheesha* pipes are packed with flavoured tobacco, such as apple, anise, strawberry, vanilla and coffee – the range of flavours is endless and good *sheesha* cafés, like good wine bars, pride themselves on the variety on offer.

Commonly enjoyed throughout the Middle East, smoking *sheesha* is a popular pastime in Dubai, and every visitor to the city wants to have a go at it. *Sheesha* first became popular in the Middle East in Turkey in the 1600s, having travelled via Iran from India, where a smoking device made use of coconuts – these days throughout the Middle East you'll see *sheesha* smoked from pineapples, mangoes and other fruit.

The *sheesha* pipes used in Dubai are similar to those found in Lebanon and Egypt, and are available in the souqs, specialised shops and even the supermarkets. If, like most visitors to Dubai, you decide to take one home as a souvenir and forget the instructions the guy in the store gives you, here's a lesson on how to use one:

- First fill your glass bowl with water and fix the metal turret into it, ensuring that the tube is underwater with the rubber stopper keeping it in position.
- Next, return the metal plate to the top of the turret and put your small ceramic or clay bowl on top of that.
- Fill the bowl with some loose *sheesha* tobacco and cover this tightly with a small piece of foil, before poking about five holes into it with a fork.
- Using tongs, heat up your Magic Coal (it's Japanese, comes in a black box and is the longest lasting coal) or other charcoal on a stove hot plate or over a gas burner, then pop it on top of the foil.
- Lastly, place the pipe into the hole on the side of the *sheesha* pipe, pop a disposable plastic mouthpiece on the end if you're planning to share, and take a long hard puff on the pipe. Recline on the Oriental cushions you bought at the souq and enjoy!

SOUQ MADINAT JUMEIRAH
Map pp214-15

☎ 366 8888; Central Plaza, Souq Madinat Jumeirah, Al-Sufouh Rd, Jumeirah; ⏰ 10am-11pm

This must be one of the most wonderful spots to smoke *sheesha* in the city – it could be the live oud player, the enchanting location, the long list of *sheesha* flavours or the balmy breezes on a cool winter's evening, but it's probably a combination of all of those that makes it so special.

TCHÉ TCHÉ Map pp220-1

☎ 355 7575; Khalid bi al-Waleed Rd (Bank St), near BurJuman Centre, Bur Dubai; ⏰ 10am-2am Sat-Thu, 3pm-2am Fri

If you tire of the 'Arabian Nights' atmosphere and the 'beautiful people' scene, head to this refreshingly ordinary neighbourhood *sheesha* café with Arabian pop and a loud TV set, frequented by Emiratis and Arabs, the occasional expat, and less often, curious travellers.

QD'S Map pp218-19

☎ 295 6000; Dubai Creek Golf & Yacht Club, Deira; ⏰ 6pm-2am

This wooden-decked, open-air bar overlooking Dubai Creek is a sublime spot for *sheesha* during the cooler winter months. It's also possible to eat here (although the food is inconsistent) and the dance floor occasionally goes off.

BARS & PUBS

Multicultural Dubai has an increasing range of cosmopolitan bars and friendly pubs to match your mood and suit your taste – you can sip a lychee martini at Asian-inspired Lotus One or drink Guinness at an Irish pub, enjoy a summery cocktail and balmy breeze at a beachside bar, or drink champagne as you count the stars above. You'll also get to listen to an extraordinary mix of music on any one night, from bhangra and Bengali to Arab-Latin fusion and Persian pop. The people you bump into at a bar will be equally as varied – while Dubai has its cliques, it isn't as segregated as some global cities. You could find yourself sharing space with young expat Iranian artists, suave Lebanese guys in suits and long-legged Russian models in not much at all.

Pubs and bars in Dubai are open until 1am or 3am and you'll find beers from all corners of the earth and the wildest cocktails conceivable. You could pay anything from Dh15 to Dh30 for a pint of beer or Dh20 to Dh50 for a glass of wine, depending on quality and vintage. Outlets in five-star hotels add a service charge although you won't always notice this as it's sometimes built into the cost. Drinks may seem expensive in dirhams, but convert the cost to your own currency and you'll find they're reasonably priced compared to Europe, and compare favourably with prices in Australia and North America. Drinks will often be accompanied by large bowls of nuts, finger food or hors d'oeuvres that are replenished often (or when asked!), making the prices seem even more reasonable. Almost all bars and pubs in Dubai have drink deals, happy hours and ladies nights (see the boxed text, p105), when women get drinks for free! Days vary and promotions change, so check what deals are on at **Mumtazz** (www.mumtazz.com) or in the entertainment mags before stepping out.

AGENCY Map p226

☎ 330 0000; Blvd at Emirates Towers, Sheikh Zayed Rd; ⏰ 12.30pm-1am Sat-Thu, 3pm-1am Fri

This cosmopolitan wine bar – the kind you find in New York and Melbourne – is a buzzy after-work spot, popular for its extensive list of old- and new-world wines and excellent wines by the glass. They have terrific, themed tasting selections of four wines for Dh75, and delicious 'wine teasers' (tapas-sized snacks) such as marinated manchega cheese with green olives and tempura-style squid with aioli.

AGENCY Map pp214-15

☎ 366 6320; Souq Madinat Jumeirah; ⏰ noon-1am

The Agency at Souq Madinat Jumeirah, while having quite a different personality to her sister-bar at Emirates Towers, is equally as stylish and sophisticated. You can expect

---

TOP FIVE DUBAI WINE BARS

- Vintage (p103), Wafi City
- Agency (above), Madinat Jumeirah
- Agency (above), Emirates Towers Hotel
- Apartment (p103), Jumeirah Beach Hotel
- Left Bank (p101), Souq Madinat Jumeirah

more of the same – a great wine list and delicious tapas menu (we love the mashed potato and chorizo!) – with the added bonus of wonderful *al fresco* seating overlooking beautiful Madinat Jumeirah's Venice-like canals, with a glimpse of the Burj Al Arab. Go to Emirates Towers midweek and Souq Madinat Jumeirah on weekends.

BAHRI BAR Map pp214-15
☎ 366 8888; Mina A' Salam, Jumeirah; ☾ noon-2am

Everybody's favourite winter bar has a wonderful big veranda covered in Persian carpets and comfy cane seats to stretch out on and admire the magical views of the Arabian sea, the Madinat Jumeirah architecture and the stunning Burj Al Arab. There are delicious wines by the glass, a great selection of icy beers on tap, potent cocktails and snacks. If it's too hot outside, the colonial-Arabian style interior is equally atmospheric, but most prefer to sweat it out!

BAR 44 Map pp214-15
☎ 399 8888; Grosvenor West Marina Beach by Le Meridien, Jumeirah; ☾ 6pm-2am

This swanky club-style bar on the 44th floor of the Grosvenor House hotel has extraordinary views of the scores of new skyscrapers and many more still under construction at 'New Dubai'. This spectacular light show, a warren of cosy rooms, live jazz and 44 types of champagne keep people coming back.

BARASTI BAR Map pp214-15
☎ 399 3333; Le Meridien Mina Seyahi Beach Resort & Marina, Al-Sufouh Rd; ☾ 6pm-2am

This casual seaside bar is the locals' top spot for laid-back sundowners on a hot afternoon. It's the kind of place you don't have to dress up for, and can head to straight after a day at the beach. It even manages to maintain its laid-back air when a DJ's on the deck spinning chilled-out sounds for Dubai's body-conscious set.

BARZAR Map pp214-15
☎ 366 6348; Souq Madinat Jumeirah, Al-Sufouh Rd, Jumeirah; ☾ noon-1am

Cheap (and sometimes free!) drinks and the chance to chill out in a beanbag by the water overlooking the magnificent Madinat Jumeirah arena is what keeps BarZar busy on weekends. The upstairs bar is often quiet, and the downstairs bar raucous, so bag a beanbag if you can.

BUDDHA BAR Map pp214-15
☎ 399 8888; Grosvenor West Marina Beach by Le Meridien, Jumeirah; ☾ 7pm-3am

Ever since Claude Challe flew to Dubai to open the new Buddha Bar, the crowd coming here has been a very stylish set. A combination of locals, expats and tourists, reflecting the global popularity of the brand and music, keep coming back for the dramatic Oriental interior, chilled-out Asian

TOP YE OLDE PUBS

Dubai's old English-style pubs were the lifeblood of expats in the 'old days', an informal social club where one could meet others who shared a love of bad food and warm beer. Given expat life today, where no-one talks to people outside their clique unless they've had one too many jelly shots, pubs (English- or American-style) are still a good place to meet for conversation and a few ales.

Boston Bar (Map pp224-5; ☎ 345 5888; Jumeirah Rotana Hotel, Al-Dhiyafah Rd; ☾ noon-2.30am Tue-Thu, noon-1.30am Fri-Mon) Head to this *Cheers*-style bar alone and you'll welcome the cricket or footy blaring on the TV, or you'll soon make friends to discuss the scores with. Happy hour, noon-8pm.

Carters (Map pp222-3; ☎ 324 0000; Wafi City; ☾ noon-2am) For better or worse this is a Dubai institution, so overlook or find humour in the kitsch Egyptian-themed décor. Happy hour, 4-8pm except Fridays.

Dubliners (Map pp218-19; ☎ 282 4040; behind Le Meridien Dubai, Airport Rd, Al-Garhoud; ☾ noon-3am) This friendly, boozy Irish bar serves reliable pub grub and Guinness, of course. Happy hour from 5-8pm. Try the pies!

Irish Village (Map pp218-19; ☎ 282 4750; Aviation Club, Dubai Tennis Stadium, Al-Garhoud Rd, Deira; ☾ 11am-1.30am Sat-Tue, 11am-3am Wed-Fri) Dubai's best Irish pub is popular with expats for its pond-side 'beer garden'. No happy hour, but hey, there's Guinness and Kilkenny draft.

Long's Bar (Map pp226; ☎ 312 2202; Tower Rotana Hotel, Sheikh Zayed Rd; ☾ noon-3am) The longest bar in town, live bands, cheap drinks and a late closure keeps this American-style bar busy. Happy hour, 4-8pm Sun-Fri.

sounds and buzzy vibe. Book a table to make sure you get in.

EL MALECON Map pp224-5
☎ 304 8281; Dubai Marine Beach Resort & Spa, Jumeirah; ⏲ 7.30pm-3am
Tipping its hat to Havana's graffiti-walled Bodeguita del Medio bar, El Malecon is the place to hit (late) when you fancy a cocktail and dancing to live Latin music. There are salsa lessons some nights, good modern Cuban food and pens on hand to add your autograph to the wall.

GINSENG Map pp222-3
☎ 324 8200; Wafi City, Bur Dubai; ⏲ 7pm-2am Fri-Wed, 7pm-3am Thu
The enormous mirrors at this uber-hip East-meets-West bar reflect a very cool crowd sipping on the best *caiparinhas* in the city and picking at the spicy Asian tapas. When there's a good DJ it's the kind of place where you want to linger for a while.

ISSIMO Map pp216-17
☎ 227 1111; Hilton Dubai Creek, Deira; ⏲ 7am-2am
Transforming from café by day to cocktail bar at night, Issimo is perfect for a martini after dinner or before heading home. Late Wednesday is best for sitting yourself on a stool and chatting with the sociable crowd or sinking into the black leather sofas and chilling to the mellow sounds.

KOUBBA Map pp214-15
☎ 366 8888; Al Qasr, Madinat Jumeirah, Jumeirah; ⏲ noon-2am
This can be one of the most romantic spots in Dubai if you can get a candlelit table on the terrace outside, overlooking the magnificent Madinat Jumeirah complex, splendidly lit at night. If you're feeling more social, the Oriental interior is atmospheric, the well-dressed crowd is sophisticated, and the music is mostly Arabian-lounge.

KU BU Map pp216-17
☎ 205 7033; InterContinental Dubai Hotel, Baniyas Rd, Deira; ⏲ 7pm-3am
A DJ spins funky tunes at this small sultry bar with African-inspired interiors that attracts couples wanting a bit of privacy (there are secluded nooks made more

TOP FIVE AL FRESCO BARS
- Bahri Bar (opposite), Mina A' Salam
- Rooftop Bar (below), One&Only Royal Mirage
- Barasti Bar (opposite), Le Meridien Mina Seyahi
- Sho Cho (p102), Dubai Marine Beach Resort
- Terrace (p102), Park Hyatt

private by plush drapes). If you're single and come here alone, be careful who you get intimate with – on some nights the place is frequented by working girls.

LEFT BANK Map pp214-15
☎ 368 6171; Souq Madinat Jumeirah, Al-Sufouh Rd, Jumeirah; ⏲ noon-2am
Left Bank's splendidly lit interior glows invitingly at night, and once inside it's hard to leave – great wines, good cocktails and an affable crowd will keep you here, whether it's a quiet midweek night or a rowdy weekend vibe.

LOTUS ONE Map p226
☎ 329 3200; World Trade Convention Centre, off Sheik Zayed Rd; ⏲ noon -2am
Super-cool Lotus One assaults your senses in the most wonderful way – there are exotic Asian-flavoured cocktails to excite your taste buds, waves of sand, pebbles and seashells glow under your feet beneath the glass floor, the fibre-optic lighting subtly shifts through a rainbow of colours, and the DJ's sultry grooves work with the sensual atmosphere.

MAI TAI LOUNGE Map p226
☎ 331 1111; Trader Vic's, Crowne Plaza Hotel; ⏲ 7pm-1.30am
If you're in the mood for a cocktail and live Latin music, this tiny bar is a perfect place to drop in to, even if you're not dining on delicious Polynesian food at the attached Trader Vic's restaurant (p88) – but don't leave without trying the tasty finger food.

ROOFTOP BAR Map pp214-15
☎ 399 9999; Arabian Court, One&Only Royal Mirage, Al-Sufouh Rd, Jumeirah; ⏲ 5.30pm-1am
With its cushion-covered banquette seating, Moroccan lanterns, Oriental carpets and chill-out music, this candle-lit rooftop bar is one of Dubai's most sublime spots.

Entertainment

BARS & PUBS

TOP FIVE BARS WITH VIEWS

- Bar 44 (p100), Grosvenor House
- Koubba (p101), Al Qasr
- Skyview Bar (below), Burj Al Arab
- Vu's (opposite), Emirates Towers Hotel
- Up on the Tenth (right), Intercontinental Hotel

Once settled in with a drink, watching the sun set over the Arabian Sea, counting the stars in the sky, it's hard to leave. People even sweat it out in summer for the experience, although the inside bar downstairs is also atmospheric.

SHO CHO Map pp224-5

☎ 346 1111; Dubai Marine Beach Resort & Spa, Jumeirah Rd; ☽ 7pm-3am

While the cool minimalist interior – with its blue lights, funky white seating and fish tanks in the walls – is attractive, during Dubai's cool winter months the outside deck is even more enticing, with a DJ spinning on the wooden deck, the salty ocean breezes and the sound of the sea. This is one of Dubai's hippest and most sublime bars – if it looks busy, act cool and walk right past the door police.

SKYVIEW BAR Map pp214-15

☎ 301 7438; Burj Al Arab, Jumeirah; ☽ 11am-2am

As drinks at the world's first 'seven star' hotel now tops most tourists' list of things to tick off, it's essential to book ahead and take a Dh200 cocktail and cold canapé package. (If you prefer wine and hot canapés, you'll still pay Dh200 for the cold package, plus the extra!) Most people seem to think the bragging rights are worth it. Fortunately the dazzling views outside distract you from the surprisingly gaudy interior.

TERRACE Map pp218-19

☎ 602 1234; Park Hyatt Dubai, next to Dubai Creek Golf & Yacht Club; ☽ noon-1am

Specialising in French oysters, caviar, champagne and vodka, the Terrace is one of Dubai's loveliest waterside lounge bars – and one of its more expensive ones. The light-filled interior is stylish, but with the boats bobbing outside at the hotel's marina, sitting on the wooden deck is divine on a cool

winter's night, and sublime in the sunshine of a warm spring day.

UP ON THE TENTH Map pp216-17

☎ 205 7333; Dubai InterContinental Hotel; ☽ 6pm-3am

This elegant bar is favoured by mature couples who enjoy the champagne, piano music and live jazz, but it's hard for anyone not to enjoy the splendid floor-to-ceiling views of Dubai Creek.

USHNA Map pp214-15

☎ 368 6506; Souq Madinat Jumeirah, Al-Sufouh Rd, Jumeirah; ☽ 12.30pm-2am

The fuchsia walls and funky hanging seats of this Indian fusion restaurant are inviting but the food still hasn't lived up to the vibe. Opt to lounge with a cocktail at the candle-lit bar outside, from where you still have views inside, or of mesmerising Madinat Jumeirah and the buzzy crowd below.

VELVET LOUNGE Map pp216-17

☎ 227 8206; Al-Khaleej Palace Hotel; ☽ 7pm-1am

This is one of Dubai's more interesting bars – with a 1970s' take on baroque style, with red velvet sofas, heavy drapes, lots of gilt and a mirrored ceiling – although it's impossible to pick the night. You might

DUBAI'S SPEAKEASIES

While certainly not illegal, these often dingy, slightly sleazy and always smoky bars can have a 'Prohibition-era' feel to them, tucked away as they often are in the back lanes of Bur Dubai and Deira's hotels. They offer an interesting insight into Dubai's different subcultures and are worth a look if you want to walk on the wild side:

Jules (Map pp218–19; ☎ 282 4040; Le Meridien Dubai, Al-Garhoud; ☽ 11am-3am) Attracting a mixed crowd and a bit 'cleaner' than the others, popular with oil workers and working girls.

Maharlika (Map pp222–3; ☎ 334 6565; President Hotel, Sheikh Khalifa bin Zayed Rd, Karama; ☽ 6pm-3am) You'll meet the whole of Manila at this Filipino bar with a vibrant floorshow and bands with names like Elvis Presley Asia.

VJs (Map pp220–1; ☎ 352 2235; Rush Inn Hotel, Khalid bin al-Waleed Rd (Bank St), Bur Dubai; ☽ 9pm-3am) A good pool table, terrible bands and lots of very friendly women.

arrive to find young Iranian expats dancing to a DJ spinning Persian pop, a more sedate cocktail crowd drinking the very cheap drinks, or at worst, it might have closed early. Take a punt.

VINTAGE Map pp222-3
☎ 324 0000; Wafi City, Bur Dubai; ☽ 6pm-1.30am
A favourite of Dubai wine aficionados for its impressive wine list, genial atmosphere and great range of grape by the glass – or by the 'flight', where tasting portions and wines from a wine-growing region are presented as a set. There is also an excellent cheese counter where you can select your own, while the fondue and wine promotion is perennially popular.

VU'S BAR Map p226
☎ 330 0000; 51st fl, Emirates Towers Hotel, Sheikh Zayed Rd; ☽ 6pm-2am
You'll get a hint at how amazing the Sheikh Zayed Rd views are at this sophisticated bar after your ears pop in the elevator on the way up. At 220m above Dubai, Vu and its drinks prices are quite amazing, but the high-ceilinged bar is super stylish and definitely worth a peek.

DANCE CLUBS
Dubai's club scene will keep the most ardent clubbers satisfied, with excellent club nights most evenings in imaginative multi-level spaces such as Trilogy and MIX, and popular weekly events like Peppermint Club and the Embassy. Dance events have really taken off with global brands such as Hed Kandi attracting the biggest crowds and regular visits from international name DJs such as Pierre Raven, Roger Sanchez and Joey Negro, with the obligatory bongo players, podium dancers and pyrotechnics.

The scene is also not as segregated as it once was, with people making an effort to venture out of their comfort zone and catch more unusual nights, such as Indian DJs spinning Bengali sounds. Although Wednesday, Thursday and Friday nights are the big nights, there's so much going on in Dubai, keen clubbers can go out anytime. But whatever evening they head out, they go out late – most dance floors don't get crowded until 1am or 2am, just an hour or two before the venue closes its doors.

SENDING OUT AN SMS
'Stanton Warriors drop sonic bombs at iBO tonight. Expect a serious assault on your senses from breakbeat's finest. Too huge for words. Get down to get down!'

Ahh, text messaging, where would we be without you? Well, in Dubai, you'd probably not be at the best clubs on the most happening nights. The club scene in the city has become so frenzied that these text messages from your favourite clubs help you plan your night. I mean, who has time to read these days?

When you get to Dubai, sign up to the mailing lists of the websites we've mentioned, leaving your mobile phone number so you don't miss a night that's too huge for words.

Most clubs don't have cover charges unless there is a big DJ in town or a special dance event. In these cases, the cover charge varies depending on the act. Like in any city in the world, Dubai clubs transform their personalities on particular nights – while some nights are perennially popular, surviving for years, others disappear after a month if they're not pulling in the punters. It's best to check out www.mumtazz.com or promoters' sites such as www.9714.com and www.fluidproduction.com before heading out.

APARTMENT Map pp214-15
☎ 406 8000; Jumeirah Beach Hotel, Jumeirah; ☽ 7pm-1.30am
Originally an exclusive club before it reinvented itself into an upmarket French restaurant and bar, the Apartment is once again a club with a bar, lounge and dance floor. Chill out in a leather armchair in the luxe lounge room or use any influence you may have to get into a plush VIP room. Dubai DJ stars like Judge Jules help to entice the self-conscious crowd on to the dance floor.

BOUDOIR Map pp224-5
☎ 345 5995; Dubai Marine Beach Resort & Spa, Jumeirah Rd; ☽ 7.30pm-4am
This decadent restaurant-cum-cocktail bar-cum-nightclub is where international celebrities and supermodels play when they're in town. Its chic Parisian-brasserie-style – think crystal chandeliers, sumptuous velvet padded booths, gilt-edged mirrors and heavy drapes – may seem odd in

Entertainment

DANCE CLUBS

Dubai, but nobody cares when DJs like Stéphane Pompougnac spin chill-out beats; they just hit the dance floor.

CHAMELEON & VICE Map pp222-3

☎ 324 0000; Wafi Pyramids, Wafi City, Oud Metha, Bur Dubai; ☾ 7pm-3am

Temporarily closed at the time of writing, while the new Raffles Hotel construction made a war zone out of the Wafi City car park, Chameleon – as its name implies – transforms throughout the night from glam cocktail bar to dinner lounge to live music venue (offering up everything from jazz to world music) to dance club. Upstairs Vice, quite simply, is a stylish vodka and champagne bar.

EMBASSY Map p226

☎ 343 8888; Shangri-La Hotel, Sheikh Zayed Rd; ☾ 10pm-3am Fri only

Just when we thought Dubai had enough exclusive clubs, the Embassy opened with a Hed Kandi night, DJ Stickyfingers on the

DUBAI'S TOP CLUB NIGHTS

- Sho Cho (p102) on Tuesday
- Trilogy (opposite) on Wednesday
- iBO (right) on Thursday
- Peppermint Club (opposite) on Friday
- Oxygen (opposite) on Monday

iBO (above) is a popular venue where international DJs perform when visiting Dubai

decks, and local celebs such as Verre chef Gordon Ramsay on the guest list. Think: dress code, valet parking, table bookings, chrome and black leather chairs, self-conscious dance floor.

IBO Map pp218-19

☎ 398 2206; Millennium Airport Hotel, Al-Garhoud Rd, Deira; ☾ 8pm-3am

This is the kind of funky club Dubai needs more of. With comfy velvet sofas, groovy white chairs, shagpile rugs on raw concrete floor, and disco ball, it epitomises casual cool. Both bar staff and clubbers are friendly, atmosphere is relaxed, and focus is on the music and dance floor with the world's most interesting DJs flying in on weekends.

KASBAR Map pp214-15

☎ 399 9999; One&Only Royal Mirage, Al-Sufouh Rd; cover charge Dh50; ☾ 9.30pm-3am Mon-Sat

With so much competition these days, Kasbar nights are inconsistent – some evenings there are queues, others you can breeze on through to an empty room. Either way, a peek at the arabesque interior of this Moroccan-style dance club is worth the admission (which includes a free drink). If the place is packed, usually not until late, it's an added bonus. If Arabian-fusion is spinning, it'll be a night you won't forget.

M-LEVEL Map pp216-17

☎ 227 1111; Hilton Dubai Creek, Deira; ☾ 9pm-3am

The stylish design, casual cool ambience and outdoor deck make dance nights here memorable, but call ahead to see what's on, as this hip space on Hilton's mezzanine level only hosts one-off events, DJ parties, music launches and private functions. There's generally something on every week, so if you're staying at the hotel or dining at one of the restaurants, ask – you'll probably get an invitation and get in for free.

MIX Map pp214-15

☎ 317 2570; Grand Hyatt Hotel, Bur Dubai; ☾ 9pm-3am, closed Sat

This was Dubai's first 'super club' and it's still going strong. Expect three levels of action, house, hip-hop and R & B, a raised bar, huge dance floor, swanky VIP rooms upstairs, top international DJs, podium dancers, bongo players and excellent people-watching opportunities. Cover charge for DJ events.

OXYGEN Map pp218-19
☎ 282 0000; Al-Bustan Rotana Hotel, Deira; ⏱ 6pm-3am

It's a shame that the beautiful faux-baroque interior of this perennially popular club goes unnoticed, but what do you expect when they have daily drink promotions like Dh2 drinks and free jelly shots all night for the ladies – it's a wonder anyone can find the door on the way out! This and good international DJs keep the expats coming back to boogie to soul, R&B, Arabic, house, hip hop and just plain pop.

PEPPERMINT CLUB Map p226
☎ 332 0037; Fairmont Hotel, Sheikh Zayed Rd; ⏱ 10pm-3am Fri

Promoters Fluid Production bring some of the biggest international DJs (Paul Van Dyk, Steve Lawler, James Lavelle, etc) to Dubai for weekly Peppermint Club nights. These are huge sweaty nights, often with over 2000 clubbers on the dance floor. There are occasionally weekend events that begin on Thursday night. Admission charge for men but women usually get in free.

TANGERINE Map p226
☎ 332 5555; Fairmont Hotel, Sheikh Zayed Rd; ⏱ 8pm-3am

One of Dubai's most popular bar-clubs, Tangerine can be relied on for a fun night out. Get there a bit early to check out the Oriental interior, as it fills up after 11pm with a well-dressed crowd. When it's busy, the power-crazed door guys are very selective about who gets in.

TRILOGY Map pp214-15
☎ 366 6917; Souq Madinat Jumeirah, Al-Sufouh Rd, Jumeirah; ⏱ 9pm-3am

Dubai's hottest dance club at the moment, hip Trilogy has dance floors and bars catering to different tastes over several levels, and visiting international DJs from around the globe. Get there early and head to Trilogy's Rooftop Bar for a drink first or buy tickets in advance to avoid the sometimes outrageous queues.

LADIES NIGHTS

Every night is Ladies Night in Dubai! It's an institution – it's just a matter of choosing the right bar or club for cheap or free drinks. Here's a sampler:

Saturday Free 'black ice' all night long at Oxygen

Sunday Unlimited free drinks at Jimmy Dix and, um, free jelly shots all night long at Oxygen…

Monday Two free drinks until 1am at Oxygen's Mademoiselles night and Dh2 after that!

Tuesday A big night in Dubai! – a bottle of sparkling stuff at Oxygen, free vodka cocktails at Mix, and free-flowing champagne at Boudoir

Wednesday Free drinks at Tangerine's Kitten Club

Thursday Free cocktails at Boudoir until midnight

Friday Three free drinks at BarZar from 4pm to 7pm and a free glass of champagne at Trilogy Rooftop bar from 7pm to 9pm

ZINC Map p226
☎ 331 1111; Crowne Plaza Hotel, Sheikh Zayed Rd; ⏱ 7pm-3am

This popular bar-restaurant-club has several drinking spaces and a decent-sized dance floor. Previously only (really) busy on Saturday nights, its glamorous Kinky Malinki nights pull in the punters for funky uplifting house, London-style. Cover charge for guys, but girls get in free.

CONCERTS, LIVE MUSIC & EVENTS

Dubai's live music and concert scene, once rather dismal, has been slowly improving due to the increasingly hip media types and creative professionals moving into the market who are demanding more, or simply organising events themselves. As a result, in recent times Dubai has seen more live jazz and R & B locally, big name acts such as Destiny's Child, Black Eyed Peas and Basement Jaxx dazzling the city, and artists like Moby and Jamiroquai on their way.

If you want to experience something different, try to catch some Arabian, Middle Eastern, Persian or Subcontinental stars if you get the chance. The legendary Fairouz, Cheb Mami, Iranian heart-throbs Daryush

Blue Bar (right) is known for its live music and excellent beers on tap

and Ebi, Persian pop sensations Arian and Shadmeher, Lebanese mega-stars Haifa and Nancy, and Pakistan's number-one selling female artist Hadiqa Kani have all performed in Dubai. On a smaller scale, there are also good Moroccan three pieces, Indian sitar players and Spanish flamenco guitarists playing live nightly in many five-star hotel restaurants, along with more unusual acts from 12-piece African collectives to rocking Filipino bands performing in back-lane bars. Classical music concerts and piano recitals are regularly organised by embassies and cultural organisations, such as Alliance Francais and the British Council, and are often held at the Crowne Plaza and Shangri-La hotels. Check with your hotel concierge.

While live music is on offer at the large hotels, concerts and big events are usually held at the Aviation Club, Dubai Tennis Stadium, Nad Al Sheba, Dubai International Convention Centre, Dubai Country Club,

the Dubai Creek Golf and Yacht Club, Al Wasl Football Stadium, the Dubai Media City Amphitheatre, Dubai Autodrome or on the beach at the Mina Seyahi or out-of-town venues. Tickets range from Dh150 for standing room to Dh750 for VVIP seats, available from the usual ticket hotlines (see p96).

BLUE BAR Map p226
☎ 310 8124; Novotel Hotel, near the Trade Centre, off Sheikh Zayed Rd; ☽ noon-1am
Another Dubai bar that has its off nights and has its moving moments too, minimalist Blue Bar has developed a reputation as a place to listen to good jazz and blues, especially on Thursday nights – it's just a shame the entertainment isn't as consistently good as the excellent Belgian beer.

JAM BASE Map pp214-15
☎ 366 6730; Souq Madinat Jumeirah, Al-Sufouh Rd, Jumeirah; ☽ 7pm-2am
Live jazz, soul and R & B – and delicious Deep South cuisine – keeps this super stylish venue buzzing, especially on weekends. It's rare that we haven't seen the dance floor packed by the end of the night.

JAZZ ON THE GREEN Map pp218-19
☎ 282 9333; Cellar, Aviation Club, Al-Garhoud, Deira; ☽ 8pm-midnight Sat
During Dubai's cooler winter months, you can listen to live jazz while you enjoy excellent food (see **Cellar**, p80) and great wine outdoors by the very pleasant duck pond.

WORLD MUSIC IN DUBAI

Multicultural Dubai offers up music from around the globe every night of the week. Mostly frequented by expat workers who just want to hear a bit of home, these venues aren't the most glam places around, but the music is interesting and they can make for a fun night out.

Ashiana (Map pp216–17; ☎ 224 0661; Ramee International Hotel, Baniyas (Al Nasr) Sq, Deira; ☎ 7pm-3am) Live Bengali band.

Club Africana (Map pp220–1; ☎ 352 2235; Rush Inn Hotel, Khalid bin al-Waleed Rd (Bank St), Bur Dubai; ☽ 9pm-3am) Twelve-piece Congolese band.

Al-Khan Sheesha Club (Map pp214–15; ☎ 266 2666; Ramada Continental Hotel, Abu Hail Rd, Deira; ☽ 9pm-3am) Singers from Egypt and Iraq and Moroccan dancers.

Saghi (Map pp216–17; ☎ 224 0661; Ramee International Hotel, Deira; ☽ 7pm-3am) Live Iranian band with dancers.

Savage Garden (Map pp220–1; ☎ 346 0111; Capitol Hotel, Bur Dubai; ☽ 6pm-3am) Latin American band from Columbia and salsa classes some nights.

Check in the entertainment magazines or call ahead as it's dependent on the weather.

MARRAKECH Map p226

☎ 343 8888; Shangri-La Hotel, Sheikh Zayed Rd; ☯ 1-3pm & 7.30pm-1am

Although Marrakech is more a restaurant than a bar, you can sit at the low tables at the front, stick to drinks and mezze, and watch the nightly performances by the magnificent three-piece traditional Moroccan band.

PEANUT BUTTER JAM Map pp222-3

☎ 324 4100; Wafi City, Bur Dubai; ☯ 8pm Fri, except summer

Sink into a beanbag, enjoy the barbecue buffet and chill out to live acoustic music on the Wafi rooftop during the cooler months. We dare you to join in for a jam.

ROCK BOTTOM CAFÉ Map pp220-1

☎ 396 3888; Regent Palace Hotel, Sheikh Khalifa bin Zayed Rd, Bur Dubai; ☯ 10am-3am

This Dubai institution is the kind of pick-up joint people end up at when common sense should tell them to go home. It has those resident cover bands that you love to hate – the ones that play daggy songs that keep you on the dance floor. (Insider tip: in Dubai, saying you ended up at the Rock Bottom Café means you drank way more than you should have.)

THEATRE, DANCE & COMEDY

Live theatre in Dubai is another part of the entertainment scene that's definitely getting healthier. Theatre companies such as the British Airways Playhouse and The British Touring Shakespeare Company tour frequently, usually performing at the Crowne Plaza Hotel, while the local Dubai Drama Group performs Tom Stoppard plays and the like at Dubai Country Club. Theatre tickets range between Dh60 and Dh250.

The Laughter Factory and Laughter House offer regular doses of comedy, with a bill of two or three visiting comedians on any one night, and occasional one-off comedy events such as Peter Searle's popular one-man show 'Hey Gringo'. These are also generally staged at the Crowne Plaza and Mövenpick Hotels. Tickets start at around Dh70 depending on who's on.

Dubai is also starting to attract big productions and popular shows like Tap Dogs, the Shaolin Monks and the Chinese State Circus.

MADINAT THEATRE/ARENA Map pp214-15

☎ 366 6546, 366 6550; Souq Madinat Jumeirah, Al-Sufouh Rd, Jumeirah; tickets Dh60-200; ☯ box office 10am-11pm, show times vary

Since the Madinat Theatre/Arena (and enchanting waterside Amphitheatre) opened, its three venues have kept Dubai's formerly culture-starved residents amused with a regular programme of entertainment that has covered everything from the Russian State Ballet to Le Petit Prince, Broadway musicals and dance spectaculars.

LAUGHTER FACTORY Map p226

☎ 331 1111, 336 8800, 800 4669; Zinc, Crowne Plaza Hotel, Sheikh Zayed Rd & Jimmy Dix, Mövenpick Hotel, Oud Metha, Bur Dubai; tickets Dh95; ☯ 9pm-1am

The Laughter Factory claims to be the city's premier comedy club (perhaps to justify the higher prices!). The stand-up comedians from London's Comedy Store generally have punters in stitches at Crowne Plaza's Zinc bar and Jimmy Dix at the Mövenpick Hotel.

LAUGHTER HOUSE Map pp218-19

☎ 282 4122; Rainbow Room, Aviation Club, Dubai Tennis Stadium, Al-Garhoud Rd, Deira; show Dh70, show plus pre-show dinner & wine Dh180; ☯ 7.30pm doors open, 9pm show starts, 1st Tue every month

Dubai's second comedy club is an offshoot of Liverpool's Laughter House, also flying stand-ups (often four) into town for the night; it's equally as popular as the Laughter Factory.

CINEMAS

Sold-out screenings at the second Dubai International Film Festival, held in December 2005, and the increasing popularity of *al fresco* film nights (see the boxed text, p108) are proof that Dubai has a large and growing number of cinephiles. Yet the city still doesn't have a cinema showing art-house

Entertainment

THEATRE, DANCE & COMEDY

or foreign films. Hollywood blockbusters still dominate, and it's next to impossible to see quality Middle East films on the big screen, except at iBO's Stella Movie Night. American movies are released simultaneously on Dubai screens, either at the same time or just a few weeks after their American release, depending on the studio's distribution strategy. As there is a large French-speaking audience in Dubai, from Europe and the Levant, French films are next in line to get the most time on screen, while **Alliance Française** (Map pp222–3; ☎ 335 8712) also shows weekly films in French and holds film festivals occasionally. A few small movie clubs operate from colleges, art galleries (such as XVA, p56) and people's homes!

Dubai once had quite a few cinemas showing films in Hindi, Tagalog, Malayalam and Tamil, catering to its large Asian expatriate population, but these have been closing down in recent years and there are only a couple left. If you've never seen a Bollywood movie on the big screen, add that to your list of things to do – they're a hoot! Running well over two hours long, they're pure spectacle, crammed with melodrama, romance and action, and frequently punctuated by song and dance routines. The plots are rarely complicated so you'll be able to understand them if they don't have sub-titles and you don't know the language. Films are subject to censorship with sex, nudity and references to Israel removed, so be prepared for occasional jump cuts. Dubai's cinemas are state-of-the-art, with comfortable seating and nachos-to-your-seat service! Movie times are published in all the newspapers, including their websites, and in the monthly entertainment mags.

CINESTAR Map pp218-19
☎ 294 9000; Deira City Centre, Deira; tickets Dh30
Showing Hollywood hits along with some independent American, British and European films, this is the place for every Emirati and expat teen to be on a weekend night.

CENTURY CINEMAS Map pp224-5
☎ 349 8765; Mercato Mall, Jumeirah Rd; tickets Dh30
A bit more intimate than the other cinemas, Century Cinemas shows the same Hollywood blockbusters, but is also host to the odd embassy-organised film week.

AL FRESCO FILMS
Dubai residents will do anything to stay outside during the cooler winter months – as a result there's a flourishing free 'cinema under the stars' scene:

Monday Mina Movies (Map pp214–15; ☎ 399 3333; Meridien Mina Seyahi Resort, ⏰ 8pm-late Mon) Free popcorn, cheap drinks, a beanbag and quality Hollywood films from *Fight Club* to *Fargo*.

Movies under the Stars (Map pp222–3; ☎ 324 0000; Wafi City Rooftop Gardens; ⏰ 8pm-late Sun) Settle into a beanbag with a bucket of beers and watch movies such as *Bend it like Beckham*.

Screen on the Beach (Map pp214–15; ☎ 348 0000; Jumeirah Beach Hotel, ⏰ 8pm-late Tue) Recline on carpets and cushions by the sea and enjoy waiter service while you watch anything from *Kingdom of Heaven* to *Jerry Maguire*.

Stella Movie Night (Map pp218–19; ☎ 398 8890; iBO, Millenium Airport Hotel; ⏰ 8pm-late Sun) Not alfresco unfortunately – under a mirror ball rather than stars at groovy iBO nightclub – but these arthouse and foreign flicks (*La Dolce Vita*, *The Apple*, *Divine Intervention* etc) are also free.

GRAND CINEPLEX Map pp214-15
☎ 324 2000; Grand Hyatt Hotel, next to Wafi City, Bur Dubai; tickets Dh25-30
This state-of-the-art 10-screen complex shows the latest release English-language movies. There's also a decent DVD/music store, café and ATM here.

GRAND MEGAPLEX
☎ 366 9898; Ibn Battuta Mall, Sheikh Zayed Rd; tickets Dh50
In addition to the usual hi-tech cinemas, you can watch documentaries and Hollywood blockbusters such as *Batman Begins* from an enormous 44ft-tall by 70ft-wide IMAX screen.

LAMCY Map pp222-3
☎ 336 8808; Lamcy Plaza, Al-Qataiyat Rd, Bur Dubai; tickets Dh20
This modern two-screen complex is one of the few remaining theatres showing Hindi, Malayalam and Tamil films. If you've never seen a Bollywood movie in the cinema, do it in Dubai on a Friday (the only day off for many Asian expatriates) and you're in for a memorable experience.

Activities

Activities

Despite the heat, most Dubaians love their outdoor activities. While the beach is the first port of call for many, others take to one of Dubai's myriad golf courses. When the mercury rises too much for even the most hardened wannabe Bedouin, the gyms and spas of Dubai are full of regulars. Of course we mustn't forget Dubai's latest novelty – dropping the kids off at school and then hitting the black run of Ski Dubai (p114) – fast becoming *the* hottest (coolest?) thing to do! So no matter what time of year you visit, Dubai has plenty of sports and activities to work off that buffet breakfast.

HEALTH & FITNESS

HEALTH CLUBS

All of Dubai's five-star and most of the city's midrange hotels have health clubs, which are usually free for guests. The facilities of the larger clubs include a gym, sauna, swimming pool, squash courts and tennis courts. Generally, if you're not a guest at the hotel you must be a member or a member's guest to use the facilities, although some accept day visitors. If you decide to use one of the hotel beach clubs for the day you'll get access to their gym facilities as well. Daily membership fees start at around Dh40 and for decent clubs hover around Dh100 to Dh200. All the clubs in the following list have treadmills, bikes, step machines, rowing machines, free weights and resistance machines, aerobics classes, as well as massage, sauna and steam room.

Griffins Health Club (Map pp218–19; ☎ 607 7755; JW Marriott Hotel; Sat-Wed Dh83, Thu-Fri Dh88; nonmembers 8-9pm Sat & Tue, Dh27)

Inter-Fitness (Map pp216–17; ☎ 222 7171; InterContinental Hotel Dubai; Sat-Wed Dh50, Thu-Fri Dh75)

Nautilus Academy (Map pp220–1; ☎ 397 4117; Al Musallah Towers, Khalid Bin Al-Waleed St, Bur Dubai; Dh40)

YOGA & PILATES

GEMS OF YOGA Map p226

☎ 331 5161; White Crown Bldg, Junction 1, Sheikh Zayed Rd

Offers several different types of yoga classes, including toning and therapeutic yoga, and group classes held in parks and on the beach.

HOUSE OF CHI & HOUSE OF HEALING Map pp220-1

☎ 397 4446; www.hofchi.com; 6th fl, Al Musallah Towers, Khalid Bin Al-Waleed St, Bur Dubai

You'll find Pilates, yoga and massage, plus a range of other conventional and alternative therapies, at this popular centre.

DAY SPAS & MASSAGE

You can book a massage at any of the clubs listed, but for a full spa treatment make an appointment at one of the following sublime spas.

> ### DUBAI'S TOP SPA TREATMENTS
>
> **Jetlag Recovery Package** (Six Senses Spa, opposite) Guaranteed to reduce swelling and improve circulation.
>
> **Canyon Love Stone Therapy** (Givenchy Spa, opposite) Get in the mood for romance with a hot stone massage.
>
> **Hopi Ear Candling** (Cleopatra's Spa, opposite) Yes, they really put hot candles in your ears.
>
> **Date Body Rub** (☎ 318 6184; The Spa, Ritz-Carlton, Al-Sufouh Rd, Jumeirah) A moisturising honey, oats, milk and orange-blossom scrub.
>
> **Sunset Sparkle** (Sensasia, opposite) Leaves your skin sparkling for that big night out!
>
> **Sunrise Body Refresher** (Willow Stream Spa, Fairmont Hotel, p148) Wake up with an exfoliating olive wash.

TREATED LIKE A PHARAOH

For gym junkies looking for something a little more exclusive, **Pharaohs Club** (Map pp222–3; ☎ 324 0000; Wafi City, Al-Qataiyat Rd) fits the bill. From the sphinxes and hieroglyphic columns at the entrance to the artificial beach and 'lazy river' on the rooftop, it's truly awesome. A week's membership costs Dh250, which is cheaper than paying Dh50 per day at the hotels or Dh200 per day to use the facilities at the beach clubs. Massages, spas and beauty treatments are available for men and women in luxurious surroundings. It has even got a climbing wall. If you are in the area, it's worth dropping in just to have a look at the facilities or to have lunch at one of the restaurants in the complex.

CLEOPATRA'S SPA Map pp222-3
☎ 324 7700; www.waficity.com; Wafi Pyramids, Wafi City, Bur Dubai
Heavenly Cleopatra's Spa was Dubai's first health spa and is still one of the most opulent, with a long list of divine treatments, including Cleopatra's (four-hour) Ritual. The rain showers are also popular.

GIVENCHY SPA Map pp214-15
☎ 315 2140; www.oneandonlyresorts.com; One&Only Royal Mirage, Al-Sufouh Rd, Jumeirah
This extravagant complex with an Oriental hammam offers Givenchy signature treatments, body scrubs, wraps, massages and facials, such as Japanese honeysuckle and green tea Sculpt Facial. You'll be checking the room rates (see the **One&Only Royal Mirage**, p149) because you won't want to leave.

SENSASIA Map pp214-15
☎ 349 8850; www.sensasiaspas.com; The Village, Jumeirah Rd, Jumeirah
The exotic 'Oriental Far East meets Middle East' style of this wonderful spa is nothing – the 'Queen for a Day' treatment (Dh1100) includes a chauffeur taking you to and from your half-day of treatments and massages.

SIX SENSES SPA Map pp214-15
☎ 366 6808; Madinat Jumeirah, Al-Sufouh Rd, Jumeirah
After a relaxing *abra* arrival, get a free health assessment at this Arabian-style spa, before choosing from a long list of heavenly treatments, such as the Jet Lag Recovery (massage, foot acupressure and eye therapy) or Sunburn Soother treatment.

BEAUTY & GROOMING

While Dubai's ladies who lunch have always had weekly massages, manicures, pedicures and facials at the top of their lists of things to do, their husbands are now following suit. In addition to women's salons, there are now a number of stylish male-only grooming salons.

1847 Map p226
☎ 330 1847; Blvd at Emirates Towers, Sheikh Zayed Rd; ⏰ 9am-9pm Sat-Thu, 1-9pm Fri
This clubby male grooming salon offers tailor-made packages, or you can opt for individual manicures, pedicures, Thai massage, or a simple cut and shave at the barber.

MALE SPA Map pp222-3
☎ 324 0000; Wafi Pyramids, next to Cleopatra's Spa, Wafi Pyramids, Wafi City; ⏰ 10am-10pm Mon-Sat, 10am-7pm Sun
Special treatments aimed at men include deep-tissue massages, shiatsu, body wraps, reflexology and facials. Their 'brainstormer scalp massage' is very popular.

OUTDOOR ACTIVITIES

Dubai has an ever-expanding range of activities and sports clubs – far too many to list in total here! *What's On* magazine has detailed information on clubs and leisure activities in the city. We've covered the activities that most visitors are likely to want to check out while in Dubai.

NIP 'N' TUCK OR TWEEZE 'N' PLUCK?

Dubai does a roaring trade in plastic surgery – rhinoplasty, liposuction, breast augmentation and the like – and these same people looking for aesthetic perfection also spend a lot of time at the gym doing weights and yoga, at the spa getting facials and massages, as well as back waxing. Back waxing? Yes, that's because we're talking about the *men* in Dubai.

Activities

OUTDOOR ACTIVITIES

DESERT SAFARIS

One of the must-dos for most visitors to Dubai, a desert safari (through an organised tour group) is great fun, and as environmentally friendly as this kind of activity can be. For a list of operators, see p155. Generally speaking, a half-day desert safari or wadi drive, with lunch/dinner, costs around Dh250 per person. They usually leave Dubai in the early afternoon so that you can watch the sun set over the desert. Overnight desert trips cost Dh350 to Dh450. This will get you some dune driving, a camel ride, a barbecue dinner (sometimes with a belly dancer for entertainment) and a night at a Bedouin-style camp site where you can peacefully sleep under the stars.

While driving over the dunes is exhilarating, some people find the experience quite frightening – let your driver know just how comfortable you are with what he's doing. While an experienced driver can still scare you silly, an inexperienced driver can leave you climbing out of the window of a rolled 4WD, so only head out with the recommended tour operators who know the terrain, know their vehicle, and know which areas are approved for these activities.

A popular event for dune driving is the Gulf News Overnight Fun Drive, held annually in December. Taking an environmentally friendly path, more than 750 vehicles take part in the two-day drive over the dunes from Dubai to Fujairah. If you are interested in the Fun Drive, details are posted on the website of Gulf News (www.gulfnews.com). You'll need to get your tickets well in advance.

MOTOR RACING

DUBAI AUTODROME KARTDROME

☎ 367 8700; www.dubaiautodrome.com; off Emirates Rd (take Interchange No 4 on Sheikh Zayed Rd), south of Dubai centre; per 15min Dh100; ☻ hours vary, call ahead

With a 17-corner, 1.4km track, electronic timing and powerful karts, along with the knowledge that this circuit might one day hold an F1 event, petrol-heads will need no further encouragement to don some driving gloves. The 'arrive and drive' package gives you 15 minutes to bring out your inner Schumacher. It also has a race and driving school at the circuit to further hone your skills.

GOLF

Dubai has become a premier golfing holiday destination over the past couple of years. While a desert city seems an unlikely destination for keen golfers, Dubai has several world-class golf courses designed by some of the world's best course designers. There's no 'members only' policy, so your chance to play some great courses is only limited by the depth of your pockets – keeping those greens green is expensive and this is reflected in the green fees. Dubai Golf (www.dubaigolf.com) has a booking service for all of the golf clubs in Dubai, and information on every course. Proof of handicap (generally the men's handicap must be under 28 and for women the maximum handicap is 36) is required, as is proper golfing attire. The following are some of the more popular courses.

DESERT COURSE

☎ 884 6777; www.thedesertcoursedubai.com; cnr Umm Suqeim St & Emirates Ring Rd, Arabian Ranches; per 18 holes Thu-Sat Dh425, Sun-Wed Dh325 (cart included)

Designed by former golf champion Ian Baker-Finch, this 18-hole course takes advantage of the natural features found in the area, and is similar to desert courses found in Palm Springs, California and Scottsdale, Arizona.

DUBAI COUNTRY CLUB Map pp214-15

☎ 333 1155; Ras al-Khor Rd; per round Sat-Thu Dh65, Fri Dh95

Yes, those really are the 'green' fees, because there are no greens, just browns! To play on 'brown' or sand golf courses, golfers are given a patch of artificial grass to slide under the ball on the fairways. The sand on the putting 'greens' is brushed smooth to approximate the rolling effect of grass. The most fun you'll ever have in a bunker.

DUBAI CREEK GOLF & YACHT CLUB

Map pp218-19

☎ 295 6000; www.dubaigolf.com; near the Deira side of Al-Garhoud Bridge; per 18 holes Thu-Sat Dh525, Sun-Wed Dh425

This former host of the Dubai Desert Classic has recently been redesigned by a former winner of the tournament, Thomas Björn.

The Creekside location is superb and real golf junkies can simply stay at the **Park Hyatt Dubai** (p145) and walk to the tee-off area. There's also a floodlit course.

EMIRATES GOLF CLUB Map pp214-15
☎ 347 3222; Interchange No 5, Sheikh Zayed Rd; 18-hole Majlis course Sun-Wed Dh625, Thu-Sat Dh425
The current site of the Dubai Desert Classic (p118), this gives you the chance to see if you can match Tiger Woods' tee shots. The club had the first grass course in the Middle East and the clubhouses, designed to resemble Bedouin tents, are quite striking.

NAD AL-SHEBA CLUB Map pp214-15
☎ 336 3666; www.nadalshebaclub.com; Nad al-Sheba District, 5km southeast of Dubai centre; peak fees 18-hole/9-hole Dh375/225, off-peak fees Dh445/270
With a floodlit 18-hole course (open until midnight!), with the back nine situated within the racecourse, it's a unique setting. Deep bunkers, double greens and plenty of water hazards await golfers here, but they also have good coaching to keep you on track. Off-peak fees apply all day Saturday and Sunday, 7.30am to 3.20pm Wednesday and 4pm to 10pm Thursday and Friday.

HORSE RIDING
EMIRATES RIDING SCHOOL
Map pp214-15
☎ 336 1394; near the Nad al-Sheba racecourse; 1hr lessons Dh125; ⏰ lessons 7-9am & 5-7pm Oct-Jun
Given the deep interest of the ruling Al-Maktoum family in all things equestrian, it's perhaps no surprise that Dubai hosts this world-class riding school. The school has dressage arenas, a floodlit main arena, training facilities and stables for 150 horses; it also gets a hoof stamp of approval by the British Horse Society.

ICE SKATING
AL-NASR LEISURELAND Map pp222-3
☎ 337 1234; www.alnasrll.com; off Oud Metha Rd, in Oud Metha; incl boot hire Dh10; ⏰ 2hr sessions at 10am, 1pm, 4pm & 7.30pm
It's certainly bigger than the rink at **Hyatt Regency** (p143), though probably not as exciting

for the kids as **Ski Dubai** (p114), but it also has a bowling alley and fast food available.

RUNNING
For at least half the year it's not as crazy as it sounds, especially when undertaken at 6am or pm. There are groups and clubs that meet regularly and there's even a marathon that now takes place in January (see City Calendar, p9). There are also 'hashing' clubs in Dubai, where the emphasis is more on the social aspects of running, OK, drinking. Visit www.creekhash.net.

DUBAI CREEK STRIDERS Map p226
☎ 321 1999; www.dubaicreekstriders.com; meet at Trade Centre car park opposite Exhibition Hall 4, Sheikh Zayed Rd
A long-established club (since 1995) running weekly on Friday mornings at 7am with shorter runs during summer (around 10km) and longer runs during the cooler months. There's no joining fee, but contact the club first before turning up.

DUBAI ROAD RUNNERS Map pp214-15
☎ 050-6243213; www.dubai-road-runners.com; north entrance to Safa Park, Al Wasl Rd; per adult Dh5; ⏰ 6.30pm Sat
The club welcomes runners of any age or ability to run one or two laps of the park (3.4km per lap), with each runner predicting the time in which they will run the course. The runner with the closest time wins a prize and funds raised are used to support events held during the year.

SANDBOARDING
If you have a burning desire to get sand wedged in every orifice, sandboarding is for you! While they'll tell you it's like surfing or snowboarding, falling off a surfboard usually doesn't hurt, and snow melts when it gets in your pants, ears, mouth – you get the picture! It's best to try it on one of the Desert Safaris (see p155) first, before booking a trip.

DESERT RANGERS
☎ 340 2408; www.desertrangers.com; per person Dh195
Starting in the morning, this half-day trip requires a minimum of four people. The

BOARD SPORTS

With the curtain finally pulled back on Ski Dubai, the city can now claim to be quite board-sport-oriented. Here's what's on offer:

Kite surfing Kite surfing is so popular that they just about own Wollongong, sorry, 'Kite' beach. See p116.

Skateboarding With all that concrete, street skating is excellent in Dubai, or head to Dubai Desert Extreme (below).

Snowboarding Head straight to Ski Dubai (right) for the quarter pipe.

Surfing During winter there are occasionally decent waves just adjacent to the Burj Al Arab! See p116.

Wakeboarding The Wakeboard School (p116) has a great reputation for getting students up and riding.

company also offers other adventure-sports activities.

ORIENT TOURS Map pp218-19

☎ 282 8238; www.orienttours.ae; Al-Garhoud Rd, Al-Garhoud; adult/child Dh180/125

Offering a similar deal of sandboarding and camel riding, they'll pick you up and drop you back at your hotel.

SKATE/INLINE/BMX

DUBAI DESERT EXTREME Map pp214-15

☎ 324 3222; off Al-Garhoud bridge, Al-Garhoud; 3hr/all day Dh15/25; ⊙ 2-10pm

Currently Dubai's only permanent skatepark, this small park is located in the Wonderland Theme and Waterpark. There's enough here to entertain most street enthusiasts for a couple of hours and you can rent equipment on site. Helmets (also for rent) are compulsory.

SKIING & SNOWBOARDING

While there's supposed to be another snowpark due to open late in 2006, given the delays with Ski Dubai we're not holding our breath. While the notion of a ski resort in the desert appears a little silly at first, keep in mind that during winter the ski resorts in Lebanon (not to mention St Moritz!) are filled with Gulf Arabs taking a break from the heat. So let it snow!

SKI DUBAI Map pp214-15

☎ 409 4000; www.skidxb.com; Sheikh Zayed Rd; Snowpark adult/child Dh50/40; Ski slope per 2hr Thu-Sat Dh130/110, Sun-Wed Dh115/100; ⊙ 10am-11pm Sat-Tue, 10am-midnight Wed-Fri

While the continuous delays had locals wondering if it was all just an expensive prank, Dubai's first indoor ski slope finally opened in late 2005. It's been an enormous success (especially on weekends); besides the novelty of snow in the desert, Ski Dubai has all the bases covered, with a great snowpark for the kids, a gentle beginners area, a permanent quarter pipe for the baggy-pant wearing snowboarders, and the world's first indoor 'black' run for those who like it steep. There's a quad lift taking skiers and boarders up to two stations, a magic carpet for beginners, and a drag lift – so it really is just like a mini ski resort! The snow uses no chemicals – it's just 'real' snow that falls overnight at around -10°C, and is then groomed, with the temperature rising to a comfortable -1°C to -2°C for the day. The best bit about it, though, is that you don't need to bring anything except gloves – all equipment is incorporated in the price, including disposable socks!

WATER SPORTS

With Dubai's beaches and sunny skies, water sports are big business. However, most water-sports facilities are based either at a big hotel or at a private club, and are priced accordingly. If you intend to spend a lot of time in the water or working on that tan, stay at one of the beach hotels (see p140).

Diving

Although the waters around Dubai are home to some coral reefs, marine life and a few modern shipwrecks, visibility in the water is not great. Dive companies prefer to take you up to the east coast to dive in the waters between Khor Fakkan and Dibba, and off the east coast of the Musandam Peninsula, which is part of Oman. For more information on diving in these areas, see Excursions, p162. Not including equipment hire, a day's diving (with two dives) costs between Dh200 and Dh500. Dives are offered to people at all levels of expertise. If you are uncertified you might want to take a diving course.

The Emirates Diving Association is the official diving body for the UAE and takes a strong interest in environmental matters. The association has a useful and detailed website (www.emiratesdiving.com). Another handy resource is the 180-page *UAE Underwater Explorer*, which has information on 30 dive sites.

AL BOOM DIVING Map pp224-5
☎ 342 2993; www.alboomdiving.com; Al-Wasl Rd, Jumeirah, just south of the Iranian Mosque
This diving centre has experienced staff (PADI certified) and can offer courses as well as dive trips (in Dubai and to the East Coast and Musandam), air fills, and maintenance for experienced divers.

SCUBATEC DIVING CENTRE
Map pp222-3
☎ 334 8988; www.scubatec.net; Sana Bldg, cnr Sheikh Khalifa bin Zayed & Al-Adhid Rds, Karama
Scubatec offers a two-dive trip off Khor Fakkan for Dh525 (including equipment), as well as dives on wrecks in the Gulf from Dh250. With a few days' notice staff can also arrange a dive on the pearling beds in the Gulf.

Fishing

While fishing in the Creek is not allowed (or advisable!), there's good fishing along Jumeirah Beach. For more serious angling, a deep-sea fishing trip is your best bet. If luck is on your side and the weather conditions are right, you're likely to catch flying fish, tuna, barracuda, kingfish and sailfish. The best time to fish off the coast of Dubai is from September to April when the water is cooler. You should try to book at least a week ahead as boats are often chartered well in advance.

DUBAI CREEK GOLF & YACHT CLUB
Map pp218-19
☎ 205 4646; near the Deira side of Al-Garhoud Bridge
The club rents out a 10m boat with skipper for up to six passengers. It costs Dh1500 for four hours or Dh2200 for eight hours, which includes fishing tackle, bait, lunch and drinks.

YACHT SOLUTIONS Map pp214-15
☎ 348 8800; Jumeirah Beach Hotel Pavilion Marina
With three fishing boats available for charter, Yacht Solutions is one of the biggest operators in Dubai. Deep-sea fishing for up to six people per boat is available and prices start from around Dh550 per hour.

Activities **OUTDOOR ACTIVITIES**

A surfer enjoys some rare clean waves during Dubai's winter months

Kite Surfing

Kite surfing has gained a solid following in Dubai and kite surfers generally congregate at Wollongong Beach, which the friendly kite crowd like to call Kite Beach (Map pp222–3), where there is a designated launch and recovery area. To regulate the sport in Dubai, the **Dubai Kite Club** (www .dubaikiteclub.com) was set up and you need a licence to practice the sport on Dubai's beaches. If you're keen to try kite surfing while in Dubai, visit the website for details on a temporary licence, and only use the recommended instructors – some phoney instructors have been reported. Kites and advice are available from **Fatima Sports** (Map pp214–15; ☎ 050-455 5216; www .fatimasport.com; Kite Beach).

Surfing

While most of the photos you see of the Burj Al Arab feature a calm sea in its reflection, there is surf that rolls into the Jumeirah Beach stretch. Swell size rarely gets above a couple of feet but there's a small and dedicated band of locals who frequently surf the often mushy conditions. The only problem as a visitor is there's nowhere to hire a surfboard. If you have access to equipment your best bet is to check out what's commonly known as Wollongong Beach or Kite Beach (Map pp214–15), near the old Wollongong University, or check out the website of **Surfers**

of Dubai (www.surfersofdubai.com) for details of swell conditions.

Waterparks

Wild Wadi Waterpark is now a Dubai landmark and an attraction in itself so we've included it in the Sights chapter; see p60 for details.

Water-skiing & Wakeboarding

If you are staying at a five-star hotel with a beach club, it costs Dh100 for a half-hour of water-skiing. If you are not a guest at one of these places you will also have to pay the daily admission fee to the beach club (usually about Dh60 to Dh200). For the best conditions and equipment, try the following Dubai Water Sports Association.

DUBAI WATER SPORTS ASSOCIATION
Map pp214-15

☎ 324 0131; Bur Dubai side of the Creek; skiing/ wakeboarding per 15min Dh45/60, plus admission Dh15; ⏲ 8am-6pm

Good equipment and staff make this the best option to get behind a boat. The admission fee is to get into the club and use the pool, deck chairs or Jacuzzi, or hang out at the bar and restaurant. To get here from the Deira side of the Creek, head along Al-Qataiyat Rd towards Al-Garhoud Bridge. Take the first exit on the right after

THE UBIQUITOUS CAMEL

When you drive out of Dubai's city limits you'll notice signs stating 'Beware of Road Surprises' and perhaps the biggest surprise (well, besides the woeful driving!) is the fact that you'll spot camels ambling along the median strip or grazing by the side of the road. The camel is of great symbolic importance to the Bedouin as their nomadic nature meant that the camel was the primary means of transport when they moved camp. The camel has enormous stamina and can go without water for up to two weeks, an asset that is vital when travelling through the Empty Quarter.

However, the camel is more than just a figurative nod to the past – you can still buy camel milk in supermarkets (verdict? it's an acquired taste…), the wool of the lamb is still used, and a calf is still slaughtered for celebrations such as weddings. There's even supposed to be camel-milk chocolate on the way! Due to the popularity of camel racing, breeding a better racing camel has seen artificial insemination and embryo transfer become an everyday thing – and yes, test-tube camels are a reality. So is a 'cama', a cross between a llama and camel, which we're not sure whether to milk, or shear and make a sweater from.

Even harder to fathom is how the robotic camel jockeys set to replace the human variety are actually going to work. Looking like *Star Wars'* 3CPO going to a fancy dress party as a jockey, these robots are fitted with shock absorbers and a GPS system and are remote controlled by their handlers from their speeding 4WDs. Quite a long way from the simple days when a good camel was the difference between making that next well or perishing in the unforgiving desert. For a wonderful account of the importance of the camel, read *The Arabian Sands* by Wilfred Thesiger.

the Dubai Police Club. Continue past the nursery and turn right just before the Dubai Docking Yard. The tarmac road ends here, but continues along a sand track for 1.4km as it skirts around a large fenced-in compound. At this point you'll see the club ahead and to your right.

WATCHING SPORT
BOAT RACING
DUBAI INTERNATIONAL MARINE CLUB Map pp214-15
☎ 399 4111; www.dimc-uae.com; Al-Sufouh Rd, Le Meridien Mina Seyahi

Outside the summer months, the Dubai International Marine Club (DIMC) has a busy calendar of boating events, from the Class One World Powerboat Championship powerboat races (usually in December) to the far gentler, more elegant dhow racing.

The Class One World Powerboat Championship races see the boats reaching speeds of up to 255km/h, with Dubai's Victory team always a strong contender.

Wooden powerboat racing is gaining popularity in Dubai as well and the races are open only to UAE nationals with the boats using standard outboard engines. Wooden boats of a slightly older vintage race under sail – large dhows similar in size to the ones you see on the Creek. Races take place every weekend from October to May at the DIMC.

Call the Race Department of the DIMC for more information and the exact dates of any of these events, or visit the website. Admission is generally free and entertainment is provided for kids.

CAMEL RACING
DUBAI CAMEL RACECOURSE
Map pp214-15
☎ 338 2324; off Oud Metha Rd, near Nad al-Sheba Club

Camel racing is a traditional sport in the UAE and was originally practised at weddings and special events. These days, however, it's a huge business with races held from October to April every Thursday and Friday. While the use of very young jockeys

Camel trainers head home after morning track work at Dubai Camel Racecourse (above)

has been a contentious issue in the past, be assured that the practice does not exist anymore in Dubai and the introduction of robot jockeys is well underway (see the boxed text, p116).

Watching these ships of the desert racing at speeds of up to 60km/h is quite a sight and really only matched by the rather erratic driving of the owners who race around the inside of the track urging on their pride and joy. Races usually start around 7am and continue until about 9am. If you miss out on a race meeting you can usually catch training sessions each morning at about the same time or at around 5.30pm – it's quite startling just how many camels there are training.

CRICKET

SHARJAH CRICKET STADIUM

☎ 06-532 2991; 2nd Industrial Rd, Industrial Area 5, Sharjah

Cricket lovers probably know about the surprising move of the International Cricket Council to Dubai after 96 years at Lord's, the home of cricket. However, at present, international cricket in the UAE is held in nearby Sharjah (p156), where matches are hosted over the winter months.

MOTOR RACING

DESERT RALLYING

Motor sports are very popular with Emiratis and the Emirates Motor Sports Federation has a calendar of events throughout the year, with the important events being

---

ALL BETS ARE OFF...

Because gambling is not permitted under Islam, you would be forgiven for thinking that the Dubai World Cup would be a rather sombre affair. However, any event where there's a purse upwards of US$20 million is going to generate a charge in the air! With all this serious money about, there are some seriously rich people who attend the event and Dubai's social set have the date of the Cup set in stone in their calendars.

While the thoroughbreds compete eagerly on the track, the 'Fashions on the Field' competition is just as hard fought. Here women fight veneered tooth and manicured nail for prizes and the opportunity for their name to be misspelt in a daily newspaper photo caption. Do we need to mention that there are an awful lot of silly hats worn? And while there's no gambling, there's plenty of free-flowing champagne, social networking and expats desperate to find out how they can upgrade from being VIP to VVIP. There's also some horse racing, but most expats don't seem to notice.

---

held in the cooler months. A round of the FIA Cross Country Rally World Cup, the **UAE Desert Challenge** (www.uaedesertchallenge.com), attracts top rally drivers from all over the world and is held in November, starting in Abu Dhabi and finishing in Dubai. There are a number of smaller rally events during February and March, including the 1000 Dunes Rally and the Spring Desert Rally, which are both 4WD events. Visit the website of the **Emirates Motor Sports Federation** (www.emsfuae.com) for more details.

CRICKET CRAZY

If you're visiting Dubai from a cricket-playing country, be prepared to at least know a little about your national team – even if you're not a cricket fan! In the years that we've lived here, nearly every conversation with an Indian or Pakistani taxi driver has gone directly from 'we're Australian' to the driver discussing the successes, failures and personal lives of the Australian cricket team, usually in more detail than we knew ourselves.

When wandering through Bur Dubai, you'll notice a sure sign that there's an international match on: the huge groups of Indians and Pakistanis gathered outside local eateries with their eyes glued to a TV. Because most of these workers can't afford the price of satellite TV, everyone meets up at their local eatery to watch the match.

But these guys aren't just couch commentators. Every afternoon and every weekend, almost every empty car park and vacant block is host to a mini test match. While the equipment might vary (we've seen everything from bricks for wickets to teams in full cricket whites!), the intensity is the same. And don't assume the heat of summer is a deterrent. Taking a taxi from the airport one roasting August night when the mercury must have been a sweat bead short of 40˚C, we saw several games underway in a floodlit car park. 'Why are they playing at 3am?', we asked the Indian taxi driver. 'Because it's cooler at night', he deadpanned.

DUBAI AUTODROME

☎ 367 8700; www.dubaiautodrome.com;
off Emirates Rd (take Interchange No 4 on Sheikh
Zayed Rd), south of Dubai centre
Probably your best chance to witness
some live motor sport (other than watching other drivers on their way from Dubai
to Abu Dhabi!) is at the new Dubai Autodrome. This 5.39km circuit and complex
is host to a round of the burgeoning A1
Grand Prix circuit (www.a1gp.com), where
drivers compete as representatives of their
country. Oddly, despite its being a Dubai
initiative, there's no UAE team – the closest
being Team Lebanon, who only occasionally manage to finish a lap. New events are
being added to the Autodrome calendar
all the time, so check the website for more
details.

HORSE RACING
NAD AL-SHEBA CLUB Map pp214-15
☎ 336 3666; www.nadalshebaclub.com;
Nad al-Sheba District, 5km southeast of Dubai centre; general admission free, admission to members'
stand from Dh60
The Dubai-based Godolphin (www.godolphin
.com) stables are well known to the many
horse-racing enthusiasts around the world,
and the love of the Arabian thoroughbred
runs deeply through the blood of the
Emiratis. While the season of racing starts
in November, the Dubai International Racing Carnival (running from late January to
the end of March) is the time when things
really hot up. The season culminates in the
Dubai World Cup (www.dubaiworldcup.com),
the world's richest horse race, with prize
money of a dizzying US$6 million and a
total purse for the event of over US$20
million.

Nad al-Sheba's races are held at night
from about 7pm, the members' stand
is licensed and there are different food
and beverage packages available. Check
the website of the Emirates Racing Association
(www.emiratesracing.com) for the exact
dates of race meetings throughout the
year. Even if you don't like horse racing the
meets will provide you with some great
people-watching experiences. Horse racing
fans should also look out for the morning stable tour (see p57) – make sure you
pencil it into your Dubai calendar.

GOLF
EMIRATES GOLF CLUB Map pp214-15
☎ 347 3222; Interchange No 5, Sheikh Zayed Rd
The Dubai Desert Classic (www.dubaidesertclassic
.com) attracts some of the best golfers in
the world. Many golf-crazy expats take the
week off to watch the competitors tackle
their local course. The event, which is held in
late February or early March at the Emirates
Golf Club, has seen some thrilling finishes
over the past couple of years, and the 18th
hole has become somewhat legendary. The
tickets are Dh175 per day for adults, but
are only available for purchase at outlets in
Dubai at present.

TENNIS

DUBAI TENNIS STADIUM Map pp218-19

☎ 316 0101; www.dubaitennischampionships
.com; Al-Garhoud

The Dubai Tennis Championships are held over two weeks from late February to early March. The tournament consists of a Women's Tennis Association (WTA) event followed by an Association of Tennis Professionals (ATP) event. After several years of the men's event not attracting the big names, it's now firmly on par with the women's event. Tennis lovers will enjoy the bonus that the small stadium offers – a close-up view of the world's best heavy hitters in action.

RUGBY

DUBAI EXILES RUGBY CLUB

Map pp214-15

☎ 333 1198; www.dubaiexiles.com;
Ras al-Khor Rd, near the Dubai Country Club

This club hosts one of the biggest events on both the sporting and social calendars, the Dubai Rugby 7s (www.dubairugby7s.com). Held every year (for over 35 years now!) in early December, the final of this three-day almost Bacchanalian festival of rugby and drinking is now host to over 30,000 spectators crammed into a temporary stadium. If you're interested in attending (highly recommended for sports fans), book well ahead. Tickets become very scarce in the days leading up to the event.

Shopping

Shopping

Just when we thought shopping in Dubai couldn't get any better, it did. But it also got a whole lot more bizarre...

Once upon a time, it all started with Mercato Mall and its preposterous Venetian-cum-Florentine architecture, but then, in true Dubai 'the land where dreams come true' style (where supermarkets regularly give away free cars and airport raffles make frequent millionaires of flyers) more and more incredible malls began to magically sprout all over the city.

The wondrous Souq Madinat Jumeirah is a modern interpretation of an old Arabian bazaar in the enchanting Madinat Jumeirah hotel and entertainment complex. If that fairy-tale world isn't 'make believe' enough, you can head to Ibn Battuta Mall, replete with starry skies, indoor palm trees, massive decorated domes, an enormous 13th-century Elephant Water Clock and a life-size Chinese junk. It's actually six different malls in one, and its design is inspired by 14th-century Arab traveller Ibn Battuta's epic journeys to China, India, Persia, Egypt, Tunisia and Andalusia. You can do an educational tour with an ancient storyteller, take a (virtual) magic carpet ride, and also do some shopping. If it isn't enough to have to travel from 'China' to 'Spain' if you want to buy some groceries and shop for electronics in the same trip, you can trek across the marble floors of the monumental Mall of the Emirates, currently the biggest shopping centre in the region, with an indoor ski park, where, of course, it snows every night. The soon-to-open gargantuan Dubai Mall will perhaps be the most amazing of them all – the largest in the world, with 12 million square feet of retail space, and the world's tallest building, Burj Dubai, towering over it.

Vilified in other parts of the world, air-conditioned malls with their trickling fountains and cold marble floors make great sense in Dubai's oppressive heat – they're oases for city dwellers. And for a city without a centre, the malls are like traditional town squares with their entertainment stages, surrounded by Starbucks cafés and their shopping arcades dotted with barrows laden with local souvenirs. When the older crowd have filled their shopping carts at Carrefour, they settle in at a café to watch the world go by. When the young Emiratis aren't sauntering by using Bluetooth to send their mobile numbers to each other, the young national women spend their pocket money or monthly salaries at ProMod or Paris Gallery, while the national guys buy the latest cool gadgets at Plug-Ins or the Mac Shop.

Shopping in Dubai is still as satisfying as exploring the extraordinary edifices that house the stores. Many of the new malls offer much more of the same – lots of glitz and glam with exclusive designers like Gucci and Dolce and Gabbana, international style franchises such as Zara and Mango, and additional branches of Dubai businesses (Damas, Magrudy's, etc). But there are also some interesting new independent shops not found elsewhere in the city, such as exotic Mumbai Se and whimsical Ginger and Lace at Ibn Battuta Mall, and funky Lebanese fashion store Aizone and sublime Norwegian skincare product house Pixi at Mall of the Emirates.

DUBAI'S SHOPPING FESTIVALS

Held every year from mid-January to mid-February, the month-long **Dubai Shopping Festival** (www.mydsf.com) brings in hoards of tourists from around the world. This is the best time to visit Dubai – aside from the massively reduced stuff on sale in the souqs and malls, the weather is gorgeous and the city is abuzz. Outdoor souqs, amusement rides, and stalls selling food from around the world are set up in many neighbourhoods, with the best on the Bur Dubai waterfront across from the British Embassy. There's family entertainment across the city, traditional performances and displays at the Heritage and Diving Villages, concerts and events in the parks, and nightly fireworks, best viewed from Creekside Park. Dubai Summer Surprises is a similar event held in July and August that mainly attracts visitors from other Gulf countries – the only people capable of surviving the soaring summer temperatures.

For many, scouring the souqs is still the quintessential Dubai shopping experience. For locals, the souqs are like the morning market for Europeans. There's the fish souq for fresh seafood, a fruit-and-vegetable souq, the spice souq for herbs and spices…and even a camel souq! For the expat an occasional visit to the souq is a reminder that there's a vibrant world in their backyard that they too often take for granted. For visitors to Dubai, nothing compares to the atmosphere and chaos of the souq – the colours and textures, the cacophony of sounds, the street hawkers competing for customers and the call to prayer echoing off the walls of the narrow lanes. You can trawl the souqs for Bedouin jewellery, Palestinian embroidery, curly-toed Aladdin slippers, Oriental perfumes, frankincense and oud, cheap electronics and fake designer brands.

Souqs are found on either side of Dubai Creek and the backstreets of Karama, while malls are scattered around the city. All are easy to reach by taxi. All malls have food-halls, restaurants, ATMs and exchange offices. The lack of duty and taxes, and cheap shipping costs, mean that visiting Dubai for shopping alone makes a trip worthwhile.

Opening Hours

Most malls in Dubai open from 10am to 10pm Saturday to Tuesday, from 10am to midnight Wednesday to Friday (weekends), and even later during Dubai Shopping Festival and Ramadan (often until 1am). Traditionally, souqs and independent shops (outside of malls) have closed during the afternoon for a few hours for prayer, lunch and rest, and haven't opened on Fridays until late afternoon, but that's changing and these days many are remaining open all day – business is just too good to close. Malls buzz on Friday nights – if you hate crowds stay clear; otherwise, mark it on your calendar for excellent people-watching.

CLOTHING SIZES
Measurements approximate only, try before you buy

Women's Clothing						
Aus/UK	8	10	12	14	16	18
Europe	36	38	40	42	44	46
Japan	5	7	9	11	13	15
USA	6	8	10	12	14	16

Women's Shoes						
Aus/USA	5	6	7	8	9	10
Europe	35	36	37	38	39	40
France only	35	36	38	39	40	42
Japan	22	23	24	25	26	27
UK	3½	4½	5½	6½	7½	8½

Men's Clothing						
Aus	92	96	100	104	108	112
Europe	46	48	50	52	54	56
Japan	S		M	M		L
UK/USA	35	36	37	38	39	40

Men's Shirts (Collar Sizes)						
Aus/Japan	38	39	40	41	42	43
Europe	38	39	40	41	42	43
UK/USA	15	15½	16	16½	17	17½

Men's Shoes						
Aus/UK	7	8	9	10	11	12
Europe	41	42	43	44½	46	47
Japan	26	27	27½	28	29	30
USA	7½	8½	9½	10½	11½	12½

Bargaining

Bargaining becomes an obsession for some, determined to save as many dirhams as they can, while others will do anything to avoid it, immediately accepting the first figure offered. Keep in mind that the first price suggested by spruikers in souqs is rarely realistic. Neither is your counter-offer of half, but that will enable the bargaining process to begin and get you closer to a compromise, and ultimately a price both parties can live with.

Confidence comes with practice. Having a friend on hand helps too. You'll get a better discount if you buy more than one piece. You can also have a go at 'good cop, bad cop', getting your pal to play the cynic, feign disinterest, and try to drag you away – the shopkeeper will reduce the price faster rather than lose a sale. Prices can drop by 20% to 50%, but once the vendor agrees to your figure, you're expected to pay. Going on to offer a lower price is an insult, and leaving the store empty-handed is impolite. Remember, you may want to return – leaving on good terms will get you a greater discount when you go back. When shopping in malls, forget bargaining in franchises, but always ask for the 'best price' in independently owned shops – you can always expect discounts on carpets, perfumes and electronics.

Best Buys

GOLD

The City of Gold's shining reputation is based on the sheer range of jewellery available (700 jewellery stores in Dubai, with almost 300 at the Gold Souq and over 100 at the Gold & Diamond Park), and low prices. Dubai's low import duties and no tax mean it's one of the cheapest places in the world to buy gold. Tradition alone keeps business booming – in India and the Gulf countries, gifts of gold for a bride's dowry must be new and brides gleam heavily with the stuff on their wedding day. And while gold souq shop windows prominently display the ornate necklaces, earrings and headpieces worn by Indian and Arabian brides – these are the ones that get jaws dropping and cameras flashing – head inside and you'll find every style conceivable, from extravagant, intricately detailed pieces to more sleek contemporary designs. Although gold glitters most in Dubai, there's also an impressive variety of silver, diamonds, pearls and gems. If you don't find anything to your taste, you can have something made. Either way you can feel confident that what you're buying is authentic: local laws are strict, Dubai Municipality does regular quality checks and gold traders wouldn't dare risk their reputation in such a competitive environment. Look for the gold purity hallmark, get a detailed invoice, and ask for a Certificate of Authenticity for diamonds and gems. While gold is sold by weight and prices fluctuate, the gold rate is fixed twice daily, according to international rates, by the Gold and Jewellery Group – check www.dubaicityofgold.com for rates. Prices still vary depending on whether the piece was made by machine or hand, and the intricacy of the design. But this is Dubai, so there's always room to bargain!

TOP FIVE GOLD & JEWELLERY STOPS

- Gold Souq (p51), Deira
- Azza Fahmy Jewellery (p134), Sheikh Zayed Rd
- Gold & Diamond Park (p135), Sheikh Zayed Rd
- Damas Jewellery (p130), Wafi City
- Tiffany & Co (p134), BurJuman Centre

Azza Fahmy Jewellery (p134) uses Arabic calligraphy in unique pieces on display

CARPETS

Dubai is a carpet-lover's paradise! Fine Persian carpets, colourful Turkish and Kurdish kilims, rough Bedouin rugs…whatever you want, they're all widely available and Dubai has a reputation in the region for having the highest-quality carpets at the best prices. The only problem is that each year the prices creep up as more and more visitors come here to shop.

GLOBAL VILLAGE

Much to the delight of Dubai residents, glorious **Global Village** (www.globalvillage.ae; adult/family Dh5/15 at time of writing, admission likely to change; 🕐 4pm–midnight), previously only open for the month-long Shopping Festival, now has a permanent home at Dubailand, from October to March each year. It's part fun fair and part world souq, where scores of countries set up pavilions to showcase their cultures and sell national products. Our favourites are Afghanistan for wild wedding jewellery, Palestine for colourful traditional cross-stitch *kandouras* (casual shirt-dresses) and cushion covers, Yemen for its authentic *khanjars* (daggers), India for the cheapest spangly slippers around (Dh25!) and Kenya for its kitsch bottle-top handbags. In between shopping you can enjoy everything from Chinese opera to Turkey's whirling dervishes. It's buzziest late at night! We can't wait until 2007 when we're promised it will be a year-round event. The only downer is the new location, best reached by car or taxi.

Bargaining is expected, but if you're having difficulty getting the price you want, just head to another store – there are hundreds of them. Dubai's malls have the greatest number of carpet shops, while the streets around Baniyas Sq and Sharjah souqs also have a good selection. When you buy a carpet ask for a certificate of authentication guaranteed by the Dubai Chamber of Commerce & Industry, so you can be sure that the carpet from Isfahan you're about to spend Dh4000 on is actually from Isfahan. For more information on carpets and what to look for when buying one, see the boxed text, below, and our recommended books (see Best Carpet Buying Books, below).

ARABIAN HANDICRAFTS & SOUVENIRS

'Arabian' handicrafts have proven as popular with Dubai visitors in recent times as carpets, gold and perfume. The Oriental décor of many of the city's fabulous hotels, restaurants and bars seems to inspire travellers to pack away little pieces of exotica to recreate their own Arabian palaces back home. If you fancy such frequent flights of the imagination, a visit to the souqs will enable you to fill your bags with coloured

> ## BEST CARPET BUYING BOOKS
>
> - *Persian Rugs and Carpets: their History and Symbolism* by Essie Sakhai
> - *Oriental Rugs, A Complete Guide* by Murray L Eiland Jr and Murray Eiland the Third
> - *The Carpets, Rugs and Kilims of the World* by Enza Milanesi
> - *Kilims, a Buyer's Guide* by Lee Allane
> - *Tribal Rugs* by James Opie

glasses and lanterns from Morocco, mother-of-pearl inlaid wooden furniture from Syria, brass Arabian coffee pots and Aladdin lamps, Turkish miniature paintings, and embroidered Indian wall hangings and cushion covers with wonderful mirror-work. Colourful Indian saris make wonderful curtains, while Kashmiri shawls look great on tables and sideboards. Add some foldable wooden legs to a decorated metal food platter and you have a cool coffee table. Get some colourful camel bags made into cube-shaped ottomans and you'll have one funky Oriental *majlis* when you get home!

Sheesha pipes (aka hubbly bubblies and nargilehs) make memorable souvenirs. The smaller pipes are generally only used for decoration and don't work, so if you intend to use it, opt for a complete *sheesha* kit in a hard case, which includes all the little accessories you'll need and makes it easy to transport. *Sheesha* pipes and the flavoured tobacco are available from souqs, specialist stores, tobacconists, supermarkets and souvenir shops. (See p98 for a lesson in how to use your *sheesha* pipe.)

If you're looking for something for family and friends, silver prayer holders, wooden inlaid boxes, tinted glass perfume bottles and kitsch souvenirs (see p126) make unique presents. For Dad, go for a framed *khanjar* (dagger) or silver gunpowder horn. Mum will appreciate a new pashmina – there are hundreds of colours and styles with beads and embroidery, and pashminas fringed with pom-poms are proving increasingly popular. For children, you can't go wrong with a cute camel gift: plush cuddly camels that play Arabian music when

Shopping

CARPET BUYING 101

You don't need to do a course to learn about buying carpets but you will learn some hard lessons and waste a lot of money if you don't do some research. Do your homework to identify what kind of carpets, rugs or kilims you like. Ask a lot of questions and bargain hard over a long time to get the best price. Patience and persistence are important. A love of tea is also essential – along with the unrolling of scores of carpets, this is part of the ritual. Visit a number of shops and compare the quality and prices. Flip the corner of the rug over – the more knots per square inch, the greater the quality. Compare carpets and examine the design – the more intricate the detail, the higher the price. Silk carpets are more valuable than wool, and natural dyes more expensive than artificial. Antique rugs are naturally dyed and appear slightly faded (this isn't a flaw). Don't hesitate to let the seller know if you saw a similar carpet for less elsewhere, but no matter how excited you are by a carpet, never show it. In fact, feign indecisiveness over several carpets and you'll probably be offered a discount for two. Take a friend – four sales are better than two and you'll get a better deal in the end.

you squeeze them, carved wooden, brass or leather stuffed camels, or camel mouse pads. The Camel Company (p136) has the best selection. For something different, check out the bright-painted pencil holders and boxes featuring Emirati scenes in a naïve style, from Gifts and Souvenirs at Karama Souq (p133). Julia Johnston's illustrated story books also make great gifts – get them from Magrudy's (p130).

Browse in the souvenir and handicraft stores in City Centre, Mall of the Emirates and Souq Madinat Jumeirah for the highest-quality stuff, but head to Karama Shopping Centre (also known as Karama Souq), Bur Dubai and Deira souqs for the lowest prices. Also check out the stalls at the Heritage and Diving Villages (p55).

> ## TOP FIVE HANDICRAFTS & SOUVENIR SHOPS
>
> - Al-Jaber Gallery (p129), Deira City Centre
> - Al-Orooba Oriental (p132), BurJuman Centre
> - 2000 Horizon Antique (p134), Karama Shopping Centre
> - Gift World (p133), Karama Shopping Centre
> - Showcase Antiques, Arts & Frames (p138)

KITSCH SOUVENIRS

While the ultimate kitsch souvenir was once a colourful mosque clock that irritatingly wakes you with the call to prayer, the souqs and souvenir shop shelves are now overflowing with lots of crazy stuff: glass Burj Al Arab paperweights, wooden Russian dolls painted as Emiratis, Barbie and Ken dolls in traditional Emirati dress, camel-sign fridge magnets, key rings dangling with miniatures of Dubai's iconic architectural highlights, a Saddam Hussein Ace of Spades Shocker Lighter, and coffee mugs and baseball caps with Sheikh Zayed or Sheikh Mohammed waving at you. Karama Souq (p133) is home to the most bizarre stuff.

BEDOUIN JEWELLERY

Bedouin jewellery is a brilliant buy in Dubai and has become increasingly popular since bo-ho ethnic style became hip again. Look out for elaborate silver necklaces and pendants, chunky earrings and rings, and wedding belts, often incorporating coral, turquoise and semiprecious stones. While some of the older Bedouin jewellery comes from the Emirates, most is from Oman, Yemen and Afghanistan. Generally, the Omani jewellery is produced with good-quality silver and is more intricate in its detail and design; the Yemeni jewellery is more elaborate and chunkier; and the Afghani jewellery, while often cheap-looking, is the most interesting, embellished with coloured beads, ribbon or tiny mirrors. Like gold, silver jewellery is sold by weight and you'll pay more for intricate workmanship and quality, but the shopkeeper often has a fixed price for these items. There is also a lot of 'Bedouin-inspired' and other beaded ethnic silver jewellery about that is made in India – you'll pay a lot less in Dubai than you will in little boutiques in London or Paris. There are some wonderful, fun necklaces, bracelets and earrings embellished with beads, charms and trinkets. You can also buy Bedouin jewellery displayed (like *khanjars*) in glass-covered picture frames, or you buy the jewellery and frame it yourself when you get home.

KHANJARS

Visit the Al Ain camel souq or the bullfights at Fujairah and you'll see old Emirati men wearing *khanjars* (daggers) over their *dishdashas* (men's shirt-dress). Traditionally, *khanjar* handles were made from rhino horn, though today they are often made from wood. Regular *khanjars* have two rings where the belt is attached, and its scabbard is decorated with thin silver wire – the intricacy of the wire thread pattern and the skill with which it is executed are what determine its value. Sayidi *khanjars* have five rings and are often covered entirely in silver sheet, with little or no wire used, and its quality is assessed by its weight and workmanship. A *khanjar* is a substantial item and ought to feel heavy when you pick it up. Don't believe anyone who tells you your *khanjar* is 'very old' – few will be more than 30 to 40 years old. Buy a *khanjar* based on quality of workmanship, but buy it most of all because you like it.

PERFUME & INCENSE

Attars (Arabian perfumes) are strong and spicy. They had to be! When there was precious little water in the Arabian deserts to wash, and before the days of air-conditioning, Arab women would smother themselves in *attars* and incense to disguise the smell of perspiration. When you pass Emirati women on the street you'll catch a whiff of their exotic perfume. If you like what you smell, you'll find Arabian perfume shops in all the Dubai malls, but it's more fun to visit the Perfume Souq (p52), a small area along Sikkat al-Khail St in Deira, just east of the Gold Souq, lined with perfume stores. Shopkeepers will daub you senseless with various perfumes, and if you buy a few – remember to bargain! – you'll go home with a gift bag of tiny samples. It is sold by the *tolah* (12mL or 12g) and prices vary, depending on the perfume. The expensive concentrated scents are made from agar wood from Malaysia. Perfume shops also sell an enormous range of incense in the form of oud (wood), rock, crystals or compressed powder. Frankincense (*luban* in Arabic) is probably the most common form of incense – the quality varies, with the best-quality product coming from the Dhofar region of southern Oman.

To burn incense, you can buy an electric incense burner or a traditional burner and a box of Magic Coal charcoal (it's Japanese, comes in a black box and is the longest-lasting coal) or heat beads. Set them alight over a gas burner or hotplate until they glow, then put a piece of frankincense on top of the charcoal. Frankincense alone might remind you of church, but add oud on top of that to get a sweet, rich log-fire smell. The colourful burners themselves make great souvenirs and many shops sell great gift sets that include everything you need.

TEXTILES

All types of vibrant (but sometimes very gaudy) textiles from India, Pakistan, Indonesia, Thailand, Korea and China are available at very cheap prices in the Bur Dubai Souq and its surrounding streets, especially along Al-Fahidi St. Costs naturally vary according to quality but silk, cotton and linen are good value. There are plenty of good tailors who work very quickly, so if you only have a few days in Dubai you'll have time to get something made. Curtain lengths could cost you as little as Dh10 a piece, while tailoring prices vary depending on the complexity of what you want, but start at around Dh30 for a shirt or skirt.

EXOTIC DELICACIES

Dubai is said to be the cheapest place outside Iran to buy Iranian caviar. It's sold at the speciality caviar shops, Caviar Classic (p136), and the deli counters at good supermarkets such as Carrefour. Saffron, from Iran and Spain, is also available for far less than you'd

---

TOP SHOPPING & EAT STREETS

Shopping and eating on these streets is best in the evening when it's buzziest, as many shops close in the afternoon.

Khalid bin al-Waleed Rd (Bank St), Bur Dubai (Map pp220–1, F4 & F5) Known as Computer Street, this is the place to head for software, hardware, laptops, personal organisers, computer accessories and shawarmas when you need to refuel.

Al-Fahidi St, Bur Dubai (Map pp220–1, F4 & G4) Textiles, tailors, saris, digital cameras and electronics, lots of cheap luggage to cart it back in, and Indian snacks to sate your appetite.

Al-Hisn St and 73 St, Bur Dubai (Map pp220–1, F4) Myriad sari shops, sequinned slippers, Asian hippy clothes, Bollywood music and movies, and food from Azerbaijan if you're feeling adventurous.

Sheikh Zayed Rd (Map p226, C4) Upmarket shopping at the Blvd at Emirates Towers and five-star hotel shopping arcades, with stylish cafés, *sheesha* spots and super restaurants in the hotels when you're hungry.

Al-Rigga Rd, Rigga (Map pp216–17, D5 & D6) Specialist *sheesha* shops, Iranian and Syrian sweet shops, discount gift stores, Al Ghurair City, Internet cafés, fast food and cheap Arabian eating at outdoor restaurants like Automatic.

Al-Dhiyafah, Satwa, between al-Satwa Rd and al-Mina Rd (Map pp224–5, H5 & H6) A giant Book Corner, sheesha pipe shops, Syrian handicrafts, Lebanese Sweet Palace, Internet cafés, outdoor restaurants and shawarma stands.

Al-Satwa Rd, Satwa, between Al-Dhiyafah Rd and Al-Hudheiba Rd (Map pp224–5, G6 & H6) The place to buy low-cost luggage, Arabic *majlis* sets, cheap *kandouras* and textiles alongside Indian sweet shops.

pay back home and can be bought in the spice souq or supermarkets. Scrumptious honey from Saudi Arabia and Oman is another wonderful product sold in Dubai. You'll find it in specialist shops in Satwa, in the spice souq and supermarkets. It ranges in colour from light golden to almost black, with the higher-priced honey collected by hand from remote areas in the mountains and deserts of Oman.

ELECTRONICS

If it plugs into a wall you can buy it in Dubai – the selection is huge and once again, due to minimal duties and the tax-free environment, Dubai is the cheapest place in the region to buy electronics and digital technology. Do your own research because the quality of service and knowledge of sales staff varies tremendously. For the lowest prices and no-name brands, head to Al-Fahidi St in Bur Dubai and an area around Al-Sabkha and Al-Maktoum

Shopping

SOUQ TO SOUQ

Bur Dubai Souq (Map pp220–1) Under the restored wooden arcades and wind-towers, you'll discover scores of shops selling textiles, cheap clothes, souvenir T-shirts and mosque alarm clocks, along with a few Arabian 'antique' stores. In the surrounding streets you can buy a sari (they make great curtains!), have a suit made, bargain for electronics, pick up some Bollywood tapes, and haggle for cheap luggage to take it all home in! Don't miss the tiniest and most atmospheric alley of them all, 'Hindi Lane' (p55), between the Hindu and Sikh temples. Little shops sell religious paraphernalia, colourful Buddhas, bindis and incense.

Deira Covered Souq (Map pp216–17) Best visited at night, Deira's souqs actually comprise a couple of sprawling markets – the covered Naif Souq (between Naif South St, 9A St and Deira St) and the Deira Covered Souq (between Al-Sabkha Rd, 67 St and Naif Rd), which isn't really 'covered' but consists of warrens of tiny shops on narrow lanes. Even if you're not keen on taking home cheap textiles, *kandouras*, kitchenware or walking sticks, just take in the bustling atmosphere. The local girls shop Naif Souq for fake Dior and YSL *shaylas*, which make stylish shawls and scarves.

Deira Gold Souq (Map pp216–17) While the entrances to the Gold Souq (on Suq Deira and Old Baladiya Sts) are easily spotted by the large wooden lattice arches, the gold glittering from the hundreds of stores within make it hard to miss. Plan on buying something – gold is a great investment. Otherwise, just enjoy ogling the elaborate jewellery displayed in the windows – that's if you can push your way past the tourists taking photos of each other! Most impressive are the ornate Indian and Arabian designs, intended for a bride's dowry – by the look of them they're too heavy to wear anyway!

Deira Spice Souq (Map pp216–17) For an authentic whiff of Arabia wander around this atmospheric Spice Souq (also known as Deira Old Souq), because you'll find more than cinnamon and saffron here. In the narrow alleys that lead to Deira Covered Souq and Gold Souq you'll find the usual plastics, polyesters and porcelain, but stick to the main 'street' and you'll see and smell sacks overflowing with spices such as cardamom, cumin and star anise, vanilla pods and pulses, and dried fruit and nuts. The essential buy here is a bag of frankincense, or better yet, a beginner's incense kit that includes a small burner, oud and coal. (Make sure to get 'Magic Coal' brand: it lasts longer than the others.)

Marina Market, Dubai Marina (Map pp214–15; ☎ 050 244 5795; New Dubai; ⏰ 11am-7pm Fri during cooler months, 2-10pm during Ramadan) Safa Park's Palm Lane Market was a novelty for locals and expats alike, but for visitors to Dubai it was nothing special, something they could find back home. Marina Market manages to please everyone with local and international arts and crafts, ethnic jewellery, home-grown fashion and a sunny waterside location. Sara Moseley's photographs of Dubai make original souvenirs and look great in expat homes while market organiser Roslynne Bargugnan's cheeky 'Made in Dubai' and 'Expat Brat' T-shirts sell like soft drinks on a summer's afternoon. Don't miss Egyptian Rania El-Farouki's stall. She's helping keep the ancient Nubian art of *talli* alive by importing the delicate gold- and silver-threaded kaftans, scarves and shawls. This is the only place you'll find these beautiful products in Dubai; each design tells a story and your purchase will help keep a dying art from extinction.

Souq Al-Arsah, Sharjah (p157) While many of the Dubai souvenir and handicrafts shops now sell the same kind of stuff you'll find at this wonderful restored Sharjah souq, none have the authentic old Arabian atmosphere. There are a few stores selling authentic Arabian antiques and collectibles, while Madiq Hormoz (☎ 06-569 6026; Shop No 61–63) has the best selection and gives the best prices on colourful camel bags, Bedouin jewellery from Oman, fabulous chunky rings from Afghanistan and beautiful, mother-of-pearl inlaid antique guns from Yemen. Avoid the Dubai–Sharjah traffic by heading there mid-morning or evening.

Hospital Rds near Baniyas Sq known as the Electronics Souq (but make sure you try before you by!). However, if you want an international warranty, you're better off paying a little extra and heading to a mall, to Carrefour or Plug-Ins. Multi-region DVD players, digital cameras, PDAs and mobile phones vary in price enormously, but will probably be cheaper than they will be back home. For software and hardware, head to Khalid bin al-Waleed Rd (Bank St) in Bur Dubai between Al-Mankhool Rd and the Falcon Roundabout, known as Computer Street. For iPods and other Apple products try the Mac Store and Virgin. Shop around and compare prices before you buy.

DESIGNER FAKES

Although the Dubai authorities have cracked down on the sale of counterfeit merchandise, many shops in the souqs in Karama, Deira and Bur Dubai openly sell fake brand name goods, such as watches, handbags, sunglasses, shoes and clothes, along with pirated CDs, DVDs and software. Those that don't, keep their imitation gear under the counter, upstairs, or in the backroom, sending their spruikers out on the streets to hiss at you from a darkened lane, 'Gucci bag, madam? Rolex watch, sir? Copy DVD?'

DEIRA

AL-GHURAIR CITY

Map ppp216-17   Shopping Centre

☎ 223 2333; cnr Al-Rigga & Omar ibn al-Khattab Rds, Deira; ☽ 10am-10pm Sat-Thu, 5-10pm Fri

Every groovy young European is wearing a checked *keffiyah* (or *gutra* as we call them in the Gulf). Whether it's for Arab solidarity or just because they look cool, grab yours at Al-Ghurair City, *the* place to shop for national dress: stylish *abayas* and *shaylas*, quality leather sandals, and *dishdashas* in chocolate and slate (popular for winter). Also, Arabian perfumes, brand-name boutiques, Book Corner, fast food and cinemas.

AL-JABER GALLERY

Map ppp218-19   Handicrafts & Souvenirs

☎ 295 4114; Deira City Centre, Al-Garhoud Rd, near Dubai Creek Golf & Yacht Club, Deira; ☽ 10am-10pm Sat-Tue, 10am-midnight Wed-Fri

As permanent tattoos are now passé, buy a henna starter kit here and design your own temporary tattoos. Jam-packed with a huge range of tacky souvenirs, it's sometimes hard to find the quality handicrafts, but we love the wonderful colourful Indian bedspreads embellished with beads, and the 'hand of Fatima' mirrors.

AMINIAN PERSIAN CARPETS

Map ppp218-19   Carpets

☎ 295 5379; Deira City Centre, Al-Garhoud Rd, near Dubai Creek Golf & Yacht Club, Deira; ☽ 10am-10pm Sat-Thu, 2-10pm Fri

This trusted Iranian carpet specialist stocks a wide and fine selection of classic Persian carpets, along with more contemporary colourful, tribal kilims. This collection is far bigger than it looks at first.

BOOK CORNER Map ppp216-17   Books

☎ 228 2835; Al-Ghurair City, cnr Omar ibn al-Khattab & Al-Rigga Rds, Deira; ☽ 10am-10pm Sat-Thu, 2-10pm Fri

Staggering in size because of its selection in English and Arabic, Book Corner stocks

SUPERMARKET SOUVENIRS

Iranian Caviar Cheaper here than anywhere bar Iran, it's well matched with straight vodka and golden sunsets from your hotel balcony.

Cardamom-flavoured condensed milk Worth weighing down the baggage for this taste of Arabia when you return home.

Natco Rose Syrup Impress your dinner-party guests with rose-flavoured sorbet.

Zaatar and sumac Add zaatar (Arabian thyme-like herb) to your croissants and sumac (Arabian spice like paprika) to your salad to remember the good eating in Dubai.

Al Jazeera Arabian coffee We just love the veiled lady on the label!

specialities in travel and children's products. Look here for the 'Quran Challenge Game'! Despite having an expansive travel section (with lots of Lonely Planet titles and maps), the same guides have been here for years – they just keep adding new ones, so make sure you check the edition you're buying.

CARREFOUR

Map ppp218-19   Supermarket

☎ 295 1010; Deira City Centre, Al-Garhoud Rd, near Dubai Creek Golf & Yacht Club, Deira;
☺ 10am-10pm Sat-Tue, 10am-midnight Wed-Fri

This enormous French supermarket is popular with everyone from Emiratis to expats, who come here for freshly baked bread, seafood that's just flown in, Iranian caviar, foie gras, cheeses and juicy olives from around the region. It also has an excellent range of mobile phones, digital cameras and electronics, and often offer the best deals around.

DAMAS Map ppp218-19   Jewellery

☎ 295 3848; Deira City Centre, Al-Garhoud Rd, near Dubai Creek Golf & Yacht Club, Deira;
☺ 10am-10pm Sat-Tue, 10am-midnight Wed-Fri

Damas may not be the most innovative designer of jewellery around, but with over 50 stores in the city, it's the most trusted jeweller, and the best place to shop for classic pieces and designer names, including Fabergé and Tiffany & Co.

DEIRA CITY CENTRE

Map ppp218-19   Shopping Centre

☎ 295 1010; Al-Garhoud Rd, near Dubai Creek Golf & Yacht Club, Deira;
☺ 10am-10pm Sat-Tue, 10am-midnight Wed-Fri

Still Dubai's most popular place to spend, despite the bigger, better and more bizarre malls. With many shops, a special arcade devoted to carpets, souvenirs and handicrafts, the city's best supermarket, food courts, and a cinema complex, it's *the* place to be on a Thursday night.

EARLY LEARNING CENTRE

Map ppp218-19   Children's Toys

☎ 295 1548; Deira City Centre, Al-Garhoud Rd, near Dubai Creek Golf & Yacht Club, Deira;
☺ 10am-10pm Sat-Tue, 10am-midnight Wed-Fri

This popular store specialises in educational stuff that stimulates kids to think

and develop key skills. They're the kind of toys that don't get discarded after a few seconds so they're ideal for keeping kids entertained if you're on the road.

MAGRUDY'S Map ppp218-19   Books

☎ 295 7744; Deira City Centre, Al-Garhoud Rd, near Dubai Creek Golf & Yacht Club, Deira;
☺ 10am-10pm Sat-Tue, 10am-midnight Wed-Fri

Head here for Dubai's widest range of English-language books plus excellent sections on travel, language and children's literature. There's also a good selection of books on Middle East history and politics, and all the coffee-table books on Dubai. Magrudy's also holds also occasional book signings. We only wish it would improve the magazine section! More branches but this is the best.

MIKYAJY Map ppp218-19   Cosmetics

☎ 295 7844; Deira City Centre, Al-Garhoud Rd, near Dubai Creek Golf & Yacht Club, Deira;
☺ 10am-10pm

The Gulf's own home-grown make-up line, Mikyaji was developed to suit the colouring of Arabian girls, but its popularity has extended to foreigners due to its fantastic vibrant colours, such as turquoise, fuchsia and tangerine. Check it out.

PLUG-INS Map ppp218-19   Electronics

☎ 295 1010; Deira City Centre, Al-Garhoud Rd, near Dubai Creek Golf & Yacht Club, Deira;
☺ 10am-10pm

From tiny digital cameras (head here when you leave yours in the back seat of a taxi cab) to home cinemas, MP3 players and personal organisers, Plug-Ins has a huge range of digital technology, and usually at the lowest prices, but always check Carrefour as well.

PRIDE OF KASHMIR

Map ppp218-19   Carpets & Handicrafts

☎ 295 0655; Deira City Centre, Al-Garhoud Rd, near Dubai Creek Golf & Yacht Club, Deira;
☺ 10am-10pm

Boasting fine Kashmiri and Persian silk carpets with 400 to1600 knots per square inch, silky pashmina shawls and whole array of luxe homeware, including velvet patchwork bedspreads, embroidered throws and sequined cushion covers.

RITUALS Map pp218-19   Cosmetics
☎ 294 1432; Deira City Centre, Al-Garhoud Rd, near Dubai Creek Golf & Yacht Club, Deira; ⏰ 10am-10pm
Head here for balance-restoring products focused around personal rituals: purifying rituals, energising rituals, relaxing rituals…even laundry rituals! Great products for travellers: energising Fujiyama mandarin and mint shower gel is invigorating after a day in the sun, lotus-flower massage oil is ideal for weary bodies, and travel-size Samurai Secret ginger and basil men's shaving balm fits snugly in the backpack.

VIRGIN MEGASTORE Map ppp218-19   Music
☎ 295 8599; Deira City Centre, Al-Garhoud Rd, near Dubai Creek Golf & Yacht Club, Deira; ⏰ 10am-10pm
Despite branches all over Dubai (including an enormous Mall of the Emirates store with a great book section), this is still our favourite for its mind-boggling selection of Middle Eastern music (traditional oud, Um Kalthoum, Fairouz, Oriental lounge and chill-out) and good selection of regional DVDs (from Egyptian musicals to Iranian

These curly-toed Aladdin slippers, found at the Bur Dubai Souq (p53), are a popular souvenir

art-house to Palestinian Elia Suleiman's *Divine Intervention*). A café and DJ booth keep things lively.

WOMEN'S SECRET
Map pp218-19   Women's Clothing
☎ 295 9665; Deira City Centre, Al-Garhoud Rd, near Dubai Creek Golf & Yacht Club, Deira; ⏰ 10am-10pm
This sassy Spanish label keeps girls coming back for more each season with its global-inspired underwear, swimwear and nightwear – expect to slip into anything from cute Mexican cross-stitched bra and pants sets to Moroccan-style kaftan-like nightdresses. More branches but we think this is the best.

ZARA Map ppp218-19   Clothing
☎ 294 0839; Deira City Centre, Al-Garhoud Rd, near Dubai Creek Golf & Yacht Club, Deira; ⏰ 10am-10pm
Another successful Spanish franchise, stylish Zara now has stores all over the city, but this one, the first in Dubai, still has the largest offering of hip, highly affordable clothes and accessories for women, men and children.

BUR DUBAI
AJMAL Map ppp220-1   Perfume
☎ 269 0102; BurJuman Centre, cnr Khalid bin al-Waleed (Bank St) & Sheikh Khalifa bin Zayed Rds, Bur Dubai; ⏰ 10am-10pm Sat-Thu, 4-10pm Fri
Often crowded with old local women in burqas waving the smoky aromas of burning oud under their *abayas*, this is the most popular maker of heady Arabian *attars* (perfumes and essential oils) in the region. Testing the perfumes is part of the fun, but try 'Zikra Al Nawaaem', an exotic spicy sandalwood-based scent in an ornate gold bottle.

AL AIN SHOPPING CENTRE
Map ppp220-1   Computers
☎ 351 6914; Al-Mankhool Rd, Bur Dubai; ⏰ 10am-2.30pm & 4.30-10pm Sat-Thu, 4.30-10pm Fri
Jam-packed with small shops selling every kind of software, hardware and accessories for PCs, this computer and electronics mall

also has a good range of digital cameras. There is an Internet café and fast-food outlets on the ground floor. Across the street, Al-Khaleej Centre has similar (but fewer) stores.

ALLAH DIN SHOES

Map ppp220-1 Handicrafts & Souvenirs
☎ 050 515 4351; Bur Dubai Souq abra station, Bur Dubai; ☺ 10am-10pm Sat-Thu, 4-10pm Fri
While every souvenir shop in Dubai now sells colourful sequined slippers and wonderful gold-threaded curly-toed shoes from Pakistan and Afghanistan, Allah Din Shoes was the first – and still has the best quality, range and prices. Evidence of how times have changed: a few years ago this stall didn't even have a name; now its owner hands out shiny business cards!

AL-OROOBA ORIENTAL

Map ppp220-1 Carpets
☎ 351 0919; BurJuman Centre, Bur Dubai; ☺ 10am-10pm Sat-Thu, 2-10pm Fri
You'll have to decide whether to enjoy the ritual of unrolling fine carpets or browsing through the interesting collection of Bedouin jewellery, prayer beads, ceramics and *khanjars* – you won't have time to do both as this is a high-quality selection of stuff that you should take time to mull over.

AMZAAN Map ppp222-3 Boutique
☎ 324 6754; Wafi City Mall, Al-Qataiyat Rd, near Al-Garhoud Bridge, Bur Dubai; ☺ 10am-10pm Sat-Thu, 4-10pm Fri
Feisty brands such as Faust, Fidel, Arrogant Cat, Antik Batik, Ed Hardy and Puzzle are reason enough to check out Sheikha Maisa Al Qassimi's funky boutique. This is also the only shop in Dubai with a good collection of Emirati labels designed by local girls: Sweet Lemon, Ice Lolly, Ilyazya, Crazy Daizy and – our favourite – Pink Sushi for fantastic bags and skirts made from checked *gutras* (men's head-dresses) and decorated with kooky trinkets.

BATEEL Map ppp220-1 Food
☎ 355 2853; BurJuman Centre, cnr Khalid bin al-Waleed (Bank St) & Trade Centre Rds, Bur Dubai; ☺ 10am-10pm Sat-Thu, 2-10pm Fri
Traditional Arabian hospitality called for the Bedouin to offer guests dates and camel

milk. Now Emiratis give Bateel's scrumptious date chocolates and truffles – made from 120 varieties of dates using European chocolate-making techniques – splendidly wrapped and on silver platters. Try the sparkling date drink and take home some date jam!

BURJUMAN CENTRE

Map ppp220-1 Shopping Centre
☎ 352 0222; cnr Khalid bin al-Waleed (Bank St) & Trade Centre Rds, Bur Dubai; ☺ 10am-10pm Sat-Thu, 2-10pm Fri
Now the most gorgeous mall of them all – after some expensive work and a new extension – BurJuman is more popular than ever. Beautiful stores include Saks Fifth Avenue, Dolce and Gabbana, Donna Karan, Kenzo, Calvin Klein, Etro, Christian Lacroix, Cartier and Tiffany's.

ETRO Map ppp220-1 Women's Clothing
☎ 351 3737; BurJuman Centre, cnr Khalid bin al-Waleed (Bank St) & Trade Centre Rds, Bur Dubai; ☺ 10am-10pm Sat-Thu, 2-10pm Fri
Italian designer Giacomo Etro's exuberant designs are inspired by his travels. Borrowing ideas from around the globe, his imaginatively exotic collections have featured colourful chiffon kaftans, Rasta shawls and textured ponchos, patchwork and mirrored skirts, sari-style tops, and embroidered belts and handbags.

FACES Map ppp220-1 Cosmetics
☎ 352 1441; BurJuman Centre, cnr Khalid bin al-Waleed (Bank St) & Trade Centre Rds, Bur Dubai; ☺ 10am-10pm Sat-Thu, 2-10pm Fri
An instant success when it opened, Faces has several branches around the city but this one was the first – here you'll find cosmetics and fragrances difficult to find elsewhere in Dubai, such as Stephane Marais, Serge Lutens, L'Artisan Parfumer, Annick Goutal, L'Erbolario, Benefit, Pout, Priorities and Smashbox, and for the boys, Zirh and Nickel Lab series.

FIVE GREEN Map ppp222-3 Boutique
☎ 336 4100; Garden Home, Oud Metha; ☺ 10am-11pm Sat-Thu, 4-11pm Fri
You'll find cool unisex labels such as Fidel, Paul Frank, BoxFresh, XLarge and Upper Playground at this urban lifestyle concept store that also sells alternative magazines,

books and music, Lomo cameras, and holds art and photography exhibitions.

GIFT WORLD

Map ppp222-3　　　　　Handicrafts & Souvenirs
☎ 335 8097; Block T, Karama Shopping Centre, Karama; ☽ 9am-10.30pm Sat-Thu, 4-10.30pm Fri
There's little space to move in this cluttered Aladdin's Cave around the corner from 2000 Horizon Antique. You'll bump your head on Moroccan lanterns and Syrian hanging lamps as you rummage through the Oriental bric-a-brac for that 'unique' piece of Bedouin jewellery or search stacks of sequined bedspreads for that perfect colour. We love the intricately patterned camel cushion covers!

KARAMA SHOPPING CENTRE

Map ppp222-3　　　　　　　Shopping Centre
Karama, Bur Dubai; ☽ 9am-10.30pm Sat-Thu, 9-11am & 4-10.30pm Fri
Also known as Karama Souq, this bustling backstreet shopping area in the heart of Karama has dozens of little shops selling handicrafts and souvenirs, fake brands and cheap clothes. While the prices are already cheap, some bargaining will reduce them more – be aggressive, as the spruikers are used to tourists here.

MOTHERCARE

Map ppp222-3　　　　　　Children's Clothing
☎ 335 9999; Lamcy Plaza, Oud Metha, Bur Dubai; ☽ 10am-10pm
One of the most popular (and affordable) stores for kid's stuff with cute clothes, cuddly toys, baby carriers, car seats and the like. Although there are several branches in Dubai, this one is close to about a dozen other shops for children on this floor of Lamcy Plaza.

OHM RECORDS Map ppp222-3　　　Music

☎ 397 3728; Trade Centre Rd, opposite BurJuman, Bur Dubai; ☽ 2-10pm
Active contributors to Dubai's developing DJ scene, Ohm records was the first to carry vinyl and has a discerning selection of house, trance, hip-hop, trip-hop and drum 'n' bass, DJ equipment and accessories. Responsible for bringing some of the more interesting DJs to Dubai, it also nurtures local talent by holding lessons for aspiring DJs.

PRAIAS Map ppp220-1　　　　Women's Clothing

☎ 351 1338; BurJuman Centre, Trade Centre Rd, Bur Dubai; ☽ 10am-10pm Sat-Thu, 2-10pm Fri
This little store might provide the only enticement for sun-worshippers to leave this pool-side spot – bold-coloured Brazilian bikinis beautifully embellished with appliqué, beading and small shells (although they aren't the only tiny things – these bikinis are minuscule!).

TAPE A L'OEIL

Map ppp220-1　　　　　　Children's Clothing
☎ 352 3223; BurJuman Centre, Trade Centre Rd, Bur Dubai; ☽ 10am-10pm Sat-Thu, 2-10pm Fri
If you're not planning on buying anything, don't dare let your kids try on these beautiful adult-like children's clothes from this

Five Green (left), one of Dubai's hippest clothing and accessory stores

delightful French store – you won't be able to resist once your kids look so adorable!

TIFFANY & CO Map ppp220-1 Jewellery
☎ 359 0101; BurJuman Centre, Trade Centre Rd, Bur Dubai; 🕑 10am-10pm Sat-Thu, 2-10pm Fri
While Tiffany's is affordable in Dubai, you may want to opt for the stunning sterling silver pieces (they won't blow the budget!), rather than the diamonds for which the jewellers are internationally renowned!

2000 HORIZON ANTIQUE Z
Map ppp222-3 Handicrafts & Souvenirs
☎ 335 3544; Block T, Karama Shopping Centre, Karama; 🕑 9am-10pm Sat-Thu, 9-11am & 4-10pm Fri
As long as you don't want antiques, you'll leave here satisfied. These guys offer the best prices in Karama Souq, and that's before you even start bargaining. The selection may be smaller than most, but you'll still find enough Orientalia to recreate the Arabian look back home, and the warm no-nonsense service is a welcome respite from the irritating spruikers outside.

WAFI GOURMET Map ppp222-3 Food
☎ 324 4555; Wafi City Mall, Al-Qataiyat Rd, near Al-Garhoud Bridge on Bur Dubai side of the Creek; 🕑 10am-10pm Sat-Thu, 2-10pm Fri
Formerly known as 'Goodies', Dubai's best Arabian deli has changed in name only. You'll still find counters of delicious Arabian delicacies – juicy olives, pickles, peppers and cheeses, freshly made hummus, *muttabal* and tabouleh, and crispy Lebanese pastries. Call in here during the cooler months, make up a mezze plate, and head creek-side to join the local families picnicking.

WHISTLES Map ppp220-1 Boutique
☎ 351 5070; BurJuman Centre, Trade Centre Rd, Bur Dubai; 🕑 10am-10pm Sat-Thu, 2-10pm Fri
The whimsical fashion at Whistles is another welcome addition to Dubai's previously glam-focused shopping scene. Now the local girls are getting the kind of eclectic and idiosyncratic style that they love.

SHEIKH ZAYED ROAD
AZZA FAHMY JEWELLERY
Map pp226 Jewellery
☎ 330 0346; Blvd at Emirates Towers, Sheikh Zayed Rd; 🕑 10am-10pm Sat-Thu, 4-10pm Fri
Egyptian Azza Fahmy claims her unique jewellery is inspired by Islamic and Arabic traditions and expresses spiritual values she believes are lost to much of the Arab world. Inscribed with classical Arabic poetry and Islamic wisdom in fine calligraphy and featuring precious gemstones, this is jewellery you'll treasure forever.

BOULEVARD AT EMIRATES TOWERS
Map pp226 Shopping Centre
☎ 330 0000, 319 8999; Sheikh Zayed Rd; 🕑 10am-10pm Sat-Thu, 4-10pm Fri
Home to dozens of exclusive designer brands such as Bulgari, Cartier, Ermenegildo Zegna, Giorgio Armani, Gucci, Jimmy Choo, Pucci and the fabulous Villa Moda. There is also the more affordable funky Barcelona brand Custo, Azza Fahmy Jewellery and some super bars and restaurants downstairs.

CUSTO Map p226 Boutique
☎ 330 0564; Blvd at Emirates Towers, Sheikh Zayed Rd; 🕑 10am-10pm Sat-Thu, 4-10pm Fri
The eclectic style of this Barcelona brand (for men and women) has been embraced by Dubai folk, fed up with the high fashion and bland franchises (all that was previously available). We love that one Custo piece, whether it be a top coat or T-shirt, is a fresh cocktail of contrasting colours, fabrics and eccentric shapes.

EMILIO PUCCI Map p226 Designerwear
☎ 330 0660; Blvd at Emirates Towers, Sheikh Zayed Rd; 🕑 10am-10pm Sat-Thu, 4-10pm Fri
Dubai's first and only Pucci store is worth visiting just to check out the groovy interior,

---

CAMEL CRAZY
Here are our top five camel gifts:
- Cute camels that play Arabic music when cuddled
- *Camelspotting* CD – cool Mid East music
- Julia Johnston's *Camel-o-shy* kids books
- A camel road-crossing sign kitchen magnet
- Intricate camel-patterned cushion covers

but you'll also find a colourful and fun range of psychedelic fashion, accessories and handbags.

GOLD & DIAMOND PARK
Map ppp214-15   Jewellery
☎ 347 7788; Sheikh Zayed Rd, near Interchange No 4; ⏰ 10am-10pm Sat-Thu, 4-10pm Fri
A cooler alternative to the Gold Souq in the hot summer months, the air-conditioned Gold and Diamond Park houses over 30 retailers and 120 manufacturers in a traditional Arabian-style building, and has a pleasant café.

ORGANIC FOODS & CAFÉ Map pp226 Food
☎ 398 9410; Al-Mankhool Rd, near Satwa Roundabout, Satwa; ⏰ 8am-10pm
Owner Nils El-Accad swears everything is 100% organic at Dubai's first organic supermarket – no genetically modified crops and all environmentally friendly. He's travelled all over the globe to source the freshest fruit, vegetables, olive oils, meat and seafood direct from small growers. He also bakes bread on site, roasts and grinds coffee, and it's one of the few places where you'll find gluten-free products.

VILLA MODA Map p226   Designerwear
☎ 330 4555; Blvd at Emirates Towers, Sheikh Zayed Rd; ⏰ 10am-10pm Sat-Thu, 4-10pm Fri
This concept store, started by Majed Al Sabah AKA Kuwait's 'Sheikh of Chic', has the coolest *2001: A Space Odyssey* interiors and hottest brands in fashion – Prada, Stella McCartney, Alexander McQueen, Chloe, Easton Pearson and Marni – along with fabulous accessories and cosmetics. Take home some Philip B White Truffle Moisturising shampoo and Commes des Garçons Ouarzazate, Jaisalmer and Zagorsk candles – divine! Amazing bargains when sales are on.

JUMEIRAH & NEW DUBAI

AIZONE Map ppp214-15   Clothing
☎ 347 9333; Mall of the Emirates, Sheikh Zayed Rd, New Dubai; ⏰ 10am-midnight
Lose yourself for hours in this large Dubai branch of hip Lebanese fashion emporium, Aizone (part of the Aishti family). Room after room hangs wonderful hard-to-find fashion from American Retro, Plenty, Bibelot, Citizens of Humanity, Lotus, Da-Nang, DSquared, Somi, Fray,

SOUVENIR SUGGESTIONS
Traditional Take-Homes
If you can't resist taking home gold, carpets, perfume and the like, here are some helpful hints:

Carpets Go for Persian, better value and finer quality than anywhere except Iran.

Gold Buy bulk. It's a great investment: you'll feel smug when it's valued back home.

Perfume No tax means French brands are cheaper than in Paris, but check the packaging to make sure it's authentic.

Pashminas Fakes are found all over the world, but bargains are to be had in the silky soft 100% pashmina shawls.

Oriental music Sure, you want to shimmy like the bellydancer on your desert safari, but listen before you buy; some are excruciating.

Cool Keepsakes
We think these Dubai-designed, home-grown and lesser-known regional products make more original mementos:

Colourful camel bags They make very groovy ottomans.

Azza Fahmy jewellery Impress your friends by explaining the Arabic inscriptions and imagery.

Arabian attars (essential oils) You can be confident no other woman in the room will be wearing the same scent.

A Pink Sushi piece Funky feminine fashion made from the traditional *gutra* (red-and-white checked men's head-dress) by an Emirati designer.

Lemonada or Blue Bedouin CDs Kick back instead to Arabian lounge and chill-out music made in Dubai.

Free People, Juicy Couture, True Religion, Shu Shu, Spy and Theory. When we were last in there we fell in love with Savage Culture colourful ponchos and embroidered Biya gymboots!

TOP SHOP-TILL-YOU-DROP MALLS

- Deira City Centre (p130)
- Mall of the Emirates (right)
- BurJuman Centre (p132)
- Souq Madinat Jumeirah (p138)
- Ibn Battuta Mall (below)

CAMEL COMPANY Map ppp214-15   Souvenirs
☎ 368 6048; Souq Madinat Jumeirah, Al-Sufouh Rd, Jumeirah; ☾ 10am-11pm
Camels are just so cute! It's those big brown eyes and eyelashes, or is it the hump? Or is it because they play music when you squeeze them? The best spot to get your camel souvenirs: plush cuddly camels, holiday-making camels in Hawaiian shirts, camels on T-shirts, coffee cups, mouse-pads, notebooks, greeting cards and more…

CAVIAR CLASSIC Map ppp214-15   Food
☎ 368 6160; Souq Madinat Jumeirah, Al-Sufouh Rd, Jumeirah; ☾ 10am-11pm
Spoil yourself with some Royal Beluga (Dh375/7000 for 50g/1kg) or the more affordable Sevruga (a mere Dh150/3000 for 50g/1kg). Either way you'll have to savour this sublime stuff from your hotel balcony with a glass of bubbly (despite the spiffy packaging and ice, it won't survive the plane trip home).

FIDEL   Boutique
☎ 368 5600; Ibn Battuta Mall, Sheikh Zayed Rd, New Dubai; ☾ 10am-10pm Sat-Tue, 10am-midnight Wed-Fri
Fidel's minimalist flagship Dubai store stocks little else but funky Fidel T-shirts – our faves are (naturally) the Destination/ New World series. There's also the no-nonsense DIM lingerie, and some quirky Japanese-style slippers and sneakers by the very hip Acupuncture.

GALLERY ONE FINE ART
PHOTOGRAPHS Map ppp214-15   Souvenirs
☎ 368 6055; Souq Madinat Jumeirah, Al-Sufouh Rd, Jumeirah; ☾ 10am-11pm
For an original souvenir of Dubai head here for colourful abstract and pop-art screen prints of Arabian images, such as camel road-crossing signs and red-and-white checked *gutras*, as well as superb black-and-white photographs of Dubai Creek activity, wind-tower architecture and street life.

GINGER & LACE   Boutique
☎ 368 5109; Ibn Battuta Mall, Sheikh Zayed Rd, New Dubai; ☾ 10am-10pm Sat-Tue, 10am-midnight Wed-Fri
Ginger & Lace stock an eclectic selection of colourful, whimsical fashion by high-spirited New York designers Anna Sui and Betsey Johnson, German-bred Ingwa, Melero (love the halters with sexy cut-out waists), Tibi (casual Capri-style chic), Indian cult-label Ananya (for signature bejewelled kaftans worn by Madonna) and Australian brand Wheels and Doll Baby (for the posh rock-chick look).

IBN BATTUTA MALL   Shopping Centre
☎ 362 1900; Sheikh Zayed Rd, New Dubai; ☾ 10am-10pm Sat-Tue, 10am-midnight Wed-Fri
The 14th-century Arab scholar Ibn Battuta travelled 75,000 miles over 30 years. You'll have a better idea how he felt after trekking from one end of the mall to the other (from China to Andalusia), but it's worth it. You can also take a virtual magic carpet ride across Dubai and take a tape home to prove it! Plus, there's some great shopping.

MALL OF THE EMIRATES
Map ppp214-15   Shopping Centre
☎ 409 9000; Sheikh Zayed Rd, New Dubai; ☾ 10am-midnight
Everyone predicted this enormous mall would be empty after we had all taken our initial curious looks, but this elegant shopping centre is now one of Dubai's busiest and it's not just the ski slope bringing people here. Along with the usual brands, there's also a Harvey Nichols and some welcome new additions to the shopping scene.

MERCATO MALL

Map ppp224-5   Shopping Centre

☎ 344 4161; Mercato Mall, Jumeira Rd, Jumeirah; ⏰ 10am-10pm Thu-Sat, 2-10pm Fri
As strange as this Italian Renaissance–style shopping centre is, its light-filled space makes it lovely to stroll around, while a good selection of stylish boutiques, make-up store Mac, a Virgin Megastore and several fine carpet shops make it difficult not to spend the dirhams.

MUMBAI SE

Boutique

☎ 366 9855; India Court, Ibn Battuta Mall, Sheikh Zayed Rd, New Dubai; ⏰ 10am-10pm Sat-Tue, 10am-midnight Wed-Fri
It's hard to leave this exotic Indian emporium empty-handed. Its collections include labels that combine contemporary elements with classic styles – a Rama red smock with Indian beading and a seashell trim or Sabeena's slinky bejewelled mandarin tunics. Meera Mahadevia's tiny handcrafted bags embellished with semi-precious stones, spiritual emblems and engravings are pretty special.

PERSIAN CARPET HOUSE & ANTIQUES Map ppp224-5   Carpets

☎ 345 6687; Mercato Mall, Jumeira Rd, Jumeirah; ⏰ 10am-10pm Thu-Sat, 2-10pm Fri
The largest carpet retailer in the country, Persian Carpet House is considered to be the best source for fine handmade Persian carpets and Oriental rugs from Turkey, Afghanistan, Pakistan, India and Kashmir. The 'antique' selection includes wonderful old gramophones, radios and telephones.

PIXI Map ppp214-15   Cosmetics

☎ 341 3833; Mall of the Emirates, Sheikh Zayed Rd, New Dubai; ⏰ 10am-midnight
This Swedish make-up and skincare line offers sublime cosmetics and beauty products for enriching your skin and sense of well-being. We highly recommend the honey almond polish (smells good enough to eat), beauty serum (with evening primrose), cucumber juice (toner) and signature scent 'El Jardin de las Figueras' – made from sun-ripened figs, it conjures up frolics through Granada fig gardens…it really does!

RAGE Map ppp214-15   Streetwear

☎ 341 3388; Mall of the Emirates, Sheikh Zayed Rd, New Dubai; ⏰ 10am-midnight
If you didn't get this guide until you arrived in Dubai, unaware the city had a surf, skate and snowboard scene, and now you want to catch some waves at Jumeirah, hit the slopes at Ski Dubai, or roll down to Creekside skate park, then head to Rage (formerly Rampage) for all your gear. This branch, close to both sea and snow, is the most convenient.

SAUCE Map ppp224-5   Boutique

☎ 344 7270; Village Mall, Jumeira Rd, Jumeirah; ⏰ 10am-10pm Thu-Sat, 4.30-10pm Fri
Sauce was the first of an increasing number of eclectic, independently owned boutiques in Dubai. Its loyal customers flock here for idiosyncratic women's fashion – skirts trimmed with ribbons and pom poms, bubblegum mini kaftans etc – from Nicola Finetti, Third Millenium, Tata-Naka, Sass and Bide, Ashish, and local designer Essa. There are also quirky accessories such as funky beads, baubles and crocheted flowers on chains.

Shopping   JUMEIRAH & NEW DUBAI

SECONDS & SECOND-HAND GEAR IN DUBAI

Fashion Factory (Map pp222–3; ☎ 336 2699; Lamcy Plaza; ⏰ 9am-10pm Sat-Tue, 9am-10.30pm Wed-Fri) High street brands such as Monsoon, Miss Selfridge and FCUK at their cheapest.

Levi's (Map pp220–1; ☎ 359 6770; Al-Khaleej Centre, Bur Dubai; ⏰ 10am-10pm Sat-Thu, 4-10pm Fri) Small factory outlet in a Levi's shop has discounted denim to satisfy boot-cut lovers.

Le Stock (Map pp224–5; ☎ 342 0211; Jumeirah Plaza, Jumeira Rd) Expensive designer gear, from Matthew Williamson to Catherine Malandrino, at low prices.

Blue Cactus (Map pp224–5; ☎ 344 7734; Jumeirah Centre, Jumeira Rd; ⏰ 10am-9pm Sat-Thu, 6-9pm Fri) Heavily discounted designers, from DKNY to Kenneth Cole.

Dubai Charity Shop (Map pp222–3; ☎ 337 8246; behind Choitrams, Karama, one block from Karama Souq; ⏰ 9am-2pm Sat-Wed) You could unearth anything from high street seconds to discarded Dior at Dubai's best second-hand store, with sales going to the Dubai Centre for Special Needs.

SHOWCASE ANTIQUES, ART & FRAMES Map ppp214-15   Art & Antiques

☎ 348 8797; Jumeirah Rd, Umm Suqeim, Jumeirah; ☽ 10am-1pm & 4-8pm Sat-Thu, 4-8pm Fri

If you enjoy a leisurely browse, visit this Jumeirah villa for antique *khanjars*, firearms, Bedouin jewellery and costumes. It's one of just a few places in Dubai to sell quality collectables and antiques, with certificates of authenticity to prove it!

SOUQ MADINAT JUMEIRAH

Map ppp214-15   Shopping Centre

☎ 348 8797; Madinat Jumeirah, Al-Sufouh Rd, Jumeirah; ☽ 10am-11pm

A must-see on your shopping tour of Dubai, for the enchanting Arabian architecture and interiors, excellent waterside eating, and dozens of excellent handicraft, souvenir and gift shops, such as Lata's and Scarabee. Prices are higher but quality is superior and shopping spruiker-free.

Sleeping

Sleeping

Befitting its status as a luxury destination, Dubai is home to an accommodation scene that leans decidedly towards the high end of the tourist market. The myriad hotel and resort projects on the drawing boards of Dubai's movers and shakers certainly aren't going to change that trend in the near future – most are five-star, although a couple of low-budget chains have longer-term plans to move in. While this is great news for travellers with a hearty budget (or no budget at all!), for those looking for

something like a hostel or budget accommodation, it's slim pickings. Fortunately for these travellers, if you're visiting in the hotter months you can get excellent discounts.

Accommodation Styles

There are two types of hotel accommodation in Dubai: the city hotels and the beach resorts. The city hotels, found in atmospheric Deira, well-situated Bur Dubai and glitzy Sheikh Zayed Rd, range from one star to five, while the beach resorts, found along Jumeirah Beach heading south, generally are five star, with one claiming to be 'seven star'. The facilities offered for the number of stars rated is generally in line with other parts of the world and all hotels listed here have air-con. For longer-term accommodation, there are furnished apartments, mainly found in Bur Dubai. While there are no official camping sites in Dubai, many residents spend weekends camping on beaches or in the desert, but given the temperatures and lack of facilities, camping is not a popular option for a Dubai holiday.

The type of hotel you should choose very much depends on what type of holiday you're after. The city hotels are great for access to the shopping malls, souqs and historic areas, but when it's really hot you might be jealous of those staying at a beach resort! Those looking for a more relaxing holiday should opt for one of the lavish beach resorts, but keep in mind you're around 30 minutes away from Dubai centre – when the traffic's good – and a taxi will cost around Dh40 to Dh50 each way. Most visitors staying at these resorts 'do the sights' in one day and spend the rest of the time soaking up the sun.

Check-in & Check-out Times

One of the most insidious trends in the hotel industry is the ever-shrinking times that you're actually able to use the room you've paid for – Dubai is no exception. Check-in is now 3pm for most hotels, but generally if you arrive early, staff will try to get you a room as soon as possible, and check-out is 11am or noon. Let hotels know exactly when you're arriving and you'll stand a better chance of not being left jet-lagged in the foyer for a couple of hours.

DON'T BELIEVE THE PRICE...

The rates quoted for some of these hotels are, quite frankly, silly. However, in the interest of comparing hotels, we have to quote the rack rates. Unless you're specifically heading to Dubai for a conference or event (when Dubai's occupancy is at its highest), you shouldn't pay anything approaching rack rates. Shop around – you can nearly always move up a ratings star or simply to a better hotel with a little bit of research. Visit the hotel websites where you can sometimes get a discount as much as half the rack rate, especially during the hotter months. Go to **Expedia** (www.expedia.com) or **Lastminute** (www.lastminute.com) and look for deals. Even if the words 'package tour' send a chill up your spine, keep in mind that the airlines and tour companies can offer the best deals – this is especially true for the resort hotels.

Price Ranges

The hotel prices we've quoted are inclusive of municipal tax (10%) and service charge (10%). It's important to note that these are the hotels' rack rates – the standard, published, high-season rates. Only at peak times and during events are you likely to pay these rates. During summer the tourist traffic really drops off so from mid-May to mid-September hotels drop their rates, often up to 50% of the published rack rate. Always ask for the best price or whether there are any deals on – generally the hotels won't tell you unless you ask. Having business cards to show will see you qualify as a corporate client, which earns a substantial discount.

All midrange and top-end hotels require you to leave your passport in their safe for the duration of your stay. They also require you to leave a credit-card authorisation of about Dh500 per night. If you don't have a credit card you will have to leave a cash deposit.

Reservations

Most reputable hotel chains have online bookings and it will save you an expensive telephone call and fax to confirm. Note that some of the less expensive hotels offer online bookings, but not through a secured server – which is akin to mailing your credit-card details on a postcard. Check out the published specials on their websites (if there are none currently available, that generally means occupancy is high) or you can try **Expedia** (www.expedia.com) or **Lastminute** (www.lastminute.com).

For the peak periods and for large events, Dubai can actually run out of hotel rooms, so you'll need to book well in advance.

> ## BOOK ACCOMMODATION ONLINE
>
> For more accommodation reviews and recommendations by Lonely Planet authors, check out the online booking service at www.lonelyplanet.com. You'll find the true, insider lowdown on the best places to stay. Reviews are thorough and independent. Best of all, you can book online.

DEIRA

Deira is Dubai's only substantial budget hotel area; if it's atmosphere and shopping you're seeking, this is for you. There are a few decent hotels with views of the Creek as well as good-value quality hotels near the airport – which isn't as bad as it sounds, particularly if you like shopping, given the proximity to the souqs and malls.

DUBAI YOUTH HOSTEL

Map pp214-15   Hostel $

☎ 298 8151/61; uaeyha@emirates.net.ae; 39 Al-Nahda Rd; New House YHA members/nonmembers s Dh140/165, d Dh150/190; Old House s Dh110/130, dm Dh50/70; ☒ ☒

While it's a fair distance from the action, it's the only hostel in town. Still, it has far better facilities than you'd expect and the new wing with spotless single and double rooms beats the Deira and Bur Dubai zero-star hotels hands down for comfort. While the dorm rooms (in the Old House) are more like pre-teen bedrooms, the New House rooms are excellent value – as long

as you are a YHA member (Dh150 per annum). Keep in mind that if you're not a member, it may be more economical to stay in a better-positioned cheapie in Deira (particularly after taking into account taxi fares – although you can take the bus). However, you won't be able to match the facilities; there's a pool and a gym, sauna, spa, Jacuzzi, tennis court and billiards room. Catch buses 3, 13, 17 or 31.

GOLD PLAZA HOTEL Map pp216-17   Hotel $

☎ 225 0240; Suq Deira St; s/d with balcony Dh125/150

This 'family' hotel is located smack bang at the entrance to the always-tempting Gold Souq. While it's in a great position, the place doesn't appear to have had a sniff of renovation in years. The rooms are quite small and simply furnished with tiled floors, and while the reception staff amusingly proclaim that they have 'no facilities' in the hotel, at least it's air-conditioned! Besides the odd lost-looking backpacker, clientele appear to be mainly East Africans here for a spot of trading.

DEIRA PALACE HOTEL

Map pp216-17   Hotel $

☎ 229 0120; marwan32@emirates.net.ae; 67 St;
s/d/tr Dh150/180/220

This large 'family hotel' (no visitors after
9pm) has been providing low-cost lodgings
one block from the Gold Souq for years.
While it's certainly no palace, it has clean
enough rooms with views of the street action. The place seems to survive on business
from African commercial travellers (coming
to do business in the souqs) and the occasional backpacker looking for Deira action.

HOTEL DELHI DARBAR

Map pp216-17   Hotel $

☎ 273 3555; Naif Rd; s/d/ste Dh175/250/350

This small, Indian-oriented establishment
is better than most of the hotels in Deira's
commercial centre, featuring spacious, clean
rooms and a popular Indian restaurant on
the ground floor. Upstairs, the 36 rooms
have the usual furniture, but are thankfully
not decorated in a chintzy manner like most
others in this price bracket. It's in a good
location too, not far from the souqs.

PACIFIC HOTEL Map pp216-17   Hotel $

☎ 227 6700; www.pacifichotel-dubai.com; 115
Al-Sabakha Rd, opposite Sabakha bus station; s/d/tr
Dh220/300/375

Close to the Creek and right in the heart of
the souq action, the clean rooms have balconies where you can check out the street
action, and while the facilities aren't up to
much, at least the management is friendly.
The beds are better than you'd expect and
there's a wall-mounted TV with satellite
stations, but it's far more interesting taking
in the action outside the window.

AL-HIJAZ HERITAGE MOTEL

Map pp216-17   Hotel $$

☎ 225 0085; www.alhijazmotel.com; next to
Al-Ahmadiya School; d Dh330; 🖵 ⊠ ♿
Located next to **Al-Ahmadiya School** (p50) and
Heritage House (p52), this modest hotel of-
fers up home-style ambience in a restored
Arabian courtyard building. Rooms are
tastefully and modestly decorated, large
(suites are huge), clean, and with satellite
TV and bar fridge (no alcohol here, though).
With the Muslim call to prayer emanating

from the mosque next door, it makes for a
unique experience in Deira.

LORDS HOTEL Map pp216-17   Hotel $$

☎ 228 9977; lords@emirates.net.ae; Al-Jazeira St;
s/d Dh350/400; 🖵

While offering plenty of superfluous nightlife, this Deira three-star is really only notable
for its clean and well-kept rooms, rooftop
pool and convenient position for souq shopping raids. Though the rooms are clean and
well-kept, they're furnished with the obligatory mismatched patterns and predictably
dull furniture. The service is friendly, but the
usual pub, club and restaurant facilities need
not delay you from checking out the Deira
shopping and the Creek action.

RAMEE INTERNATIONAL HOTEL

Map pp216-17   Hotel $$

☎ 224 0222; rameedxb@emirates.net.ae;
9C St; s/d Dh360/480

A busy hotel off bustling Baniyas Sq, it at-
tracts large tour groups doing Dubai on a budget.
While it's the usual bland three-star, the
rooms are very clean, come with satellite TV
and bar fridges, and 24-hour room service.
The hotels of the Ramee Group (which has
several properties in the UAE) always seem
to have plenty of Indian-focused entertain-
ment that's fun to drop in and take a peek
at. This hotel is no exception, but perhaps
in a gesture towards world peace, one bar
features a Pakistani band!

SUN AND SAND HOTEL

Map pp218-19   Hotel $$

☎ 223 9000; www.sunsandhotel.com; 37 St;
s/d Dh468/536; 🖵

Appreciably better than the other hotels in
this three-star ghetto is this small, reasonably well-equipped hotel that's short on
sand (you'll have to take a beach shuttle
bus for that), but offers plenty of sun at its
rooftop pool. Though a little less alarming
than the garish Arabian chintz décor of
the foyer, the rooms are still mired in the
mixed-patterned '90s.

NIHAL HOTEL Map pp218-19   Hotel $$

☎ 295 7666; nihalhtl@emirates.net.ae; 40C St;
s/d/ste Dh 390/540/780

One of Deira's uninspired three-star cube-
shaped hotels, the Nihal is well-positioned

for shopping and checking out Dubai's heritage attractions. Some of the spacious rooms are the type only an Arab grandma could embrace and she'd probably say *aiwa* (yes) in approval of the plastic covering on the bed headboards! Some of these suites also strangely feature saunas, perhaps so you can recreate Dubai's summer conditions if you visit in the cooler months.

RIVIERA HOTEL Map pp216-17   Hotel $$$
☎ 222 2131; www.rivierahotel-dubai.com; Baniyas Rd; s/d Dh605/678, Creek view extra Dh74; 🖵 🕭

While this Creek stalwart pretends that the design clock stopped about 20 years ago, it is hard to argue with the address. If you care more about being in the centre of the Creek action than sheet thread count, this isn't a bad choice, although after a wander through the souqs, you might long for the swimming pool of the Carlton Tower, virtually next door. The TV, bar fridge and good service sweeten the deal.

AL-BUSTAN ROTANA
Map pp218-19   Hotel $$$
☎ 282 0000; www.rotana.com; Casablanca Rd, Al-Garhoud; d Dh700; 🖵 ✕ 🕭 ♨ 🕭
Away from the plush lobby, it's not the most impressive hotel in the looks department,

TAXI SIR?
Many four- and five-star hotels in Dubai have taxis that operate from the hotel. These 'taxis' have no taxi signage, generally cost more than a 'normal' taxi and often operate without a meter. Tell the bell captain you want a normal taxi (you might have to insist), unless you are craving limo luxury.

but it makes amends with its convenient airport access and excellent facilities (such as wi-fi in the public areas) and affable service. While the rooms are a decent size and well-equipped, they're a smidgen uninspired – book a pool-view room or suite. The hotel's restaurant, **Blue Elephant** (p81) and nightclub, **Oxygen** (p105) are both Dubai favourites.

HYATT REGENCY DUBAI
Map pp216-17   Hotel $$$
☎ 209 1234; www.dubai.regency.hyatt.com; off Al-Khaleej Rd; s/d Dh672/744; 🖵 ✕ 🕭 ♨ 🕭
The granddaddy of Dubai's huge five-star hotels has undergone a stylish renovation and its key attributes – good shopping and extensive amenities – have been brought back into focus. The rooms are large and comfortable with superb views over the Gulf, Dubai and Sharjah, and the food outlets worth staying in for.

Bab al-Shams Desert Resort & Spa (p151), a luxury retreat located in Margham, 45 minutes from Dubai

SHERATON DUBAI CREEK

Map pp216-17   Hotel $$$

☎ 228 1111; www.starwood.com; Baniyas Rd;
s/d Dh700/750; 🖥 ✖ 🛒 🐾 ♿

After an extensive renovation, this hotel is
once again a desirable Creekside address.
There are plenty of room options, some with
superb floor-to-ceiling windows providing
an excellent atmospheric Creek vista, with
the Towers floors being the best. There are
also inexplicable Japanese-themed rooms,
which are obviously not the best choice
if you're after arabesque atmosphere! The
breakfasts are generous and the restaurants,
particularly the Indian **Ashiana** (p81) and the
Japanese **Creekside** (p80), are notable.

CARLTON TOWER HOTEL

Map pp216-17   Hotel $$$

☎ 222 7111; www.carltontower.net; Baniyas Rd;
s/d/ste Dh800/900/1200, Creek view extra Dh100;
🖥 ✖ 🛒 ♿

A long-time favourite with Russian tour-
groups, this old hotel has a great outlook
right on the Creek. The renovated rooms

are fine – pony up the extra cash for the
Creek-view rooms. Probably the best features of this hotel are its position close
to souqs and the decent-sized outdoor
swimming pool – heaven after a hot day of
sightseeing. In true old-Dubai style, there
are numerous bars and restaurants in the
hotel, all of them endearingly cheesy.

HILTON DUBAI CREEK

Map pp216-17   Hotel $$$$

☎ 227 1111; www.hilton.com; Baniyas Rd, Rigga;
r from Dh1440; 🖥 ✖ 🛒 ♿

Perhaps the closest the Hilton chain has
come to creating a design hotel, these
sleek city digs represent the best of Deira's
accommodation. The waterside location
offers amazing views down the Creek
(insist on a room with a view) and its restaurant, **Verre** (p82), is still the most refined
dining in town. While we think that the
ultramodern design and cool atmosphere
offer relief from the in-your-face opulence
of Dubai's other five-star hotels, some
guests want a bit more 'fuss' for their
dirham.

THE CALL TO PRAYER

If you're staying in the older parts of Deira or Bur Dubai, be prepared to be woken at about 4.30am each morning by
an inimitable wailing. This is the azan, the call to prayer. At the first sign of dawn, you'll hear a cacophony of sounds
as muezzins chant the call to prayer through speakers positioned on the minaret of each mosque. Back in the old days,
the muezzins used to climb a ladder to the minarets and call out from the top.

Muslims pray five times a day: at dawn; when the sun is directly overhead; when the sun is in the position that
makes the shadow of an object the same length as that object; at the beginning of sunset; and at twilight, when the
last light of the day disappears over the horizon. In addition to the muezzins' call, the exact times are printed in the
daily newspapers and on websites. Once the call has been made, Muslims have half an hour in which to pray. There
is an exception for the dawn prayer; after the call they have about an hour and 20 minutes in which to wake up and
pray, before the sun has risen.

Muslims don't need to be near a mosque to pray; they just need to face Mecca. If someone cannot get to a mosque,
they will stop wherever they are to pray – by the side of the road, in hotel lobbies, in shops – so if you see someone
praying, just be as unobtrusive as you can, and if possible don't walk in front of them. All public buildings, such as
government departments, libraries, shopping centres, airports, etc, have prayer rooms or designated areas where
people can pray. You'll find a qibla (a niche that indicates the direction of Mecca) in every hotel room in Dubai, usually
on the ceiling, desk or bedside table.

The phrase that you'll be able to make out most often during the call to prayer is *Allah-u-akbar* which means 'God
is Great'. This is repeated four times at the start of the azan. Next comes *Ashhadu an la illallah ha-illaah* – 'I testify there
is no god but God'. This is repeated twice. So is the next line, *Asshadu anna muhammadan rasuulu-ilaah* – 'I testify that
Mohammed is His messenger'. Then come two shorter lines, also sung twice: *Hayya ala as-salaah* (Come to prayer) and
Hayya ala al-falaah (Come to salvation). *Allah-u-akbar* is repeated two more times, and then comes the last line *Laa
ilaah illa allah* – 'There is no god but God'.

The only prayer call with a difference is the one at dawn. In this azan, after the exhortation to come to salvation,
comes the gently nudging extra line, also repeated, *As-salaatu khayrun min al nawn*, which translates as 'It is better
to pray than to sleep'. If you're not in a hotel where you can hear the call to prayer, just head to the souqs and buy a
mosque alarm clock – it's almost guaranteed to get you out of bed!

PARK HYATT DUBAI

Map pp218-19   Hotel $$$$

☎ 602 1234; dubai.park.hyatt.com; Dubai Creek Golf & Yacht Club; d/ste Dh1420/3220; 🖳 ⊠ 🖳 🖈 ⅋

This elegant, Moroccan-styled (and thankfully low-rise) hotel, right on the Creek, completes a trinity of Hyatts in Dubai and this is the smallest and most stylish of the three. Huge, well-appointed rooms are standard, as are wonderful views of Dubai Creek. It's a lovely, airy hotel to hang out in and it's the perfect resort for golf-club wielding visitors as the **Dubai Creek Golf & Yacht Club** (p112) is right next door.

INTERCONTINENTAL DUBAI

Map pp216-17   Hotel $$$$

☎ 222 7171; www.intercontinental.com; Baniyas Rd; s/d Dh1400/1540; 🖳 ⊠ 🖳 🖈 ⅋

This Creek legend has recently had a face-lift that has seen the introduction of some fantastic restaurants and some much-needed TLC to the rooms. It's still a comfortable Creek address, although it's not the leading hotel it once was. All the rooms have great views, although standard rooms are still a very tight fit and rather anonymously decorated. The suites are better for those with a fear of tight spaces, but not particularly great value. On the plus side, the heath club is excellent and business facilities have been keeping guests happily communicating for years. Both **China Club** (p80) and **Yum!** (p79) restaurants are worth a visit.

BUR DUBAI

Bur Dubai is a great location for hitting the heritage sights and traversing the Creek. (Deira is only a short *abra* ride away.) However, except for the Bastakia and Bur Dubai souq, much of the area is rather bland and full of soulless low-rise apartments.

FOUR POINTS SHERATON

Map pp220-1   Hotel $$

☎ 397 7444; www.starwood.com; Khalid bin al-Waleed Rd; s/d from Dh475; 🖳 ⊠ 🖳 🖈 ⅋

This boxy 125-room, four-star might be oriented towards business travellers, but it's also well located for sightseeing. While the rooms won't have you groping for your camera, a walk around the interesting

neighbourhood might. The rooms themselves are standard old-school Sheraton and don't skimp on amenities (hairdryer, stocked mini bar and satellite TV) but nonsmokers should make certain to book a nonsmoking room. The hotel has a gym and a rooftop swimming pool; while we're not so sure about chancing the in-house beauty salon, you should check out the excellent **Antique Bazaar** (p84) Indian restaurant.

RYDGES PLAZA   Map pp224-5   Hotel $$

☎ 398 2222; www.rydges.com; Satwa Roundabout; s/d/ste Dh450/500/1200; 🖳 ⊠ 🖳 🖈 ⅋

While this Aussie chain is unquestionably old-fashioned, the position of the hotel allows you to explore the interesting neighbourhood and experience some local colour, but still be just a short taxi ride from the five-star strips of Sheikh Zayed and Jumeirah. The hotel itself is of the 1990s midrange chain variety, but rooms are well-equipped with mini bar, hairdryer, safe, tea- and coffee-making facilities, as well as decent satellite TV. There's a health club, swimming pool and spa, and plenty of food and beverage outlets, including a couple of well-regarded restaurants.

CAPITOL HOTEL   Map pp220-1   Hotel $$$

☎ 346 0111; www.capitol-hotel.com; Al-Mina Rd, Satwa; s/d Dh605/697; 🖳 🖳

This four-star is strategically located near the start of the Jumeirah strip and only a few minutes away from the Creek. The huge rooms are attractively furnished (and very quiet), and facilities are good. Unlike Deira or way down the beach, nothing is too far away by taxi from here – but you will need to catch taxis. The rooms are generous in size with satellite TV, mini bar and Internet connection. There's a reasonable gym, sauna and steam room as well as a rooftop pool to cool down in.

MÖVENPICK HOTEL BUR DUBAI

Map pp222-3   Hotel $$$

☎ 336 6000; www.moevenpick-hotels.com; 19 St; s/d Dh650/750; ⊠ 🖳 🖈 ⅋

Well positioned for shopping excursions, this modern hotel has fine business facilities including wi-fi enabled and smoke-free rooms. There is a rooftop fitness centre and temperature-controlled pool.

However, the hotel position means that there's nothing worth opening your blinds for, apart from some sun, and the décor is a little bland. The rooftop is home to a pool and large deck area and, oddly, a running track that would drive you batty after a couple of laps, so it's probably better to get exercise in the health club or nearby Creekside Park.

XVA Map pp220-1 — Boutique Hotel $$$

☎ 353 5383; www.xvagallery.com; behind Basta Art Café, Al-Musallah Roundabout; d/ste Dh650/750
This small hotel in an old courtyard building is a triple treat, with its gallery, café and boutique hotel rooms. While the café and well-respected art gallery are arranged around the lovely central courtyard, the rooms are upstairs. They're uniquely furnished in an attractive but minimalist Oriental style, with no distractions like TV, and suites are larger and more comfortable for a longer stay.

REGENT PALACE HOTEL
Map pp220-1 — Hotel $$$
☎ 396 3888; www.ramee-group.com; Sheikh Khalifa bin Zayed Rd; s/d from Dh700/800;
🖳 🗙 🖳 ⛐
Conveniently located opposite the upmarket **BurJuman Centre** (p132), this hotel is decorated in an old-fashioned style that bears no relation to the hotel exterior. Business travellers love the location and the facilities such as the fitness club and outdoor swimming pool. Rooms are best on the upper floors and we recommend the deluxe rooms over the standard ones. It's also in a great position for heading down to the Creek sights.

REGAL PLAZA HOTEL
Map pp220-1 — Hotel $$$
☎ 355 6633; www.ramee-group.com; Al-Mankhool Rd; s/d from Dh830/1060; 🖳 🗙 🖳 ⛐
Located amid the shops and banks of Bur Dubai, this Indian-run hotel has modern rooms and good facilities for a three-star, including a swimming pool and gym. The rooms are very clean and decorated in your average business hotel manner (including mini bar), but nonsmokers should make sure they book the nonsmoking rooms. Rooms on the upper floors have

HOTEL APARTMENTS

While on the surface the plethora of hotel apartments in the Bur Dubai area makes sense for a longer stay in Dubai, unless you really feel the need to cook, they don't represent great value. Prices start from around Dh500 for a studio in one of the better hotel apartments, but prices can drop significantly if you're staying longer than a week. **Dubai Tourism** (www.dubaitourism.ae) has a full listing.

interesting neighbourhood views and there are a couple of unintentionally amusing bars.

RAMADA HOTEL
Map pp220-1 — Hotel $$$
☎ 351 9999; www.ramadadubai.com; Al-Mankhool Rd; s/d Dh960/1080; 🖳 🖳
The most notable aspect of this refurbished hotel is its striking late-1970s stained-glass feature stretching the height of the atrium. The 172 rooms that rise up around the feature have been recently renovated and we especially like the business-class rooms which are large and split level. All rooms have tea- and coffee-making facilities, broadband Internet and mini bar, and are decorated in an inoffensive modern hotel style. There's a welcome rooftop pool with a large deck area and a gym with good facilities overlooking the pool. While the food and beverage outlets are fairly innocuous (including the obligatory English pub), any nightclub named 'Rumours' is going to be a tragic affair. The one at this hotel is no exception.

GRAND HYATT DUBAI
Map pp214-15 — Hotel $$$$
☎ 317 1234; www.dubai.grand.hyatt.com; Al-Qataiyat Rd; s & d from Dh1200;
🖳 🗙 🖳 ⛐ ⛐
This gigantic resort-style hotel is large enough to have its own postcode. Once inside the hotel it's hard not to be impressed by the indoor 'rainforest' – and the dhow (boat) hulls hanging from the ceiling. The rooms, all 674 of them, are conservatively but tastefully furnished, with nice touches such as original artwork by local artists. Facilities thoughtfully include broadband Internet and a 24-hour

'technology concierge' to help you get online. The hotel is always buzzing and it's fun just wandering around the huge area that houses the numerous eateries and checking out the chefs working in the open kitchens of the stylish restaurants.

SHEIKH ZAYED ROAD

The Sheikh Zayed strip has several excellent five-star properties along with some great dining options and plenty of nightlife. While the road is strategically positioned for both the beach and the Deira sights, the traffic can be a heartbreaker at certain times of the day.

IBIS WORLD TRADE CENTRE

Map p226   Hotel $

☎ 332 4444; www.ibishotel.com; behind World Trade Centre, Sheikh Zayed Rd; d from Dh295; 🖳 ⊗ 🏊 ♿

Surprisingly stylish, this hotel's groovy lobby makes promises the smallish rooms can't keep. But at this price it's fantastic value for the Sheikh Zayed strip and the best-value digs in Dubai. Sure, it'll probably be filled with convention-goers here for a plastics conference, and there are no views or a pool, but if our next cancelled flight sees us shuttled to an Ibis as good as this, we'll sleep happy.

CROWNE PLAZA HOTEL

Map p226   Hotel $$$

☎ 331 1111; www.dubai.crowneplaza.com; Sheikh Zayed Rd; d from Dh690; 🖳 ⊗ 🖭 🏊 ♿

While this is a very popular and long-standing business hotel, the huge complex is starting to feel more worn out than worn in. Though it doesn't seem to bother the regular business clientele, the tired carpets, small standard rooms and standing room–only bathrooms will be noticeable to the discerning traveller. The health club (featuring two squash courts) and outdoor pool are generously-sized, the views are great, and it's still a fabulous address with the beach and the Creek a short complimentary shuttle away. There's plenty on offer within the hotel complex, with numerous bars and restaurants and a pretty decent shopping centre.

The Ibis World Trade Centre hotel (left) is a stylish affair

DUSIT DUBAI Map p226   Hotel $$$

☎ 343 3333; www.dusit.com; Sheikh Zayed Rd, next to Interchange No 1; s/d from Dh850;

This startling blue-glass edifice, shaped like an upside-down tuning fork, adds yet another architecturally intriguing shape to the Sheikh Zayed Rd strip. While staying at a hotel that is determinedly Thai seems a little odd in Dubai, the warmth of the traditional Thai greeting, the smell of fresh jasmine, and live Thai music played in the foyer of this hotel sets you at ease. The rooms are stylish with exquisite Thai touches, and the top two floors house executive rooms and suites. All rooms have high-speed Internet and there's wi-fi throughout most of the public areas of the hotel. The views from the gym are enough to make you don your running shoes for a look and both the **Benjarong** (p88) Thai restaurant and the **Pax Romana** (p92) Italian restaurant are fine Dubai eateries.

FAIRMONT Map p226   Hotel $$$

☎ 332 5555; www.fairmont.com; Sheikh Zayed Rd; d from Dh960;

This hotel is a distinctive sight at night when its illuminated four-poster towers and colour-cycling lighting scheme joins the glowing chorus of Sheikh Zayed properties. Inside it's busy both architecturally and with guests heading to the numerous restaurants. The standard rooms are of a contemporary design and feature outstanding toiletries and a room safe that allows you to charge your laptop while it's locked away. All rooms have great views and there's a bewildering array of spacious one- and two-bedroom suites. As well as a pool, there's a gym and the Willow Stream Spa with its wide range of treatments, along with some excellent dining options.

NOVOTEL WORLD TRADE CENTRE

Map p226   Hotel $$$

☎ 332 0000; www.novotel.com; behind World Trade Centre; d from Dh969;

This no-nonsense Novotel, situated behind the Sheikh Zayed strip, is kept busy with the business, trade and convention set. The contemporary design and decent breakfasts are both welcome, and it's only a short taxi ride to Dubai's sights and shopping. The swimming pool also makes a welcome sight after enduring the dizzying heat of a souq shopping expedition.

SHANGRI-LA Map p226   Hotel $$$$

☎ 343 8888; www.shangri-la.com; Sheikh Zayed Rd; s/d from Dh1100/1200;

One of the newer breed on the Sheikh Zayed strip, this chic hotel has spacious, comfortable rooms and stunning views of either the city or the sea. Considering that it's a hotel and not a resort, there is

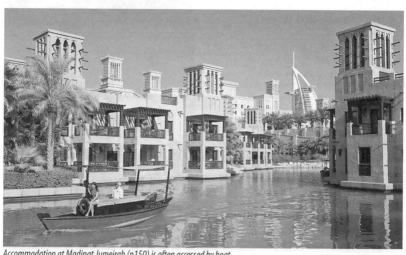

Accommodation at Madinat Jumeirah (p150) is often accessed by boat

a surprising amount of facilities on offer, including a squash and tennis court, a well-equipped gym, separate aerobics room and spa. There are plenty of dining options, with the wonderful Vietnamese/French cuisine of **Hoi An** (p88) a standout.

EMIRATES TOWERS

Map p226   Hotel $$$$
☎ 330 0000; www.emiratestowershotelcom; Sheikh Zayed Rd; d from Dh2160;
🖥 ✕ 🖩 ♨ ♿
While this is arguably the best business hotel in the Middle East, there's plenty here to entertain those with more relaxing things in mind. The standard (rightly called Deluxe) rooms are large and contemporary in style, with touches like a mini hi-fi system, great toiletries, comfy bathrobes and city or desert views. The Tower rooms are the same size but on higher floors, while the suites are much larger and offer thoughtful extras such as limo transfers and airport welcome service. If you're still pining for sand between your toes you have access to facilities at their beach resorts. Apart from that, there's pretty much all you need right in the complex.

JUMEIRAH & NEW DUBAI

The luxury resort hotels along this strip are perfect for a relaxing beach holiday – especially in a city with guaranteed sunshine most of the year! While there's no real budget accommodation here, the summer discounts can be breathtakingly good, although the heat will be just as breathtaking… Keep in mind that you're a long way from the heritage sights, if you can drag yourself away from the hotel wet bar.

DUBAI MARINE BEACH RESORT &

SPA Map pp224-5   Beach Resort $$$
☎ 346 111; www.dxbmarine.com; Jumeirah Rd, Jumeirah; s/d Dh780/840
The somewhat-dated rooms at this resort are set in a series of 33 villas among attractive tropical gardens, small fountains and ponds. There is a petite but well-protected private beach, three pools, a spa and a well-equipped gym. The best

aspect of the resort, however, is the myriad bars, restaurants and clubs – this is a good place to stay if you're after a slice of hedonistic Dubai, especially during the cooler months.

ONE&ONLY ROYAL MIRAGE

Map pp214-15   Resort $$$$
☎ 399 9999; www.oneandonlyresorts.com; Al-Sufouh Rd; Palace/Arabian Court Deluxe from Dh1158/1278, Residence & Spa Prestige from Dh1255; 🖥 ✕ 🖩 ♨ ♿
Even with competition from Madinat Jumeirah in the Arabian-themed resort stakes, this is arguably the most romantic resort on the beach strip. While all the rooms have sea views, you'll spend most of your time just wandering around the resort discovering new alcoves and niches, restaurants and bars. The resort consists of three parts: the Palace, where rooms lean towards a Moorish style; Arabian Court, which is more pan-Arabian; and the Residence & Spa, with its majestic spa and hammam. We'd happily hole up in any of them for as long as our credit cards could hold out – it's the kind of resort that has you rescheduling your flight out.

LE MERIDIEN MINA SEYAHI RESORT

Map pp214-15   Resort $$$$
☎ 399 3333; www.lemeridien-minaseyahi.com; Al-Sufouh Rd; r from Dh1200, with sea view from Dh1400; 🖥 ✕ 🖩 ♨ ♿
This graceful and delightfully landscaped 210-room resort is a prime choice for water-sports enthusiasts – as well as for those who refer to the occasional swim to the wet bar as exercise. The rooms are large, the eateries are good, and service is relaxed and friendly. There's a great gym, a PADI-certified dive centre, sailing craft for hire, and plenty of activities for those who have babies on board.

HILTON DUBAI JUMEIRAH

Map pp214-15   Resort $$$$
☎ 399 1111; www.hilton.com; Al-Sufouh Rd; s/d Dh1250/1350; 🖥 ✕ 🖩 ♨ ♿
This laid-back resort is literally being overshadowed by the massive Jumeirah Beach Residence development inland behind the resort (thankfully, most of the 400 rooms have Gulf views). There's also a generous

stretch of beach and good casual eateries. If you're travelling with children, there are kids' activities, menus, a playground and a baby-sitting service, making it an excellent family resort. The hotel's best restaurant, BiCE (p92), serves the most authentic Italian in Dubai, and after several years still packs in hotel guests and Dubai regulars.

JUMEIRAH BEACH HOTEL
Map pp214-15   Beach Resort $$$$
☎ 348 0000; www.jumeirahbeachhotel.com; Jumeirah Rd, Umm Suqeim; s/d Dh1600/1700;
🖥 ❌ 🖥 🛁 ♿

In spite of its beachside position, this resort-hotel serves a diverse clientele, from beachcombing families to conference-goers pretending that staying here is somehow related to work. The hotel's public areas are full of sun cream–smelling families bumping into PDA-wielding executives planning their afternoon escape to a Dubai golf course. There's nearly a kilometre of private beach (with fantastic views of stablemate Burj Al Arab, p152), but if that's too tame, the Wild Wadi Waterpark (p60) is adjacent. The Deluxe rooms are huge and have views of the Gulf and the Deluxe Balcony rooms are the same apart from the balcony. There are suites of all shapes and sizes, but perhaps the pick of the bunch is the Junior Suite with its personal sun terrace so you don't have to mix it with bucket- and spade-wielding kids. There are enough bars, cafés and restaurants to keep guests of all ages happy.

LE ROYAL MERIDIEN BEACH RESORT
Map pp214-15   Resort $$$$
☎ 399 5555; www.leroyalmeridien-dubai.com; Al-Sufouh Rd; s/d/ste Dh1500/1600/3000;
🖥 ❌ 🖥 🛁 ♿

A lovely stretch of beach and elegant gardens are the standout features of this Arabian-accented resort. There are plenty of water sports on offer, a great spa, extensive health-club facilities and numerous delicious dining options. A great resort for families (there's a popular children's club) or those who want an active holiday. Note that building activity from the nearby Dubai Marina can be heard and seen from many of the rooms.

MINA A' SALAM, MADINAT
JUMEIRAH Map pp214-15   Resort $$$$
☎ 366 8888; www.jumeirahinternational.com; Al-Sufouh Rd; s/d from Dh1750/1850;
🖥 ❌ 🖥 🛁 ♿

This 'harbour of peace' is part of the huge Madinat Jumeirah resort (which also includes Al-Qasr and Dar al-Masyaf) and was developed in a convincing 'old-Arabian' style. It's a breathtakingly beautiful hotel with luxurious, generous-sized sea-facing rooms and excellent service. The resort has some fantastic restaurants and bars, a wonderfully atmospheric souq, Six Senses Spa (p111) and a brilliant health club. Sitting on the balcony of the hotel's Bahri Bar, looking across the lake to the Burj Al Arab, is an experience not to be missed – if you can drag yourself away from your own balcony.

DUBAI'S DRAWING BOARD...

Hotel openings are a common event in Dubai. Here's a short list of the more attention-grabbing hotels coming soon to a city where no idea is too outlandish or expensive.

Armani Hotel (www.armanihotels.com) It speaks volumes for Dubai's kudos these days that when Armani finally decided to go into the hotel business he teamed up with a Dubai-based company, with its first hotel project to be located in the world's tallest building, the Burj Dubai (p29). Due 2008.

Hydropolis (www.hydropolis.com) The world's first underwater hotel promises guests the healing power of water. If that doesn't work there's also a cosmetic surgery clinic opening at this aquatically audacious resort. Due 2007.

Palazzo Dubai (www.palazzoversace.ae) It's fitting that the Versace brand's second hotel property should be located in Dubai, when the first was at Australia's glitzy and gaudy Gold Coast. The papered and pedicured feet of the guests in Dubai, though, won't have to endure the city's hot sands – plans are afoot for temperature-controlled sand. Due 2008.

Trump Tower It was almost inevitable that publicity-loving real-estate developer Donald Trump would come to Dubai. It was also predictable that the project would be as silly as a gold tulip–shaped structure located on The Palm, Jumeirah, proving that you can't buy taste, no matter how rich you are. Opening TBA.

AL-QASR, MADINAT JUMEIRAH

Map pp214-15   Hotel $$$$

☎ 366 8888; www.madinatjumeirah.com;
Al-Sufouh Rd, Umm Suqeim; d from Dh1910;
🖵 ✖ ⊠ ♿ ☕

Surrounded by man-made waterways, this
hotel stands alone literally and figuratively.
The centrepiece of the extraordinary Madinat Jumeirah resort, it's a majestic hotel
with fabulous views and attentive service.
Built like a magnificent palace and far more
opulent than its sister hotel **Mina A' Salam**
(opposite), Al-Qasr boasts deluxe rooms
with ocean views (we'd happily retire in
one) and club rooms that offer the usual
executive floor perks. While it shares facilities (such as the health club) with Mina
A' Salam, the splendid public areas of this
five-star deluxe hotel feel more private, as
much of the dining and drinking take place
over at Mina A' Salam. You get the feeling
that it's just how they want it.

GROSVENOR WEST MARINA BEACH

Map pp214-15   Beach Resort $$$$

☎ 399 8888; www.grosvenorhouse.lemeridien.com;
Dubai Marina; s & d Dh2100; 🖵 ✖ ⊠ ♿ ☕

Grosvenor House takes the prize as the first
hotel opened among the jumble of cloud-
busting buildings of the Marina. While
there is a disconcerting amount of building
going on around the hotel, all the hotel
rooms face The Palm development, which

*A friendly welcome at the Burj Al Arab (p152) awaits the
guests of this 'seven star' hotel*

is a fascinating sight in itself. The 'standard'
rooms are rightly called deluxe as they are
spacious and have balconies – perfect for
a champagne toast after buying one of
Dubai's man-made islands. The rooms are
well-appointed with huge plasma TVs and

DESERT DREAMS

Dubai now has two outstanding desert escapes, the **Al-Maha Desert Resort & Spa** (Map p154; ☎ 303 4224; www
.al-maha.com; Margham; ste incl meals & activities Dh4770; 🖵 ✖ ⊠ ☕) and the recently opened **Bab al-Shams
Desert Resort & Spa** (Map p154; ☎ 832 6699; www.babalshams.com; Margham; r Dh1400; 🖵 ✖ ⊠ ♿ ☕). If
your stay in Dubai is going to be longer than five days, we heartily recommend a couple of nights at one of these two
resorts – budget permitting, of course!

Al-Maha is an eco-tourism resort and spa, located 65km southeast of Dubai, which is part of the Dubai Desert
Conservation Reserve (DDCR). The resort is named after the Arabic word for the endangered scimitar-horned oryx, bred
successfully as part of the DDCR's program. The resort has 40 suites and two Royal suites, each a luxurious, stand-alone,
tent-roofed structure complete with a large, chilled private plunge pool. Privacy is at a premium here – private vehicles,
visitors and children under 12 are not allowed at the resort – so it's a very romantic getaway. While there are activities
such as fascinating desert wildlife drives and sunset camel rides (ending with a glass of bubbly), the finest activity is
having dinner on your balcony looking out at the beautiful desert landscape of peach-coloured dunes, dotted by the
shapes of the beautiful white oryx happily grazing.

Less exclusive is the Bab al-Shams resort. While the activities list at this newish resort is still growing, it makes a
great retreat for some serious downtime. With its Gulf décor and labyrinthine layout, it's quite the desert medina. The
pool is the main focus of daytime activity, with a superb bar for sunset *sheesha* and a view of the falconry exhibition
and pretty parading camels. The traditional Al-Hadheerah desert restaurant offers the over-the-top Arabian experience
complete with belly dancer, band and endless *sheesha*.

a very cool networked music and DVD playback system. The suites lose the balcony but gain an extra plasma TV and plenty of en-suite space, and the executive floors give you access to a hip lounge and all-day snacks and drinks. Heading downstairs, there are plenty of eateries to choose from, as well as the **Buddha Bar** (p100).

BURJ AL ARAB Map pp214-15   Hotel $$$$
☎ 301 7111; www.burj-al-arab.com; Jumeirah Rd, Umm Suqeim; d from Dh3859; 🖳 ⊠ 🖳 🔧 ⬇️
If you like to name-drop hotels you've stayed at, this one affords you the ultimate bragging rights – after all, how many self-appointed seven-star hotels are there in the world? Its ostentatious opulence will leave you reeling, as will the unbeatable views from the two-storey suites of this Dubai icon. If you're contemplating staying at the world's tallest dedicated hotel and you're thinking 'Is it worth the money?' you're asking the wrong question. Seeking a good-value five-star in Jumeirah? Search again. Looking for a once-in-a-lifetime experience? Let that Rolls-Royce gently glide you up to the entrance. But while it's sleek and stylish from the outside, prepare yourself for a shock once you feast your eyes on the gaudy, post-modern Arabian interior. Having left taste exhausted at the door, the décor seeks to impress with its sheer extravagance. With 202 suites and over 1200 staff, service is never anything less than personal and whatever you desire is never more than a 'genie's lamp rub' away. As for the décor of the rooms themselves, suffice it to say you half expect an Arabian Joan Collins to make an entrance via the internal staircase…

Excursions

Strait of Hormuz

Kumzar

Tumb
Kubra

Ras Sheikh Masud

Khasab

Musandam
Peninsula

Bukha

THE
GULF

Tibat
Sham

Abu
Musa

Khor Khowair

OMAN

Rams

Gulf of Oman

Ras al-Khaimah   Habab

Al-Jazirah al-Hamra   RAS
AL-KHAIMAH

Al-Rafaah   Hamraniyah   Habab

Digdagga

Umm al-Qaiwain

Ras al-Khaimah
International
Airport

Dibba

FUJAIRAH

Dadna
Al-Aqah
Sharam

Hamriya   UMM
AL-QAIWAIN

Az-Zora   AJMAN

Al-Hilew   Biatah

Al-Uyaynah

Bidiya

Shumayliyah Mountains

Ajman   Sharjah
International
Airport

Nabgha

Tayyibah

SHARJAH

Rikaisa
Dam

Khor Fakkan

Manama

AJMAN

OMAN   Qidfa

Sharjah   Al-Dhaid   Masafi   Madha   Mirbah

Dubai   Dubai
International
Airport

Al-Awir

SHARJAH   Siji

FUJAIRAH

Bithnah   Fujairah

Al-Haba

Mileiha   Fiji

Fujairah
International
Airport

Kalba

Jebel Ali Port   Jebel Ali Village

Bahuth
Ruwayyah

Al-Madam

Hajar Mountains

Khor Kalba
Conservation
Reserve

Al-Liseli   Big Red

Al-Ghirefah

RAS AL-
KHAIMAH

Khatmat
Malahah

Margham

Mazeirah

AJMAN   Wahlah

Muraqqab

Bab al-Shams
Desert Resort
& Spa

Al Maha Desert
Resort & Spa

Ash-Shuayb

Masfout

DUBAI

Al-Wajajah

Al-Samha

DUBAI   Al-Faqa

Hatta

Hatta Rock Pools

Ajban

Al-Haiyi

Sumayni

Fa'iyyah

Al-Juwayf

Abu Dhabi

Sharm   Zaymi

Al-Ain
International
Airport

Sweihan

Mahdah

Al Hijr al-Gharbi   Western

Al-Ohah

ABU DHABI

Al-Saad

Buraimi Oasis

Wadi
al-Jizzi

Hajar

Al-Khatam   Al-Khawrah

Zakhir

Al-Ain   Buraimi

Al-Wasit

Al-Khaznah

Al-Zahir

Jebel Hafit

(1160m)   Hafit

UNITED ARAB
EMIRATES

OMAN

0   40 km
0   20 miles

Mudaysis

Excursions

Dubai is dazzling – and difficult to leave. But if you're staying in Dubai for more than a few days, or if your threshold for shopping and swimming is low, there are plenty of excursions that can reveal to you the many different facets of the UAE.

You can witness the almost mythical haze of the edge of the Empty Quarter of the desert and jagged mountains painted in multiple shades of ochre and violet, subtly changing colour. You'll pass camels wandering down the road and tiny roadside mosques, and you can visit an oasis city replete with plantations of date palms burdened with fruit, and swim at pristine white sandy beaches with barely a hotel in sight.

All the trips mentioned here can be arranged with any tour company in Dubai (see p48). However (apart from visiting Sharjah, to which you can take a taxi), we suggest you hire a car to go further afield (see p175) – that way you can pull over and get those classic camel shots! We don't, however, recommend hiring a 4WD to go off-road unless you have experience driving in dunes and wadis.

One of the wonderful things about these trips is how quickly the feel of your surroundings changes once outside the city limits of Dubai. So no matter what type of experience you're craving, given the excellent road network in the UAE, nothing's further away than a three-hour drive from Dubai. Enjoy!

DESERT SAFARI

There's nothing like getting out into the desert, especially at sunset. Don't leave Dubai without doing a desert safari. We strongly recommend an overnighter – sleeping under the stars is magic! Tours by the companies listed all offer roughly the same experience: departing in the afternoon, they travel out to the desert and, after an exhilarating bit of 4WD 'dune-bashing', you reach the camp with enough time for sand-boarding and a camel ride before sunset. After working up an appetite, you can enjoy an Arabian/Lebanese barbecue dinner. (While there is no alcohol provided, people have been known to sneak a bottle or two on the trip to drink under the stars, but you didn't hear that from us!) Dinner is followed by a belly dancer and *sheesha* before returning to Dubai. This kind of trip can cost around Dh320 and upwards per person, and if you haven't experienced the desert before it's a must! If you're a time-poor traveller, the trip is worthwhile because you can tick off several must-do activities in one hit. But if you really want that Bedouin experience, we highly recommend staying overnight at the camp and sleeping under the stars (generally for an extra fee).

Arabian Adventures (Map pp214–15; ☎ 343 9966; www.arabian-adventures.com; Emirates Holidays Bldg, Interchange No 2, Sheikh Zayed Rd, Dubai)

Net Tours & Travels (Map pp218–19; ☎ 266 8661; www.nettoursdubai.com; Al-Bakhit Centre, Abu Baker al-Siddiq Rd, Hor al-Anz)

Orient Tours (Map pp218–19; ☎ 282 8238; www.orienttours.co.ae; Al-Garhoud Rd, Deira)

MOUNTAIN RETREAT

Head to scenic **Hatta** (p159), deep in the rugged Hajar Mountains, for a relaxing break away from the city. Half the fun of Hatta is getting there – driving on a freeway surrounded by red-tinged dunes and arid, craggy mountains is definitely part of the adventure.

CULTURAL JOURNEY

While Dubai's architecture and resort ideas keep getting wilder, arty **Sharjah** (p156) opts for a different kind of creative outlet. Dubai's next-door neighbour has positioned itself as the cultural capital of the UAE and was named by Unesco as the cultural capital of

Excursions

the Arab world. Galleries and artists abound and Sharjah even has an International Art Biennale.

LUSH OASIS

Al-Ain (p164) will provide you with that 'oasis in the desert' feel, as both Al-Ain and neighbouring Buraimi in Oman lie within the Buraimi Oasis, a lush area of date plantations. While the road is excellent, it passes through enough sand dunes to give you a feeling of just how welcome the oasis must have been after a couple of weeks' travel by camel. The cooler, drier temperature and delicious dates don't hurt either.

BEACHES & FISHING VILLAGES

Head for the **East Coast** (p160). The scenic drive takes you to some beautiful beaches and rocky headlands, home to a string of fishing villages, rugged wadis, crumbling watchtowers, restored forts, dive sites, and the busy ports of Khor Fakkan and Fujairah.

SHARJAH

Arty Sharjah, Dubai's closest neighbour, has positioned itself as the cultural capital of the UAE, and was named by Unesco as the cultural capital of the Arab world. With its proliferation of superb museums and galleries, the tag is deserved, but it's an ironic choice considering that there is a deepening conservatism in the emirate (see the boxed text, below). In addition to the cultural highlights, Sharjah also offers wonderful souq shopping and many quality souvenirs that are less expensive than in Dubai.

The city was the most important port on the Arabian side of the lower Gulf, and during the latter half of the century its rulers vied with those of Abu Dhabi for the area's leading political role. However, this changed in the 1980s with Dubai's ascendancy in wealth and political power. Today, Sharjah is responsible for some 45% of the UAE's total industrial production, and it's increasingly becoming a dormitory suburb for Dubai, as rents and the general cost of living are much lower.

Most visitors to Dubai tend to miss out on Sharjah, but it's easy to get to (provided you travel mid-morning or mid-evening to avoid the traffic jams) and the main sights can be covered in a few hours.

The centre of Sharjah is the area between the Corniche and Al-Zahra Rd, from the Central Market to Sheikh Sultan bin Saqr al-Qasimi Rd. It's not a huge area and it's pretty easy to get around on foot if the heat's not too debilitating. Sharjah can be hellish to navigate when driving. Al-Wahda Rd, the main link with Dubai, is gridlocked during peak hours, especially at the King Faisal Sq overpass. The proliferation of roundabouts, lengthy street names, and the absence of directions to Ajman or Dubai (except on the outskirts) make it easy to get lost once you're in the centre. Street signs tend to be written in very small print

---

DECENCY LAWS

When you're visiting Sharjah, keep in mind that in late 2001 Sharjah's government introduced new laws on 'decency and public conduct'. These are the strictest laws governing dress in the UAE, and along with Sharjah's ban on alcohol, they represent the deep conservatism in the emirate. For men, the laws mean no bare chests or 'short' shorts in public or in commercial or public offices. Knee-length shorts are OK, if not exactly welcomed. For women, the laws forbid clothing that exposes the stomach, upper arms, shoulders, and back, clothing above the knee, and 'tight and transparent clothing that describes the body'. If you're going for a dip, only strip down to your swimwear at the beach, remembering to cover up before you leave. While this is all pretty straightforward, the next bit is a little more intriguing...

The laws also forbid 'a man and woman who are not connected by a legally acceptable relationship to be alone in a vehicle, in public places, or in suspicious times or circumstances'. The interpretation of the laws is up to Sharjah's police and courts and can involve anything from a warning to jail time.

and have similar-sounding names – Sheikh Mohammed bin Sultan al-Qasimi Rd versus Sheikh Khalid bin Mohammed al-Qasimi Rd, for example. The website www .sharjah-welcome.com is a comprehensive resource aimed at tourists and it also has a decent map that's worth printing (once you click on the map of the world, the map of the country, the map of the emirate, and so on!).

Make imposing **Al-Hisn Fort** your first stop. Sitting somewhat forlornly in the middle of Burj Ave, the fort was once the residence of the ruling family of Sharjah. Originally built in 1820, it has been fully restored and houses a fascinating collection of photographs, weapons, jewellery, currency, documents, and items used in the pearl trade. Many of the photos from the 1930s show members of the ruling Al-Qasimi family and the British Trucial Oman Scouts who were stationed here at the time. There's also some fascinat-

TRANSPORT – SHARJAH

Distance from Dubai 10km

Direction Northeast

Travel time 20 to 60 minutes, traffic dependent

Car Avoid peak hours (8am to 10am, 1pm to 2pm and 4pm to 7pm), which are horrendous. Take Al Ittihad Rd, which is signposted E11. The 'E' represents an inter-emirate highway and this one takes you up the coast as well as back through to Abu Dhabi.

Taxi & Minibus Minibuses (Dh5) go from the Deira taxi and minibus stand (Map pp216–17) on Omar ibn al-Khattab Rd. A taxi will cost you about Dh25. You won't be able to get a minibus back to Dubai though – instead, take a taxi from the stand at the north end of Rolla Sq, which should cost around Dh30.

ing footage of the first Imperial Airways flights from London, which landed here in 1932 on their way to India. The difference between Sharjah then and now is astonishing.

Next, we suggest you do our Arts Amble (p65) through Sharjah, taking in both the Heritage and Arts areas and their many charming renovated buildings and wonderful museums. Most of the buildings have been faithfully constructed incorporating traditional designs and materials, such as sea rock and gypsum. See p27 to learn more about traditional architecture.

If you prefer to explore on your own, coming from Burj Ave you'll arrive at the Heritage Area that really consists of two tiny neighbourhoods, Al Sheyoukh and Al Maraija, now linked since the area has been fully restored and pedestrianised. Coming from Burj Ave, you should arrive at **Literature Square** and the **House of Poetry**. There are a number of interesting little museums around here that come under the umbrella of the Sharjah Heritage Museum. The main museum is housed in the former home of the Al-Naboodah family, a beautiful courtyard house with displays of clothing and jewellery. The small **Sharjah Islamic Museum** is also worth a peek for its collection of coins from all over the Islamic world and a number of handwritten Qurans and old writing implements. There are also some impressive ceramics from Turkey, Syria and Afghanistan, as well as a display on the covering of the Kaaba stone at Mecca, the most holy sacred shrine for Muslims, including a copy of the embroidered cloth and the original bag that once held the holy key to the Kaaba. While there are a number of other tiny museums in this area, many of them don't have any signage in English and would only warrant 10 minutes of your time in each.

Make your next stop the charming **Souq Al-Arsah**, located on the south side of Burj Ave, which was restored by the government after large sections of it fell to pieces during the 1970s and '80s. *Arsah* (although the sign on the souq says 'Arsa'!) means a large open space or courtyard and was originally a stop for travellers. The *areesh* (palm frond) roof and wooden pillars give it a real traditional feel and it's a wonderful place to wander around and look for unusual Arabian 'antiques' and curios and Bedouin jewellery – you're sure to find some amazing stuff that you won't see elsewhere. Also take the time to look at **Dar al Dhyafa**, at the back of the souq, the beautifully restored house that is now an atmospheric hotel. It's the only hotel like it in the UAE – you might just decide to stay!

From the hotel's rooftop (ask nicely!) you'll get a great view of the only round wind-tower in the Gulf, at the **Majlis of Ibrahim Mohammed al-Midfa**. Ibrahim Al Midfa started the first newspaper in the UAE in 1927 and was an advisor to the ruling family. The main **Al Midfa House**, across from the *majlis* (formal meeting room), has an elephant engraved on its door that's worth a look.

> **DID YOU KNOW?**
>
> *Bait* means house in Arabic. You'll see it on signs a lot in the Sharjah Heritage area – eg Beit Al Naboodah, Bait Al Garbi, and so on.

When you're done with shopping, refuel at the souq's traditional coffeehouse before following our walk back to Burj Ave to the atmospheric Arts Area. Here you'll find the excellent **Sharjah Art Museum**, with a good permanent collection of art that originally belonged to the Ruler of Sharjah, including Orientalist painting and some provocative contemporary art, as you'd expect from a museum that hosts the cutting-edge Sharjah International Art Biennale (see p30). This is by far the finest art gallery in the UAE. There's also a library and a stylish, cool-looking coffee shop in the foyer, that offers quick tasty meals.

In the small area around the peaceful main square in front of the museum – a lovely place to relax in cooler weather – are a number of arts centres and small museums that are also worth a look, including the **Very Special Arts Centre**, a workshop and gallery for disabled artists, and the **Emirates Fine Arts Society**, which also displays the works of local artists.

Near Cultural Sq, you'll find the fairly hi-tech **Sharjah Archaeological Museum**, displaying the earliest archaeological finds in the emirate, dating from 5000 BC, and up to the beginning of the Islamic era. Video, audio and multimedia are used creatively, fortunately avoiding the crushingly dull experience often associated with small-town archaeological museums. Here you'll enjoy engaging exhibitions of tombs, mud-brick and *areesh* houses, along with weapons, pottery, tools, coins and jewellery.

If you're in the mood for more shopping, check out the **Central Market**, also known as the 'Blue Souq', located on the Corniche near the King Faisal Mosque. Consisting of two grand halls connected by an overhead bridge, it has the lowest prices (although no longer the best selection) of carpets in the country, as well as dozens of shops selling handicrafts, souvenirs, 'antiques' and jewellery from Oman, India and Iran.

The gold-domed **Al Majarrah Souq** on the Corniche has about 50 shops selling textiles, perfumes and clothes, while the **Gold Centre** at the crossing of Al-Qassimia and Al-Wahda Sts has about 40 shops selling jewellery. The **Fruit & Vegetable Souq**, **Animal Souq**, **Plant Souq** and **Fish Souq** are also great places to wander around and check out the local action.

Sights & Information

To telephone from outside Sharjah, you need to use the area code ☎ 06.

Al Majarrah Souq (Sharjah Creek, close to Holiday Inn Resort; ⊕ 9am-1pm & 4.30-10pm)

Al-Hisn Fort (☎ 06-568 5500; Burj Ave; ⊕ 9am-1pm & 5-8pm Tue-Sun, 5pm-8pm Fri, women only Wed)

Central Market (Al Majaz, end of Corniche Rd, close to Khaled Lagoon; ⊕ 9am-1pm & 4-11pm Sat-Thu, 4-11pm Fri)

Gold Centre (Al Yarmook, at the crossing of Al-Qassimia & Al-Wahda Sts; ⊕ 10am-1pm & 4.30-10pm)

Sharjah Archaeological Museum (☎ 06-566 5466; Al-Abar Rd, near Cultural Sq; ⊕ 9am-1pm & 5-8pm Mon-Sat, 5-8pm Fri, women only Wed afternoon)

Sharjah Art Museum (☎ 06-568 8222; Al Shwaiheyn, close to Burj Ave; ⊕ 9am-1pm & 5-8pm Sat-Thu, 5-8pm Fri, women only Wed afternoon)

Souq Al-Arsah (Al Muraija, Heritage Area; ⊕ 9am-1pm & 4.30-8.30pm, some shops open later)

Eating

Souq Al-Arsah Coffeehouse (Al-Muraija, Heritage Area; mains Dh10) Visiting this atmospheric old coffeehouse is tradition for many. For Dh10 you'll get a large biryani as well as some fresh dates for dessert. Backgammon sets are available and sweet tea is served out of a huge urn. Make sure to greet the locals inside with *A salaam a'laykum* as you enter!

Kitchen (☎ 06-568 8101; Sarah Centre, near Al-Hisn Fort; mains Dh10) A simple yet tasty Indian spot between the Arts and Heritage areas, close to the Corniche.

Automatic Restaurant (☎ 06-572 7335; Buhairah Corniche; mains Dh20) This is an excellent branch of the reasonably priced tasty Lebanese chain.

Al-Fawar (☎ 06-559 4662; King Faisal Rd; mains Dh20) A popular, long-standing Lebanese restaurant with a cheaper cafeteria-style section next door, which also offers takeaway.

Sanobar Restaurant (☎ 06-528 3501; Al-Khan Rd; mains Dh20) An exceptional Lebanese and seafood restaurant with a Mediterranean atmosphere and prices far lower than what you'd find in Dubai.

OFF-ROADING

If you're experienced at four-wheel driving and driving off-road – whether along wadis or on sand dunes – then get hold of Dariush Zandi's excellent guide *Off-Road in the Emirates*. This has the most accurate, up-to-date and detailed directions of any of the guides around, and it's often better than asking for directions – many times people will offer directions that may not always be accurate, just to save face. If you don't have experience driving on dunes or in the desert, then we don't encourage it (it can be dangerous!) and strongly suggest you go on an organised tour instead (see p155). These can be lots of fun, you get to meet new people, and the guide will often share knowledge with you about the area that you wouldn't have been able to find out on your own.

Sleeping

Dar al Dhyafa (☎ 06-528 3501/569 6111; fax 569 6222; Souq Al-Arsah; price on request) If you're enchanted by the ambience of the souq area, this charming boutique style hotel offers a rare opportunity for you to enjoy it overnight, and prices are negotiable depending on how busy the hotel is. The 'bridal' suite is the pick of the rooms on offer, but all of the rooms are decorated in traditional style and Emirati food is served in the *majlis*. Staying here is a truly special experience.

Beach Hotel (☎ 06-528 3501; beachtl@emirates.net .ae, Al-Khalidia area; r Dh350; ☒) If you want the sun and sand but don't want to pay Dubai prices, this low-rise seaside hotel with a huge swimming pool and a pristine white sandy beach is a good midrange option and close to all the Sharjah sights. Just remember it's dry, so you will need to bring the duty-free!

HATTA

An enclave of Dubai spectacularly nestled in the Hajar Mountains, Hatta is a popular weekend getaway spot – so if you want to explore it peacefully avoid going on a weekend! About 105km from Dubai by road (20km of which runs through Omani territory), Hatta makes a good overnight stop on a two- or three-day itinerary. There is no customs check as you cross the border, but if you're driving a rental car your insurance does not cover accidents in Oman.

This mountain town was once an important source of tobacco, as well as a vital staging post on the trade route between Dubai and Oman. Today, Hatta's main drawcards are its relatively cool, humidity-free climate and the dramatic mountain scenery. Unfortunately, the rock pools near Hatta, which were once one of the UAE's highlights, are now polluted, dirty, covered in graffiti and generally very disappointing. Hatta itself, however, makes a good base for off-road trips through the mountains and is a wonderful place to relax.

The **Heritage Village** is Hatta's main attraction. While nowhere near as impressive as the Heritage Village at Shindagha in Dubai, this one is worth a quick look if you have some time. It's a re-creation of a traditional mountain village, with traditional buildings dedicated to weaponry, local songs and dances, palm-tree products, handicrafts, weaving, traditional dress, social life and old village society. There's also a watchtower you can climb for some great views over the valley, along with a functioning *falaj* (traditional irrigation channel) that waters small but lush agricultural plots just below the village. The turn-off for the Heritage Village is signposted on the main street, about 3km from the Fort Roundabout.

Despite the **Hatta rock pools'** sorry state, most people still come to visit this once lovely site, about 20km south of Hatta town across the border in Oman (but access is from Hatta). The miniature canyon has cold, clear water year-round, and while most people find a visit to Hatta disappointing these days, some people still find the experience of leaping off the rocks into the icy water enjoyable. Be warned: the area gets crowded at weekends. You don't *need* a 4WD to get to the rock pools from Hatta, although it's strongly advised.

INSURANCE WARNING

Unless you make specific arrangements, your rental car insurance will not cover you when in Oman. This means that if you go to Hatta, which involves passing through about 20km of Omani territory, or visit Buraimi on an excursion to Al-Ain, you will not be covered for any accident while in Omani territory. Coverage for Oman increases the insurance rate as well as increasing the rental rate significantly.

TRANSPORT – HATTA

Distance from Dubai 105km

Direction Southeast

Travel time 90 minutes

Car From Trade Centre roundabout, take the Za'abeel exit in the direction of Nad Al Sheeba – there are signs for Hatta and Oman – to take the E44, which you follow all the way to Hatta.

Public Transport From Dubai, buses leave every hour for Hatta from 6.10am to 9pm (Dh10, one hour) departing from the Deira bus station (Map pp216–17). In Hatta, the buses depart from the red bus shelter near the Hatta Mountains Restaurant, leaving Hatta for Dubai every hour from 6am to 9pm. You can buy tickets from the driver. Shared taxis leave from Bur Dubai bus station (Map pp220–1) and cost Dh30, or you can negotiate the whole car and driver for around Dh150.

However, if you want to continue past the pools and on to Al-Ain, only attempt it with a 4WD and an experienced driver behind the wheel. If you don't have your own transport, the **Hatta Fort Hotel** offers a 4WD safari to the rock pools. A three-hour trip for six people costs Dh600, including soft drinks and towels. A seven-hour trip for six people costs Dh1400 including a picnic lunch.

Sights & Information

Heritage Village (admission free; 🕑 8am-7.30pm Sat-Thu, 3-9pm Fri)

Sleeping & Eating

To telephone from outside Hatta, you need to use the area code ☎ 04.

Hatta Fort Hotel (☎ 04-852 3211; www.jebelali-international.com; r Dh550; 🏊) The only place to stay in Hatta. However, that's not a bad thing – the rooms are spacious, comfortable and well equipped.

Built in 1986, the hotel is renowned for its dramatic setting amid lush green gardens with arid mountains all around. It has a lovely swimming pool and extensive sports facilities, including a modest nine-hole golf course.

Gazebo Coffee Shop (mains Dh40) A popular lunch stop in a lovely spot overlooking the Hatta Fort Hotel pool.

Jeema Restaurant (mains Dh65) Has great views overlooking the Hajar mountains and serves fine French cuisine; on a cool winter's evening the hotel also does good buffets around the pool.

EAST COAST

The Hajar Mountains provide a stunning backdrop to the East Coast waters of the Gulf of Oman, making this one of the most beautiful parts of the UAE, and one of our favourite spots. We'd be happy just to drive through the spectacular arid mountains, but it also gets green here because the run-off from the hills provides irrigation for most of the year. There are wadis to explore in the mountains, and water holes that are full year-round.

Masafi has a colourful Friday market (on every day) that's worth a pitstop just to check out the activity. Dibba is a pretty seaside town that's worth a brief detour on the way to the wonderful long, wide beach of Al-Aqah. Bidiya mosque is the oldest in

BIKING UP BIG RED

Midway between Dubai and Hatta is the 100m-high dune known as Big Red. The highway cuts right between the towering peach-coloured dune. This is a popular spot for local 4WD fanatics to let down their tyres and tackle the slopes. On weekends, dozens of vehicles crawl up and down the soft sands and it gets very crowded. Presumably any wildlife here has long since fled. If you want to hire a quad bike, both **Al-Badayer Motors** (☎ 050 655 5447) and **Al-Ramool Motors** (☎ 050 453 4401/050 698 5678) hire them from Dh60 for 30 minutes. Both are open from 8am until sunset daily. You can also put the kids on the back of a camel or pony, and there's a small kiosk.

the country, nestled beneath a hill dotted with watchtowers. The whole area north of Khor Fakkan is well known for diving and snorkelling, while south of Khor Fakkan the sea is somewhat less inviting – the port nearby at Fujairah is the second-busiest bunkering (refuelling) port in the world, and at any time there are hundreds of ships queued up offshore, a line of them running the entire length of the coast! A special effort should be made to check out the Friday afternoon bullfights (p163) at Fujairah – trust us, there is nothing like them! And just a short drive south from there is the atmospheric old settlement of Kalba and the gorgeous Khor Kalba mangroves.

The small town of **Masafi**, an enclave of Ajman Emirate, 35km from Fujairah, is at the junction where the road from Dubai to the East Coast splits into two and heads north to Dibba and south to Fujairah.

Known as the location of the Masafi water-bottling factory, the town is also famous for its **Friday market**. Despite its name, the market is actually open every day of the week and has an enormous range of carpets, some handicrafts and souvenirs, plants, fruit and vegetables and cold drinks for sale. Some of the carpets send the kitsch-meter off the scale, such as the one of Sheikh Zayed, but they make fun souvenirs for people with a sense of humour. You'll get an excellent deal here, depending on the traffic, and especially compared to Dubai (but keep in mind these carpets are machine-made).

When you arrive at the split in the road, we recommend heading north in the direction of **Dibba**. Although there are no actual sights at Dibba, it's worth a quick look for its traditional way of life, quiet laid-back atmosphere, pretty bay and swimming beaches, and abandoned old boats on the shore.

A short distance down the coast is **Al-Aqah Beach**.

Just offshore from the **Sandy Beach Motel** is **Snoopy Island**, a popular diving and snorkelling spot. There are stonefish around the island, so wear shoes if you're planning to go for a swim.

The charming fishing village of **Bidiya** is one of the oldest towns in the Gulf. Archaeological digs have shown that the site of the town has been settled more or less continuously since the 3rd millennium BC. Today it's best known for its restored **mosque**, a small structure of stone, mud brick and gypsum; it's is still in use and is the oldest in the UAE. It's said to have been built around AD 640, although other sources date it as far back as 1449 BC. Built into a low hillside along the main road just north of the village, and on the hillside above and behind it, are several restored **watchtowers**.

Bidiya Mosque (above) is the oldest existing in the country, but its construction date is unknown

One of Sharjah Emirate's enclaves, **Khor Fakkan** is the largest town on the East Coast after Fujairah, and sits on the prettiest bay in the UAE. Unfortunately, the development of tourism has been somewhat held back by Sharjah's ban on alcohol, which is why most visitors stay at the Meridien Al-Aqqa or the Hilton in Fujairah.

Khor Fakkan's picturesque Corniche is bounded by the port and fish market at the southern end, and the faded Oceanic Hotel to the north. There is a lovely beach in between, fronted by a lush strip of parkland. **Sharq Island**, at the entrance to Khor Fakkan's bay, is another popular diving spot – contact any of the diving operators listed (see above) to arrange a diving excursion. (And don't worry: *sharq* means 'east' in Arabic!)

The prosperous but small city of **Fujairah** is the capital of the emirate of the same name, and while there's not a great deal to see in Fujairah itself, it makes a good base for exploring the rest of the East Coast if you want to take your time. The main shopping strip is Hamad bin Abdullah Rd, between the Fujairah Trade Centre and the coast. Along this road, at the intersection with the coast road, is the Central Market.

It's worth taking a walk through the **old town**. Many of the buildings here have been restored (including the recently renovated 300-year-old **Fujairah Fort**, overlooking the old town) and have wonderful decorative elements and carved wooden doors with fabulous big brass handles. While the Fort was not open at the time of research, it's still possible to take a walk around the area, and to get a fairly close look. It's not known when it will be possible to visit, as it was due to open some time ago.

Nearby, the unexciting **Fujairah Museum** has some limited exhibits on maritime activities, archaeological finds from around the emirate (such as items from tombs near Qidfa dating from 1500 BC), displays of heritage jewellery and a collection of photographs showing local life in the pre-oil era.

IT'S PADI TIME!

To check out the wonderful sea life in this region it's best to go diving with PADI (Professional Association of Diving Instructors) approved dive centres. As well as a full open-water diving course (which costs around Dh1700), they all offer 'discover diving' courses that include instruction, pool diving and often a shallow open-water dive for around Dh250. Below is a list of PADI-certified dive centres on the East Coast.

Al Boom Diving (☎ 09-204 4925; www.alboomdiving.com; Le Meridian Al-Aqah Beach resort)

Divers Down Khor Fakkan Dive Centre (☎ 09-237 0299; Oceanic Hotel, Khor Fakkan)

Sandy Beach Diving Centre (☎ 09-244 5555; www.sandybm.com; Sandy Beach Motel, Al-Aqah Beach)

Scuba International Diving College (☎ 09-220 0060; www.scubainternational.net; Fujairah International Marine Club)

TRANSPORT – EAST COAST

Distance from Dubai 130km

Direction East

Travel time 90 minutes

Car Take the E11 towards Sharjah and then head in the direction of Dhaid, on the E88. At Masafi you can take the E89 road heading north to Dibba or south to Fujairah. We recommend going north first to Dibba and then driving south along the coast. If you're heading here on a Thursday morning, this would give you enough time to take a quick look at the market at Masafi and see Dibba, check into a hotel such as the Meridien Al-Aqqa for the night, then complete your sightseeing of the southern coast in the morning, arriving for the Fujairah bullfights right on time!

Public Transport Minibuses leave from the Deira taxi and minibus station (Map pp216–17) and cost Dh25. Long-distance taxis cost Dh25 shared or around Dh200 to hire the whole car. In Fujairah the taxi station is on the road to Sharjah and Dubai. Minibuses from Dubai continue as far as Khor Fakkan. A shared taxi costs Dh10 (or around Dh30 for the whole car) from Fujairah to Khor Fakkan and Dh20 (or Dh70 for the whole vehicle) to Dibba. However, depending on the day/time, you should be able to negotiate a discount. You can get a taxi from Fujairah to Al-Aqah Beach Resort for Dh75.

The most exciting thing to do on a visit to Fujairah is to watch the **bullfighting** (see below). On the road to Kalba, near Al Rughailat Bridge, it's easy to find – just look for all the 4WDs.

If you keep heading south you'll arrive at the traditional fishing village of **Kalba** (part of the Sharjah emirate), which remains wonderfully true to what life would have been like on the Gulf coast earlier this century. *Shasha* (small canoe-shaped fishing boats made from stripped palm fronds) and crayfish baskets line the beach, and fishermen set out every morning and pull in their nets each evening.

The **Khor Kalba Conservation Reserve** (*khor* means inlet in Arabic) is just south of town and is the site of the oldest mangrove forest in Arabia. Birdlife is abundant in the reserve – the only place in the world that the Khor Kalba white-collared kingfisher is found! It's possible to hire boats from the local fishermen and paddle up the inlets into the mangroves.

On Friday afternoons a mostly local and enthusiastic crowd gathers for the bull-on-bull action at Fujairah (below)

Sights & Information

Ain al-Madhab Garden (🕑 10am-1pm)

Fujairah Bullfights (on the road to Kalba, near Al Rughailat Bridge; ☎ 4.30pm Fri) It's best to arrive by 4pm if you want to park your vehicle with the locals!

Fujairah Museum (admission Dh1; 🕑 8.30am-1.30pm & 4.30-6.30pm Sun-Thu, 2-6.30pm Fri)

Masafi Friday Market (🕑 8am-10pm daily)

BULLFIGHTING, FUJAIRAH STYLE

We knew we had arrived at the site of the Fujairah bullfights when we saw what appeared to be a thousand Land Cruisers abandoned at odd angles at the side of the road. It was 4.30pm on a Friday afternoon and the bullring was surrounded by local Emiratis (both men and women) four-deep around the ring, which measured about 100m across. We'd been to bullfights in Mexico, Spain and Portugal, but had never seen anything quite like this and it felt more than a little surreal. While you could sit happily in the stands and order a *cerveza* (beer) at a Spanish bullfight, with little risk of coming face to face with the sad, snarling bull, here you passed the bull on your way to the ring, praying to any god who'd listen that the knot in the rope securing the bull to the utility truck was secure.

There's no fanfare here, no picadors, no matadors, and no deaths as a metaphor for life. The contest is blunt-horned bull against blunt-horned bull. They push each other around until one exits the ring or loses the will to fight and wanders off. One tradition has it that the Portuguese introduced bullfighting to Fujairah, though other sources say that the bullfights predate the arrival of Islam. A more colourful legend holds that long ago two young men came into conflict over their desire to marry the same woman, so their families decided to let battling bulls settle the matter.

It's kind of ironic that in this version of the bullfight, the riskiest thing to be here is not a bull, but a spectator, as the second fight of the afternoon proved. The two black bulls were tied up on opposite sides of the ring when the MC, a national guy with a megaphone and voice of sandpaper, introduced the next fight. The handlers released the bulls and they were soon in the centre of the ring butting heads, their powerful necks straining. The weaker of the two bulls started going backwards and the more powerful one pushed harder and harder, sending both bulls out of the ring and into a group of national men sitting on a picnic blanket. Dirt, drinks and *dishdashas* flying in all directions, the two bulls made their triumphant exit from the ring. Bulls one, locals nil.

Eating

To telephone from outside the East Coast, you need to use the area code ☎ 09.

Diner's Inn (☎ 09-222 6351; Al-Faseel Rd; mains Dh8) Across from Fujairah Hilton, this inn serves large portions of decent, cheap Indian and Chinese food.

Taj Mahal (☎ 09-222 5225; Hamad bin Abdullah Rd, Fujairah, back of bldg opposite Etisalat office; mains from Dh10) Good quality Indian in a clean, comfortable place.

Taj Khorfakkan Restaurant (☎ 09-222 5995; inland from Central Market, across from Saheel Market, Khor Fakkan; mains Dh10-15) Reasonably priced food at this casual restaurant.

Lebanon Cafeteria (☎ 09-238 5631; Corniche, Khor Fakkan; mains Dh20) Has a good range of grills and Lebanese mezze as well as the usual Indian fare of biryanis and tikka dishes.

Sailors (☎ 09-222 2411; Hilton Fujairah; mains Dh30) A casual seafood restaurant and bar overlooking the beach – sublime setting!

Taste (☎ 09-244 9000; Le Meridien Al-Aqah Beach Resort, Al-Aqah Beach; mains from Dh45; dinner only) This stylish Thai-Indonesian resort is the best restaurant in the whole region (and one of the best in the country). Reservations essential.

Sleeping

Hilton Fujairah (☎ 09-222 2411; www.hilton.com; Al-Faseel Rd, Fujairah; s/d Dh750/805;) This stylish, white low-rise hotel complex has a lovely swimming pool, beautiful gardens, a superbly positioned beachfront bar (which is a wonderful spot for a drink on a breezy winter's evening!) and excellent discounts from the rack rate.

Le Meridien Al-Aqah Beach Resort (☎ 09-244 9000; www.alaqah.lemeridien.com; Al-Aqah beach; d Dh1050;) While this enormous hotel doesn't exactly blend in with its surroundings, it's easily the best hotel on the East Coast and the views are magnificent. While some prefer the ageing and overpriced Sandy Beach Hotel, Le Meridien is far better value with its large, luxurious sea-facing rooms that overlook the most beautiful beach on the coast. The extensive hotel facilities include a large swimming pool, gym, tennis courts and terrific water sports. The standard rooms are spacious, while deluxe rooms are regal, some with enormous balconies. The restaurants and cafés are also excellent, while finishing the night with a *sheesha* at the outdoor café-bar by the water is a must. Note that special Internet packages can be had for as low as Dh500 including breakfast, cocktails, three-course meal and room upgrade. Book ahead and get excellent Internet deals from the website.

AL-AIN & BURAIMI

Al-Ain and Buraimi lie within the Buraimi Oasis, and the border between the UAE and Oman wriggles through the two towns and a lush collection of interconnected oases. In the days before the oil boom, Al-Ain (in Abu Dhabi emirate on the UAE side of the border) was a five-day overland journey by camel from Abu Dhabi. Today the trip takes just under 90 minutes on a tree-lined freeway, or just over an hour from Dubai. In barely 30 years Al-Ain has been transformed from a series of rustic villages into a suburbanised garden city. It's best to make an overnight trip, but if you are really pressed for time, get an early start, zip around the sights, and you can get back to Dubai in a day. Once in the oasis, you can cross freely between the UAE and Oman – the official frontier post to enter Oman is 50km east of Buraimi – and UAE currency is accepted in Buraimi at a standard rate (at the time of writing) of OR1 = Dh9.55.

One of Al-Ain's main attractions during summer is its dry air, which is a welcome change from the humidity of the coast. The temperate climate has ensured that many sheikhs from around the Emirates have their summer palaces here. The lovely, cool, quiet date-palm oases all over town are pleasant to wander through at any time of the year.

Distances in both Al-Ain and Buraimi are large, but taxis are abundant and cheap if you haven't hired a car. It's easy to find most of the things worth seeing in Al-Ain by following the big, purple tourist signs. Unless you're skilful at bargaining, it's better to use the gold-and-white Al-Ain taxis than the orange-and-white Buraimi ones, which don't have meters.

The **Al-Ain Palace Museum** is located on the edge of the oasis, in the centre of town – just follow the signs. The majestic fort was the birthplace of the UAE's late president, Sheikh Zayed; it's one of the best museums in the country, and a highlight of a visit to

TRANSPORT – AL-AIN & BURAIMI

Distance from Dubai 160km

Direction Southeast

Travel time 90 minutes

Car From the centre of Dubai, take the exit next to the World Trade Centre in the direction of Za'abeel. There are plenty of signs here and all the way to Al-Ain.

Public Transport Minibuses (Dh30, 90 minutes) to Al-Ain leave from the Bur Dubai bus station (Map pp220–1). A shared taxi from here costs Dh30. To return to Dubai you'll need to catch a shared taxi (the taxi stand is next to the bus station), as the minibuses don't take passengers in the other direction. Shared taxis take four to seven passengers to Dubai (Dh30). Hiring a taxi of your own will cost about Dh150, depending on your negotiating skills.

Al-Ain. As you enter the museum, take a look at the *majlis* (formal meeting room) and be sure to check out the display of photographs of Al-Ain in the 1960s – it's unrecognisable. There are many wonderful rooms, decorated as they probably used to be, and beautiful gardens.

The colourful **livestock souq**, across from the museum and fort parking lot, is worth a visit. While it sells everything from Brahmin bulls to goats and chickens, it attracts people from all over the eastern UAE and northern Oman, and it's worth a visit more for the characters you'll meet. Don't be surprised if you see an Emirati loading goats into the back seat of a late-model Mercedes! The souq is at its buzziest before 9am, when trading is heaviest; remember to greet people with a *Sa'alam* and ask before you take photos.

Near the souq, you will see entrances to the date palm-plantations, and signs indicating that only tourists and date farmers can enter. Take advantage of the privilege to explore these gorgeous oases, either on foot or by car – they're a couple of degrees cooler and make a fabulous respite from the heat in summer.

The beautifully restored **Jahili Fort & Park** is set inside a walled park, next to the public gardens, near the Al-Ain Rotana Hotel. Built in 1898, the fort is a handsome piece of traditional architecture. Notice that the main corner tower is graced with three concentric rings of serrated battlements. While the fort itself is not open you can wander round the lush gardens.

Excursions

AL-AIN & BURAIMI

THE DATE PALM

If you visit Al-Ain, Dubai or Abu Dhabi in early summer, one of the things you will be struck by is the enormous number of date clusters hanging off the date palms that line many of the streets and parks. The ubiquitous date palm has always held a vital place in the life of Emiratis. For centuries, dates were one of the staple foods of the Bedouin, along with fish, camel meat and camel milk. Not a great deal of variety you might think, but consider the fact that there are over 80 different kinds of dates in the UAE. Dates are roughly 70% sugar, which prevents them from rotting, making them edible for longer than other fruits.

Apart from providing a major foodstuff, the date palm was also used to make all kinds of useful items. Its trunk was used to make columns and ceilings for houses, while its fronds (called *areesh*) were used to make roofs and walls. The date palm provided the only shade available in desert oases. Livestock were fed with its seeds and it was burned as fuel. Palm fronds were, and still are, used to make bags, mats, boats (called *shasha*), shelters, brooms and fans.

A wonderfully restored fort that you can fully explore is Buraimi's **Al-Khandaq Fort**, which is said to be around 400 years old. Here you can explore the beautifully renovated rooms and climb the battlements for a view of the surrounding oasis. Unusually for an Omani fort, there are both inner and outer defence walls. The large enclosed yard just east of the fort is **Buraimi's Eid prayer ground**, where people gather to pray during the holidays marking the end of Ramadan and the end of the pilgrimage season.

The **Buraimi Souq** is housed in the large brown building at the Horse Roundabout, sells fruit, vegetables, meat and household goods, and includes a few shops that sell Omani silver jewellery and *khanjars*, the ornate daggers worn by many Omani and some Emirati men (see the boxed text, p126).

The **Hili Gardens & Archaeological Park**, consisting of a public park and archaeological site, is about 8km north of the centre of Al-Ain, off the Dubai road. The main attraction is the **Round Structure**, a building dating from the 3rd millennium BC. It has two porthole entrances and is decorated with relief carvings of animals and people. Although this structure is locally referred to as a tomb, it may not have been a tomb at all. No bones were ever found here, just remnants of pottery, and there are suggestions that it may have been a temple. There have also been ongoing excavations on a tomb dating back to somewhere between 2300 and 2000 BC. The tomb is 8m in length and adjoins the older Round Structure. More than 250 skeletons were found here.

Do make time to visit the working, atmospheric **Al-Ain Camel Souq**. The camel handlers will be happy to show you around, although they'll expect a hefty tip at the end – a few words of Arabic will help you get a good discount. The variety and size of the big brown-eyed creatures are overwhelming, and if you can find a handler who can speak some English he'll tell you where they come from and how much they cost, just in case you have room in your vehicle! To get to the souq on Bainyas Rd, drive over the Al-Ain–Buraimi border, past the souq, then over the border again and turn right, continuing until you see the souq.

Sights & Information

To telephone from outside these towns, you need to use the area code for Al-Ain, ☎ 03, and Buraimi, ☎ 00 968.

Al-Khandaq Fort (750m past the border, near Buraimi Souq; ☺ 8am-6pm Sat-Wed, 8am-1pm & 4-6pm Thu & Fri)

Al-Ain Palace Museum (☎ 03-715 7755; Sultan bin Zayed St; ☺ 9am-7.30pm Sun-Thu, 3-7.30pm Fri)

Hili Gardens & Archaeological Park (8km north of Al-Ain centre, off the Dubai road; admission Dh1; ☺ 9am-10pm)

Jahili Fort & Park (next to public gardens, near Al-Ain Rotana Hotel; admission Dh1; ☺ 9am-10pm)

Eating

You won't have any trouble finding cheap eats in the centre of Al-Ain. In Buraimi your options are limited to the standard

IN AN ARAB HOME

If you're invited into an Emirati's home, the following tips may be useful.

- Take a small gift of chocolates, dates or sweets – while not expected, it's appreciated.
- Don't sit in such a way that the soles of your feet are pointing at someone else.
- Don't eat or offer things with your left hand.
- It's considered polite to let your host set the pace in any conversation.
- Be wary of openly admiring any of your host's ornaments or other such things. It's an Arab custom to make a gift of anything that a guest admires.
- It's polite to take a second or third helping, but don't leave your plate completely empty. This implies that you are still hungry and that your host has not been attentive to your needs.
- It's considered very impolite to refuse an offer of coffee or tea in any social or business setting. After finishing your coffee, hold out the cup in your right hand for more. If you have had enough, rock the cup gently back and forth to indicate that you're through. Note that it's generally considered impolite to drink more than three cups, unless the conversation drags on for an extended period of time.
- Don't overstay your welcome. If you are dining at someone's house it's best to leave soon after coffee is served.

cheap fare of a helping of biryani for about Dh10 at any of the places along the main street or around the market.

Golden Fork (☎ 03-766 9033; Khalifa St; mains Dh10) This branch of the ubiquitous Filipino restaurant chain has tasty noodle and rice dishes and mixed grills.

Al-Ain Oasis Restaurant (☎ 03-766 5340; Al-Ain Oasis; mains Dh20) In a beautiful setting in the heart of the oasis, about a 500m walk from the old Al-Ain Museum. Offers tasty mixed grills and the recommended fish biryani.

Al-Mallah (☎ 03-766 9928; Khalifa St; mains Dh30) Serves generous portions of excellent Lebanese cuisine. Highly recommended are the mezzes and shish *tawooq*.

Al-Khayam (☎ 03-768 6666; Hilton Al-Ain, Al-Sarooj district; mains Dh30) Authentic Persian cuisine with delicious bread done in a clay oven and traditional *majlis* seating – very special!

Luce (☎ 03-768 6686; Al-Ain InterContinental Hotel, Khalid bin Sultan St; mains Dh50) This stylish restaurant has delicious Italian cuisine and a very cool atmosphere for Al-Ain.

Sleeping

If you're on a tight budget you'll want to stay in Buraimi (but note that no hotels serve alcohol); you can get excellent Internet deals on the five-star resorts.

Hamasa Hotel (☎ 00 968-651 200, Abu Bakr al-Siddiq St, Buraimi; r Dh150) The better of the cheap hotels in Buraimi, it's about 100m north of the border, on your right as you enter Buraimi from Al-Ain. The rooms are larger than at the nearby Al-Dhahrah Hotel, though not quite as clean.

DIVERSIONS: JEBEL HAFIT

South of Al-Ain is **Jebel Hafit**, a jagged 1160m-high limestone mountain that rears out of the plain. The views across the desert from the top of this mountain are worth the effort of the rather twisty drive up. The summit is about 30km by road from the centre of Al-Ain. To get there, head south from the Clock Tower Roundabout and turn right at Khalid bin Sultan St. From there follow the purple tourist signs. There are no buses to Jebel Hafit and a taxi would cost around Dh50 for the round trip.

Al-Masa Hotel (☎ 00 968-653 007; Abu Bakr al-Siddiq St, Buraimi; r Dh300) A decent midrange hotel with clean rooms with small balconies and satellite TV, about 500m from the border, after you enter Buraimi from Al-Ain.

Hilton Al-Ain (☎ 03-768 6666; www.hilton.com; Al Surooj District; r Dh600) The oldest of the three 'name hotels'. While very comfortable, it doesn't quite match up to its rivals. Excellent discounts available on the Internet off-season.

Al-Ain InterContinental (☎ 03-768 6686; www.ichotelsgroup.com; Khalid bin Sultan St; s & d Dh700; 🏊) With spacious gardens, an Olympic-sized pool as well as a smaller family pool, lots of sports facilities and several good restaurants and bars, this is an excellent choice, especially if you can get a good Internet rate.

Al-Ain Rotana Hotel (☎ 03-754 5111; www.rotana.com; Sheikh Zayed Rd; r Dh760; 🏊 🍸) This is a splendid hotel with lots of marble, a huge atrium with palm trees, spacious comfortable rooms, a good pool and excellent facilities.

Al-Ain Palace Museum (p165), the former palace of His Highness Sheikh Zayed bin Sultan Al-Nahyan

ABU DHABI

The capital of the UAE is highly underrated. Although it doesn't have many tourist attractions as such, it's a pretty, lush, green city on an island, with a breathtaking Corniche and a laid-back, traditional feel to it. In comparison to Dubai, Abu Dhabi keeps it real – it's a modest, down-to-earth city that's very much focused on family, heritage and culture, rather than tourism and big business. This is a city where it's actually possible to walk down the street and bump into people you know, and to see Emiratis going about their business – and to actually get to meet some! Not all Dubai expats can say they've done that, even after many years in the country.

Like Dubai, the city has a multicultural feel, with a large Indian, Arab and European expat population. With close ties to Europe, the city has a great deal of French, Germans and Swiss contributing to what is already a vibrant intellectual and arts scene.

One of the city's main attractions is its active **Abu Dhabi Cultural Foundation** where it's always possible to walk in off the street on any given evening and catch an exhibition, concert, ballet, theatre performance or art-house film. There is also a small display of old photos, *khanjars*, costumes and crafts – the city takes great pride in the traditional Emirati way of life, its culture and heritage. In the grounds of the Cultural Foundation, you will also find **Al-Hosn fort**, once the residence

TRANSPORT – ABU DHABI

Distance from Dubai 150km

Direction Southwest

Travel time 90 minutes

Car Head along Sheikh Zayed Rd (E11) and it will take you directly to Abu Dhabi.

Public Transport Minibuses (Dh30, 90 minutes) to Abu Dhabi leave from the Bur Dubai bus station (Map pp220–1). A shared taxi from here costs Dh30, and taking a car on your own will be around Dh150. To return to Dubai, catch a shared taxi (the taxi stand is next to the bus station), which takes four to seven passengers, and costs Dh30; getting your own taxi will cost around Dh150, depending on your negotiating skills. For the same price as a shared taxi, you can take a less-cramped Intercity Bus service, also leaving from the bus and taxi station.

of Sheik Zayed and the Nahyan family; the small gardens here are worth a wander.

The **Corniche** is popular for rollerblading, cycling, walking and jogging, and the ideal time to go is sunset, especially on a Friday.

Down by the *mina* (port) – similar to Dubai's dhow wharfage and fascinating in itself – is an interesting **Iranian souq**, which operates in the evenings (head there after sunset). Here you'll find Persian miniature paintings and wonderful enamel hand-crafted photo frames, among a lot of plastic

The skyline of Abu Dhabi (above), as seen from the city's Heritage Village

junk and cheap carpets. There are also some interesting backstreets to wander, with tiny Afghan hole-in-the-wall bakeries, tailors, sari shops, Russian grocery stores, pet shops and oud makers.

As the late Sheikh Zayed (former UAE President and Ruler of Abu Dhabi) was set on greening the emirate, the city is amazingly green with date palms in the centre of main roads, and expansive parks scattered all over the city. As it's also a very family-oriented town, during cool winter evenings and Ramadan you'll find families picnicking late into the night in the Corniche parks.

Head to one of the city's finest spots – a point just beyond the tiny Heritage Village (not worth much of your time), near Marina Mall, where you'll see a giant flagpole. From here you'll have gorgeous views of the whole city skyline and turquoise sea. Sublime.

Sights & Information

To telephone from outside Abu Dhabi, you need to use the area code ☎ 02.

Abu Dhabi Cultural Foundation (☎ 02-619 5223; opposite Etisalat bldg, Airport Rd, Centre; 8am-2pm & 5-9.30pm Sat-Thu, 5-8pm Fri) Home to the Emirates Film Competition, this cultural centre regularly hosts art and photography exhibitions, theatre, opera, ballet, concerts and screens art-house films in a small theatre.

Eating

There are plenty of cheap eats all over town, as well as some excellent midrange and fine-dining restaurants in all of the hotels.

Automatic (cnr Hamdan & Najda St, Centre; shawarmas Dh3.50) Head here after dark for the tastiest shawarmas in the UAE at this shawarma stand!

India Palace (☎ 02-644 8777; Salam St, Centre; mains Dh30) Delicious quality Indian food served in a palatial Indian interior – you won't find better chicken tikka anywhere!

Royal Orchid (☎ 02-644 4400; Salam St, Centre; mains Dh30) Delicious authentic Thai (and Mongolian!) in a beautiful Thai-style interior. No alcohol.

Prego's (☎ 02-644 3000; Beach Rotana Hotel, Tourist Club area; mains Dh40) If the weather is cool, eat outside by the beach at this stylish Italian restaurant with authentic cuisine. If this is full, the hotel also has an excellent Trader Vic's.

Jazz Bar (☎ 02-681 1900; Hilton Abu Dhabi; mains Dh50) This has long been a favourite of many Abu Dhabi expats for its wonderfully creative fine cuisine, the buzzy atmosphere and excellent resident jazz bands that always get people up and dancing after dinner.

DO THE RIGHT THING

Although tourism in Dubai has not reached the heights it has in other cities in the region, it does have an impact on the environment and society. There are a number of things you can do to be a responsible traveller and this list is particularly pertinent outside Dubai on an excursion:

- Preserve natural resources. Try not to waste water. Switch off air-con when you go out – except in midsummer, of course!
- Ask before taking photographs of people, especially women. Don't worry if you don't speak Arabic. A smile and gesture will be understood and appreciated.
- Remember that the UAE is a Muslim country, and although Dubai is the most international and cosmopolitan city of the Gulf, revealing clothes will cause offence to most local people.
- Similarly, public displays of affection between members of the opposite sex are inappropriate.
- Learning something about Dubai's history and culture helps prevent misunderstandings and frustrations.

Be aware of environmental issues. Desert safaris in a 4WD make a popular day excursion for visitors, but they are not environmentally sound activities. Expats are just as guilty of 'dune-bashing' the environment as tourists are, as the sport is becoming an increasingly popular weekend pastime. If you are taking part in any desert activities, keep in mind the following guidelines:

- To minimise your impact on the land, stick to the tracks and avoid damaging the all-too-rare vegetation that is such an important part of the fragile desert ecosystem.
- Driving in wadis (seasonal rivers) should be avoided to ensure that they are not polluted with oil and grease. They are sometimes important sources of irrigation and drinking water.
- When diving or snorkelling, avoid touching or removing any marine life, especially coral.
- If you plan to camp out, remember to take your own wood – don't pull limbs from trees or uproot shrubs. Plants in the desert may look dead but usually they are not.

Sleeping

There are countless accommodation options in Abu Dhabi for every budget.

International Rotana Inn (☎ 02-677 9900; btwn Al-Salam & Hamdan Sts; d Dh200) A decent budget-to-midrange option, depending on what kind of discounts you can get, right in the centre of town.

Khalidia Palace (☎ 02-666 2470; Corniche Rd; d Dh300; 🍴 🏊) This is a decent midrange option, with good facilities and a great little Korean-Japanese restaurant on site.

Beach Rotana Hotel (☎ 02-644 3000; www.rotana.com; Tourist Club area; d Dh1000; 🍴 🏊) The swishest hotel in the capital after renovation a couple of years ago – spacious comfortable rooms, lots of great restaurants, bars and a club to choose from, plus there's a swanky mall next door!

Emirates Palace (☎ 02-690 9000; www.emiratespalace.com; Corniche Rd; s & d Dh2900; 🍴 💻) Abu Dhabi's 'Burj Al Arab' – this magnificent luxury Kempinski hotel easily rivals Dubai's 'seven star' hotel in every way with splendid, regal rooms fitted out with the latest hi-tech entertainment systems, and fabulous views of the turquoise sea. A grand palace suite is Dh51,000 a night! The only other problem is that the hotel is so enormous it can often feel like you're the only one there!

Directory

Directory

TRANSPORT

Flights, tours and rail tickets can be booked online at www.lonelyplanet.com/travel _services.

AIR

There are direct flights to Dubai from most European countries and hubs in Asia. From North America, however, you'll need to change flights in Europe or Asia. Dubai's ever expanding airport is increasingly the major stopover hub between Europe and Asia. For general airport information in Dubai call ☎ 224 5555; for flight inquiries dial ☎ 206 6666; or for both, visit the website (www.dubaiairport.com).

The national carrier is **Emirates Airlines** (www.emirates.com), which flies to more than 70 destinations in the Middle East, Europe, Australia, Africa and the subcontinent. The secondary carrier is the regional airline, **Gulf Air** (www.gulfairco.com). It flies to many of the same destinations as Emirates, although all flights go via Bahrain. While Emirates' famed service appears to have wilted (especially in Economy), Emirates has a perfect safety record, which is more than you can say about Gulf Air. Local budget airline **Air Arabia** (www.airarabia.com) flies out of neighbouring Sharjah; a return trip to Beirut is usually less than half the price of Emirates.

Remember when buying air tickets that direct flight routes are generally more expensive than non-direct routes. This means that flying Emirates or British Airways between London and Dubai, for instance, is going to be more expensive than flying Gulf Air via Bahrain or Qatar Airways via Doha. Sometimes, however, connecting flights can be more trouble than they're worth and you should check how long you'll be stuck at an airport before you buy that cheaper ticket. For all the talk of free markets, air fares out of the UAE are just as strictly regulated as anywhere else. There are no bucket shops.

High season for air travel varies from airline to airline. Generally, it is from late May or early June to the end of August, and from the beginning of December to the end of January. Low season is generally any other time. Regardless, special fares are offered throughout the year by different airlines and travel agents, so it pays to shop around.

Airlines

The following is a selection of carriers that fly to and from Dubai. Many of them also have desks at the **Dubai National Air Travel Agency Airline Centre** (DNATA; Map pp218–19; ☎ 295 1111; Al-Maktoum Rd, Deira).

Air France (Map pp218–19; ☎ 294 5899; Al-Shoala Complex, cnr Al-Maktoum Rd & 9 St, Deira)

Air India (Map pp218–19; ☎ 227 6787; Al-Maktoum Rd, Deira)

Alitalia (Map pp218–19; ☎ 224 2256; 16th fl, Green Tower, Baniyas Rd, Deira)

British Airways (Map p226; ☎ 307 5777; 21st fl, Al Attar Business Tower, Sheikh Zayed Rd)

Cathay Pacific Airways (Map pp218–19; ☎ 295 0400; Al-Shoala Complex, cnr Al-Maktoum Rd & 9 St, Deira)

EgyptAir (Map pp218–19; ☎ 224 7055; Al-Maktoum Rd, Deira)

Emirates Deira (Map pp218–19; ☎ 295 1111; DNATA Airline Centre, Al-Maktoum Rd); Sheikh Zayed Rd (Map pp214–15; ☎ 214 4444; Sheikh Zayed Rd, near Interchange No 2)

Gulf Air (Map pp216–17; ☎ 800 2200; Salahuddin Rd, Deira)

KLM (Map pp222–3; ☎ 800 4744; 9th fl, Gulf Towers, cnr Oud Metha Rd & 20 St, Oud Metha)

Lufthansa Airlines (Map pp214–15; ☎ 343 2121; 2nd fl, Lufthansa Bldg, Sheikh Zayed Rd)

Malaysia Airlines (Map pp220–1; ☎ 397 0250; 1st fl, National Bank of Umm al-Qaiwain Bldg, Khalid bin al-Waleed Rd, Bur Dubai)

Middle East Airlines (Map pp216–17; ☎ 203 3761; 3rd fl, Dubai Tower, Baniyas Sq, Deira)

Oman Air (Map pp220–1; ☎ 351 8080; Mezzanine fl, Al-Rais Centre, Al-Mankhool Rd, Bur Dubai)

Qatar Airways (Map pp216–17; ☎ 221 4448; Doha Centre, Al-Maktoum Rd, Deira)

Royal Brunei Airlines (Map pp220–1; ☎ 351 4111; 3rd fl, Rais Hassan Saadi Bldg, Al-Mankhool Rd, Bur Dubai)

Singapore Airlines (Map pp216–17; ☎ 223 2300; 3rd fl, Pearl Bldg, 18 St, Deira)

SriLankan Airlines (Map pp218–19; ☎ 203 3666; 3rd fl, DNATA Airline Centre, Al-Maktoum Rd, Deira)

Swiss (Map pp218–19; ☎ 294 5051; 1st fl, Al-Yamamah Towers, cnr Baniyas Rd & 9 St, Deira)

Thai Airways International (Map pp218–19; ☎ 268 1702; Al-Muraqqabat Rd, Deira)

Airport

Dubai international airport (Map pp218–19) is the busiest in the Middle East, with nearly 25 million passengers passing through the airport in 2005. With double-digit growth in passengers the airport authority is finalising another building programme costing US$2.5 billion, due to be completed in late 2006. The new structures will be for the exclusive use of Emirates Airlines, including a new underground third terminal and a doubling in size of the concourse. A third concourse will be built to accommodate the huge new Airbus A380.

The major international airlines, including Emirates, use Terminal 1, the main terminal. Smaller airlines, mostly en route to East Africa or the countries of the former Soviet Union, use the much smaller Terminal 2.

BICYCLE

While you can now hire bicycles in Dubai we can't really recommend cycling as a way to get around the city. With drivers more concerned with the mobile phone held in one hand, the cigarette in the other and knee-steering across three lanes in as many metres, you, dear cyclist (and pedestrian for that matter), are way down on the list of driver priorities. You will see cyclists around and if you do want to ride a bike in Dubai remember to monitor your fluid intake in the heat and humidity. And always yield to cars. For hire and repairs, contact **Wolfi's Bike Shop** (Map pp214–15; ☎ 339 4453; Sheikh Zayed Rd).

BOAT

Around 150 *abra*s (small motorboats) cross the Creek from early morning until around midnight, taking two routes. The routes link **Bur Dubai Abra Station** (Map pp220–1; near Bank of Baroda Bldg) with the **Deira Old Souq Abra Station** (Map pp220–1; cnr Old Baladiya St & Baniyas Rd). The other route, further up the Creek, connects the **Dubai Old Souq Abra Station** (Map pp220–1; Dubai Souq) with the **Sabakha Abra Station** (Map pp220–1; cnr Al-Sabkha & Baniyas Rds) on the Deira side. Be aware, however, that the *abra* stations were undergoing refurbishment at the time of writing and that routes were subject to slight changes.

Like shared taxis, *abra*s leave when full (around 20 passengers), but it never takes more than a few minutes for one of them to fill up. The fare is a measly 50 fils – and has been for years – easily making it the most rewarding 50 fils you'll spend in Dubai!

GETTING INTO TOWN

To get to/from the airport you can choose from Dubai municipality buses, airport buses or taxi. Remember, if you're staying at one of the beach hotels along the Jumeirah strip, ask about transfers when booking your accommodation. All transport leaves outside the arrivals hall, and the areas are signposted (bus, taxi, limo etc). Refreshingly, unlike most other Middle East destinations there's virtually no spruiking.

Airport bus 401 goes via DNATA Airline Centre, Union Sq, Baniyas Rd, Al-Sabakha bus station and Deira bus station. Airport bus 402 goes via Deira City Centre and al-Karama. The airport buses are Dh3.

Dubai municipality buses leave from the **Deira bus station** (Map pp218–19); buses 4, 11 and 15 go to the airport every 15 to 20 minutes for Dh1.50. From the **Bur Dubai bus station** (Map pp220–1), buses 33 and 44 go to the airport for Dh2, but 44 takes a circuitous route via Karama. Only bus 2 goes to Terminal 2, leaving from the **Gold Souq** (Map pp216–17), but there's a shuttle service between the two terminals.

Only the sand-coloured Dubai Transport taxis are allowed to pick up passengers from the arrivals area. There's a Dh20 charge levied on these taxis for the run from the airport (welcome to Dubai!). While you could try to save money and head to the arrivals area to attempt to flag down a taxi after a drop-off, taxis are not allowed to pick up passengers here and the taxi driver can end up in trouble. A ride to the Deira souq area will cost about Dh30 to Dh35 while to Bur Dubai it costs around Dh40 to Dh45. A ride to the beginning of the Jumeirah hotel area starts at around Dh60. Going the other way, a taxi ride from the Deira souq area to the airport costs Dh12 to Dh25; from Bur Dubai it's about Dh17 to Dh20.

Note that it can be quite tricky getting on and off the *abra*s – not something to attempt wearing high heels.

BUS

Local buses operate out of the two main stations in Deira and Bur Dubai. The **Deira bus station** (Map pp218–19) is off Al-Khor St, near the Gold Souq. The **Bur Dubai bus station** (Map pp220–1), Dubai's main bus station, is on Al-Ghubaiba Rd. In the official timetables the two stations appear as 'Gold Souq Bus Station' and 'Al-Ghubaiba Bus Station', respectively. Numbers and routes are posted on the buses in English as well as Arabic. Fares are Dh1 to Dh3.50, depending on the distance travelled. You pay the driver, so keep some change handy. A free schedule and route map can be picked up from either bus station, or from the tourist office in Baniyas Sq.

Note that most buses start and finish their days a bit later on Friday. You can count on there being no Friday service from about 11.30am until about 1.30pm (except on routes 16, 90 and 91) while noon prayers, the most important of the week, are under way. From Saturday to Thursday, buses run from approximately 5.45am to 11.15pm, at intervals of 15 to 20 minutes.

If you're going to regularly use the buses, get an e-Go Card. The card costs Dh5 to purchase and then you must recharge it with credit – Dh20 for the first time and multiples of Dh10 after that. The amount for each bus ride is deducted each time you use the ticket machine on the bus. Purchase the e-Go Cards from the major bus stations.

While the buses are a very economical way to get around Dubai, outside the cooler months they're not a lot of fun to catch or wait for. While they are air-conditioned, the people waiting for them are not. Also, there have been reports of some men taking advantage of the close proximity of women on crowded buses, as there are only a few seats for 'women only'.

For information on public buses you can call the 24-hour **Dubai Municipality hotline** (☎ 800 4848).

CAR & MOTORCYCLE

If you are planning on taking a day or overnight excursion from Dubai, hiring a car is the best and cheapest way to do it. If you decide to hire a car to get around the city, you're not going to have much of a relaxing holiday! Traffic congestion in Dubai can be a real problem at peak hours, which occur three times a day (although everyone will say that it's all day!): between 7am and 9am, 1pm and 2pm and most of the evening from 6pm onwards. The worst congestion is around the approaches to Al-Maktoum and Al-Garhoud

MOTORING MAYHEM

Driving in Dubai is not for the faint of heart. Although it's not as chaotic as in other parts of the Middle East (yes, we're looking at you Beirut!), drivers tend to cut in front of you, turn without indicating and view roundabouts as a lane-less free for all. Out on the freeway, driving in the lane closest to the centre of the road at speeds of less than 160km/h will invoke some serious headlight flashing from the latest model Mercedes trying to break the Dubai–Abu Dhabi land speed record. It's no wonder that Sheikh Zayed Rd is the deadliest road in Dubai.

So it's no surprise that UAE has one of the world's highest rates of road deaths per capita. Inappropriate speed and reckless driving are the major causes as well as pedestrians crossing against the lights or not at crossings. At the beginning of 2006, there was nearly one death per day on Dubai's roads. The worst aspect of this is that there doesn't seem to be sufficient incentive not to drive badly. Although speeding fines are meted out, most people view speed cameras as toll booths they don't have to stop at! Causing a death through an accident requires the payment of blood money (*dhiyya*) to the victim's family. Although this is a large sum (up to Dh200,000), nationals are insured against it. This often means that the only punishment for causing death or injury through reckless driving is an increased insurance premium.

If you're used to counting drinks down at the local to see whether you're over the alcohol limit or not, we'll make it easy for you – if you've had one, you've had one too many! Dubai has a zero-tolerance policy on drink-driving and if your vehicle is stopped and you're found to have been driving under the influence of alcohol, you'll be a guest of Dubai Police for at least one night. If you have been involved in an accident and have been drinking, your insurance will be voided whether you were responsible for the accident or not.

Bridges and along Al-Ittihad Rd towards Sharjah. Accidents are frequent, so it's a good idea to tune into the radio to get traffic updates.

It is compulsory to wear seatbelts in the front and it is illegal to use a hand-held mobile phone while driving – although you'll find in Dubai that it appears to be mandatory rather than illegal.

As you would expect, Dubai is not short on petrol stations. However, after many years of the government subsidising the price of petrol at the pumps, petrol prices rose by 30% in late 2005. Petrol is sold by the imperial gallon (an imperial gallon is just over 4.5L) and now costs around Dh6.5 per gallon.

It is not possible to hire motorcycles in Dubai – which is probably just as well after you've seen a couple wedged under trucks. Before you drive in Dubai, read the boxed text, opposite, for some important safety messages.

Hire

Like most countries, a credit card is essential for hiring a car at a reputable rental company in Dubai. If you do find a car-rental company that will take a cash deposit instead, not only will you probably have to leave your passport with them, they may not offer full insurance. Some agencies insist on a credit-card deposit as well as your passport. Find another agency if this is the case. You do not have to leave your passport with them. A photocopy of it is sufficient.

For tourists, most foreign driving licences are accepted in Dubai so long as you are either a citizen or a resident of the country that issued the licence. However, some companies insist on an international licence, so it's worth getting one of these before you leave home.

At large international agencies, small cars such as a Toyota Corolla start at about Dh130 per day with another Dh20 to Dh25 for collision damage waiver (CDW) insurance. These rates fall to about Dh120 per day including insurance for a week's hire, and around Dh100 per day with insurance for a month. If you have taken out CDW, the larger agencies do not charge an excess in the case of an accident that is your fault. Always call the police if you are involved in an accident; see the boxed text, p176, for more details.

At the smaller agencies, you should be able to negotiate a net rate of around Dh120 per day, including CDW insurance. With these agencies, no matter what they tell you, you may still be liable for the first Dh1000 to Dh1500 of damage in the event of an accident that is your fault, even if you have CDW. Sometimes this excess is only Dh200 if you have paid CDW. Ask questions and read the small print on the contract carefully.

The first 100km or 150km per day are usually free with additional kilometres costing 40 or 50 fils each. If you rent a car for more than three days you should be given unlimited mileage.

Most agencies have free pick-up and delivery within Dubai, either to/from a hotel or the airport. They also offer a chauffeur service, but you'll pay around Dh180 per eight hours for this privilege. If you are just moving around Dubai for the day it is much cheaper to use taxis.

Although smaller agencies are generally cheaper than the larger chain companies, it's worth considering the convenience of being able to contact the local office of a reliable company if you are driving out of Dubai and something goes wrong. It's also worth ensuring complete insurance cover (zero liability).

There are dozens of car-rental firms in Dubai, including all the major international chains as well as plenty of local companies. The highest concentrations of local companies are on Abu Baker al-Siddiq Rd, just north of the Clock Tower Roundabout, and on Omar ibn al-Khattab St. They are also found opposite the minibus and taxi station on Omar ibn al-Khattab St in Deira; on the Bur Dubai side of the Creek on Sheikh Khalifa bin Zayed Rd, just north of Al-Adhid Rd; and on Kuwait St in Karama. The following major companies will generally deliver the car to you.

Avis (www.avis.com) Airport (Map pp218–19; ☎ 224 5219; Airport arrivals hall; ☼ 24hr); Deira (Map pp218–19; ☎ 295 7121; Al-Maktoum Rd, Deira)

Budget (www.budget.com) Airport (Map pp218–19; ☎ 224 5192; Airport arrivals hall; ☼ 24hr); Airport Rd (Map pp218–19; ☎ 282 3030; Airport Rd, just before Cargo Village)

Diamondlease (Map p226; ☎ 343 4330; www .diamondlease.com; Sahara Towers, Sheikh Zayed Rd)

Europcar (Map pp218–19; ☎ 224 5240; www .europcar-dubai.com; Airport arrivals hall; ⊗ 24hr)

Hertz (www.hertz-uae.com) Airport (Map pp218–19; ☎ 224 5222; Airport arrivals hall; ⊗ 24hr); Airport Rd (Map pp218–19; ☎ 282 4422; Airport Rd, just before Cargo Village)

Thrifty (☎ 355 6732; www.thrifty.com) Airport (Map pp218–19; ☎ 224 5404; Airport arrivals hall; ⊗ 24hr) Plus various locations around Dubai.

Road Rules

Most people drive on the right in Dubai, which is the side you're supposed to drive on. The speed limit is 60km/h on city streets and 80km/h on major city roads – if you actually reach these limits, send us a postcard. On Sheikh Zayed Rd and on other dual-lane highways around the UAE the official speed limit is 100km/h on some sections, but otherwise it's 120km/h. If you are caught speeding, you will be fined, but in some cases you will simply be sent a bill by the police. For this reason, most car-rental companies require customers to sign a statement acknowledging that they are aware of this and authorising the rental company to charge their credit card for any tickets that turn up after they have left town. So if you see a flash of light while powering down Sheik Zayed Rd, check your credit-card statements when you get home! There are also speed cameras on the major highways.

Increasingly, the busier city streets have a strictly enforced four-hour limit on parking. Tickets must be purchased from

ACCIDENT ALERT

If you are unfortunate enough to have an accident, no matter how small, you are required to wait at the scene and report it to the **traffic police** (☎ 999). Unless your car is causing a major traffic jam, do NOT move it until the traffic police get there. If there has been an injury, or it's not blindingly obvious who was at fault, don't move the vehicles at all. For insurance-claim purposes you must have a police report and if you move your car, the police may not be able to issue a complete report. Outside Dubai you should leave your car exactly where it is, no matter how bad an obstruction it is causing, and call the police immediately. If you are driving a hire car and you have a crash, your insurance will not cover any damage unless a police report is written.

SLOW TRAIN COMING

For visitors stuck in traffic, as they become increasingly late for that dinner booking, help is at hand. A light-rail system for Dubai has been approved. While the details are still a little light (the Dubai Municipality website has some fascinating insights, such as 'the trains will be fast and will run on tracks'), the light-rail system will consist of two lines, the first running from the border with Sharjah, going under the Creek and emerging to run parallel to Sheikh Zayed Rd down to Jebel Ali. The second line will be more of a local line serving Dubai city and the airport. The system will be fully automatic with no drivers – no great loss considering how dangerously the public transport buses are sometimes driven in Dubai! And this being Dubai, there will be a 1st-class section, which will probably be renamed 'VIP' to try to encourage Dubai's social set to use it…

one of the many orange ticket-dispensing machines, and displayed on your dashboard. Rates start at Dh2 for an hour. Parking rates apply from 8am to 1pm and from 4pm to 9pm Saturday to Thursday. Compliment the parking inspectors on their groovy safari suits all you like, but good luck getting out of a fine. Parking in the centre of Dubai is free on Friday and holidays. Fines for not buying a ticket start at Dh100, and you can't re-register your car until you've paid up.

TAXI

Taxis are generally the most popular way to get around for visitors to Dubai, and you can usually find one without too long a wait. The city has a large, modern fleet of taxis with meters; the starting fare is Dh3 plus Dh1.43 per kilometre, rising to Dh3.50 plus Dh1.70 per kilometre between 10pm and 6am. Drivers are sometimes keen to help themselves to an excellent tip, so keep some smaller notes (5s and 10s) and coins handy for taxi trips. While Dubai might have rid the streets of the old meter-less taxis (and thank heaven for that!), there has been an increasing number of illegal car lift services operating. If you're waiting for a taxi, occasionally an unmarked car will pull up and attempt to pick up passengers. To combat this, Dubai transport has just introduced a new City Taxi service. These are small vans that pick up and drop off passengers anywhere on a fixed route for a flat fee of Dh5. Routes are initially operating from Shindagha to convenient locations such as Jumeirah, and other routes may follow.

Dubai Transport Corporation has women taxi drivers and if you book in advance it can provide wheelchair-accessible taxis.

Taxi companies include the following:

Cars Taxis (☎ 269 3344)

Dubai Transport Company (☎ 208 0808)

Metro Taxis (☎ 267 3222)

National Taxis (☎ 339 0002)

PRACTICALITIES

ACCOMMODATION

Accommodation in the Sleeping chapter (p140) is listed by neighbourhood, with all listings sorted by price (from lowest to highest). With several hundred hotels and a new one seemingly announced every week, Dubai isn't lacking in accommodation options – except for quality cheap sleeps, which are still thin on the ground. Accommodation prices quoted in the Sleeping chapter are rack rates (the standard published rates) and you can expect to pay these rates during any of the holidays, festivals and events that frequently occur in Dubai. During summer the tourist traffic really drops off so from mid-May to mid-September hotels drop their rates, often up to 40% of the published rack rate. Always ask for the best price or about current deals – generally the hotels won't tell you these unless you ask. The hotels publish specials on their websites (if there are none currently available, that generally means occupancy is high). Alternatively, you can try online **Expedia** (www .expedia.com) or **Lastminute** (www.lastminute .com). If you do arrive in Dubai and need accommodation, there's an office to your left just after you pass through Customs – but really, what were you thinking?

BUSINESS HOURS

Business hours and even working days are not fixed in Dubai. Government departments generally work from Saturday to Wednesday between 7am and 2pm, but offices that deal

---

ESSENTIAL READING

Globalisation may have provided Dubai with a multicultural workforce, but it's proven no match for traditional Arab customs. Business, social and cultural practices are still noticeably different from those of the West. To avoid embarrassment in a social situation or even blowing a business deal with your poor meeting etiquette, here are some books that will help:

- *The Arab Way: How to Work More Effectively With Arab Cultures* (Dr Jehad Al Omari) Want to know how to make small talk or avoid confrontation? This excellent cross-cultural guide provides practical tips to avoid faux pas while addressing Western misconceptions of Arabs, Islam and the Arab world.
- *Teach Yourself Islam* (Ruqaiyyah Waris Maqsood) Written by a practising Muslim, this basic introduction to Islam, its teachings and Islamic society is an easy and fascinating read and a must for travellers to the UAE.
- *Understanding Arabs: A Guide for Modern Times* (Margaret K Nydell) A superb cross-cultural handbook for people who want to better appreciate Arab culture, society, beliefs and values.
- *Don't They Know it's Friday* (Jeremy Williams) Straightforward advice on social and business etiquette written by an expat who has worked all over the Gulf and runs courses on doing business with Arabs – compulsory reading for those moving to the UAE.
- *Serve Them Right* (Kate Dickens) A very practical guide to working with and serving Dubai's multicultural population.
- *Culture Shock! United Arab Emirates: A Guide to Customs and Etiquette* (Gina Crocetti) Created primarily for expats and business travellers with good detail on UAE culture, society, customs and etiquette.
- *UAE: A Meed Practical Guide* A comprehensive guide to the country with good background on UAE business, finance and trade.
- *Living and Working in the Gulf States and Saudi Arabia* (Robert Hughes, Graeme Chesters, Jim Watson) A detailed guide for anyone planning to move to Dubai; it covers everything you need to know about living, working and studying in the Gulf.
- *Live and Work in Saudi and the Gulf* (Louise Whetter) Aimed at people looking for work, starting a business or buying a home in the Gulf – good detail on jobs and how to get them, the way of life, law, health and education systems.

with the public often have extended business hours and are sometimes open on Thursday. Private companies generally work an 8am to 5pm or 9am to 6pm day but may take Friday and Saturday as the weekend – especially international companies who have a base in Dubai. Meetings in Dubai take a little getting used to as you're expected to arrive punctually, but can end up waiting a long time for your host. Meetings, when they do eventually start, can go for hours without seemingly achieving anything tangible! See the boxed text, p177, for more info.

CHILDREN

All across the Middle East, families are well catered for – Dubai's no exception. All the parks mentioned in this book have kids' playgrounds and there are plenty of grassy stretches where they can expend energy – just make sure the kids are getting enough fluids in the heat. All the shopping centres have nurseries or play areas for little kids though most of the time you won't be able to leave them unattended. For the best children's activities, check the Top Ten for Kids (p47). *Family Explorer* (Dh55) lists dozens of fun things for kids to do around the UAE. Lonely Planet's *Travel with Children* by Cathy Lanigan is a good book that prepares you for the joys and pitfalls of travelling with the little ones.

Baby-sitting

Most of the large hotels have baby-sitting services and these tend to be reliable as they are very used to large numbers of children visiting. Locals and expats with children generally have maids, and those who don't often 'borrow' a maid from a neighbour for the night if they want to go out – the maids are more than happy to earn the extra money.

CLIMATE

For most of the year Dubai's weather is warm and humid; the sky is rarely cloudy. So far, so good. However, the summer months (May to September) are extremely hot with daytime temperatures in the low to mid-40s (Celsius). July and August are the hottest months, with average temperatures around 43°C with 85% humidity. Sometimes the heat reaches 48°C and the

humidity 95% – and rumours always swirl around in the heat that it has reached 50°C somewhere in the UAE. The sea temperature in the height of summer (June to August) is about 37°C, which provides no relief, and hotel swimming pools have to be cooled during this time so the guests don't assume they're being parboiled for dinner.

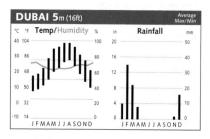

During October, November, March and April the weather is much more bearable, with temperatures in the low to mid-30s. In winter (December to February), Dubai enjoys perfect weather with an average temperature of 24°C, though it can get quite windy. Unlike the desert area inland, Dubai doesn't get too cold on winter nights, with the lowest temperature hovering around 15°C, but bring a warm jacket if you're visiting at that time of year as Dubaians love to spend winter nights out enjoying the cooler weather.

It doesn't rain often, or heavily, although when it does (usually in December, January or February), getting around can suddenly become difficult as streets turn into rivers and traffic becomes chaotic, with traffic accidents everywhere. Drivers here are not used to wet road conditions, and the city planners decided Dubai didn't need a drainage system, so there are no gutter or storm-water drains. The average annual rainfall is about 6.5cm per year (and it rains only five days a year on average), but rainfall varies widely from one year to the next. In winter there can be fog in the early mornings.

Sandstorms can occur during March and April, although Dubai is protected from the swirling dust and sand to some degree by its ever-increasing number of tall buildings. Driving out through the desert while there's a sandstorm is quite an experience!

COURSES

Language

Most language courses on offer are for English. There are only a few places where English speakers can study Arabic. This is because of the great demand by national students and expats from the subcontinent who want to improve their employment opportunities in the world of business, which is dominated by the English language. The following centres offer Arabic courses:

Arabic Language Centre (Map p226; ☎ 308 6036; alc@dwtc.com; Dubai World Trade Centre, Sheikh Zayed Rd) Runs five courses a year in Arabic from beginner to advanced levels.

Berlitz Language School (Map pp224–5; ☎ 344 0034; Jumeirah Beach Rd) Offers courses in a number of languages, including Arabic and Urdu. The latter is useful to know to some extent as this is the language of so many of the Pakistani expats in the UAE.

Polyglot Language Institute (Map pp216–17; ☎ 222 3429; www.polyglot.co.ae; Al-Masaeed Bldg, Al-Maktoum Rd, Deira) Beginner courses and conversation classes in Arabic, French, German and English. A 10-week Arabic course with three classes per week costs Dh1000.

Cultural

Ballet Centre (Map pp224–5; ☎ 344 9776; Street 39B, Jumeirah) Offers one hour belly-dancing lessons for beginners (of course they have *ballet* lessons as well…) at 7pm Sundays and 8pm Wednesdays for Dh25.

Dubai International Art Centre (Map pp224–5; ☎ 344 4398; Villa 27, Street 75B, near Town Centre, Jumeirah Beach Rd) Offers a plethora of art-related courses, but it's the Arabic Calligraphy courses that are the most fascinating to us.

Music Chamber (Map p226; ☎ 331 6416; Holiday Centre, Crowne Plaza Hotel, Sheikh Zayed Rd) Offers oud (Arabic lute) lessons if you want to try your hand at learning to play this difficult instrument. Has a good selection of student to professional quality ouds in stock as well.

CUSTOMS

The duty-free allowances for tobacco are huge: 2000 cigarettes, 400 cigars or 2kg of loose tobacco (this is still *not* a country cracking down on smoking). Non-Muslims are allowed to import 2L of wine and 2L of spirits. You are generally not allowed to bring in alcohol if you cross into the UAE by land. No customs duties are applied to personal belongings. If videos are found in your bag, officials will remove them and they will be checked. Officials have a list of banned videos and other materials. It is also illegal to bring in materials that insult Islam (this includes books like Salman Rushdie's *The Satanic Verses*) or materials that might be used to convert Muslims to another religion – so leave that stack of bibles at home.

DISABLED TRAVELLERS

Dubai's **Department of Tourism & Commerce Marketing** (DTCM; ☎ 223 0000; www.dubaitourism .co.ae) has a highly detailed list of facilities for disabled people at dozens of hotels, which they will fax to you on request. All the major shopping centres have wheelchair access, but ramps in car parks and into most buildings in the city are few and far between. There are a number of car parks for disabled drivers.

You can order taxis that are equipped to carry wheelchairs from **Dubai Transport** (☎ 208 0808). The airport has facilities for the disabled, including low check-in counters, but things get more difficult once you are out of the airport. While many hotels in Dubai now claim that they are disabled-friendly, we have noted in individual reviews the hotels that have specifically paid attention to the details of what this actually means. Dubai Museum has ramps; however, other tourist attractions are difficult places for disabled visitors to get around on their own. Dubai airport has modern facilities for people with disabilities, including lounges and carts for getting around the concourse.

ELECTRICITY

The electric voltage is 220V AC. British-style three-pin wall sockets are standard, although most appliances are sold with two-pin plugs. Adaptors are inexpensive and available in small grocery stores and supermarkets. The two-pin plugs will go into the three-pin sockets, but this does involve a technique that won't be seen in a workplace safety video anytime soon.

EMBASSIES & CONSULATES

It's important to realise what your own embassy can and can't do to help you if you get into trouble.

Generally speaking, the embassy will not be much help in emergencies if the trouble you're in is remotely your own fault. Remember that you are bound by the laws of the UAE. Your embassy will not be very sympathetic if you end up in jail after committing a crime locally, even if such actions happen to be legal in your own country.

In genuine emergencies you might get some assistance, but only if other channels have been exhausted. For example, if you need to get home urgently, a free ticket home is exceedingly unlikely – the embassy would expect you to have insurance. If you have all your money and documents stolen, it might assist with getting a new passport, but a loan for onward travel is out of the question.

UAE Embassies & Consulates

Contact details for UAE diplomatic missions include the following:

Australia (☎ 02 6286 8802; 36 Culgoa Circuit, O'Malley, ACT 2606)

Bahrain (☎ 723 737; House No 221, Rd 4007 – Complex 340, Manama)

Egypt (☎ 02 360 9722; 4 Ibn Seena Street, Giza, Cairo)

France (☎ 01 45 53 94 04; 3 Rue de Lota, 75116 Paris)

Germany (☎ 3051 6516; 18-20, D-10785, Berlin)

India (☎ 11 2467 0830; EP 12 Chandra Gupta Marg, Chanakyapuri, New Delhi 11002)

Iran (☎ 21 878 8515; Wali Asr St, Shaheed Waheed Dastakaardi St No 355, Tehran)

Kuwait (☎ 252 6356; Al-Istiqlal St, Qaseema 7, Al-Assaffa, PO Box 1828, Kuwait 13019)

Oman (☎ 600 302; Al-Khuwair, PO Box 551 code 111, Muscat)

Qatar (☎ 483 8880; 22 Al-Markhiyah St, Khalifa Northern Town, PO Box 3099, Doha)

Saudi Arabia (☎ 01 482 6803; Abu Bakr al-Karkhi Zone, Amr bin Omayad St, PO Box 94385, Riyadh 11693)

UK (☎ 20 75811281; 30 Princes Gate, London SW7 1PT)

USA (☎ 202 363 3009; 3522 International Court, NW Washington DC 20008)

Embassies & Consulates in Dubai

Most countries have diplomatic representation in the UAE. Dubai is home to the consulates and one embassy, the British embassy; other embassies are in Abu Dhabi and are listed in the front pages of the Dubai phone book. The telephone area code for Dubai is ☎ 04.

Australia (Map pp214–15; ☎ 331 3444; 6th fl, Dubai World Trade Centre, Sheikh Zayed Rd, Za'abeel; ⏰ 8am-3.30pm Sat-Tue, 8am-2.45pm Wed)

Canada (Map pp220–1; ☎ 352 1717; dubai@dfait-maeci .gc.ca; 7th fl, United Bank Bldg, Khalid bin al-Waleed Rd, Bur Dubai; ⏰ 8-11.30am Sat-Wed)

Egypt (Map pp222–3; ☎ 397 1122; 11 St, Bur Dubai; ⏰ 9am-noon Sat-Wed)

France (Map p226; ☎ 332 9040; fransula@emirates.net .ae; 18th fl, API World Tower, Sheikh Zayed Rd, Za'abeel; ⏰ 8.30am-1pm Sat-Wed)

Germany (Map pp222–3; ☎ 397-2333; aadubai@emirates .net.ae; 1st fl, Sharaf Bldg, Khalid bin al-Waleed Rd, near BurJuman Centre, Bur Dubai; ⏰ 9am-noon Sat-Wed)

India (Map pp222–3; ☎ 397 1222; cgidubai@emirates .net.ae; 7B St, Bur Dubai; ⏰ 8am-4.30pm Sun-Thu)

Iran (Map pp224–5; ☎ 344 4717; irancons@emirates.net .ae; cnr Al-Wasl Rd & 33 St, Jumeirah; ⏰ 8am-1pm Sat-Wed)

Italy (Map p226; ☎ 331 4167; consulit@emirates.net .ae; 17th fl, Dubai World Trade Centre, Sheikh Zayed Rd, Za'abeel; ⏰ 9am-1pm Sat-Wed)

Jordan (Map pp222–3; ☎ 397 0500; jorconslt@emirates.net .ae; 11 St, Bur Dubai; ⏰ 8am-12.30pm Sat-Wed)

Kuwait (Map pp216–17; ☎ 228 4111; kuwait@emirates .net.ae; Baniyas Rd, Deira; ⏰ 8.30am-2.30pm Sat-Wed)

Lebanon (Map pp222–3; ☎ 397 7450; lebconsd@emirates .net.ae; 3 St, Bur Dubai; ⏰ 9am-noon Sat-Wed)

Netherlands (Map pp222–3; ☎ 352 8700; nlgovdba@emirates.net.ae; 5th fl, ABN-Amro Bank Bldg, Khalid bin al-Waleed Rd, Bur Dubai; ⏰ 9am-3pm Sat-Wed)

Oman (Map pp222–3; ☎ 397 1000; general@ocodubai .com; 11 St, Bur Dubai; ⏰ 8am-2pm Sat-Wed)

Pakistan (Map pp222–3; ☎ 397 0412; parepdub@emirates .net.ae; 11 St, Bur Dubai; ⏰ 8am-noon Sat-Wed)

Qatar (Map pp222–3; ☎ 398 2888; qatar98@emirates .net.ae; cnr Al-Adhid Rd & 52 St, Al-Jafiliya; ⏰ 8-11.30am Sat-Wed)

Saudi Arabia (Map pp220–1; ☎ 266 3383; 28 St, Hor al-Anz; ⏰ 8.30-11.30am Sat-Wed)

South Africa (Map pp222–3; ☎ 397 5222; sacons@emirates.net.ae; 3rd fl, Sharaf Bldg, Khalid bin al-Waleed Rd, near Bur Juman Centre, Bur Dubai; ⏲ 8.30am-12.30pm Sat-Wed)

Syria (Map pp214–15; ☎ 266 3354; cnr 15 & 10C Sts, Al-Wuheida, Deira; ⏲ 8.30am-2.30pm Sat-Wed)

Turkey (Map p226; ☎ 331 4788; tcdubkon@emirates.net .ae; 11th fl, Dubai World Trade Centre, Sheikh Zayed Rd, Za'abeel; ⏲ 9am-noon Sat-Thu)

UK (Map pp220–1; ☎ 309 4444; britemb@emirates.net .ae; Al-Seef Rd, Bur Dubai; ⏲ 8am-1pm Sat-Wed)

USA (Map p226; ☎ 311 6000; 21st fl, Dubai World Trade Centre, Sheikh Zayed Rd, Za'abeel; ⏲ 8.30am-5pm Sat-Wed)

Yemen (Map pp222–3; ☎ 397 0131; 7B St, Bur Dubai; ⏲ 8.30-11.30am Sat-Wed)

EMERGENCY

In an emergency, you can try calling one of the following numbers:

Ambulance (☎ 998/999)

Electrical faults (☎ 991)

Fire department (☎ 997)

Operator (☎ 181)

Police (☎ 999)

GAY & LESBIAN TRAVELLERS

Homosexuality is illegal in the UAE and can incur a jail term. You will see men walking hand in hand but that's a sign of friendship and is no indication of sexual orientation. While Dubai has made a huge effort to promote itself as a tolerant, safe tourist destination, open displays of homosexuality can land you in trouble. Note that any specifically gay-focused websites are blocked in the UAE.

HOLIDAYS

See the Islamic Holidays table (below) for the approximate dates of the religious holi-

days observed in Dubai. Lailat al-Mi'raj is the celebration of the Ascension of Prophet Mohammed. Eid al-Fitr is a three-day celebration that occurs after Ramadan, and Eid al-Adha is a four-day celebration that occurs after the main pilgrimage to Mecca, or *haj*.

Secular holidays are New Year's Day (1 January) and National Day (2 December). The death of a minister, a member of the royal family or the head of state of another Arab country is usually marked by a three-day holiday. Newspaper websites (p184) are the quickest way to find details when this occurs. If a public holiday falls on a weekend (ie, Thursday or Friday), the holiday is usually taken at the beginning of the next working week.

The Islamic calendar starts at the year AD 622, when Prophet Mohammed fled Mecca for the city of Medina. It is called the Hejira calendar (hejira means 'flight'). As it is a lunar calendar, it's roughly 11 days shorter than the Gregorian (Western) calendar, which means that Islamic holidays fall 11 days earlier each year. However, this is not a fixed rule, as the exact dates of Islamic holidays depend upon the sighting of the moon at a particular stage in its cycle. This can be as informal as a group of elderly imams being taken on a night-time drive into the desert to confer on whether or not the new moon is visible. This is why Islamic holidays are not announced until a day or two before they occur, and why they differ from country to country.

Ramadan

This is the month during which Muslims fast during the daylight hours. They must also refrain from sex, swearing, smoking or any other indulgence. This is to clean the mind and body to better focus on the relationship with Allah. The breaking of the fast – the meal is called Iftar – is usually done at the mosque, or with friends and

ISLAMIC HOLIDAYS

Hejira Year	New Year	Prophet's Birthday	Ramadan	Eid al-Fitr	Eid al-Adha
1427	31.01.06	11.04.06	24.09.06	24.10.06	31.12.06
1428	20.01.07	31.03.07	13.09.07	13.10.07	20.12.07
1429	10.01.08	20.03.08	02.09.08	01.10.08	08.12.08
1430	29.12.08	09.03.09	22.08.09	21.09.09	28.11.09

family. For most Muslims in Dubai the rest of the long evening is split between visiting friends, eating and shopping. For good restaurants to visit at Iftar, see p85.

During Ramadan, government offices ease back to about six hours' work (well, attendance) a day. Bars and pubs are closed until 7pm each night; live music is prohibited and dance clubs are closed throughout the month. Camel racing ceases too. Some restaurants do not serve alcohol during this month. Everyone, regardless of their religion, is required to observe the fast in public. That means no eating, drinking or smoking.

Some hotels still serve breakfast and lunch to guests, but this is in specially designated rooms and most of the time eating during the day means room service or self-catering. Non-Muslims offered coffee or tea when meeting a Muslim during the day in Ramadan should initially refuse politely. If your host insists, and repeats the offer several times, you should accept as long as it does not look as though you are going to anger anyone else in the room who may be fasting.

For visitors interested in Islam or religion in general, this is a fascinating time to visit Dubai. If you walk the backstreets of areas like Satwa at Iftar, you'll see mosques with mats and carpets laid out with food ready for mosque attendees, and witness the streets come to life – well into the wee hours.

INSURANCE

A travel-insurance policy to cover theft, loss and medical problems is a good idea. Some policies offer both lower and higher medical-expense options; the higher ones are chiefly for countries such as the USA, which have extremely high medical costs. There are a wide variety of policies available, so check the small print. Some policies specifically exclude 'dangerous activities', which can include scuba diving and motorcycling – and probably hitting the slopes at Ski Dubai.

You may prefer a policy that pays doctors or hospitals directly rather than you having to pay on the spot and claim later. If you have to claim later make sure you keep all documentation. Some policies ask you to call back (reverse charges) to a centre in your home country where an immediate assessment of your problem is made.

Check that the policy covers ambulances or an emergency flight home.

INSURANCE WARNING

Unless you make specific arrangements, your rental-car insurance will not cover you when in Oman. This means that if you go to Hatta, which involves passing through about 20km of Omani territory, or visit Buraimi on an excursion to Al-Ain, you will not be covered for any accident while in Omani territory. Ask for this coverage if you intend to head into Oman.

INTERNET ACCESS

For visitors, Etisalat will be your sole provider of Internet access in Dubai. For most expats, any mention of Etisalat's 'service' will often set off a flood of tears and recitation of a hard luck story. The introduction of the latest Internet services such as broadband and wi-fi have either been handled haphazardly or are very slow to come. In the UAE the Internet is accessed through a proxy server in an attempt to block out pornography and other 'unsuitable' material. Many hotels and hotel residences offer Internet access to their guests, though sometimes this is only available to executive guests who are paying a premium for their rooms. Broadband is becoming common in hotels and there are now a few hotels offering wireless access – these have been noted in the reviews. For wired connections, hotels generally have the necessary cables to get connected, but many can't offer help beyond 'the cable thingy goes into the computer'.

If you wish to access the Internet with your own modem, Etisalat has a 'Dial 'n' Surf' service at ☎ 500 5555; all you need is a modem and a phone line. No account number or password is needed. It is charged at 12 fils per minute directly to the telephone you are connected to. If you're staying at a hotel you should check whether the hotel will charge you an additional fee for using their phone line.

Etisalat has also introduced a wi-fi service (iZone) that is available at most malls and many hotels and coffee shops (including all Starbucks cafés). For a full list, visit the website (www.izone.ae)...and yes, we understand the irony of this if you're actually looking for a place to get connected. For assistance, just call ☎ 800 6100. The iZone Prepaid Cards are available as one-/three-/24-hour cards (Dh15/30/70) where the usage duration runs continuously from the first login time. There's also a 12-hour (Dh120) card that is valid for 60 days from the time of first login. Note that you need to SMS Etisalat to receive a password for the service.

There are a few specialist Internet cafés around the city and rates are around Dh10 to Dh15 per hour; the following are the most reliable ones in Dubai:

Al-Jalssa Internet Café (Map pp220–1; ☎ 351 4617; Al-Ain Shopping Centre, Al-Mankhool Rd; ☺ 9am-1am) Has wireless.

F1 Net Café (Map pp224–5; ☎ 345 1232; Palm Strip Shopping Centre, Jumeirah Rd; ☺ 10am-10pm)

LEGAL MATTERS

Dubai maintains the death penalty for drug importation, although the penalty usually ends up being a very long jail term. Jail sentences for being involved in drugs by association are also likely. That means that even if you are in a room where there are drugs, but are not partaking, you could be in as much trouble as those who are. The UAE has a small but growing drug problem, and the authorities are cracking down hard on it. The secret police are pervasive, and they include officers of many nationalities. Theft and writing bad cheques are also taken pretty seriously and usually involve jail and deportation.

If you are arrested you have the right to a phone call, which you should make as soon as possible (ie, before you are detained in a police cell or prison pending investigation, where making contact with anyone could be difficult). Call your embassy or consulate first. If there is an accident, it's a case of being guilty until proven innocent. This means that if you are in a road traffic accident, you may be held under police guard until an investigation reveals whose fault the accident was.

Note that drinking alcohol in a public place that is not a licensed venue is illegal. The penalties vary from a warning to a fine. If the police should approach you when you're camping, put away any alcohol.

MAPS

Maps of Dubai are available from the bigger bookshops around town (see the Shopping chapter, p122). All the maps mentioned here should also be available in the bookshops at five-star hotels. The *Dubai Tourist Map* (Dh45), published by the municipality, is the best of the local maps. Geoprojects publishes a map of Dubai which is not bad, but it's becoming increasingly outdated and it doesn't include the names of all the minor streets. It is available from most bookshops and hotels for Dh30.

MEDICAL SERVICES

There are pharmacies on just about every street in Dubai. See the daily newspapers for a list of pharmacies that are open 24 hours on that particular day, or if you need to get to a pharmacy urgently call ☎ 223 2323, a hotline that will tell you where the nearest open pharmacy is. As a visitor you will receive medical care, but you will be charged for it. It's important to have health cover for your trip as a lengthy stay in a hospital in Dubai will be expensive. Generally the standard of medical services is good.

The following government hospitals have emergency departments:

Al-Maktoum Hospital (Map pp216–17; ☎ 222 1211; Al-Maktoum Hospital Rd, near cnr Omar ibn al-Khattab Rd, Rigga)

Al-Wasl Hospital (Map pp222–3; ☎ 324 1111; Oud Metha Rd, south of Al-Qataiyat Rd, Za'abeel)

New Dubai Hospital (Map pp216–17; ☎ 222 9171; Abu Baker al-Siddiq Rd, near cnr Al-Khaleej Rd, Hor al-Anz)

Rashid Hospital (Map pp222–3; ☎ 337 4000; off Oud Metha Rd, near Al-Maktoum Bridge, Bur Dubai)

If you need nonurgent care, ask your consulate for the latest list of recommended doctors and dentists. Some are listed here in case you need to find one and your consulate is closed:

Al-Zahra Private Medical Centre (Map p226; ☎ 331 5000; Zaabeel Tower, Sheikh Zayed Rd)

Dubai London Clinic (Map pp224–5; ☎ 344 6663; Al-Wasl Rd, Jumeirah) The clinic also has an emergency section and dental services.

Manchester Clinic (Map pp224–5; ☎ 344 0300; Jumeirah Rd, just north of McDonald's)

MONEY

The UAE dirham (Dh) is divided into 100 fils. Notes come in denominations of five, 10, 20, 50, 100, 200, 500 and 1000. There are Dh1, 50 fils, 25 fils, 10 fils and 5 fils coins (although the latter two are rarely used today). A few years ago the government issued new coins, which are smaller than the old ones. Both types remain legal tender, but you should look at your change closely as the new Dh1 coins are only slightly smaller than the old 50 fils coins. The coins only show the denomination in Arabic, so it's a great way to learn; turn to p191 for the numerals.

The UAE dirham is fully convertible and – for better or worse depending where you're coming from – pegged to the US dollar. See the Quick Reference on the inside front cover for a list of exchange rates.

ATMs & Credit Cards

There are globally linked ATMs all over Dubai, at banks, shopping malls and at the upmarket hotels. Visa, MasterCard and American Express are widely accepted at shops, hotels and restaurants throughout Dubai and debit cards are accepted at bigger retail outlets.

Changing Money

Don't exchange money at the airport; the rates are terrible. Once in the city, there is no shortage of banks and exchange houses. In central Deira, especially along Sikkat al-Khail St, and around Baniyas Sq, every other building seems to contain a bank or a moneychanger. In Bur Dubai there are plenty of moneychangers (though most of them only take cash and not travellers cheques) around the *abra* dock. Thomas Cook Al-Rostamani has a number of branches around the city, including one on **Sheikh Zayed Rd** (Map p226), south of the Crowne Plaza Hotel; on **Kuwait St** (Map pp222–3) in Bur Dubai; and on **Rd 14** (Map pp216–17) in Deira, near Al-Khaleej Hotel.

If you are changing more than US$250 it might pay to do a little shopping around. Moneychangers sometimes have better rates than banks, and some don't charge a commission. The problem with moneychangers is that some of them either will

not take travellers cheques or will take one type only. Some places will only exchange travellers cheques if you can produce your original purchase receipt. If you don't have the receipt try asking for the manager.

Currencies of neighbouring countries are all recognised and easily changed with the exception of the Yemeni rial.

American Express (Amex) is represented in Dubai by **Kanoo Travel** (Map pp222–3; ☎ 336 5000; Sheikh Khalifa bin Zayed Rd, Karama; ✆ 8.30am-1pm & 3-6.30pm Sat-Thu). The office is on the 1st floor of the Hermitage Building, next to the main post office. It won't cash travellers cheques but will hold mail for Amex clients. Address mail to: c/o American Express, Client's Mail, PO Box 290, Dubai, UAE.

NEWSPAPERS & MAGAZINES

The newspaper scene has changed dramatically in Dubai in the last couple of years. New newspapers such as the free *7days* (www.7days.ae – amusingly published six days a week!) and also the government-sponsored *Emirates Today* (www.emiratestodayonline.com) have been breaking stories the established dailies (*Gulf News*, *Khaleej Times* and *Gulf Today*) dare not touch. For more on this, see p18.

Gulf News, *Khaleej Times* and *Gulf Today*, all published in Dubai, are the three English-language newspapers in Dubai. They cost Dh2 and carry pretty much the same international news, though *Gulf News* is the best of a pretty average bunch. Local news consists largely of 'business' stories, which are little more than recycled press releases masquerading as news. The local papers tend to have fairly comprehensive coverage of the Indian, Pakistani and Filipino political and entertainment scenes. *Gulf Business* (Dh15) is a glossy business magazine published locally, as is the English-language fashion and lifestyle magazine *Emirates Woman* (Dh15).

International newspapers and news magazines such as the *International Herald Tribune* (Dh15) and the *Economist* (Dh28) are fairly easy to find, though not cheap and sometimes several days or a week out of date. Many newsagencies and bookshops sell Indian newspapers such as *Malayalam Manorama* and the *Times of India* (Dh2 to Dh3).

The Arabic dailies are *Al-Bayan* (published in Dubai), *Al-Khaleej* and *Al-Ittihad* (both published in Abu Dhabi). Foreign newspapers are available in larger bookshops and hotels as well as Spinney's and Choitrams supermarkets.

Time Out Dubai is produced weekly and has decent listings and stories on upcoming events. It costs Dh10 although you'll find it free in Dubai's better hotel rooms. *What's On* is another listings monthly for Dh10, although it's not as 'hip' as *Time Out Dubai*.

Connector is a monthly publication aimed at Western expats with plenty of advertisements but also useful listings pages in the green section at the back of the book.

PHOTOGRAPHY & VIDEO

Dubai loves technology, so memory cards, batteries and other accessories for digital cameras are available everywhere. The best range and prices are usually found at **Carrefour** (p130) or **Plug-Ins** (p130). The UAE uses the PAL video system and all imaginable accessories are available from Carrefour and Plug-Ins.

POST

Emirates Post is the UAE's official postal service. There are post boxes at most of the major shopping centres. There are also a number of fax and postal agencies dotted along the small streets around Deira Souq and Dubai Souq. Letters up to 20g cost Dh3 to Europe and to most African countries; Dh3.50 to USA, Australia and the Far East; Dh2.50 to the subcontinent; Dh1.50 to Arab countries and Dh1 within the Gulf. Double these rates for letters weighing 20g to 50g. For letters weighing 50g to 100g, rates to these destinations are Dh13/11/9/6/4. Postcard rates are Dh2 to Europe, the USA, Australia and Asia; Dh1 to Arab countries and 75 fils within the Gulf.

Parcels weighing between 500g and 1kg cost Dh68 to the USA, Australia and the Far East; Dh45 to Europe and Africa; Dh36 to the subcontinent; Dh34 to other Arab countries; and Dh23 within the Gulf. For parcels weighing between 1kg and 2kg, the rates to these destinations are Dh130/85/68/64/45. Rates for surface mail are roughly half those for airmail.

Here are the most useful post offices in Dubai:

Al-Musalla Post office (Map pp220–1; ☼ 8am-1pm & 4-7pm Sat-Thu) At Al-Fahidi Roundabout in Bur Dubai.

Al-Rigga Post Office (Map pp218–19; ☼ 8am-1pm & 4-7pm Sat-Thu) Near the Clock Tower Roundabout.

Deira Post Office (Map pp216–17; Al-Sabkha Rd; ☼ 8am-midnight Sat-Wed, 8am-1pm & 4-8pm Thu) Near the intersection with Baniyas Rd.

Main Post Office (Map pp222–3; Za'abeel Rd; ☼ 8am-11.30pm Sat-Wed, 8am-10pm Thu, 8am-noon Fri) On the Bur Dubai side of the Creek in Karama. It also has a philatelic bureau.

Satwa Post Office (Map pp224–5; Al-Satwa Rd; ☼ 8am-1pm & 4-7pm Sat-Thu)

Mail generally takes about a week to 10 days to Europe or the USA and eight to 15 days to Australia. There does not seem to be any way of tracing packages that have gone missing, though. If you need to send something in a hurry, it's best to use one of the following courier agencies:

Aramex (☎ 286 5000)

DHL (☎ 800 4004)

FedEx (☎ 800 4050)

Poste-restante facilities are not available in Dubai. The Amex office will hold mail for Amex clients; see Changing Money (opposite) for the Amex office address. If you are staying at a five-star hotel, the reception desk will usually hold letters and small packages for two or three days prior to your arrival. It's a good idea to mark these 'Guest in Hotel' and, to be sure, 'Hold for Arrival'.

RADIO

The quality of radio programming is improving in Dubai (especially talk radio), but it's generally a cringe-worthy affair wherever you point the dial.

Channel 4 FM (104.8) Contemporary Top 40.

Dubai Eye FM (103.8) News, talk and sport.

Dubai FM (92) Classic hits from the '80s, '90s etc as well as dance and lounge on weekends.

Emirates 1 FM (100.5 and 104.1) Popular music.

Emirates 2 FM (90.5 and 98.5) Eclectic programming.

It's worth searching through the dial as there are stations playing Hindi, Arabic and Indian regional music, as well as stations where you can hear recitations of the Quran – very soothing when you're stuck in Dubai's horrific traffic.

SAFETY

On the whole, Dubai is a very safe city, but you should exercise the same sort of caution with your personal safety as you would anywhere. One very real danger in Dubai is bad driving; see the boxed text, p174. We don't recommend that you swim, water-ski or jet-ski in the Creek. The tides in the Gulf are not strong enough to flush the Creek out on a regular basis so it is not a clean waterway, despite what the tourist authorities might tell you. Also, be careful when swimming in the open sea. Despite the small surf, currents can be very strong and drownings are not uncommon.

TAXES & REFUNDS

When people say there is 'no tax' in Dubai, what they are referring to is the fact that there is no tax on incomes in Dubai – at this time. Prices are generally cheaper for most goods as there is less tax on goods before they arrive in the shops. Prices on many items in Dubai's shops are cheaper than at Dubai Duty Free and there is no tax refund that applies when you depart.

TELEPHONE & FAX

The UAE has an efficient telecommunications system. Calls within Dubai Emirate, not including Hatta, are free. The state telecommunications monopoly is **Etisalat** (Map pp216–17; cnr Baniyas & Omar ibn al-Khattab Rds; ☽ 24hr), recognisable by the giant, white golf ball on top of its headquarters. There is another office in **Al-Khaleej Shopping Centre** (Map pp220–1; Al-Mankhool Rd).

If you need to make a call from the airport, there are telephones at the far end of the baggage-claim area. Some of the lounges at the gates in the departures area also have phones from which you can make free local calls. Coin phones have almost completely been taken over by cardphones. Phonecards are available in various denominations from grocery stores, supermarkets and petrol stations – do not buy them from street vendors. Note that there

are two phonecards, one for cardphones and one for mobile phones operating on the Wasel GSM service.

To phone another country from the UAE, dial ☎ 00 followed by the country code. If you want to call the UAE, the country code is ☎ 971. The area code for Dubai is ☎ 04, though if you are calling from outside UAE you drop the zero.

There are Home Country Direct services to 43 countries. Dialling these codes connects you directly to an operator in the country being called. A list of access codes to these countries is in the Etisalat Services section of the phone book.

Call Charges

The following are some direct-dial rates per minute from the UAE:

To	Peak (Dh)	Off-peak (Dh)
Australia	4.19	2.54
Canada	4.19	2.54
France	4.19	3.21
Germany	4.19	3.60
India	4.29	3.67
Japan	4.19	3.60
Netherlands	5.45	4.50
UK	4.19	3.21
USA	4.19	3.00

There is a complete list of rates in the green pages section at the back of the Dubai phone book. The off-peak rates apply from 9pm to 7am daily and all day on Friday and national holidays.

Faxes

Most Etisalat offices are equipped to send and receive faxes. They may ask for your local address and contact number before they'll send a fax, and though the service is fairly good, it is expensive at Dh10 per page to most international destinations. Most typing and photocopying shops also have fax machines you can use. You'll find the highest concentration of these just north of the Clock Tower Roundabout on Abu Baker al-Siddiq Rd.

Mobile Phone

Mobile numbers begin with 050 in the UAE. Often people will give their seven-digit mobile number without mentioning this prefix as mobiles have almost become the standard means of communication in Dubai!

If you don't have a worldwide roaming service and want to use your mobile phone in Dubai, you can buy a prepaid SIM card from Etisalat, Dubai Duty Free or one of Dubai's myriad mobile phone shops. This excellent-value Ahlan Visitor's Mobile Package lasts 90 days, costs Dh90 and includes 90 minutes of UAE-based calls as well as a free three-minute international call. Recharge cards are available for purchase from grocery stores, supermarkets and petrol stations – once again, do not buy them from street vendors.

The UAE has introduced Wireless Application Protocol (WAP) services, which are available to Wasel GSM users as well as to normal UAE-based GSM subscribers. All you need to do is dial ☎ 125 and follow the instructions provided. Details about actually setting up access are available from **Etisalat** (www.etisalat.co.ae). Once you have done this, and as long as you have credit on the Wasel account, wireless application services are available.

TELEVISION

Local TV consists of several Arabic-language channels and one English-language station. However, all hotels you're likely to stay at in Dubai will have satellite TV. For news channels this will generally include BBC World and CNN. American sitcoms, copious reality TV shows and sport generally make up the rest of the programming.

TIME

Dubai is four hours ahead of GMT. The time does not change during the summer. Not taking daylight saving into account, when it's noon in Dubai, the time elsewhere is as follows:

City	Time
Auckland	8pm
London	8am
Los Angeles	midnight
New York	3am
Paris, Rome	9am
Perth, Hong Kong	4pm
Sydney	6pm

TIPPING

Tips are not generally expected since a service charge is added to your bill (this goes to the restaurant, not the waiter, though). If you want to leave a tip, 10% is sufficient for good service – if you don't get good service, don't leave it.

TOILET

The best advice is to go when you can. The very few public toilets on the streets are usually only for men. Public toilets in shopping centres, museums, restaurants and hotels are Western style and are generally well maintained. On an excursion outside Dubai you might have to contend with 'hole in the ground' loos at the back of restaurants or petrol stations.

TOURIST INFORMATION
Local Tourist Offices

The **Department of Tourism & Commerce Marketing** (DTCM; ☎ 223 0000; www.dubaitourism .co.ae) is the official tourism board of the Dubai government. It is also the sole regulating, planning and licensing authority for the tourist industry in Dubai. It has three main welcome bureaus you can call for information or for help in booking hotels, tours and car hire: the airport arrivals area (just after customs, on your left), Baniyas Sq and way down Sheikh Zayed Rd on the way to Abu Dhabi (around 40km out of Dubai). The quality of information they give largely depends on the enthusiasm of the person behind the desk. There are also smaller information desks at all the major shopping malls.

Airport (Map pp218–19; ☎ 224 5252/224 4098; ⏲ 24hr)

Baniyas Square (Map pp216–17; ☎ 228 5000; Baniyas Sq; ⏲ 9am-11pm)

Sheikh Zayed Road (☎ 883 3397; Sheikh Zayed Rd; ⏲ 9am-9pm)

Dubai National Travel & Tourist Authority (DNATA) is the quasi-official travel agency in Dubai; it has the monopoly on travel services at a wholesale level. The **DNATA head office** (Map pp218–19; ☎ 295 1111; Al-Maktoum Rd, Deira) is at the DNATA Airline Centre. There are other branches opening around the city.

Tourist Offices Abroad

The DTCM has a number of branches overseas that are vigorously promoting Dubai as an upmarket tourist destination. These branches go by the name of the Dubai Tourism & Commerce Promotion Board and include the following:

Australia & New Zealand (☎ 02 9956 620; dtcm_aus@dubaitourism.ae; Level 6, 75 Miller St, North Sydney, NSW 2060 Australia)

Far East (☎ 02 2827 5221; dtcm_hk@dubaitourism.ae; 19th fl, 148 Electric Rd, North Point, Hong Kong)

France (☎ 01 44 95 85 00; dtcm-france@dubai.fr; 15 bis, rue de Marignan, 75008 Paris, France)

Germany (☎ 069 71 000 20; dtcm_ge@dubaitourism .ae; Bockenheimer Landstrasse 23 D 60325, Frankfurt/Main, Germany)

India (☎ 022-22833497; dtcm_in@dubaitourism.ae; A/121, Mittal Court, Nariman Point, Mumbai 400 021, India)

Italy (☎ 02 5740 3036; dtcm_it@dubaitourism.ae; Via Pietrasanta 14, 20141, Milano, Italy)

Japan (☎ 03 5367 5450; dtcm_ja@dubaitourism.ae; Woody 21 Bldg, Aizumi-cho 23, Shinjuku-ku, Tokyo 160 0005, Japan)

Nordic Countries (☎ 08 411 11 35; dtcm_sca@ dubaitourism.ae; Skeppsbron 30, SE-111 30, Stockholm, Sweden)

Russia, CIS & Baltic States (☎ 095-980 0717; dtcm_cis@ dubaitourism.ae; 2, 8th fl, 10 Bldg, Letnikovskaya St, 115114, Moscow, Russia)

South Africa (☎ 011 785 4600; dtcm_sa@dubaitourism .ae; 1 Orchard Lane, PO Box 698, Rivonia, 2128 Johannesburg)

Switzerland & Austria (☎ 031 924 75 99; dtcm_ch@ dubaitourism.ae; Hinterer Schermen 29, CH-3063 Ittigen-Bern, Switzerland)

UK & Ireland (☎ 020 7839 0580; dtcm_uk@ dubaitourism.ae; 125 Pall Mall, London SW1Y 5EA, UK)

USA (☎ 212 575 2262; dtcm_usa@dubaitourism.ae; 5 West 45th St, Suite No 405 New York, NY 10036, USA)

VISAS

To visit Dubai your passport must have at least six months validity from your date of arrival. Officially, you will be denied entry if your passport shows any evidence of travel to Israel, and Israeli passport holders are not permitted to enter. Visit visas valid for 60 days are available on arrival in the UAE at approved ports of entry, including all airports and ports, for citizens of most developed countries. These include all Western European countries (except Malta and Cyprus), Australia, Brunei, Canada, Hong Kong, Japan, Malaysia, New Zealand, Singapore, South Korea and the USA. Tourist visas are valid for 60 days despite the fact that the stamp on your passport, which is in Arabic, says it is valid for 30 days. No fee is charged for tourist visas.

Citizens of the other Gulf Cooperative Council (GCC) countries do not need visas to enter the UAE, and can stay pretty much as long as they want. For citizens of other countries, a transit or tourist visa must be arranged through a sponsor. This can be a hotel, a company or a resident of the UAE. Most hotels charge a fee for arranging a visa, of around Dh200.

VIS-À-VIS OMAN

Coming from Dubai, many nationalities can enter Oman without visa charges if they have tourist visas or entry stamps issued by Dubai authorities. They are also free to depart for, or return from, a third destination through land or air facilities in either country.

If you are visiting Oman on a tourist visa, these same nationalities can enter the UAE by land, air or sea without visa charges.

Visa Extensions

Visit visas can be extended once for 30 days by the **Department of Immigration and Naturalisation** (Map pp222–3; ☎ 398 1010; Sheikh Khalifa bin Zayed Rd), near the Za'abeel Roundabout, for Dh500 and a fair amount of paperwork. You may be asked to provide proof of funds.

For longer periods, you have to leave the country and come back again to get a new stamp. People have been known to stay in Dubai for a year or more simply by flying out to Bahrain, Doha or Kish (an island off the Iranian coast) every two months and picking up a new visa on their return at a total cost of about Dh400 per trip. Visas can only be extended in the city or emirate you arrived in, so if you landed in Sharjah you can't get your visa extended in Dubai.

WOMEN TRAVELLERS

Attitudes Towards Women

In general, Dubai is one of the best Middle East destinations for women travellers. Checking into hotels is not usually a problem, but unaccompanied women might want to think twice about taking a room in some of the budget hotels in Deira and Bur Dubai – of course these hotels are not included in our Sleeping chapter.

Although things might be better in Dubai than in other parts of the Gulf, it does not mean that some of the problems that accompany travel in the Middle East will not arise here as well, such as unwanted male attention and long, lewd stares. You may be beeped at by men in passing cars, but most times these are taxi drivers touting for business. Try not to be intimidated; it helps to retain a sense of humour.

Safety Precautions

Dubai is a very liberal place and people here are used to Western women. While it *is* liberal, do yourself a favour and wear more than a skimpy tank top to places like shopping malls where local Emiratis will be present. While they're too good a host to actually say anything, most Emiratis find this disrespectful. When it comes to beach parties and nightclubs almost anything goes, but take a taxi there and back. Keep in mind also that many of Dubai's bars and clubs (even the notable ones) have 'working women' operating in them.

If you travel outside Dubai, keep in mind that everywhere else in the UAE is far more conservative. Apply common sense – don't wear tight and revealing clothes that are just going to make your life difficult. Women should always sit in the back seat of taxis. You'll find that you'll often be asked to take the front seat in buses or be asked to sit next to other women. This is so you can avoid the embarrassment of men's stares.

In banks, Etisalat offices, post offices and libraries there are usually separate sections or windows for women – great when there's a queue – so take advantage of it! In small Arab and Indo-Pakistani restaurants you will often be ushered into the 'family room'. You don't have to sit here but the room is there to save you from being stared at by men. Trust us, it's usually a good idea to follow their advice.

Organisations

International Business Women's Group (www .ibwgdubai.com) Operating since 1983, this is a networking support group for women in the UAE who are in senior management or who own their own companies. It meets on the second Monday of each month and is open to all nationalities.

WORK

You can pre-arrange work in the UAE, but if you enter the country on a visit visa and then find work, you will have to leave the country for one day and re-enter under your employer's sponsorship.

If you have arranged work in Dubai you will enter the country on a visit visa sponsored by your employer while your residence visa is processed. This process involves a blood test for HIV/AIDS and lots of paperwork. Those on a residence visa who are sponsored by a spouse who is in turn sponsored by an employer are not officially permitted to work. This rule is often broken, and it is possible to find work in the public or private sector. If you are in this situation, remember that your spouse, and not the company you work for, is your sponsor. One effect of this is that you may only be able to apply for a tourist visa to another Gulf Arab country with a consent letter from your spouse. In some cases you will need to be accompanied by your spouse, who has company sponsorship. Similarly, if you want to apply for a driving licence you will also need a consent letter from your spouse.

If you obtain your residence visa through an employer and then quit because you've found something better, you may find yourself under a six-month ban from working in the UAE. This rule is designed to stop people from job hopping.

If you are employed in Dubai and have any work-related problems you can call the Ministry of Labour Helpline (☎ 269 1666) for advice.

Finding Work

While plenty of people turn up in Dubai on a visit visa, decide they like the look of the place and then scout around for a job, this isn't really the most effective way to go about it. Firstly, most employees are on a contract that's generally for three years. Secondly, there are a lot of sums to be done before you can really figure out whether the amount you're offered is going to make financial sense. Things such as a housing allowance, medical coverage, holidays and schooling (for those with kids) have to be taken into account before you can decide.

Target who you want to work with and try to set up meetings before you arrive. Email and follow up with a phone call or two. Employers in Dubai are very fond of people with qualifications. However, it's of little consequence *which* higher learning establishment you attended – it's of lesser importance than the paper it's written on. Teachers, nurses and those in engineering are highly valued in Dubai and well paid.

The *Khaleej Times* and the *Gulf News* publish employment supplements several times a week. When you find a job, you will be offered an employment contract in Arabic and English. Get the one in Arabic translated before you sign it.

Business Aid Centre (☎ 337 5747; www.bacdubai.com; PO Box 8743, Dubai)

Clarendon Parker (☎ 331 1702; www.clarendonparker .com; PO Box 26359, Dubai)

SOS Recruitment Consultants (☎ 396 5600; www.sos .co.ae; PO Box 6948, Dubai)

Language

Language

It's true – anyone can speak another language. Don't worry if you haven't studied languages before or that you studied a language at school for years and can't remember any of it. It doesn't even matter if you failed English grammar. After all, that's never affected your ability to speak English! And this is the key to picking up a language in another country. You just need to start speaking.

Learn a few key Arabic phrases before you go. Write them on pieces of paper and stick them on the fridge, by the bed or even on the computer – anywhere that you'll see them often.

You'll find that locals appreciate travellers trying to speak Arabic, no matter how muddled you may think you sound. So don't just stand there, say something!

SOCIAL
Meeting People
Hello/Welcome.
marHaba
Peace be upon you.
al-salaam alaykum
Peace be upon you. (response)
wa alaykum e-salaam
How are you?
kay fahlak?
Good, thanks.
zein, shukran
Goodbye.
fl'man ullah or ma'al salaama
Goodbye. (response)
(to a man) alla ysalmak
(to a woman) alla ysalmich
Goodbye.
(to a man) Hayyaakallah
(to a woman) Hayyachallah
Goodbye. (response)
(to a man) alla yHai'eek
(to a woman) alla yHai'eech
Please.
(to a man) min fadhlak
(to a woman) min fadhlich
Thank you (very much).
shukran (jazeelan)
You're welcome.
al-afu
Excuse me.
(to a man) lau tismaH
(to a woman) lau tismaHin
Yes.
na'am
No.
la'
If God is willing.
insha'allah

Do you speak English?
titkallam ingleezi?
Do you understand (me)?
Hal bitifhaam (alay)?
I understand.
(by a man) ana fahim
(by a woman) ana fahma
I don't understand.
(by a man) ana mu fahim
(by a woman) ana mu fahma

Could you please ...?
mumkin min fadhlak ...?
repeat that	a'id Hatha
speak more slowly	takalam shwai shwai
write it down	iktbHa lee

Going Out
What's on ...?
maza yaHdos ...?
locally	mahaleeyan
this weekend	fee nihayet Hatha alesboo'a
today	al-yom
tonight	al-layla

Where are the places to eat?
wayn el maHalat al-aakl?

PRACTICAL
Question Words
Who?	mnu?
What?	shu?
When?	mata?
Where?	wayn?
How?	chayf?
How many?	cham?

Numbers & Amounts

0	sifr
1	waHid
2	ithneen
3	thalatha
4	arba'a
5	khamsa
6	sitta
7	sab'a
8	thimania
9	tis'a
10	ashra
11	Hda'ash
12	thna'ash
13	thalathta'ash
14	arba'ata'ash
15	khamista'ash
16	sitta'ash
17	sabi'ta'ash
18	thimanta'ash
19	tisi'ta'ash
20	'ishreen
21	waHid wa 'ishreen
22	ithneen wa 'ishreen
23	thalatha wa 'ishreen
30	thalatheen
40	arbi'een
50	khamseen
60	sitteen
70	saba'een
80	thimaneen
90	tis'een
100	imia
101	imia waHid
102	imia wa-ithneen
103	imia wa-thalatha
200	imiatain
300	thalatha imia
1000	alf
2000	alfayn
3000	thalath-alaf

Days

Monday	yom al-ithneen
Tuesday	yom al-thalath
Wednesday	yom al-arbaa'
Thursday	yom al-khamis
Friday	yom al-jama'a
Saturday	yom as-sabt
Sunday	yom al-Had

Banking

I want to ...
ana areed an ...
 cash a cheque
 asref el-chek

change money
asref beezat
change some travellers cheques
asref chekat siyaHeeya

Where's the nearest ...?
wayn aghrab ...?
 automatic teller machine (ATM)
 alet saref/sarraf alee
 foreign exchange office
 maktab al-serafa

Post

Where is the post office?
wayn maktab el-bareed?

I want to send a ...
ana areed an arsell an ...

fax	faks
parcel	barsell/ta'rd
postcard	beetaga bareediya/kart

I want to buy ...
ana areed an ashtaree ...

an aerogram	reesala jaweeya
an envelope	zaref
a stamp	tab'eh bareed

Phones & Mobiles

I want to buy a (phone card).
ana areed ashtaree (beetaget Hatef/
 kart telefon)
I want to make a call (to ...)
ana areed an atsell (bee ...)
I want to make a reverse-charge/collect call.
ana areed taHweel kulfet al-mukalama ila
 al-mutagee

Where can I find a/an ...?
wayn mumkin an ajed ...?
I'd like a/an ...
ana areed ...
 adaptor plug
 maakhaz tawseel
 charger for my phone
 shaHen leel Hatef
 mobile/cell phone for hire
 mobail ('mobile') leel ajar
 prepaid mobile/cell phone
 mobail moos baq aldaf'
 SIM card for your network
 seem kart lee shabaket al-itsalaat

Internet

Where's the local Internet café?
wayn magHa al-internet?
I'd like to ...
ana abga an ...
    check my email   chayk al-emayl malee
    get online   ahsaal ala khat internet

Transport

When does the ... leave?
mata yamshi ...
When does the ... arrive?
mata yusal ... (m)
    boat   il-markab
    train   il-qittar
mata tusal ... (f)
    bus   il-bas
    plane   il-tayara

What time's the ... bus?
mata ... bas?
    first   awal
    last   akhar

What time's the next bus?
mata il-bas al-thani?
Are you free? (taxi)
anta fathee?
Please put the meter on.
lau samaHt shagal al-addad
How much is it to ...?
bcham la ...?
Please take me to (this address).
lau samaHt wasalni la (Hadha elonwan)

FOOD

breakfast   futtoor
lunch   ghadha
dinner   asha
snack   akal khafif
eat   kol
drink   ishrab

Can you recommend a ...
mumkin an tansaHanee ala ...?
    bar/pub   baar
    café   magha
    restaurant   mata'am

Is service/cover charge included in the bill?
Hal al-fattoora tashmole al-khadma aidan?

For more detailed information on eating and dining out, see 'Eating' on p75.

EMERGENCIES

It's an emergency!
Halet isa'af!
Could you please help me/us?
mumkin an toosaadnee min fadhlak?
Call the (police/a doctor/an ambulance)!
etasell bil (shurta/tabeeb/sayyaret al-isa'af)!
Where's the police station?
wayn marekaz al-shurta?

HEALTH

Where's the nearest ...?
wayn aghrab ...?
    chemist (night)   saydalee (laylee)
    dentist   tabeeb asnan
    doctor   tabeeb
    hospital   mustashfa

Symptoms

I have (a) ...
ana andee ...
    diarrhoea   is-haal
    fever   sukhoona
    headache   suda or waja' ras
    pain   alam/waja'

GLOSSARY

This glossary contains a list of Arabic terms that you may hear on your travels through Dubai. For food terms you'll commonly find in the city, check out the Lebanese Food Lingo 101 (p15) and Persian Plates (p14) boxed texts.

abaya - woman's full-length black robe
abra - small, flat-decked boat; water taxi
agal - headropes used to hold a *gutra* in place
areesh - palm fronds used to construct houses
attar - perfume

ayyalah - Bedouin dance
azan - call to prayer

baggara - traditional pearling boat
baglah - large dhow used for long-distance journeys
baiti - romantic Arabic poetry style
barasti - traditional Gulf method of building palm-leaf houses; house built with palm leaves
bateel - young shoot of date-palm plant
boom - large dhow used for long-distance journeys
burj - tower

dalla - traditional copper coffeepot
dhow - traditional sailing vessel of the Gulf
dishdasha - man's shirt-dress

falaj - traditional irrigation channel

galalif - dhow builder
gutra - white headcloth

habban - Arabian bagpipes
haj - Muslim pilgrimage to Mecca
halal - meat from animals killed according to Islamic law
hammam - bathhouse
hammour - common species of fish found in Gulf waters
haram - forbidden by Islamic law
hawala - written order of payment
housh - courtyard

imam - prayer leader, Muslim cleric

jasr - drum covered with goatskin, which is slung around the neck and hit with sticks
jebel - hill, mountain

kandoura - casual shirt-dress worn by men and women
khaleeji - traditional Gulf-style music
khanjar - traditional curved dagger
khor - inlet or creek

liwa - traditional dance performed to a rapid tempo and loud drumbeat; it is usually sung in Swahili and most likely brought to the Gulf by East African slaves

majlis - formal meeting room or reception area
Majlis - parliament
manior - percussion instrument of a belt decorated with dried goat hooves
masayf - traditional summer house incorporating a wind-tower
mashait - traditional winter house incorporating a court-yard
masjid - mosque
mathaf - museum

mihrab - niche in a mosque indicating the direction of Mecca
mimzar - oboe-like instrument
mina - port
Muallaqat - collection of pre-Islamic Arabic odes
muezzin - mosque official who sings the *azan*
mullah - Muslim scholar, teacher or religious leader

nabati - Arabic vernacular poetry

oud – wooden Arabian lute, also the wood used to burn with frankincense

qibla - the direction of Mecca, indicated in a mosque by the *mihrab*

Ramadan - Muslim month of fasting

sambuq - boat mainly used for fishing
shasha - small fishing boat made of palm fronds
sheesha - tall, glass-bottomed smoking implement; also called a water pipe or hubbly-bubbly
sheikh - venerated religious scholar, tribal chief, ruler or elderly man worthy of respect
sheikha - daughter of a *sheikh*
somok - wooden incense

tafila - prose-style Arabic poetry
tamboura - harplike instrument with five horse-gut strings that are plucked with sheep horns
Trucial States - former name of the United Arab Emirates; also called Trucial Coast, Trucial Oman and Trucial Sheikdoms

wasta - influence gained by way of connections in high places
wind-tower - architectural feature of *masayf* houses designed to keep the house cool
wudu - practice of ritual washing before daily prayer

Behind the Scenes

THE LONELY PLANET STORY

The story begins with a classic travel adventure: Tony and Maureen Wheeler's 1972 journey across Europe and Asia to Australia. There was no useful information about the overland trail then, so Tony and Maureen published the first Lonely Planet guidebook to meet a growing need.

From a kitchen table, Lonely Planet has grown to become the largest independent travel publisher in the world, with offices in Melbourne (Australia), Oakland (USA) and London (UK). Today Lonely Planet guidebooks cover the globe. There is an ever-growing list of books and information in a variety of media. Some things haven't changed. The main aim is still to make it possible for adventurous travellers to get out there – to explore and better understand the world.

At Lonely Planet we believe travellers can make a positive contribution to the countries they visit – if they respect their host communities and spend their money wisely. Every year 5% of company profit is donated to charities around the world.

THIS BOOK

This 4th edition was written by Terry Carter and Lara Dunston, as was the previous edition. The 2nd edition was revised and updated by Richard Plunkett. The 1st edition was researched and written by Lou Callan. This guidebook was commissioned in Lonely Planet's Melbourne office, and produced by the following:

Commissioning Editor Stefanie Di Trocchio, Kerryn Burgess

Coordinating Editors Susie Ashworth, Sarah Stewart

Coordinating Cartographer Julie Sheridan

Coordinating Layout Designer Evelyn Yee

Managing Editor Jennifer Garrett

Managing Cartographer Shahara Ahmed

Assisting Cartographers Jack Gavran, Amanda Sierp

Cover Designer Yukiyoshi Kamimura

Project Manager Eoin Dunlevy

Language Content Coordinator Quentin Frayne

Thanks to Helen Christinis, Sally Darmody, Laura Jane, Wayne Murphy, Stephanie Pearson, Raphael Richards, Jane Thompson, Marg Toohey, Celia Wood

Cover photographs: Golf Club, Dubai, United Arab Emirates, Jon Arnold/Photolibrary (top); Arab man with a camel, Pankaj Shah/Getty (bottom); Skateboarding in Dubai, Terry Carter/Lonely Planet Images (back).

Internal photographs by Lonely Planet Images and Terry Carter. All images are the copyright of the photographers unless otherwise indicated. Many of the images in this guide are available for licensing from Lonely Planet Images: www.lonelyplanetimages.com.

All images are copyright of the photographer unless otherwise indicated. Many of the images in this guide are available for licensing from Lonely Planet Images: www.lonelyplanetimages.com.

THANKS
TERRY CARTER & LARA DUNSTON

There are just so many people to thank for their help on this book – both with the editorial and photography – that the music would start playing and we'd be escorted off the stage before we could mention about a third of you. You know who you are, we've already told you how much we appreciate your help, but once again a big *shukran* to all of you. However, we must make an exception to this for commissioning editor Kerryn Burgess who came up with the crazy idea to commission Terry for the photography as

LONELY PLANET AUTHORS

Why is our travel information the best in the world? It's simple: our authors are independent, dedicated travellers. They don't research using just the Internet or phone, and they don't take freebies in exchange for positive coverage. They travel widely, to all the popular spots and off the beaten track. They personally visit thousands of hotels, restaurants, cafés, bars, galleries, palaces, museums and more – and they take pride in getting all the details right, and telling it how it is. For more, see the authors section on www.lonelyplanet.com.

well as writing, and to the eternally floating editor Stefanie Di Trocchio for seeing it through.

OUR READERS

Many thanks to the travellers who used the last edition and wrote to us with helpful hints, useful advice and interesting anecdotes:

Jackie Ainsworth, Luis Amaral, Greg Andrews, Andrew Bartram, Sven Berger, Jacqueline Black, Philip Bowell, Ken & Rosemary Brooks, J W Byrom, Burt Candy, Vipan Chopra, M Digel, Magdalena Dral, John Lee Fagence, Brian Furner, Craig Gemmell, Dede Ghiradi, Daniel Happell, M Harris, Mathias Heinemann, L J Hill, Peter Hore, Trygve & Karen Inda, Adeel Jamil, Stephanie Johnston, Jens Juhl, Elisabeth Knap, Marnix Koets, Lin Lee, Peter Lindholm, Renae Lindwall, Megan Loutfi, Thorsten Luttger, Astrid, Heidi, Winston & Jacquelyn Marshall, Nick Massey, Tony Meagher, Rachel Metcalfe, Michele Moore, Jennifer Mundy, Aylin Ozcanli, Rolf Palmberg, Prakash Parmar, Simon Peters, Ceri Powell, Deborah Ruff, Henryk Sadura, Carla Santos, Beate Schmahl, Maggie Seeliger, Khaled Shivji, John Smith, Kim Stevens, Jenny Storti, Guelsah Taskin, Louie Tham, James Tisdale, Miquel Trujillo, Shabnam Walji, Stephen G Wesley & Lydia Wilson.

SEND US YOUR FEEDBACK

We love to hear from travellers – your comments keep us on our toes and help make our books better. Our well-travelled team reads every word on what you loved or loathed about this book. Although we cannot reply individually to postal submissions, we always guarantee that your feedback goes straight to the appropriate authors, in time for the next edition. Each person who sends us information is thanked in the next edition – and the most useful submissions are rewarded with a free book.

To send us your updates – and find out about Lonely Planet events, newsletters and travel news – visit our award-winning website: www.lonelyplanet.com/feedback.

Note: We may edit, reproduce and incorporate your comments in Lonely Planet products such as guidebooks, websites and digital products, so let us know if you don't want your comments reproduced or your name acknowledged. For a copy of our privacy policy visit www.lonelyplanet.com/privacy.

Notes

Notes

Notes

Notes

Notes

Notes

Index

See also separate indexes for Eating (p210), Entertainment (p210), Shopping (p210) and Sleeping (p211).

000 map pages
000 photographs

Index

SLEEPING

Index

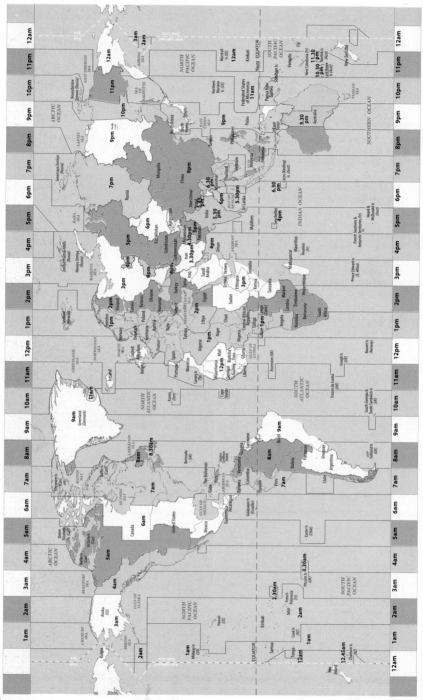

MAP LEGEND

ROUTES

............Tollway	............One-Way Street
............Freeway	............Mall/Steps
............Primary Road	............Tunnel
............Secondary Road	............Walking Tour
............Tertiary Road	............Walking Tour Detour
............Lane	............Walking Trail
............Under Construction	............Walking Path
............Track	............Pedestrian Overpass
............Unsealed Road	

TRANSPORT

............Ferry	............Rail
............Bus Route	

HYDROGRAPHY

............River, Creek	............Water

BOUNDARIES

............International	............Regional, Suburb
............State, Provincial	............Ancient Wall
............Disputed	............Cliff

AREA FEATURES

............Airport	............Forest
............Area of Interest	............Land
............Beach, Desert	............Mall
............Building, Featured	............Park
............Building, Information	............Reservation
............Building, Other	............Rocks
............Building, Transport	............Sports
............Cemetery, Christian	............Urban
............Cemetery, Other	

POPULATION

CAPITAL (NATIONAL)	**CAPITAL (STATE)**
Large City	**Medium City**
Small City	Town, Village

SYMBOLS

Sights/Activities	Eating	Information
Beach	Eating	Bank, ATM
Castle, Fortress	**Drinking**	Embassy/Consulate
Hindu	Drinking	Hospital, Medical
Islamic	**Entertainment**	Information
Monument	Entertainment	Internet Facilities
Museum, Gallery	**Shopping**	Police Station
Other Site	Shopping	Post Office, GPO
Ruin	**Sleeping**	Telephone
Sikh	Sleeping	
Zoo, Bird Sanctuary	**Transport**	**Geographic**
	Airport, Airfield	Oasis
	Border Crossing	
	Bus Station	
	Parking Area	

Maps

GREATER DUBAI

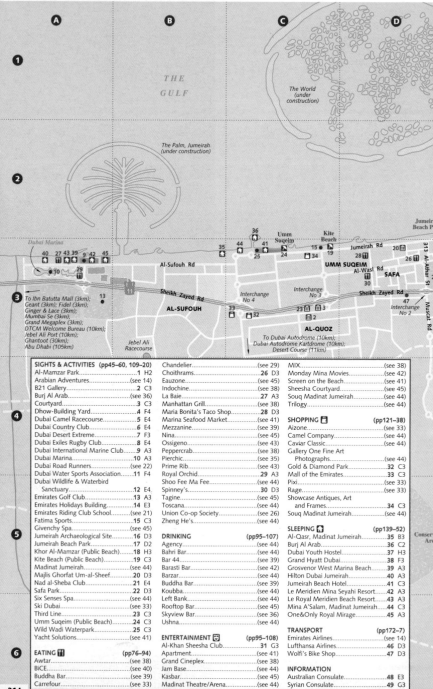

THE GULF

The World (under construction)

The Palm, Jumeirah (under construction)

Dubai Marina

Al-Sufouh Rd

AL-SUFOUH

Sheikh Zayed Rd

To Ibn Batutta Mall (3km);
Geant (3km); Fidel (3km);
Ginger & Lace (3km);
Mumbai Se (3km);
Grand Megaplex (3km);
DTCM Welcome Bureau (10km);
Jebel Ali Port (10km);
Ghantoot (30km);
Abu Dhabi (105km)

Jebel Ali Racecourse

Interchange No 4

To Dubai Autodrome (10km);
Dubai Autodrome Kartdrome (10km);
Desert Course (11km)

AL-QUOZ

Interchange No 3

Umm Suqeim

Kite Beach

Jumeirah Rd

UMM SUQEIM

Al-Wasl Rd

SAFA

Sheikh Zayed Rd

Interchange No 2

Jumeirah Beach Park

Muscat Rd

Conservation Area

214

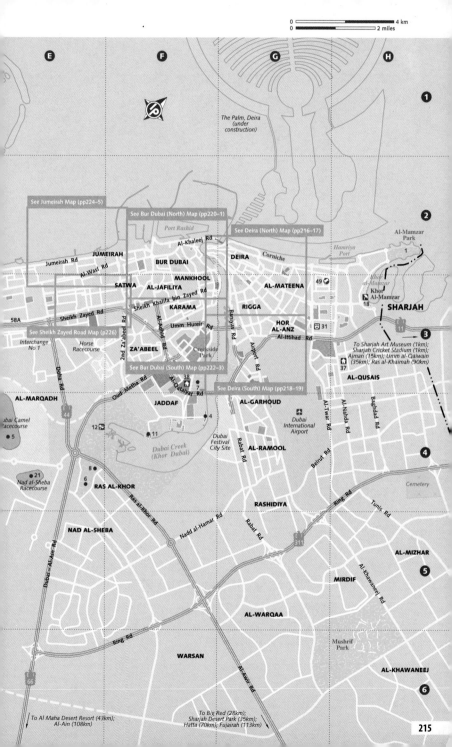

0 ————— 4 km
0 ————— 2 miles

E   **F**   **G**   **H**

1

The Palm, Deira
(under
construction)

Al-Mamzar
Park

See Jumeirah Map (pp224–5)

See Bur Dubai (North) Map (pp220–1)

See Deira (North) Map (pp216–17)

Port Rashid

Al-Khalee̅ Rd

Corniche

*Hamriya
Port*

2

Jumeirah Rd

JUMEIRAH

Al-Wasl Rd

DEIRA

*Khor
al-Mamzar*

Khor
Al-Mamzar

BUR DUBAI

18

SHARJAH

MANKHOOL

SATWA

AL-JAFILIYA

Sheikh Khalifa bin Zayed Rd

AL-MATEENA

49

58A

Sheikh Zayed Rd

KARAMA

2nd Za'abeel Rd

RIGGA

Banyyas Rd

To Sharjah Art Museum (1km);
Sharjah Cricket Stadium (1km);
Ajman (15km); Umm al-Qaiwain
(35km); Ras al-Khaimah (90km)

Interchange
No 1

Horse
Racecourse

Umm Hureir Rd

**HOR
AL-ANZ**

31

Al-Ittihad Rd

3

See Sheikh Zayed Road Map (p226)

Al-Ada Rd

Al-Ittihad Rd

37

ZA'ABEEL

Creekside
Park

Airport Rd

AL-QUSAIS

See Bur Dubai (South) Map (pp222–3)

See Deira (South) Map (pp218–19)

AL-MARQADH

Oud Metha Rd

38

Al-Qataiyat Rd

7

4

JADDAF

AL-GARHOUD

*Dubai Camel
Racecourse*

44

12

AL-RAMOOL

Rabat Rd

Al-Twar Rd

Al-Nahda Rd

Baghdad Rd

5

11

*Dubai
International
Airport*

4

*Dubai Creek
(Khor Dubai)*

*Dubai
Festival
City Site*

Cemetery

8

21

*Nad al-Sheba
Racecourse*

6

RAS AL-KHOR

RASHIDIYA

Ring Rd

Tunis Rd

NAD AL-SHEBA

Ras al-Khor Rd

Nadd al-Hamar Rd

Rabat Rd

31

Dubai – Al-Ain Rd

AL-MIZHAR

5

Al-Khawaneej Rd

MIRDIF

AL-WARQAA

Ring Rd

*Mushrif
Park*

WARSAN

Al-Awir Rd

AL-KHAWANEEJ

6

To Al Maha Desert Resort (43km);
Al-Ain (108km)

To Big Red (28km);
Sharjah Desert Park (35km);
Hatta (70km); Fujairah (113km)

DEIRA (NORTH)

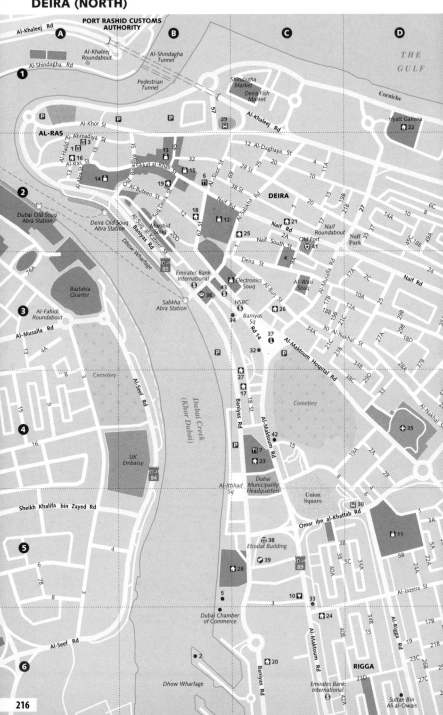

PORT RASHID CUSTOMS AUTHORITY

Al-Khaleej Rd   **Ⓐ**   **Ⓑ**   **Ⓒ**   **Ⓓ**

Al-Khaleej Roundabout   Al-Shindagha Tunnel

Al-Shindagha Rd   Al-Shindagha Tunnel   *THE GULF*

❶   Pedestrian Tunnel

Shindagha Market

Deira Fish Market

Corniche

57   Al-Khaleej Rd

29   Hyatt Galleria   **22**

AL-RAS   Al-Khor St

Al-Ahmadiya St   12 Al-Daghaya St

1 16 Al-Ras   13   20   4

Al-Hadd   Al-Barsha   15   32   28 St   10   11A

14   Sikkat al-Khail   15   6   38 St   **DEIRA**   15   16B

❷   19   Al-Buteen St   Naif Rd   20   21B   27   14A   10   8

Dubai Old Souq Abra Station   18   Naif Rd   **Naif Rd** **21**   17   6C

Deira Old Souq Abra Station   Murshid Souq   12   **25**   Naif South St   Old Fort   Naif Park   35 37   45 18B

❸   Al-Fahidi Roundabout   Baniyas Rd   Deira St   4   Al-Musalla Rd   2C   24

Al-Musalla Rd   D 85   Emirates Bank International   43   Electronics Souq   Al-Wasi Souq   17B   10A   12A   25   29B

   36   HSBC   Al-Buri Souq   **26**   18B 19B   12C   2   29B 18D

   Sabkha Abra Station   34   Baniyas Sq   34A   30   21C   27A

   37   Rd 14   Al-Nakhal St   23B   34B   29D 28A

   32   Al-Maktoum Hospital Rd   15   21C   38C

Cemetery   27   18 St   Cemetery   19A   2A   Al-Nakhal St

❹   Al-Seef Rd   17   Baniyas Rd   42   **35**

   Al-Maktoum Rd

UK Embassy   D 84   7   23   15

Al-Ittihad Sq   Dubai Municipality Headquarters   Union Square

Sheikh Khalifa bin Zayed Rd   Omar ibn al-Khattab Rd   30   3A

❺   38   Etisalat Building   11   5A

   39   D 89   34A   5B

   28   Al-Jazeira St

   5   10 33   24

Dubai Chamber of Commerce   **RIGGA**

❻   Al-Seef Rd   2   20   Emirates Bank International   23D   17B

Dhow Wharfage   Baniyas Rd   Sultan Bin Ali al-Owais

| 0 | 500 m |
| 0 | 0.3 miles |

E **F** **G** **H**

SIGHTS & ACTIVITIES	(pp49–52, 109–20)
Al-Ahmadiya School	**1** A2
Creekside Leisure	**2** B6
Deira Covered Souq	(see 12)
Deira Gold Souq	(see 13)
Deira Spice Souq (Old Souq)	(see 14)
Heritage House	**3** A2
Inter-Fitness	(see 23)
Naif Souq	**4** C1
National Bank of Dubai	**5** B5
Perfume Souq	(see 15)

EATING 🍽	(pp79–82)
Ashiana	(see 28)
Ashwaq Cafeteria	**6** B2
China Club	**7** C4
Creekside	(see 28)
Glasshouse Mediterranean Brasserie	(see 20)
Minato	(see 7)
Miyako	(see 22)
Shabestan	(see 7)
Shahrzad	(see 22)

Spinney's	**8** F6
Verre	(see 20)
Wholesale Market	**9** G2
YUM!	(see 7)

DRINKING 🍷	(pp95–107)
Issimo	(see 20)
Ku Bu	(see 23)
M-Level	(see 20)
Up on the Tenth	(see 23)
Velvet Lounge	**10** C5

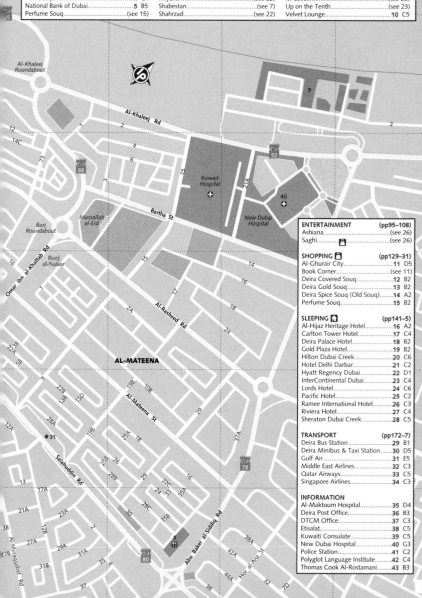

ENTERTAINMENT	(pp95–108)
Ashiana	(see 26)
Saghi	(see 26)

SHOPPING 🛍	(pp129–31)
Al-Ghurair City	**11** D5
Book Corner	(see 11)
Deira Covered Souq	**12** B2
Deira Gold Souq	**13** B2
Deira Spice Souq (Old Souq)	**14** A2
Perfume Souq	**15** B2

SLEEPING 🛏	(pp141–5)
Al-Hijaz Heritage Hotel	**16** A2
Carlton Tower Hotel	**17** C4
Deira Palace Hotel	**18** B2
Gold Plaza Hotel	**19** B2
Hilton Dubai Creek	**20** C6
Hotel Delhi Darbar	**21** C2
Hyatt Regency Dubai	**22** D1
InterContinental Dubai	**23** C4
Lords Hotel	**24** C6
Pacific Hotel	**25** C2
Ramee International Hotel	**26** C3
Riviera Hotel	**27** C4
Sheraton Dubai Creek	**28** C5

TRANSPORT	(pp172–7)
Deira Bus Station	**29** B1
Deira Minibus & Taxi Station	**30** D5
Gulf Air	**31** E5
Middle East Airlines	**32** C3
Qatar Airways	**33** C5
Singapore Airlines	**34** C3

INFORMATION	
Al-Maktoum Hospital	**35** D4
Deira Post Office	**36** B3
DTCM Office	**37** C3
Etisalat	**38** C5
Kuwaiti Consulate	**39** C5
New Dubai Hospital	**40** G3
Police Station	**41** C2
Polyglot Language Institute	**42** C4
Thomas Cook Al-Rostamani	**43** B3

217

A **B** **C** **D**

1

Dhow Wharfage

17
16 23 42A
33C 33B
36A
14
37
Al-Maktoum Rd
Baniyas Rd
Al-Rigga Rd
26C 43
12
41C 40C
34C 41B
45B
18
40D
36B
45C
Clock Tower
Roundabout
27
Abu Baker al-Siddiq Rd

2

Dubai
TV

Dubai
Courts

81
Riyadh St

Al-Maktoum
Bridge

1C
3C
28A
30
32
34A
36
38
21
11D

15
20
13
10
25
9
15
4
Airport Rd
6B

3

Creekside
Park

Dubai Creek
(Khor Dubai)

85

17
12B
14
24
19
23

Deira City Centre
10

25
27

4

13

2

Al-Garhoud Rd
2
4A

5

Dubai Creek
Golf Course

11

6

6
7

11

Casablanca Rd
35

6
25A
3

Dubai Aviation
College

Emirates
Training
Building

Al-Garhoud
Bridge

To Al-Garhoud
Bridge (300m)

25A

SIGHTS & ACTIVITIES (pp49–52, 109–20)
Dhow Wharfage..................................**1** B1
Dubai Creek Golf &
Yacht Club......................................**2** B4
Dubai Tennis Stadium.......................**3** C6
Griffins Health Club...........................**4** F1
Net Tours & Travels............................**5** E1
Orient Tours.......................................**6** C6

EATING 🍴 (pp79–82)
Blue Elephant.................................(see 11)
Café Havana....................................(see 10)
Carrefour..(see 10)
Casa Mia...(see 8)
Cellar..(see 3)
More..**7** D5
M's Beef Bistro...................................**8** E6
Thai Kitchen....................................(see 13)
Traiteur...(see 13)

DRINKING (pp95–107)
Dubliners..(see 8)
Irish Village....................................(see 3)
Jules...(see 8)
Terrace...(see 13)

ENTERTAINMENT 🎭 (pp95–108)
Cinestar...(see 10)
iBO..**9** E5
Jazz on the Green...........................(see 3)
Laughter House...............................(see 3)
Oxygen...(see 11)
QD's..(see 2)
Stella Movie Night..........................(see 9)

SHOPPING 🛍 (pp129–31)
Al-Jaber Gallery..............................(see 10)
Aminian Persian Carpets.................(see 10)
Damas...(see 10)
Deira City Centre..............................**10** C4
Early Learning Centre......................(see 10)

Magrudy's.......................................(see 10)
Mikyajy...(see 10)
Plug-Ins..(see 10)
Pride of Kashmir.............................(see 10)
Rituals..(see 10)
Virgin Megastore.............................(see 10)
Women's Secret..............................(see 10)
Zara...(see 10)

SLEEPING 🛏 (pp141–5)
Al-Bustan Rotana..............................**11** D6
Nihal Hotel.......................................**12** D1
Park Hyatt Dubai...............................**13** B4
Sun and Sand Hotel..........................**14** D1

TRANSPORT (pp172–7)
Air France...**15** D2
Air India..**16** C1
Alitalia..**17** C1
Avis...**18** C1
Avis...(see 22)
Budget..**19** D3
Budget..(see 22)
Cathay Pacific Airways......................**20** D2
DNATA Airline Centre........................**21** D2
DNATA Head Office..........................(see 21)
Dubai International Airport................**22** G3
EgyptAir..**23** C1
Emirates Airlines.............................(see 21)
Europcar...(see 22)
Hertz...**24** D3
Hertz...(see 22)
SriLankan Airlines...........................(see 21)
Swiss...**25** C3
Thai Airways International..................**26** E1
Thrifty...(see 22)

INFORMATION
Al-Rigga Post Office..........................**27** D1
DTCM Office....................................(see 10)
DTCM Office....................................(see 22)

A **B** **C** **D**

SIGHTS & ACTIVITIES (pp52–6, 109–20)
Ali bin Abi Taleb Mosque..............1 G3
Bastakia Quarter.............................2 G4
Bateaux Dubai.................................3 H6
Bin Suroor Mosque.........................4 F2
Bur Dubai Souq..............................5 G4
Danat Dubai Cruises.......................6 H6
Diwan...7 G4
Dubai Museum................................8 G4
Grand Mosque.................................9 G4
Heritage & Diving Villages............10 G2
Hindi Lane....................................11 G4
House of Chi & House of Healing....12 F5
Majlis Gallery.................................13 G4
Nautilus Academy....................(see 12)
Sheikh Saeed al-Maktoum House.....14 G2
Wonder Bus Tours....................(see 32)
XVA...(see 39)

EATING (pp82–6)
Antique Bazaar.........................(see 35)
Automatic......................................15 F5
Basta Art Café...............................16 G4
Bastakiah Nights...........................17 G4
Carrefour......................................18 F2
Choithrams....................................19 E4
Dôme..20 F6
Kan Zaman.............................(see 28)
Kwality..21 E3
Lebanese Village...........................22 F5

Shindaga Market...........................23 F2
Spinney's......................................24 E6
Spinney's......................................25 F5
Troyka..26 E4
Yakitori..................................(see 26)

DRINKING (pp95–107)
VJs.......................................(see 27)

ENTERTAINMENT (pp95–108)
Club Africana................................27 F4
Kan Zaman....................................28 G2
Rock Bottom Café...................(see 38)
Savage Garden.......................(see 34)
Tché Tché......................................29 F5

SHOPPING (pp131–4)
Ajmal.....................................(see 32)
Al Ain Shopping Centre.................30 F5
Al-Khaleej Shopping Centre....(see 33)
Al-Orooba Oriental.................(see 32)
Allah Din Shoes......................(see 31)
Bateel...................................(see 32)
Bur Dubai Souq.............................31 G3
BurJuman Centre...........................32 F6
Etro.......................................(see 32)
Faces.....................................(see 32)
Levi's...33 F4
Praias....................................(see 32)
Tape A L'oeil..........................(see 32)

Tiffany & Co..........................(see 32)
Whistles.................................(see 32)

SLEEPING (pp145–7)
Capitol Hotel................................34 A4
Four Points Sheraton....................35 F5
Ramada Hotel................................36 E5
Regal Plaza Hotel..........................37 F5
Regent Palace Hotel......................38 F6
XVA...39 G4

TRANSPORT (pp172–7)
Bur Dubai Abra Station.................40 F3
Bur Dubai Bus Station...................41 F3
Deira Old Souq Abra Station.........42 H3
Dubai Old Souq Abra Station.........43 G3
Malaysia Airlines...........................44 F5
Oman Air......................................45 E4
Royal Brunei Airlines.....................46 E4
Sabkha Abra Station......................47 H4

INFORMATION
Al-Jalssa Internet Café............(see 30)
Al-Musallah Post Office.................48 G4
British Embassy.............................49 H6
Canadian Consulate.......................50 F6
DTCM Office..........................(see 32)
Dutch Consulate...........................51 F5
Etisalat..................................(see 33)
Saudi Arabian Consulate...............52 H6

3 Jumeirah Rd
94

**PORT RASHID
CUSTOMS AUTHORITY**

92

Al-Mina Rd

10B 19
12B
Cemetery
14B

34
Al-Mina Rd
Cemetery

4 28
DEC Gas
Power Station
75
4A
6A
3B
8A
Al-Mankhool Rd
338
Kuwait St
Cemetery

4B
13
6B

8C
Al-Mankhool Rd
90
2A
4A
6A
2B
4E
43A 41A
39A
37A
35A
2A
4D
77
23A 19A
6 25A
8C
MANKHOOL

5 2C
4C
27A 25A
29A 23A 21
31A
12 12C
19 14C 15A
11
10D
12C
43A
10C
12B
16C
27
Kuwait St
23B

12D
14B

35
33A
22
31B
258
30A
32
3
Al-Adhid Rd
33
AL-JAFILIYA
22
24
31
27
23
25B

6 24A
398
388
42
258
25C
46
7C
44
43B
48
24
26C
28C 23C
30A

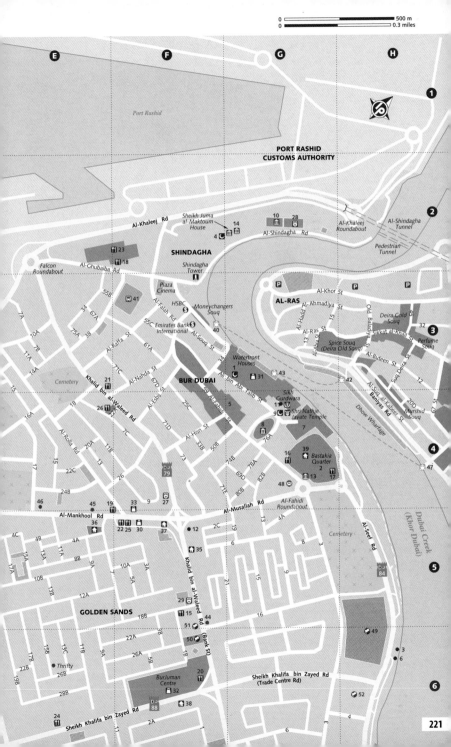

0 ▬▬▬▬▬▬▬▬ **500 m**
0 ▭▭▭▭▭▭▭▭ **0.3 miles**

E   F   G   H

1

Port Rashid

**PORT RASHID
CUSTOMS AUTHORITY**

2

Al-Khaleej Rd

Sheikh Juma al-Maktoum House

14

4

10   28

Al-Shindagha Rd

Al-Khaleej Roundabout

Al-Shindagha Tunnel

Pedestrian Tunnel

23

18

SHINDAGHA

Shindagha Tower

Al-Ghubaiba Rd

Falcon Roundabout

Plaza Cinema

P

Al-Khor St

AL-RAS

Al-Ahmadiya St

P   P

55B

41

Al-Falah Rd

HSBC

Moneychangers Souq

Al-Hadd St

Al-Ras St

Al-Ahira St

Deira Gold Souq

Old Baladiya St

Sikkat al-Khail St

32

3

7A

6YA

10A

75A

38

55C

Emirates Bank International

61A

40

Al-Souq St

13

Spice Souq (Deira Old Souq)

Al-Buteen St

Perfume Souq

Souq Deira St

7B

11A

14A

Al-Raffa St

7IC

Al-Nahda St

Waterfront Houses

1

31

43

42

Al-Sikka al-Kabeer St

2OD

Murshid Souq

4

15

16A

21

26

Khalid bin al-Waleed Rd

Al-Esbij

Cemetery

25C

BUR DUBAI

Al-Fahidi St

5

Sikh Gurdwara

11

9

Shri Nathje Jayate Temple

8

7

16

39

Bastakia Quarter

2

13

17

Dhow Wharfage

Banyas Rd

47

Al-Rolla Rd

20A

11B

7C

71D

Al-Hisn St

33B

5QB

74B

79A

63D

50B

71E

80B

52B

76A

48

Bur Dubai

(Khor Dubai)

22C

24B

79

27

5

46

45

19

33

9

Al-Mankhool Rd

36

22 25 30

37

12

2C

19

Al-Musallah Rd

Al-Fahidi Roundabout

13

4A

6

Cemetery

Al-Seef Rd

84

4C

4B

4A

8B

9A

35

10A

3A

5A

15

9

16

5

15A

17A

10B

13B

12A

GOLDEN SANDS

18B

29

15

44

51

3B

50

Bank St

Khalid bin al-Waleed Rd

49

17B

15B

13C

11B

9A

22A

26A

1B

3

6

22B

26B

Thrifty

BurJuman Centre

20

32

38

Sheikh Khalifa bin Zayed Rd (Trade Centre Rd)

52

6

28B

88

24

Sheikh Khalifa bin Zayed Rd

2A

1

3

4

221

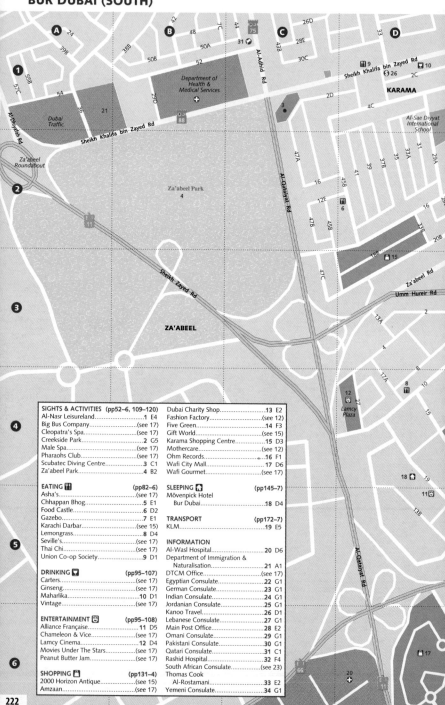

SIGHTS & ACTIVITIES (pp52–6, 109–120)	
Al-Nasr Leisureland	1 E4
Big Bus Company	(see 17)
Cleopatra's Spa	(see 17)
Creekside Park	2 G5
Male Spa	(see 17)
Pharaohs Club	(see 17)
Scubatec Diving Centre	3 C1
Za'abeel Park	4 B2

EATING (pp82–6)	
Asha's	(see 17)
Chhappan Bhog	5 E1
Food Castle	6 D2
Gazebo	7 E1
Karachi Darbar	(see 15)
Lemongrass	8 D4
Seville's	(see 17)
Thai Chi	(see 17)
Union Co-op Society	9 D1

DRINKING (pp95–107)	
Carters	(see 17)
Ginseng	(see 17)
Maharlika	10 D1
Vintage	(see 17)

ENTERTAINMENT (pp95–108)	
Alliance Française	11 D5
Chameleon & Vice	(see 17)
Lamcy Cinema	12 D4
Movies Under The Stars	(see 17)
Peanut Butter Jam	(see 17)

SHOPPING (pp131–4)	
2000 Horizon Antique	(see 15)
Amzaan	(see 17)

Dubai Charity Shop	13 E2
Fashion Factory	(see 12)
Five Green	14 F3
Gift World	(see 15)
Karama Shopping Centre	15 D3
Mothercare	(see 12)
Ohm Records	16 F1
Wafi City Mall	17 D6
Wafi Gourmet	(see 17)

SLEEPING (pp145–7)	
Mövenpick Hotel Bur Dubai	18 D4

TRANSPORT (pp172–7)	
KLM	19 E5

INFORMATION	
Al-Wasl Hospital	20 D6
Department of Immigration & Naturalisation	21 A1
DTCM Office	(see 17)
Egyptian Consulate	22 G1
German Consulate	23 G1
Indian Consulate	24 G1
Jordanian Consulate	25 G1
Kanoo Travel	26 D1
Lebanese Consulate	27 G1
Main Post Office	28 E2
Omani Consulate	29 G1
Pakistani Consulate	30 G1
Qatari Consulate	31 C1
Rashid Hospital	32 F4
South African Consulate	(see 23)
Thomas Cook Al-Rostamani	33 E2
Yemeni Consulate	34 G1

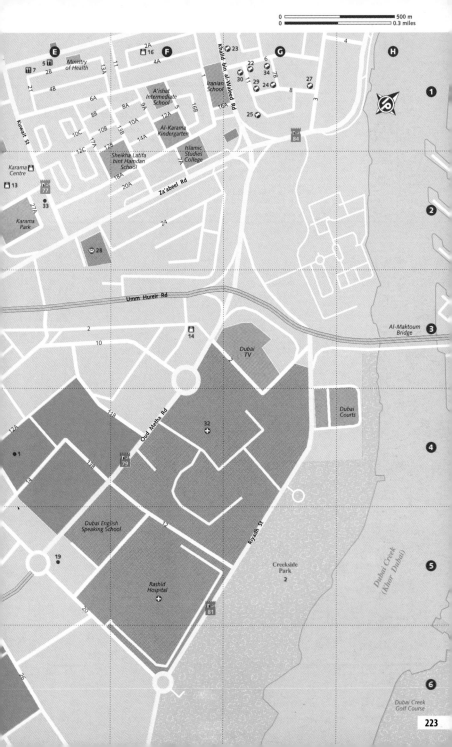

0   500 m
0   0.3 miles

E   **F**   **G**   **H**

5   Ministry
of Health
7   2B
21   4B
13A
11
2A
16
4A
23

22
6
30   11   29   34   7B
24
27
8
3
25

1

A'ishat
Intermediate
School
6A
8B   8A   9A
5
10C   10B   10A
12C   17A
12B
13B
14A
Al-Karama
Kindergarten
12A
Iranian
School
16A
16B

Kuwait St
Sheikha Latifa
bint Hamdan
School
18A
20A
Islamic
Studies
College
Za'abeel Rd

Karama
Centre
13
77
33
27A
Karama
Park
28
24

84

2

Umm Hureir Rd

Al-Maktoum
Bridge   **3**

2
10
14
Dubai
TV
2
Dubai
Courts

11B
12A
1
79
32
13B

4

19
Dubai English
Speaking School
12
Riyadh St
Creekside
Park
2

Dubai Creek
(Khor Dubai)

5

Rashid
Hospital
20
81

2B

6

Dubai Creek
Golf Course

223

A   **B**   **C**   **D**

SIGHTS & ACTIVITIES (pp58–60, 109–20)
Al-Boom Diving................................1 F5
Green Art Gallery.............................2 D5
Iranian Mosque................................3 F5
Jumeirah Mosque.............................4 F4
Russian Beach (Public Beach).........5 E4
Sensasia...6 F4

EATING (pp89–94)
Al Mallah...7 H6
Automatic....................................(see 25)
Beirut..8 H5
Bella Donna.................................(see 16)
Coconut Grove............................(see 19)
Il Rustico.....................................(see 19)
Johnny Rockets...............................9 E4
Lime Tree Café..............................10 F4

Ravi..11 H6
Spinney's..12 E4
Spinney's.....................................(see 16)

DRINKING (pp95–107)
Boston Bar.....................................13 H5
El Malecon..................................(see 18)
Sho Cho......................................(see 18)

ENTERTAINMENT (pp95–108)
Boudoir.......................................(see 18)
Century Cinemas.........................(see 16)

SHOPPING (pp135–8)
Blue Cactus....................................14 E5
Le Stock...15 E5
Mercato Mall.................................16 A5

Persian Carpet House
  & Antiques..............................(see 16)
Sauce..17 E4
Virgin Megastore........................(see 16)

SLEEPING (pp149–52)
Dubai Marine Beach Resort & Spa..18 H3
Rydges Plaza..................................19 H6

INFORMATION
Ballet Centre..................................20 E5
Berlitz Language School.................21 C5
Dubai International Art Centre.......22 E4
Dubai London Clinic.......................23 A6
Iranian Consulate...........................24 E5
Manchester Clinic..........................25 D5
Satwa Post Office...........................26 G6

1
2
3

THE

GULF

4

5

Jumeirah Rd

Town
Centre

14D

Jumeirah
Kindergarten

32C

6

32C

Al-Wasl Rd

Beach
Centre

8A • 21

Dubai
Zoo

6D

14A

10D

45A

16C

51

59A

2

20B

75A

69A

75B

79

77B

26C

28B

69B

65B

2D

81

79

75

2C

63

43A

41A

94

92

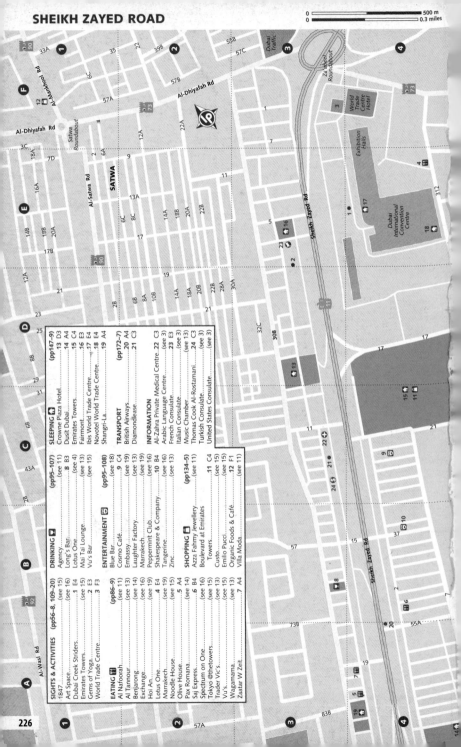

0 — 500 m
0 — 0.3 miles